The Complete Kubernetes Guide

Become an expert in container management with the power of Kubernetes

Jonathan Baier
Gigi Sayfan
Jesse White

BIRMINGHAM - MUMBAI

The Complete Kubernetes Guide

First published: May 2019

Production reference: 1160519

Published by Packt Publishing Ltd.
Livery Place
35 Livery Street
Birmingham
B3 2PB, UK.

ISBN 978-1-83864-734-6

www.packtpub.com

`mapt.io`

Mapt is an online digital library that gives you full access to over 5,000 books and videos, as well as industry leading tools to help you plan your personal development and advance your career. For more information, please visit our website.

Why subscribe?

- Spend less time learning and more time coding with practical eBooks and Videos from over 4,000 industry professionals

- Improve your learning with Skill Plans built especially for you

- Get a free eBook or video every month

- Mapt is fully searchable

- Copy and paste, print, and bookmark content

Packt.com

Did you know that Packt offers eBook versions of every book published, with PDF and ePub files available? You can upgrade to the eBook version at `www.packt.com` and as a print book customer, you are entitled to a discount on the eBook copy. Get in touch with us at `customercare@packtpub.com` for more details.

At `www.packt.com`, you can also read a collection of free technical articles, sign up for a range of free newsletters, and receive exclusive discounts and offers on Packt books and eBooks.

Contributors

About the authors

Jonathan Baier is an emerging technology leader living in Brooklyn, New York. He has had a passion for technology since an early age. When he was 14 years old, he was so interested in the family computer (an IBM PCjr) that he pored over the several hundred pages of BASIC and DOS manuals. Then, he taught himself to code a very poorly-written version of Tic-Tac-Toe. During his teenage years, he started a computer support business. Throughout his life, he has dabbled in entrepreneurship. He currently works as Senior Vice President of Cloud Engineering and Operations for Moody's Corporation in New York.

Gigi Sayfan is a principal software architect at Helix, and he has been developing software professionally for more than 22 years in domains, such as instant messaging and morphing. He has written production code every day in many programming languages, such as Go, Python, C/C++, C#, Java, Delphi, JavaScript, and even Cobol and PowerBuilder for operating systems, such as Windows, Linux, macOS, Lynx (embedded), and more. His technical expertise includes databases, networking, distributed systems, unorthodox user interfaces, and general software development life cycles.

Jesse White is a 15-year veteran and technology leader in New York City's very own Silicon Alley, where he is a pillar of the vibrant engineering ecosystem. As the founder of DockerNYC and an active participant in the open source community, you can find Jesse at a number of leading industry events, including DockerCon and VelocityConf, giving talks and workshops.

Packt is searching for authors like you

If you're interested in becoming an author for Packt, please visit `authors.packtpub.com` and apply today. We have worked with thousands of developers and tech professionals, just like you, to help them share their insight with the global tech community. You can make a general application, apply for a specific hot topic that we are recruiting an author for, or submit your own idea.

Table of Contents

Preface

If you are running more containers or want automated management of your containers, you need Kubernetes at your disposal.

This Learning Path focuses on core Kubernetes constructs, such as pods, services, replica sets, replication controllers, and labels. You'll learn to integrate your build pipeline and deployments in a Kubernetes cluster. As you move ahead in the Learning Path, you'll orchestrate updates behind the scenes, avoid downtime on your cluster, and deal with underlying cloud provider instability in your cluster. Using real-world use cases, you'll explore the options for network configuration, and understand how to set up, operate, and troubleshoot various Kubernetes networking plugins. In addition to this, you'll also get to grips with custom resource development and utilization in automation and maintenance workflows.

By the end of this Learning Path, you'll know everything you need to graduate from intermediate to advanced level of understanding Kubernetes.

Who this book is for

This Learning Path is ideal for you if you are a developer or a system administrator with an intermediate understanding of Kubernetes and want to master its advanced features. Basic knowledge of networking is required to easily understand the concepts explained here.

What this book covers

Chapter 1, *Introduction to Kubernetes*, is a brief overview of containers and the how, what, and why of Kubernetes orchestration, exploring how it impacts your business goals and everyday operations.

Chapter 2, *Understanding Kubernetes Architecture*, will help you understand the design of the Kubernetes systems and appreciate why some of these design choices have been made.

Chapter 3, *Building a Foundation with Core Kubernetes Constructs*, uses a few simple examples to explore core Kubernetes constructs, namely pods, services, replication controllers, replica sets, and labels. Basic operations, including health checks and scheduling, will also be covered.

Chapter 4, *Working with Networking, Load Balancers, and Ingress,* covers cluster networking for Kubernetes and the Kubernetes proxy. It also takes a deeper dive into services and shows a brief overview of some higher-level isolation features for multi-tenancy.

Chapter 5, *Using Critical Kubernetes Resources,* will help you use almost all the latest Kubernetes resources for appropriate use cases in production. You will also learn how to define, version, and deliver them.

Chapter 6, *Exploring Kubernetes Storage Concepts,* covers storage concerns and persistent data across pods and the container life cycle. We will also look at new constructs for working with stateful applications in Kubernetes.

Chapter 7, *Monitoring and Logging,* teaches how to use and customize built-in and third-party monitoring tools on your Kubernetes cluster. We will look at built-in logging and monitoring, the Google Cloud Monitoring/Logging service, and Sysdig.

Chapter 8, *Monitoring, Logging, and Troubleshooting,* will help you set up and understand monitoring and metering in Kubernetes clusters, and will enable you to identify and troubleshoot typical problems that administrators encounter during day-to-day operations.

Chapter 9, *Operating Systems, Platforms, and Cloud and Local Providers,* starts off by covering Open Container Project and its mission to provide an open container specification, looking at how having open standards encourages a diverse ecosystem of container implementations (such as Docker, rkt, Kurma, and JetPack). The second half of this chapter will cover available OSes, such as CoreOS, Project Atomic, and their advantages as a host OSes, including performance and support for various container implementations.

Chapter 10, *Creating Kubernetes Clusters,* will make you understand the different options for creating Kubernetes clusters. You will create several clusters using the tools and examine the clusters.

Chapter 11, *Cluster Federation and Multi-Tenancy,* explores the new federation capabilities and how to use them to manage multiple clusters. We will also cover the federated version of the core constructs and the integration to public cloud vendor DNS.

Chapter 12, *Cluster Authentication, Authorization, and Container Security,* get into the options for container security, from the container run-time level to the host itself. We will discuss how to apply these concepts to workloads running in a Kubernetes cluster and some of the security concerns and practices that relate specifically to running your Kubernetes cluster.

Chapter 13, *Running Stateful Applications with Kubernetes,* will teach you how to transform monolithic stateful applications to microservices running on Kubernetes, suitable for production workload. They will also learn several ways that this can be done with or without the PetSet resource prior to Kubernetes release 1.3. You will be able to fill in the gaps in the available documentation resources.

Chapter 14, *Rolling Updates, Scalability, and Quotas,* will teach you how rolling updates and horizontal pod autoscaling behave. You will learn how to customize and run scaling testing at production environment. You will be able to use resource quotas for CPU and memory.

Chapter 15, *Advanced Kubernetes Networking,* will help you determine which networking plugin is suitable in different deployments, and you will learn how to deploy Kubernetes with different network plugins. You will be able to understand iptables load balancing and how to extend them.

Chapter 16, *Kubernetes Infrastructure Management,* focuses on how to make changes to the infrastructure that powers your Kubernetes infrastructure, whether it be a purely public cloud platform or a hybrid installation. We'll discuss methods for handling underlying instance and resource instability, and strategies for running highly available workloads on the partially available underlying hardware.

Chapter 17, *Customizing Kubernetes – API and Plugins,* will help you implement third-party resources, understand concepts of enhancing the Kubernetes API, and show you how to integrate resources with existing environments. You will learn how schedulers work and how to implement your own scheduling engine. Finally, you will also learn how to implement custom external load balancing for on-premise deployments based on common services such as haproxy or nginx.

Chapter 18, *Handling the Kubernetes Package Manager,* explains how to handle Kubernetes applications as packages. The chapter starts with Helm Classic and goes through Helm for Kubernetes, and finally covers real-world examples of how to create and update packages in a Helm repository in order to be able to maintain them for production application deployments.

Chapter 19, *The Future of Kubernetes,* will help you create your own Kubernetes packages and store them in Helm repository. You will get an understanding of delivery pipelines for Kubernetes packages, from repositories to clusters.

To get the most out of this book

This book will cover downloading and running the Kubernetes project. You'll need access to a Linux system (VirtualBox will work if you are on Windows) and some familiarity with the command shell. To follow the examples in each chapter, you need a recent version of Docker and Kubernetes installed on your machine, ideally Kubernetes 1.10. If your operating system is Windows 10 Professional, you can enable hypervisor mode; otherwise, you will need to install VirtualBox and use a Linux guest OS.

Additionally, you should have a Google Cloud Platform account. You can sign up for a free trial here: https://cloud.google.com/.

Also, an AWS account is necessary for a few sections of the book. You can sign up for a free trial here: https://aws.amazon.com/.

Download the example code files

You can download the example code files for this book from your account at www.packt.com. If you purchased this book elsewhere, you can visit www.packt.com/support and register to have the files emailed directly to you.

You can download the code files by following these steps:

1. Log in or register at www.packt.com.
2. Select the **SUPPORT** tab.
3. Click on **Code Downloads & Errata**.
4. Enter the name of the book in the **Search** box and follow the onscreen instructions.

Once the file is downloaded, please make sure that you unzip or extract the folder using the latest version of:

- WinRAR/7-Zip for Windows
- Zipeg/iZip/UnRarX for Mac
- 7-Zip/PeaZip for Linux

The code bundle for the book is also hosted on GitHub at https://github.com/PacktPublishing/Getting-Started-with-Kubernetes-third-edition. In case there's an update to the code, it will be updated on the existing GitHub repository.

We also have other code bundles from our rich catalog of books and videos available at `https://github.com/PacktPublishing/`. Check them out!

Conventions used

There are a number of text conventions used throughout this book.

`CodeInText`: Indicates code words in text, database table names, folder names, filenames, file extensions, pathnames, dummy URLs, user input, and Twitter handles. Here is an example: "The last two main pieces of the Master nodes are `kube-controller-manager` and `cloud-controller-manager`."

A block of code is set as follows:

```
"conditions": [
  {
    "type": "Ready",
    "status": "True"
  }
```

When we wish to draw your attention to a particular part of a code block, the relevant lines or items are set in bold:

```
"conditions": [
  {
    "type": "Ready",
    "status": "True"
  }
```

Any command-line input or output is written as follows:

```
$ kubectl describe pods/node-js-pod
```

Bold: Indicates a new term, an important word, or words that you see onscreen. For example, words in menus or dialog boxes appear in the text like this. Here is an example: "Click on **Jobs** and then **long-task** from the list, so we can see the details."

Warnings or important notes appear like this.

 Tips and tricks appear like this.

Get in touch

Feedback from our readers is always welcome.

General feedback: If you have questions about any aspect of this book, mention the book title in the subject of your message and email us at customercare@packtpub.com.

Errata: Although we have taken every care to ensure the accuracy of our content, mistakes do happen. If you have found a mistake in this book, we would be grateful if you would report this to us. Please visit www.packt.com/submit-errata, selecting your book, clicking on the Errata Submission Form link, and entering the details.

Piracy: If you come across any illegal copies of our works in any form on the Internet, we would be grateful if you would provide us with the location address or website name. Please contact us at copyright@packt.com with a link to the material.

If you are interested in becoming an author: If there is a topic that you have expertise in and you are interested in either writing or contributing to a book, please visit authors.packtpub.com.

Reviews

Please leave a review. Once you have read and used this book, why not leave a review on the site that you purchased it from? Potential readers can then see and use your unbiased opinion to make purchase decisions, we at Packt can understand what you think about our products, and our authors can see your feedback on their book. Thank you!

For more information about Packt, please visit packt.com.

Introduction to Kubernetes

1

In this book, we will help you build, scale, and manage production-ready Kubernetes clusters. Each section of this book will empower you with the core container concepts and the operational context of running modern web services that need to be available 24 hours of the day, 7 days a week, 365 days of the year. As we progress, you'll be given concrete, code-based examples that you can deploy into running clusters in order to get real-world feedback on Kubernetes' many abstractions. By the end of this book, you will have mastered the core conceptual building blocks of Kubernetes, and will have a firm understanding of how to handle the following paradigms:

- Orchestration
- Scheduling
- Networking
- Security
- Storage
- Identity and authentication
- Infrastructure management

This chapter will set the stage for *why Kubernetes?* and give an overview of modern container history, diving into how containers work, as well as why it's important to schedule, orchestrate, and manage a container platform well. We'll tie this back to concrete objectives and goals for your business and product. This chapter will also give a brief overview of how Kubernetes orchestration can enhance our container management strategy and how we can get a basic Kubernetes cluster up, running, and ready for container deployments.

In this chapter, we will cover the following topics:

- Introducing container operations and management
- The importance of container management
- The advantages of Kubernetes

- Downloading the latest Kubernetes
- Installing and starting up a new Kubernetes cluster
- The components of a Kubernetes cluster

Technical requirements

You'll need to have the following tools installed:

- Python
- AWS CLI
- Google Cloud CLI
- Minikube

We'll go into the specifics of these tools' installation and configuration as we go through this chapter. If you already know how to do this, you can go ahead and set them up now.

A brief overview of containers

Believe it or not, containers and their precursors have been around for over 15 years in the Linux and Unix operating systems. If you look deeper into the fundamentals of how containers operate, you can see their roots in the chroot technology that was invented all the way back in 1970. Since the early 2000s, FreeBSD, Linux, Solaris, Open VZ, Warden, and finally Docker all made significant attempts at encapsulating containerization technology for the end user.

While the VServer's project and first commit (*running several general purpose Linux server on a single box with a high degree of independence and security* (`http://ieeexplore.ieee.org/document/1430092/?reload=true`)) may have been one of the most interesting historical junctures in container history, it's clear that Docker set the container ecosystem on fire back in late 2013 when they went full in on the container ecosystem and decided to rebrand from dotCloud to Docker. Their mass marketing of container appeal set the stage for the broad market adoption we see today and is a direct precursor of the massive container orchestration and scheduling platforms we're writing about here.

Over the past five years, containers have grown in popularity like wildfire. Where containers were once relegated to developer laptops, testing, or development environments, you'll now see them as the building blocks of powerful production systems. They're running highly secure banking workloads and trading systems, powering IoT, keeping our on-demand economy humming, and scaling up to millions of containers to keep the products of the 21st century running at peak efficiency in both the cloud and private data centers. Furthermore, containerization technology permeates our technological zeitgest, with every technology conference in the world devoting a significant portion of their talks and sessions devoted to building, running, or developing in containers.

At the beginning of this compelling story lies Docker and their compelling suite of developer-friendly tools. Docker for macOS and Windows, Compose, Swarm, and Registry have been incredibly powerful tools that have shaped workflows and changed how companies develop software. They've built a bridge for containers to exist at the very heart of the **Software Delivery Life Cycle** (**SDLC**), and a remarkable ecosystem has sprung up around those containers. As Malcom McLean revolutionized the physical shipping world in the 1950s by creating a standardized shipping container, which is used today for everything from ice cube trays to automobiles, Linux containers are revolutionizing the software development world by making application environments portable and consistent across the infrastructure landscape.

We'll pick this story up as containers go mainstream, go to production, and go big within organizations. We'll look at what makes a container next.

What is a container?

Containers are a type of operating system virtualization, much like the virtual machines that preceded them. There's also lesser known types of virtualization such as Application Virtualization, Network Virtualization, and Storage Virtualization. While these technologies have been around since the 1960s, Docker's encapsulation of the container paradigm represents a modern implementation of resource isolation that utilizes built-in Linux kernel features such as chroot, **control groups** (**cgroups**), UnionFS, and namespaces to fully isolated resource control at the process level.

Containers use these technologies to create lightweight images that act as a standalone, fully encapsulated piece of software that carries everything it needs inside the box. This can include application binaries, any system tools or libraries, environment-based configuration, and runtime. This special property of isolation is very important, as it allows developers and operators to leverage the all-in-one nature of a container to run without issue, regardless of the environment it's run on. This includes developer laptops and any kind of pre-production or production environment.

This decoupling of application packaging mechanism from the environment on which it runs is a powerful concept that provides a clear separation of concerns between engineering teams. This allows developers to focus on building the core business capabilities into their application code and managing their own dependencies, while operators can streamline the continuous integration, promotion, and deployment of said applications without having to worry about their configuration.

At the core of container technology are three key concepts:

- cgroups
- Namespaces
- Union filesystems

cgroups

cgroups work by allowing the host to share and also limit the resources each process or container can consume. This is important for both resource utilization and security, as it prevents **denial-of-service (DoS)** attacks on the host's hardware resources. Several containers can share CPU and memory while staying within the predefined constraints. cgroups allow containers to provision access to memory, disk I/O, network, and CPU. You can also access devices (for example, `/dev/foo`). cgroups also power the soft and hard limits of container constraints that we'll discuss in later chapters.

There are seven major cgroups:

- **Memory cgroup**: This keeps track of page access by the group, and can define limits for physical, kernel, and total memory.
- **Blkio cgroup**: This tracks the I/O usage per group, across the read and write activity per block device. You can throttle by group per device, on operations versus bytes, and for reads versus writes.
- **CPU cgroup**: This keeps track of user and system CPU time and usage per CPU. This allows you to set weights, but not limits.

- **Freezer cgroup**: This is useful in batch management systems that are often stopping and starting tasks in order to schedule resources efficiently. The SIGSTOP signal is used to suspend a process, and the process is generally unaware that it is being suspended (or resumed, for that matter.)
- **CPUset cgroup**: This allows you to pin a group to a specific CPU within a multi-core CPU architecture. You can pin by application, which will prevent it from moving between CPUs. This can improve the performance of your code by increasing the amount of local memory access or minimizing thread switching.
- **Net_cls/net_prio cgroup**: This keeps tabs on the egress traffic class (net_cls) or priority (net_prio) that is generated by the processes within the cgroup.
- **Devices cgroup**: This controls what read/write permissions the group has on device nodes.

Namespaces

Namespaces offer another form of isolation for process interaction within operating systems, creating the workspace we call a container. Linux namespaces are created via a syscall named unshare, while clone and setns allow you to manipulate namespaces in other manners.

 unshare() allows a process (or thread) to disassociate parts of its execution context that are currently being shared with other processes (or threads). Part of the execution context, such as the mount namespace, is shared implicitly when a new process is created using FORK(2) (for more information visit http://man7.org/linux/man-pages/man2/fork.2.html) or VFORK(2) (for more information visit http://man7.org/linux/man-pages/man2/vfork.2.html), while other parts, such as virtual memory, may be shared by explicit request when creating a process or thread using CLONE(2) (for more information visit http://man7.org/linux/man-pages/man2/clone.2.html).

Namespaces limit the visibility a process has on other processes, networking, filesystems, and user ID components. Container processes are limited to seeing only what is in the same namespace. Processes from containers or the host processes are not directly accessible from within this container process. Additionally, Docker gives each container its own networking stack that protects the sockets and interfaces in a similar fashion.

If cgroups limit how much of a thing you can use, namespaces limit what things you can see. The following diagram shows the composition of a container:

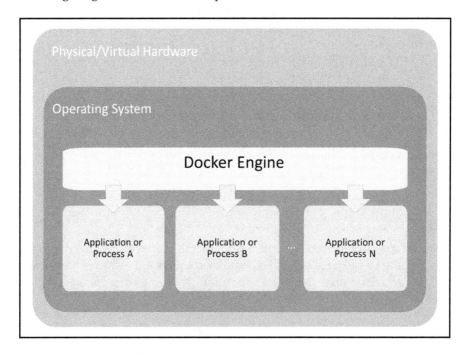

In the case of the Docker engine, the following namespaces are used:

- `pid`: Provides process isolation via an independent set of process IDs from other namespaces. These are nested.
- `net`: Manages network interfaces by virtualizing the network stack through providing a loopback interface, and can create physical and virtual network interfaces that exist in a single namespace at a time.
- `ipc`: Manages access to interprocess communication.
- `mnt`: Controls filesystem mount points. These were the first kind of namespaces created in the Linux kernel, and can be private or shared.
- `uts`: The Unix time-sharing system isolates version IDs and kernel by allowing a single system to provide different host and domain naming schemes to different processes. The processes `gethostname` and `sethostname` use this namespace.
- `user`: This namespace allows you to map UID/GID from container to host, and prevents the need for extra configuration in the container.

Union filesystems

Union filesystems are also a key advantage of using Docker containers. Containers run from an image. Much like an image in the VM or cloud world, it represents state at a particular point in time. Container images snapshot the filesystem, but tend to be much smaller than a VM. The container shares the host kernel and generally runs a much smaller set of processes, so the filesystem and bootstrap period tend to be much smaller—though those constraints are not strictly enforced. Second, the union filesystem allows for the efficient storage, download, and execution of these images. Containers use the idea of *copy-on-write storage*, which is able to create a brand new container immediately, without having to wait on copying out a whole new filesystem. This is similar to thin provisioning in other systems, where storage is allocated as needed:

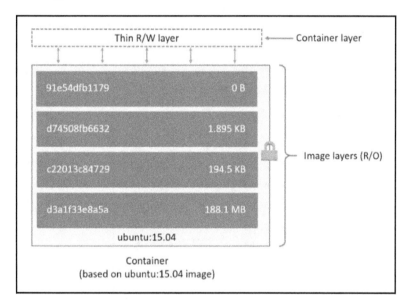

Copy-on-write storage keeps track of what's changed, and in this way is similar to **distributed version control systems** (**DVCS**) such as Git. There are a number of options available to the end user that leverage copy-on-write storage:

- AUFS and overlay at the file level
- Device mapper at the block level
- BTRFS and ZFS and the filesystem level

The easiest way to understand union filesystems is to think of them like a layer cake with each layer baked independently. The Linux kernel is our base layer; then, we might add an OS such as Red Hat Linux or Ubuntu.

Next, we might add an application such as nginx or Apache. Every change creates a new layer. Finally, as you make changes and new layers are added, you'll always have a top layer (think frosting) that is a writable layer. Union filesystems leverage this strategy to make each layer lightweight and speedy.

In Docker's case, the storage driver is responsible for stacking these layers on top of each other and providing a single pane of glass to view these systems. The thin writable layer on the top of this stack of layers is where you'll do your work: the writable container layer. We can consider each layer below to be container image layers:

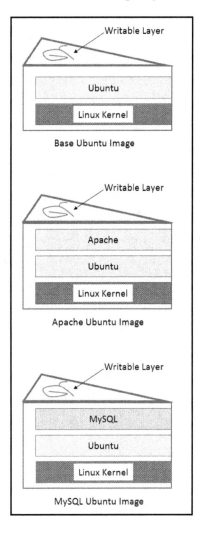

What makes this truly efficient is that Docker caches the layers the first time we build them. So, let's say that we have an image with Ubuntu and then add Apache and build the image. Next, we build MySQL with Ubuntu as the base. The second build will be much faster because the Ubuntu layer is already cached. Essentially, our chocolate and vanilla layers, from the preceding diagram, are already baked. We simply need to bake the pistachio (MySQL) layer, assemble, and add the icing (the writable layer).

Why are containers so cool?

What's also really exciting is that not only has the open source community embraced containers and Kubernetes, but the cloud providers have also deeply embraced the container ecosystem and invested millions of dollars in supporting tooling, ecosystem, and management planes that can help manage containers. This means you have more options to run container workloads, and you'll have more tools to manage the scheduling and orchestration of the applications running on your clusters.

We'll explore some specific opportunities available to Kubernetes users, but at the time of this book's publishing, all of the major **cloud service providers** (**CSPs**) are offering some form of hosted or managed Kubernetes:

- **Amazon Web Services**: AWS offers **Elastic Container Service for Kubernetes** (**EKS**) (for more information visit `https://aws.amazon.com/eks/`), a managed service that simplifies running Kubernetes clusters in their cloud. You can also roll your own clusters with kops (for information visit `https://kubernetes.io/docs/setup/custom-cloud/kops/`). This product is still in active development:

Provision an EKS cluster	Deploy worker nodes	Connect to EKS	Run Kubernetes apps
EKS automatically deploys Kubernetes masters	Add worker nodes to your EKS cluster	Point your favorite Kubernetes tooling at your EKS cluster	Deploy your Kubernetes applications to your EKS cluster

- **Google Cloud Platform**: GCP offers the **Google Kubernetes Engine** (**GKE**) (for more information visit `https://cloud.google.com/kubernetes-engine/`), a powerful cluster manager that can deploy, manage, and scale containerized applications in the cloud. Google has been running containerized workloads for over 15 years, and this platform is an excellent choice for sophisticated workload management:

- **Microsoft Azure**: Azure offers the **Azure Container Service** (**AKS**) (for more information visit `https://azure.microsoft.com/en-us/services/kubernetes-service/`), which aims to simplify the deployment, management, and operations of a full-scale Kubernetes cluster. This product is still in active development:

When you take advantage of one of these systems, you get built-in management of your Kubernetes cluster, which allows you to focus on the optimization, configuration, and deployment of your cluster.

The advantages of Continuous Integration/Continuous Deployment

ThoughtWorks defines Continuous Integration as a development practice that requires developers to integrate code into a shared repository several times a day. By having a continuous process of building and deploying code, organizations are able to instill quality control and testing as part of the everyday work cycle. The result is that updates and bug fixes happen much faster and the overall quality improves.

However, there has always been a challenge in creating development environments that match those of testing and production. Often, inconsistencies in these environments make it difficult to gain the full advantage of Continuous Delivery. Continuous Integration is the first step in speeding up your organization's software delivery life cycle, which helps you get your software features in front of customer quickly and reliably.

The concept of Continuous Delivery/Deployment uses Continuous Integration to enables developers to have truly portable deployments. Containers that are deployed on a developer's laptop are easily deployed on an in-house staging server. They are then easily transferred to the production server running in the cloud. This is facilitated due to the nature of containers, which build files that specify parent layers, as we discussed previously. One advantage of this is that it becomes very easy to ensure OS, package, and application versions are the same across development, staging, and production environments. Because all the dependencies are packaged into the layer, the same host server can have multiple containers running a variety of OS or package versions. Furthermore, we can have various languages and frameworks on the same host server without the typical dependency clashes we would get in a VM with a single operating system.

This sets the stage for Continuous Delivery/Deployment of the application, as the operations teams or the developers themselves can focus on getting deployments and application rollouts correct, without having to worry about the intricacies of dependencies.

Continuous Delivery is the embodiment and process wherein all code changes are automatically built, tested (Continuous Integration), and then released into production (Continuous Delivery). If this process captures the correct quality gates, security guarantees, and unit/integration/system tests, the development teams will constantly release production-ready and deployable artifacts that have moved through an automated and standardized process.

It's important to note that CD requires the engineering teams to automate more than just unit tests. In order to utilize CD in sophisticated scheduling and orchestration systems such as Kubernetes, teams need to verify application functionality across many dimensions before they're deployed to customers. We'll explore deployment strategies that Kubernetes has to offer in later chapters.

Lastly, it's important to keep in mind that utilizing Kubernetes with CI/CD reduces the risk of the many common problems that technology firms face:

- **Long release cycles**: If it takes a long time to release code to your users, then it's a potential functionality that they're missing out on, and this results in lost revenue. If you have a manual testing or release process, it's going to slow down getting changes to production, and therefore in front of your customers.
- **Fixing code is hard**: When you shorten the release cycle, you're able to discover and remediate bugs closer to the point of creation. This lowers the fixed cost, as there's a correlation between bug introduction and bug discovery times.
- **Release better**: The more you release, the better you get at releasing. Challenging your developers and operators to build automation, monitoring, and logging around the processes of CI/CD will make your pipeline more robust. As you release more often, the amount of difference between releases also decreases. A smaller difference allows teams to troubleshoot potential breaking changes more quickly, which in turn gives them more time to refine the release process further. It's a virtuous cycle!

Because all the dependencies are packaged into the layer, the same host server can have multiple containers running a variety of OS or package versions. Furthermore, we can have various languages and frameworks on the same host server without the typical dependency clashes we would get in a VM with a single operating system.

Resource utilization

The well-defined isolation and layer filesystem also makes containers ideal for running systems with a very small footprint and domain-specific purpose. A streamlined deployment and release process means we can deploy quickly and often. As such, many companies have reduced their deployment time from weeks or months to days and hours in some cases. This development life cycle lends itself extremely well to small, targeted teams working on small chunks of a larger application.

Microservices and orchestration

As we break down an application into very specific domains, we need a uniform way to communicate between all the various pieces and domains. Web services have served this purpose for years, but the added isolation and granular focus that containers bring have paved the way for microservices.

A definition for microservices can be a bit nebulous, but a definition from Martin Fowler, a respected author and speaker on software development, says this:

> *In short, the microservice architectural style is an approach to developing a single application as a suite of small services, each running in its own process and communicating with lightweight mechanisms, often an HTTP resource API. These services are built around business capabilities and independently deployable by fully automated deployment machinery. There is a bare minimum of centralized management of these services, which may be written in different programming languages and use different data storage technologies.*

As the pivot to containerization and as microservices evolve in an organization, they will soon need a strategy to maintain many containers and microservices. Some organizations will have hundreds or even thousands of containers running in the years ahead.

Future challenges

Life cycle processes alone are an important piece of operation and management. How will we automatically recover when a container fails? Which upstream services are affected by such an outage? How will we patch our applications with minimal downtime? How will we scale up our containers and services as our traffic grows?

Networking and processing are also important concerns. Some processes are part of the same service and may benefit from proximity to the network. Databases, for example, may send large amounts of data to a particular microservice for processing. How will we place containers near each other in our cluster? Is there common data that needs to be accessed? How will new services be discovered and made available to other systems?

Resource utilization is also key. The small footprint of containers means that we can optimize our infrastructure for greater utilization. Extending the savings started in the Elastic cloud will take us even further toward minimizing wasted hardware. How will we schedule workloads most efficiently? How will we ensure that our important applications always have the right resources? How can we run less important workloads on spare capacity?

Finally, portability is a key factor in moving many organizations to containerization. Docker makes it very easy to deploy a standard container across various operating systems, cloud providers, and on-premise hardware or even developer laptops. However, we still need tooling to move containers around. How will we move containers between different nodes on our cluster? How will we roll out updates with minimal disruption? What process do we use to perform blue-green deployments or canary releases?

Whether you are starting to build out individual microservices and separating concerns into isolated containers or you simply want to take full advantage of the portability and immutability in your application development, the need for management and orchestration becomes clear. This is where orchestration tools such as Kubernetes offer the biggest value.

Our first clusters

Kubernetes is supported on a variety of platforms and OSes. For the examples in this book, I used an Ubuntu 16.04 Linux VirtualBox (`https://www.virtualbox.org/wiki/Downloads`) for my client and **Google Compute Engine** (**GCE**) with Debian for the cluster itself. We will also take a brief look at a cluster running on **Amazon Web Services** (**AWS**) with Ubuntu.

> To save some money, both GCP (`https://cloud.google.com/free/`) and AWS (`https://aws.amazon.com/free/`) offer free tiers and trial offers for their cloud infrastructure. It's worth using these free trials for learning Kubernetes, if possible.
>
> Most of the concepts and examples in this book should work on any installation of a Kubernetes cluster. To get more information on other platform setups, refer to the Kubernetes getting started page, which will help you pick the right solution for your cluster: `http://kubernetes.io/docs/getting-started-guides/`.

Running Kubernetes on GCE

We have a few options for setting up the prerequisites for our development environment. While we'll use a Linux client on our local machine in this example, you can also use the Google Cloud Shell to simplify your dependencies and setup. You can check out that documentation at `https://cloud.google.com/shell/docs/`, and then jump down to the `gcloud auth login` portion of the tutorial.

Getting back to the local installation, let's make sure that our environment is properly set up before we install Kubernetes. Start by updating the packages:

```
$ sudo apt-get update
```

You should see something similar to the following output:

```
$ sudo apt update
[sudo] password for user:
Hit:1 http://archive.canonical.com/ubuntu xenial InRelease
Ign:2 http://dl.google.com/linux/chrome/deb stable InRelease
Hit:3 http://archive.ubuntu.com/ubuntu xenial InRelease
Get:4 http://security.ubuntu.com/ubuntu xenial-security InRelease [102 kB]
Ign:5 http://dell.archive.canonical.com/updates xenial-dell-dino2-mlk
InRelease
Hit:6 http://ppa.launchpad.net/webupd8team/sublime-text-3/ubuntu xenial
InRelease
Hit:7 https://download.sublimetext.com apt/stable/ InRelease
Hit:8 http://dl.google.com/linux/chrome/deb stable Release
Get:9 http://archive.ubuntu.com/ubuntu xenial-updates InRelease [102 kB]
Hit:10 https://apt.dockerproject.org/repo ubuntu-xenial InRelease
Hit:11 https://deb.nodesource.com/node_7.x xenial InRelease
Hit:12 https://download.docker.com/linux/ubuntu xenial InRelease
Ign:13 http://dell.archive.canonical.com/updates xenial-dell InRelease
<SNIPPED...>
Fetched 1,593 kB in 1s (1,081 kB/s)
Reading package lists... Done
Building dependency tree
Reading state information... Done
120 packages can be upgraded. Run 'apt list --upgradable' to see them.
$
```

Install Python and `curl` if they are not present:

```
$ sudo apt-get install python
$ sudo apt-get install curl
```

Install the `gcloud` SDK:

```
$ curl https://sdk.cloud.google.com | bash
```

We will need to start a new shell before `gcloud` is on our path.

Configure your GCP account information. This should automatically open a browser, from where we can log in to our Google Cloud account and authorize the SDK:

```
$ gcloud auth login
```

If you have problems with login or want to use another browser, you can optionally use the `--no-launch-browser` command. Copy and paste the URL to the machine and/or browser of your choice. Log in with your Google Cloud credentials and click **Allow** on the permissions page. Finally, you should receive an authorization code that you can copy and paste back into the shell, where the prompt will be waiting.

A default project should be set, but we can verify this with the following command:

```
$ gcloud config list project
```

We can modify this and set a new default project with the following command. Make sure to use project ID and not project name, as follows:

```
$ gcloud config set project <PROJECT ID>
```

We can find our project ID in the console at the following URL: `https://console.developers.google.com/project`. Alternatively, we can list the active projects with `$ gcloud alpha projects list`.

You can turn on API access to your project at this point in the GCP dashboard, `https://console.developers.google.com/project`, or the Kubernetes script will prompt you to do so in the next section:

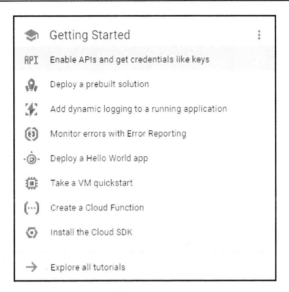

Next, you want to change to a directory when you can install the Kubernetes binaries. We'll set that up and then download the software:

```
$ mkdir ~/code/gsw-k8s-3
$ cd ~/code/gsw-k8s-3
```

Installing the latest Kubernetes version is done in a single step, as follows:

```
$ curl -sS https://get.k8s.io | bash
```

It may take a minute or two to download Kubernetes depending on your connection speed. Earlier versions would automatically call the kube-up.sh script and start building our cluster. In version 1.5, we will need to call the kube-up.sh script ourselves to launch the cluster. By default, it will use the Google Cloud and GCE:

```
$ kubernetes/cluster/kube-up.sh
```

If you get an error at this point due to missing components, you'll need to add a few pieces to your local Linux box. If you're running the Google Cloud Shell, or are utilizing a VM in GCP, you probably won't see this error:

```
$ kubernetes_install cluster/kube-up.sh...
Starting cluster in us-central1-b using provider gce
... calling verify-prereqs
missing required gcloud component "alpha"
missing required gcloud component "beta"
$
```

You can see that these components are missing and are required for leveraging the `kube-up.sh` script:

```
$ gcloud components list
Your current Cloud SDK version is: 193.0.0
The latest available version is: 193.0.0

┌─────────────────────────────────────────────────────────────────────────┐
│                                Components                                 │
├───────────────┬──────────────────────────────────┬──────────┬───────────┤
│    Status     │               Name               │    ID    │   Size    │
├───────────────┼──────────────────────────────────┼──────────┼───────────┤
│ Not Installed │ App Engine Go Extensions         │ app-engine-go │ 151.9 MiB │
│ Not Installed │ Cloud Bigtable Command Line Tool │ cbt      │ 4.5 MiB   │
│ Not Installed │ Cloud Bigtable Emulator          │ bigtable │ 3.7 MiB   │
│ Not Installed │ Cloud Datalab Command Line Tool  │ datalab  │ < 1 MiB   │
│ Not Installed │ Cloud Datastore Emulator         │ cloud-datastore-emulator │ 17.9 MiB │
│ Not Installed │ Cloud Datastore Emulator (Legacy) │ gcd-emulator │ 38.1 MiB │
│ Not Installed │ Cloud Pub/Sub Emulator           │ pubsub-emulator │ 33.4 MiB │
│ Not Installed │ Emulator Reverse Proxy           │ emulator-reverse-proxy │ 14.5 MiB │
│ Not Installed │ Google Container Local Builder   │ container-builder-local │ 3.8 MiB │
│ Not Installed │ Google Container Registry's Docker credential helper │ docker-credential-gcr │ 3.3 MiB │
│ Not Installed │ gcloud Alpha Commands            │ alpha    │ < 1 MiB   │
│ Not Installed │ gcloud Beta Commands             │ beta     │ < 1 MiB   │
│ Not Installed │ gcloud app Java Extensions       │ app-engine-java │ 118.9 MiB │
│ Not Installed │ gcloud app PHP Extensions        │ app-engine-php │ │
│ Not Installed │ gcloud app Python Extensions     │ app-engine-python │ 6.2 MiB │
│ Not Installed │ gcloud app Python Extensions (Extra Libraries) │ app-engine-python-extras │ 27.8 MiB │
│ Not Installed │ kubectl                          │ kubectl  │ 12.3 MiB  │
│ Installed     │ BigQuery Command Line Tool       │ bq       │ < 1 MiB   │
│ Installed     │ Cloud SDK Core Libraries         │ core     │ 7.3 MiB   │
│ Installed     │ Cloud Storage Command Line Tool  │ gsutil   │ 3.3 MiB   │
└───────────────┴──────────────────────────────────┴──────────┴───────────┘
```

```
To install or remove components at your current SDK version [193.0.0], run:
  $ gcloud components install COMPONENT_ID
  $ gcloud components remove COMPONENT_ID
To update your SDK installation to the latest version [193.0.0], run:
  $ gcloud components update
```

You can update the components by adding them to your shell:

```
$ gcloud components install alpha beta
Your current Cloud SDK version is: 193.0.0
Installing components from version: 193.0.0
```

```
┌─────────────────────────────────────────────────────────────────────
│ ─────────┐
│ │ These components will be installed. │
│ ├────────────────────────────────────┬──────────────┬──────────────
│ ──┐
│ │ Name  │ Version  │ Size  │
│ ├──────────────────────────┬─────────┼──────────┬──────────
│ ──┐
│ │ gcloud Alpha Commands  │ 2017.09.15  │ < 1 MiB  │
│ │ gcloud Beta Commands   │ 2017.09.15  │ < 1 MiB  │
│ └──────────────────────────────────────────┴──────────
│ ──┘
```

```
For the latest full release notes, please visit:
  https://cloud.google.com/sdk/release_notes
Do you want to continue (Y/n)? y
```

```
├═══ Creating update staging area ═══╣

├═══ Installing: gcloud Alpha Commands ═══╣

├═══ Installing: gcloud Beta Commands ═══╣

├═══ Creating backup and activating new installation ═══╣
```

```
Performing post processing steps...done.
Update done!
```

After you run the `kube-up.sh` script, you will see quite a few lines roll past. Let's take a look at them one section at a time:

```
... Starting cluster in us-central1-b using provider gce
... calling verify-prereqs

All components are up to date.

All components are up to date.

All components are up to date.
```

 If your `gcloud` components are not up to date, you may be prompted to update them.

The preceding screenshot shows the checks for prerequisites, as well as making sure that all components are up to date. This is specific to each provider. In the case of GCE, it will verify that the SDK is installed and that all components are up to date. If not, you will see a prompt at this point to install or update:

```
... calling kube-up
Your active configuration is: [default]

Project: dynamic-nomad-152102
Zone: us-central1-b
gs://kubernetes-staging-549d6b8d9c/kubernetes-devel/
+++ Staging server tars to Google Storage: gs://kubernetes-staging-549d6b8d9c/kub
ernetes-devel
+++ kubernetes-server-linux-amd64.tar.gz uploaded (sha1 = 5df19e3745bbc8c7d1a5bf6
d61d9e1b0d189db64)
+++ kubernetes-salt.tar.gz uploaded (sha1 = 95e855d893e4549b935aed8736f3a2372ae7c
cd3)
+++ kubernetes-manifests.tar.gz uploaded (sha1 = e9c52530a14612c91f45e017743925a0
dba6dcc8)
INSTANCE_GROUPS=
NODE_NAMES=
```

Now, the script is turning up the cluster. Again, this is specific to the provider. For GCE, it first checks to make sure that the SDK is configured for a default project and zone. If they are set, you'll see those in the output:

 You may see an output that the bucket for storage hasn't been created. That's normal! The creation script will go ahead and create it.

```
BucketNotFoundException: 404 gs://kubernetes-staging-22caacf417 bucket does
not exist.
```

Next, it uploads the server binaries to Google Cloud storage, as seen in the **Creating gs:...** lines:

```
Looking for already existing resources
Starting master and configuring firewalls
Created [https://www.googleapis.com/compute/v1/projects/dynamic-nomad-152102/zon
es/us-central1-b/disks/kubernetes-master-pd].
NAME                    ZONE            SIZE_GB  TYPE     STATUS
kubernetes-master-pd  us-central1-b  20        pd-ssd   READY

New disks are unformatted. You must format and mount a disk before it
can be used. You can find instructions on how to do this at:

https://cloud.google.com/compute/docs/disks/add-persistent-disk#formatting

Created [https://www.googleapis.com/compute/v1/projects/dynamic-nomad-152102/glo
bal/firewalls/kubernetes-master-https].
NAME                        NETWORK  SRC_RANGES   RULES      SRC_TAGS   TARGET_TAGS
kubernetes-master-https  default  0.0.0.0/0    tcp:443               kubernetes-mast
er
Created [https://www.googleapis.com/compute/v1/projects/dynamic-nomad-152102/reg
ions/us-central1/addresses/kubernetes-master-ip].
Generating certs for alternate-names: IP:23.251.158.223,IP:10.0.0.1,DNS:kubernet
es,DNS:kubernetes.default,DNS:kubernetes.default.svc,DNS:kubernetes.default.svc.
cluster.local,DNS:kubernetes-master
```

It then checks for any pieces of a cluster already running. Then, we finally start creating the cluster. In the output in the preceding screenshot, we can see it creating the master server, IP address, and appropriate firewall configurations for the cluster:

```
+++ Logging using Fluentd to gcp
WARNING: You have selected a disk size of under [200GB]. This may result in poor
 I/O performance. For more information, see: https://developers.google.com/compu
te/docs/disks#pdperformance.
Created [https://www.googleapis.com/compute/v1/projects/dynamic-nomad-152102/glo
bal/firewalls/kubernetes-minion-all].
NAME                  NETWORK  SRC_RANGES      RULES                    SRC_TAG
S  TARGET_TAGS
kubernetes-minion-all  default  10.244.0.0/14   tcp,udp,icmp,esp,ah,sctp
    kubernetes-minion
Created [https://www.googleapis.com/compute/v1/projects/dynamic-nomad-152102/zon
es/us-central1-b/instances/kubernetes-master].
NAME              ZONE          MACHINE_TYPE    PREEMPTIBLE  INTERNAL_IP  EXTER
NAL_IP      STATUS
kubernetes-master  us-central1-b  n1-standard-1                10.128.0.2  23.25
1.158.223  RUNNING
Creating minions.
Attempt 1 to create kubernetes-minion-template
WARNING: You have selected a disk size of under [200GB]. This may result in poor
 I/O performance. For more information, see: https://developers.google.com/compu
te/docs/disks#pdperformance.
Created [https://www.googleapis.com/compute/v1/projects/dynamic-nomad-152102/glo
bal/instanceTemplates/kubernetes-minion-template].
NAME                      MACHINE_TYPE    PREEMPTIBLE  CREATION_TIMESTAMP
kubernetes-minion-template  n1-standard-2                2016-12-10T04:25:37.527-
08:00
Created [https://www.googleapis.com/compute/v1/projects/dynamic-nomad-152102/zon
es/us-central1-b/instanceGroupManagers/kubernetes-minion-group].
NAME                     LOCATION       SCOPE  BASE_INSTANCE_NAME       SIZE  TA
RGET_SIZE  INSTANCE_TEMPLATE          AUTOSCALED
kubernetes-minion-group  us-central1-b  zone   kubernetes-minion-group  0     3
           kubernetes-minion-template  no
Waiting for group to become stable, current operations: creating: 3
Waiting for group to become stable, current operations: creating: 3
Waiting for group to become stable, current operations: creating: 1
Group is stable
```

Finally, it creates the minions or nodes for our cluster. This is where our container workloads will actually run. It will continually loop and wait while all the minions start up. By default, the cluster will have four nodes (minions), but K8s supports having more than 1,000 (and soon beyond). We will come back to scaling the nodes later on in this book:

```
Attempt 1 to create kubernetes-minion-template
WARNING: You have selected a disk size of under [200GB]. This may result in
poor I/O performance. For more information, see:
https://developers.google.com/compute/docs/disks#performance.
Created
[https://www.googleapis.com/compute/v1/projects/gsw-k8s-3/global/instanceTe
mplates/kubernetes-minion-template].
```

```
NAME MACHINE_TYPE PREEMPTIBLE CREATION_TIMESTAMP
kubernetes-minion-template n1-standard-2 2018-03-17T11:14:04.186-07:00
Created
[https://www.googleapis.com/compute/v1/projects/gsw-k8s-3/zones/us-central1
-b/instanceGroupManagers/kubernetes-minion-group].
NAME LOCATION SCOPE BASE_INSTANCE_NAME SIZE TARGET_SIZE INSTANCE_TEMPLATE
AUTOSCALED
kubernetes-minion-group us-central1-b zone kubernetes-minion-group 0 3
kubernetes-minion-template no
Waiting for group to become stable, current operations: creating: 3
Group is stable
INSTANCE_GROUPS=kubernetes-minion-group
NODE_NAMES=kubernetes-minion-group-176g kubernetes-minion-group-s9qw
kubernetes-minion-group-tr7r
Trying to find master named 'kubernetes-master'
Looking for address 'kubernetes-master-ip'
Using master: kubernetes-master (external IP: 104.155.172.179)
Waiting up to 300 seconds for cluster initialization.
```

Now that everything is created, the cluster is initialized and started. Assuming that everything goes well, we will get an IP address for the master:

```
... calling validate-cluster
Validating gce cluster, MULTIZONE=
Project: gsw-k8s-3
Network Project: gsw-k8s-3
Zone: us-central1-b
No resources found.
Waiting for 4 ready nodes. 0 ready nodes, 0 registered. Retrying.
No resources found.
Waiting for 4 ready nodes. 0 ready nodes, 0 registered. Retrying.
Waiting for 4 ready nodes. 0 ready nodes, 1 registered. Retrying.
Waiting for 4 ready nodes. 0 ready nodes, 4 registered. Retrying.
Found 4 node(s).
NAME STATUS ROLES AGE VERSION
kubernetes-master Ready,SchedulingDisabled <none> 32s v1.9.4
kubernetes-minion-group-176g Ready <none> 25s v1.9.4
kubernetes-minion-group-s9qw Ready <none> 25s v1.9.4
kubernetes-minion-group-tr7r Ready <none> 35s v1.9.4
Validate output:
NAME STATUS MESSAGE ERROR
etcd-1 Healthy {"health": "true"}
scheduler Healthy ok
controller-manager Healthy ok
etcd-0 Healthy {"health": "true"}
Cluster validation succeeded
```

Also, note that configuration along with the cluster management credentials are stored in home/<Username>/.kube/config.

Then, the script will validate the cluster. At this point, we are no longer running provider-specific code. The validation script will query the cluster via the kubectl.sh script. This is the central script for managing our cluster. In this case, it checks the number of minions found, registered, and in a ready state. It loops through, giving the cluster up to 10 minutes to finish initialization.

After a successful startup, a summary of the minions and the cluster component health is printed on the screen:

```
Done, listing cluster services:
Kubernetes master is running at https://104.155.172.179
GLBCDefaultBackend is running at
https://104.155.172.179/api/v1/namespaces/kube-system/services/default-http
-backend:http/proxy
Heapster is running at
https://104.155.172.179/api/v1/namespaces/kube-system/services/heapster/pro
xy
KubeDNS is running at
https://104.155.172.179/api/v1/namespaces/kube-system/services/kube-dns:dns
/proxy
kubernetes-dashboard is running at
https://104.155.172.179/api/v1/namespaces/kube-system/services/https:kubern
etes-dashboard:/proxy
Metrics-server is running at
https://104.155.172.179/api/v1/namespaces/kube-system/services/https:metric
s-server:/proxy
Grafana is running at
https://104.155.172.179/api/v1/namespaces/kube-system/services/monitoring-g
rafana/proxy
InfluxDB is running at
https://104.155.172.179/api/v1/namespaces/kube-system/services/monitoring-i
nfluxdb:http/proxy
To further debug and diagnose cluster problems, use 'kubectl cluster-info
dump'.
```

Finally, a kubectl cluster-info command is run, which outputs the URL for the master services, including DNS, UI, and monitoring. Let's take a look at some of these components.

If you'd like to get further debugging and/or diagnose cluster problems, you can use `kubectl cluster-info dump` to see what's going on with your cluster. Additionally, if you need to pause and take a break and want to conserve your free hours, you can log into the GUI and set the `kubernetes-minion-group` instance group to zero, which will remove all of the instances. The pencil will edit the group for you; set it to zero. Don't forget to set it back to three if you want to pick up again!

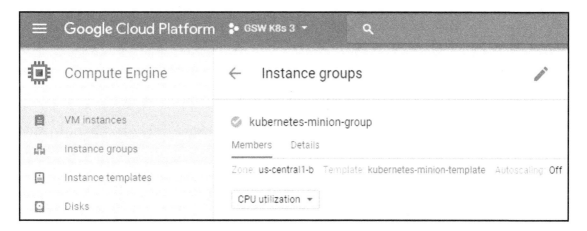

You can simply stop the manager as well. You'll need to click the stop button to shut it down:

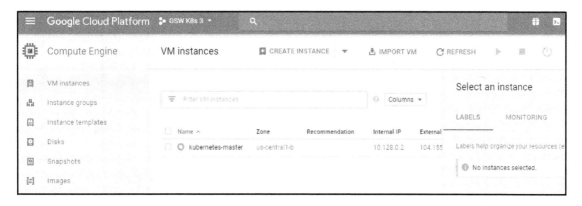

If you'd like to start the cluster up again, start the servers again to keep going. They'll need some time to start up and connect to each other.

If you want to work on more than one cluster at a time or you want to use a different name than the default, see the `<kubernetes>/cluster/gce/config-default.sh` file for more fine-grained configuration of your cluster.

Kubernetes UI

Since Kubernetes v1.3.x, you can no longer authenticate through public IP addresses to the GUI. To get around this, we'll use the `kubectl proxy` command. First, grab the token from the configuration command, and then we'll use it to launch a local proxy version of the UI:

```
$ kubectl config view |grep token
  token: RvoYTIn4rExi1bNRzk56g0PU0srZbzOf
$ kubectl proxy --port=8001
```

Open a browser and enter the following URL: `https://localhost/ui/`.

You can also type these commands to open a browser window automatically if you're on macOS: `$ open https://localhost/ui/` or `$ xdg-open https://localhost/ui` if you're on Linux.

The certificate is self-signed by default, so you'll need to ignore the warnings in your browser before proceeding. After this, we will see a login dialog:

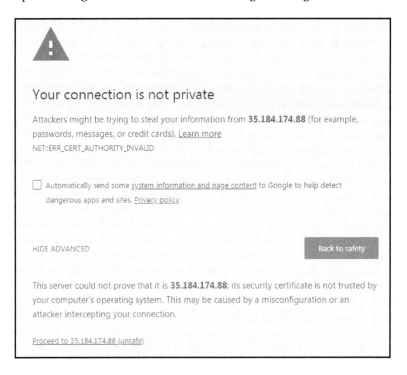

At this login dialog, you'll need to input the token that you grabbed in the aforementioned command.

This is where we use the credentials listed during the K8s installation. We can find them at any time by simply using the `config` command $ `kubectl config view`.

Use the **Token** option and log in to your cluster:

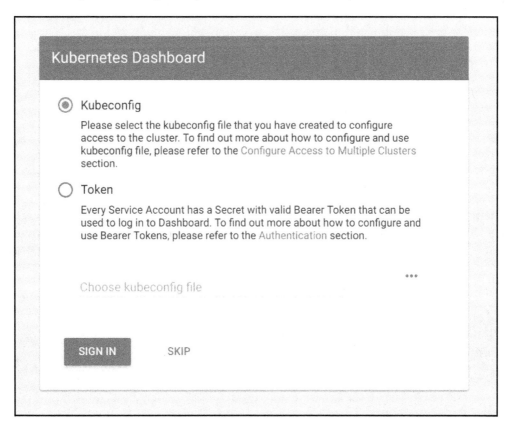

Now that we have entered our token, you should see a dashboard like the one in the following screenshot:

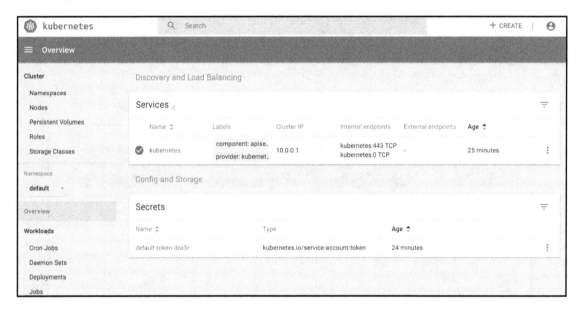

The main dashboard takes us to a page with not much display at first. There is a link to deploy a containerized app that will take you to a GUI for deployment. This GUI can be a very easy way to get started deploying apps without worrying about the YAML syntax for Kubernetes. However, as your use of containers matures, it's a good practice to use the YAML definitions that are checked in to source control.

If you click on the **Nodes** link on the left-hand side menu, you will see some metrics on the current cluster nodes:

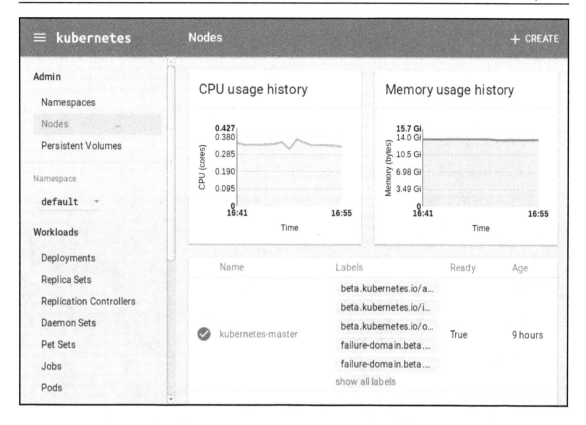

At the top, we can see an aggregate of the CPU and memory use followed by a listing of our cluster nodes. Clicking on one of the nodes will take us to a page with detailed information about that node, its health, and various metrics.

The Kubernetes UI has a lot of other views that will become more useful as we start launching real applications and adding configurations to the cluster.

Grafana

Another service installed by default is Grafana. This tool will give us a dashboard to view metrics on the cluster nodes. We can access it using the following syntax in a browser:

```
https://localhost/api/v1/proxy/namespaces/kube-system/services/monitoring-g
rafana
```

The Grafana dashboard should look like this:

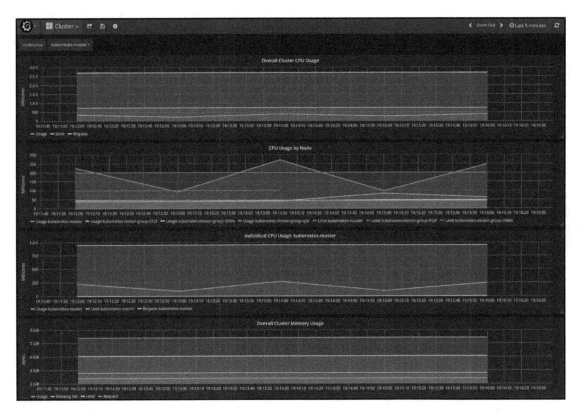

From the main page, click on the **Home** drop-down and select **Cluster**. Here, Kubernetes is actually running a number of services. Heapster is used to collect the resource usage on the pods and nodes, and stores the information in InfluxDB. The results, such as CPU and memory usage, are what we see in the Grafana UI. We will explore this in depth in Chapter 7, *Monitoring and Logging*.

Command line

The `kubectl` script has commands for exploring our cluster and the workloads running on it. You can find it in the `/kubernetes/client/bin` folder. We will be using this command throughout the book, so let's take a second to set up our environment. We can do so by putting the binaries folder on our `PATH`, in the following manner:

```
$ export PATH=$PATH:/<Path where you downloaded K8s>/kubernetes/client/bin
$ chmod +x /<Path where you downloaded K8s>/kubernetes/client/bin
```

> **TIP**
>
> You may choose to download the `kubernetes` folder outside your home folder, so modify the preceding command as appropriate. It is also a good idea to make the changes permanent by adding the `export` command to the end of your `.bashrc` file in your home directory.

Now that we have `kubectl` on our path, we can start working with it. It has quite a few commands. Since we have not spun up any applications yet, most of these commands will not be very interesting. However, we can explore two commands right away.

First, we have already seen the `cluster-info` command during initialization, but we can run it again at any time with the following command:

```
$ kubectl cluster-info
```

Another useful command is `get`. It can be used to see currently running services, pods, replication controllers, and a lot more. Here are the three examples that are useful right out of the gate:

- Lists the nodes in our cluster:

```
$ kubectl get nodes
```

- Lists cluster events:

```
$ kubectl get events
```

- Finally, we can see any services that are running in the cluster, as follows:

```
$ kubectl get services
```

To start with, we will only see one service, named `kubernetes`. This service is the core API server for the cluster.

For any of the preceding commands, you can always add a -h flag on the end to understand the intended usage.

Services running on the master

Let's dig a little bit deeper into our new cluster and its core services. By default, machines are named with the `kubernetes-` prefix. We can modify this using `$KUBE_GCE_INSTANCE_PREFIX` before a cluster is spun up. For the cluster we just started, the master should be named `kubernetes-master`. We can use the `gcloud` command-line utility to SSH into the machine. The following command will start an SSH session with the master node. Be sure to substitute your project ID and zone to match your environment:

```
$ gcloud compute ssh --zone "<your gce zone>" "kubernetes-master"

$ gcloud compute ssh --zone "us-central1-b" "kubernetes-master"
Warning: Permanently added 'compute.5419404412212490753' (RSA) to the list
of known hosts.

Welcome to Kubernetes v1.9.4!

You can find documentation for Kubernetes at:
  http://docs.kubernetes.io/

The source for this release can be found at:
  /home/kubernetes/kubernetes-src.tar.gz
Or you can download it at:
https://storage.googleapis.com/kubernetes-release/release/v1.9.4/kubernetes
-src.tar.gz

It is based on the Kubernetes source at:
  https://github.com/kubernetes/kubernetes/tree/v1.9.4

For Kubernetes copyright and licensing information, see:
  /home/kubernetes/LICENSES

jesse@kubernetes-master ~ $
```

If you have trouble with SSH via the Google Cloud CLI, you can use the console, which has a built-in SSH client. Simply go to the **VM instances details** page and you'll see an **SSH** option as a column in the `kubernetes-master` listing. Alternatively, the VM instance details page has the SSH option at the top.

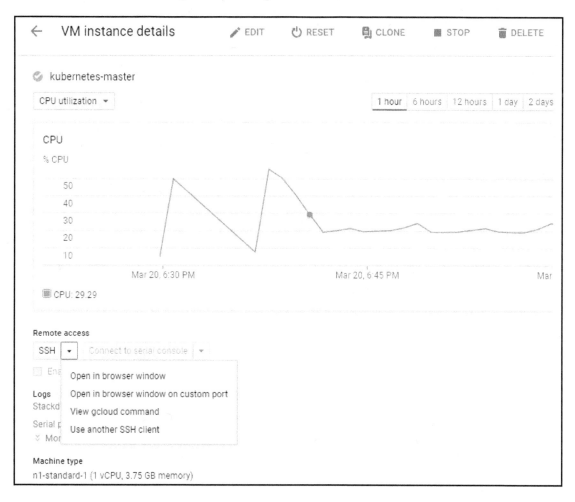

Once we are logged in, we should get a standard shell prompt. Let's run the `docker` command that filters for `Image` and `Status`:

```
$ docker container ls --format 'table {{.Image}}\t{{.Status}}'
```

```
IMAGE                                                                    STATUS
gcr.io/google_containers/node-problem-detector:v0.1                      Up 13 hours
gcr.io/google_containers/pause-amd64:3.0                                 Up 13 hours
gcr.io/google_containers/fluentd-gcp:1.21                                Up 13 hours
gcr.io/google_containers/kube-apiserver:fa481b6112db7dcce46bfc8cfbf149a2 Up 13 hours
gcr.io/google_containers/etcd:2.2.1                                      Up 13 hours
gcr.io/google_containers/etcd:2.2.1                                      Up 13 hours
gcr.io/google_containers/rescheduler:v0.2.1                             Up 13 hours
gcr.io/google_containers/glbc:0.8.0                                     Up 13 hours
gcr.io/google-containers/kube-addon-manager:v5.1                        Up 13 hours
gcr.io/google_containers/etcd-empty-dir-cleanup:0.0.1                   Up 13 hours
gcr.io/google_containers/kube-controller-manager:9b1fc8f7afac597ccb49e34778214c49 Up 13 hours
gcr.io/google_containers/kube-scheduler:67b73a442b6a6f362a086ea4ab8dc1cd Up 13 hours
gcr.io/google_containers/pause-amd64:3.0                                 Up 13 hours
gcr.io/google_containers/pause-amd64:3.0                                 Up 13 hours
gcr.io/google_containers/pause-amd64:3.0                                 Up 13 hours
gcr.io/google_containers/pause-amd64:3.0                                 Up 13 hours
gcr.io/google_containers/pause-amd64:3.0                                 Up 13 hours
gcr.io/google_containers/pause-amd64:3.0                                 Up 13 hours
gcr.io/google_containers/pause-amd64:3.0                                 Up 13 hours
gcr.io/google_containers/pause-amd64:3.0                                 Up 13 hours
gcr.io/google_containers/pause-amd64:3.0                                 Up 13 hours
```

Even though we have not deployed any applications on Kubernetes yet, we can note that there are several containers already running. The following is a brief description of each container:

- `fluentd-gcp`: This container collects and sends the cluster logs file to the Google Cloud Logging service.
- `node-problem-detector`: This container is a daemon that runs on every node and currently detects issues at the hardware and kernel layer.
- `rescheduler`: This is another add-on container that makes sure critical components are always running. In cases of low resource availability, it may even remove less critical pods to make room.
- `glbc`: This is another Kubernetes add-on container that provides Google Cloud Layer 7 load balancing using the new Ingress capability.
- `kube-addon-manager`: This component is core to the extension of Kubernetes through various add-ons. It also periodically applies any changes to the `/etc/kubernetes/addons` directory.
- `etcd-empty-dir-cleanup`: A utility to clean up empty keys in `etcd`.

- `kube-controller-manager`: This is a controller manager that controls a variety of cluster functions, ensuring accurate and up-to-date replication is one of its vital roles. Additionally, it monitors, manages, and discovers new nodes. Finally, it manages and updates service endpoints.
- `kube-apiserver`: This container runs the API server. As we explored in the Swagger interface, this RESTful API allows us to create, query, update, and remove various components of our Kubernetes cluster.
- `kube-scheduler`: This scheduler takes unscheduled pods and binds them to nodes based on the current scheduling algorithm.
- `etcd`: This runs the `etcd` software built by CoreOS, and it is a distributed and consistent key-value store. This is where the Kubernetes cluster state is stored, updated, and retrieved by various components of K8s.
- `pause`: This container is often referred to as the pod infrastructure container and is used to set up and hold the networking namespace and resource limits for each pod.

 I omitted the `amd64` for many of these names to make this more generic. The purpose of the pods remains the same.

To exit the SSH session, simply type `exit` at the prompt.

 In the next chapter, we will also show how a few of these services work together in the first image, *Kubernetes core architecture*.

Services running on the minions

We could SSH to one of the minions, but since Kubernetes schedules workloads across the cluster, we would not see all the containers on a single minion. However, we can look at the pods running on all the minions using the `kubectl` command:

```
$ kubectl get pods
No resources found.
```

Since we have not started any applications on the cluster yet, we don't see any pods. However, there are actually several system pods running pieces of the Kubernetes infrastructure. We can see these pods by specifying the kube-system namespace. We will explore namespaces and their significance later, but for now, the --namespace=kube-system command can be used to look at these K8s system resources, as follows:

```
$ kubectl get pods --namespace=kube-system
jesse@kubernetes-master ~ $ kubectl get pods --namespace=kube-system
NAME READY STATUS RESTARTS AGE
etcd-server-events-kubernetes-master 1/1 Running 0 50m
etcd-server-kubernetes-master 1/1 Running 0 50m
event-exporter-v0.1.7-64464bff45-rg88v 1/1 Running 0 51m
fluentd-gcp-v2.0.10-c4ptt 1/1 Running 0 50m
fluentd-gcp-v2.0.10-d9c5z 1/1 Running 0 50m
fluentd-gcp-v2.0.10-ztdzs 1/1 Running 0 51m
fluentd-gcp-v2.0.10-zxx6k 1/1 Running 0 50m
heapster-v1.5.0-584689c78d-z9blq 4/4 Running 0 50m
kube-addon-manager-kubernetes-master 1/1 Running 0 50m
kube-apiserver-kubernetes-master 1/1 Running 0 50m
kube-controller-manager-kubernetes-master 1/1 Running 0 50m
kube-dns-774d5484cc-gcgdx 3/3 Running 0 51m
kube-dns-774d5484cc-hgm9r 3/3 Running 0 50m
kube-dns-autoscaler-69c5cbdcdd-8hj5j 1/1 Running 0 51m
kube-proxy-kubernetes-minion-group-012f 1/1 Running 0 50m
kube-proxy-kubernetes-minion-group-699m 1/1 Running 0 50m
kube-proxy-kubernetes-minion-group-sj9r 1/1 Running 0 50m
kube-scheduler-kubernetes-master 1/1 Running 0 50m
kubernetes-dashboard-74f855c8c6-v4f6x 1/1 Running 0 51m
17-default-backend-57856c5f55-21z6w 1/1 Running 0 51m
17-lb-controller-v0.9.7-kubernetes-master 1/1 Running 0 50m
metrics-server-v0.2.1-7f8dd98c8f-v9b4c 2/2 Running 0 50m
monitoring-influxdb-grafana-v4-554f5d97-17q4k 2/2 Running 0 51m
rescheduler-v0.3.1-kubernetes-master 1/1 Running 0 50m
```

The first six lines should look familiar. Some of these are the services we saw running on the master, and we will see pieces of these on the nodes. There are a few additional services we have not seen yet. The kube-dns option provides the DNS and service discovery plumbing, kubernetes-dashboard-xxxx is the user interface for Kubernetes, 17-default-backend-xxxx provides the default load balancing backend for the new layer-7 load balancing capability, and heapster-v1.2.0-xxxx and monitoring-influx-grafana provide the Heapster database and user interface to monitor resource usage across the cluster.

Finally, `kube-proxy-kubernetes-minion-group-xxxx` is the proxy, which directs traffic to the proper backing services and pods running on our cluster. The `kube-apiserver` validates and configures data for the API objects, which include services, replication controllers, pods, and other Kubernetes objects. The `rescheduler` guarantees the scheduling of critical system add-ons, given that the cluster has enough available resources.

If we did SSH into a random minion, we would see several containers that run across a few of these pods. A sample might look like the following:

```
IMAGE                                                               STATUS
gcr.io/google_containers/exechealthz-amd64:1.2                      Up 13 hours
gcr.io/google_containers/kube-dnsmasq-amd64:1.4                     Up 13 hours
gcr.io/google_containers/heapster_grafana:v3.1.1                    Up 13 hours
gcr.io/google_containers/kubedns-amd64:1.8                          Up 13 hours
gcr.io/google_containers/heapster_influxdb:v0.7                     Up 13 hours
gcr.io/google_containers/defaultbackend:1.0                         Up 13 hours
gcr.io/google_containers/pause-amd64:3.0                            Up 13 hours
gcr.io/google_containers/pause-amd64:3.0                            Up 13 hours
gcr.io/google_containers/pause-amd64:3.0                            Up 13 hours
gcr.io/google_containers/fluentd-gcp:1.25                           Up 13 hours
gcr.io/google_containers/node-problem-detector:v0.1                 Up 13 hours
gcr.io/google_containers/kube-proxy:b87ffd2bf726a72a00bbc021970cb855 Up 13 hours
gcr.io/google_containers/pause-amd64:3.0                            Up 13 hours
gcr.io/google_containers/pause-amd64:3.0                            Up 13 hours
gcr.io/google_containers/pause-amd64:3.0                            Up 13 hours
```

Again, we saw a similar lineup of services on the master. The services we did not see on the master include the following:

- `kubedns`: This container monitors the service and endpoint resources in Kubernetes and synchronizes any changes to DNS lookups.
- `kube-dnsmasq`: This is another container that provides DNS caching.
- `dnsmasq-metrics`: This provides metric reporting for DNS services in cluster.
- `l7-defaultbackend`: This is the default backend for handling the GCE L7 load balancer and Ingress.
- `kube-proxy`: This is the network and service proxy for your cluster. This component makes sure that service traffic is directed to wherever your workloads are running on the cluster. We will explore this in more depth later in this book.
- `heapster`: This container is for monitoring and analytics.
- `addon-resizer`: This cluster utility is for scaling containers.

- `heapster_grafana`: This tracks resource usage and monitoring.
- `heapster_influxdb`: This time series database is for Heapster data.
- `cluster-proportional-autoscaler`: This cluster utility is for scaling containers in proportion to the cluster size.
- `exechealthz`: This performs health checks on the pods.

 Again, I have omitted the `amd64` for many of these names to make this more generic. The purpose of the pods remains the same.

Tearing down a cluster

Alright, this is our first cluster on GCE, but let's explore some other providers. To keep things simple, we need to remove the one we just created on GCE. We can tear down the cluster with one simple command:

```
$ cluster/kube-down.sh
```

Working with other providers

By default, Kubernetes uses the GCE provider for Google Cloud. In order to use other cloud providers, we can explore a rapidly expanding tool set of different options. Let's use AWS for this example, where we have two main options: kops (`https://github.com/kubernetes/kops`) and kube-aws (`https://github.com/kubernetes-incubator/kube-aws`). For reference, the following KUBERNETES_PROVIDER are listed in this table:

Provider	KUBERNETES_PROVIDER value	Type
Google Compute Engine	gce	Public cloud
Google Container Engine	gke	Public cloud
Amazon Web Services	aws	Public cloud
Microsoft Azure	azure	Public cloud
Hashicorp vagrant	vagrant	Virtual development environment
VMware vSphere	vsphere	Private cloud/on-premise virtualization
libvirt running CoreOS	libvirt-coreos	Virtualization management tool
Canonical Juju (folks behind Ubuntu)	juju	OS service orchestration tool

CLI setup

Let's try setting up the cluster on AWS. As a prerequisite, we need to have the AWS CLI installed and configured for our account. The AWS CLI installation and configuration documentation can be found at the following links:

- Installation documentation:
  `http://docs.aws.amazon.com/cli/latest/userguide/installing.html#instal l-bundle-other-os`
- Configuration documentation:
  `http://docs.aws.amazon.com/cli/latest/userguide/cli-chap-getting-start ed.html`

You'll also need to configure your credentials as recommended by AWS (refer to `https:// docs.aws.amazon.com/sdk-for-go/v1/developer-guide/configuring-sdk. html#specifying-credentials`) in order to use kops. To get started, you'll need to first install the CLI tool (refer to `https://github.com/kubernetes/kops/blob/master/docs/ install.md`). If you're running on Linux, you can install the tools as follows:

```
curl -Lo kops https://github.com/kubernetes/kops/releases/download/$(curl -
s https://api.github.com/repos/kubernetes/kops/releases/latest | grep
tag_name | cut -d '"' -f 4)/kops-darwin-amd64
chmod +x ./kops
sudo mv ./kops /usr/local/bin/
```

If you're installing this for macOS, you can use `brew update && brew install kops` from the command-line Terminal. As a reminder, you'll need `kubectl` installed if you haven't already! Check the instructions in the preceding links to confirm the installation.

IAM setup

In order for us to use kops, we'll need an IAM role created in AWS with the following permissions:

```
AmazonEC2FullAccess
AmazonRoute53FullAccess
AmazonS3FullAccess
IAMFullAccess
AmazonVPCFullAccess
```

Once you've created those pieces manually in the AWS GUI, you can run the following commands from your PC to set up permissions with the correct access:

```
aws iam create-group --group-name kops

aws iam attach-group-policy --policy-arn
arn:aws:iam::aws:policy/AmazonEC2FullAccess --group-name kops
aws iam attach-group-policy --policy-arn
arn:aws:iam::aws:policy/AmazonRoute53FullAccess --group-name kops
aws iam attach-group-policy --policy-arn
arn:aws:iam::aws:policy/AmazonS3FullAccess --group-name kops
aws iam attach-group-policy --policy-arn
arn:aws:iam::aws:policy/IAMFullAccess --group-name kops
aws iam attach-group-policy --policy-arn
arn:aws:iam::aws:policy/AmazonVPCFullAccess --group-name kops

aws iam create-user --user-name kops

aws iam add-user-to-group --user-name kops --group-name kops

aws iam create-access-key --user-name kops
```

In order to use this newly created kops user to interact with the kops tool, you need to copy down the `SecretAccessKey` and `AccessKeyID` from the output JSON, and then configure the AWS CLI as follows:

```
# configure the aws client to use your new IAM user
aws configure # Use your new access and secret key here
aws iam list-users # you should see a list of all your IAM users here
# Because "aws configure" doesn't export these vars for kops to use, we
export them now
export AWS_ACCESS_KEY_ID=$(aws configure get aws_access_key_id)
export AWS_SECRET_ACCESS_KEY=$(aws configure get aws_secret_access_key)
```

We're going to use a gossip-based cluster to bypass a kops configuration requirement of public DNS zones. This requires kops 1.6.2 or later, and allows you to create a locally registered cluster that requires a name ending in `.k8s.local`. More on that in a bit.

 If you'd like to explore how to purchase and set up publicly routable DNS through a provider, you can review the available scenarios in the kops documentation here: `https://github.com/kubernetes/kops/blob/master/docs/aws.md#configure-dns`.

Cluster state storage

Since we're building resources in the cloud using configuration management, we're going to need to store the representation of our cluster in a dedicated S3 bucket. This source of truth will allow us to maintain a single location for the configuration and state of our Kubernetes cluster. Please prepend your bucket name with a unique value.

You'll need to have kubectl, kops, the aws cli, and IAM credentials set up for yourself at this point!

Be sure to create your bucket in the us-east-1 region for now, as kops is currently opinionated as to where the bucket belongs:

```
aws s3api create-bucket \
  --bucket gsw-k8s-3-state-store \
  --region us-east-1
```

Let's go ahead and set up versioning as well, so you can roll your cluster back to previous states in case anything goes wrong. Behold the power of Infrastructure as Code!

```
aws s3api put-bucket-versioning --bucket gsw-k8s-3-state-store --versioning-configuration Status=Enabled
```

Creating your cluster

We'll go ahead and use the .k8s.local settings mentioned previously to simplify the DNS setup of the cluster. If you'd prefer, you can also use the name and state flags available within kops to avoid using environment variables. Let's prepare the local environment first:

```
$ export NAME=gswk8s3.k8s.local
$ export KOPS_STATE_STORE=s3://gsw-k8s-3-state-store
$ aws s3api create-bucket --bucket gsw-k8s-3-state-store --region us-east-1
{
    "Location": "/gsw-k8s-3-state-store"
}
$
```

Let's spin up our cluster in Ohio, and verify that we can see that region first:

```
$ aws ec2 describe-availability-zones --region us-east-2
{
  "AvailabilityZones": [
  {
  "State": "available",
  "ZoneName": "us-east-2a",
  "Messages": [],
  "RegionName": "us-east-2"
  },
  {
  "State": "available",
  "ZoneName": "us-east-2b",
  "Messages": [],
  "RegionName": "us-east-2"
  },
  {
  "State": "available",
  "ZoneName": "us-east-2c",
  "Messages": [],
  "RegionName": "us-east-2"
  }
  ]
}
```

Great! Let's make some Kubernetes. We're going to use the most basic kops cluster command available, though there are much more complex examples available in the documentation (https://github.com/kubernetes/kops/blob/master/docs/high_availability.md):

```
kops create cluster --zones us-east-2a ${NAME}
```

With kops and generally with Kubernetes, everything is going to be created within **Auto Scaling groups (ASGs)**.

 Read more about AWS autoscaling groups here—they're essential: https://docs.aws.amazon.com/autoscaling/ec2/userguide/AutoScalingGroup.html.

Once you run this command, you'll get a whole lot of configuration output in what we call a dry run format. This is similar to the Terraform idea of a Terraform plan, which lets you see what you're about to build in AWS and lets you edit the output accordingly.

At the end of the output, you'll see the following text, which gives you some basic suggestions on the next steps:

```
Must specify --yes to apply changes
Cluster configuration has been created.

Suggestions:
* list clusters with: kops get cluster
* edit this cluster with: kops edit cluster gwsk8s3.k8s.local
* edit your node instance group: kops edit ig --name=gwsk8s3.k8s.local
nodes
* edit your master instance group: kops edit ig --name=gwsk8s3.k8s.local
master-us-east-2a

Finally configure your cluster with: kops update cluster gwsk8s3.k8s.local
--yes
```

 If you don't have an SSH keypair in your `~/.ssh` directory, you'll need to create one. This article will lead you through the steps: `https://help.github.com/articles/generating-a-new-ssh-key-and-adding-it-to-the-ssh-agent/`.

Once you've confirmed that you like the look of the output, you can create the cluster:

```
kops update cluster gwsk8s3.k8s.local --yes
```

This will give you a lot of output about cluster creation that you can follow along with:

```
I0320 21:37:34.761784 29197 apply_cluster.go:450] Gossip DNS: skipping DNS
validation
I0320 21:37:35.172971 29197 executor.go:91] Tasks: 0 done / 77 total; 30
can run
I0320 21:37:36.045260 29197 vfs_castore.go:435] Issuing new certificate:
"apiserver-aggregator-ca"
I0320 21:37:36.070047 29197 vfs_castore.go:435] Issuing new certificate:
"ca"
I0320 21:37:36.727579 29197 executor.go:91] Tasks: 30 done / 77 total; 24
can run
I0320 21:37:37.740018 29197 vfs_castore.go:435] Issuing new certificate:
"apiserver-proxy-client"
I0320 21:37:37.758789 29197 vfs_castore.go:435] Issuing new certificate:
"kubecfg"
I0320 21:37:37.830861 29197 vfs_castore.go:435] Issuing new certificate:
"kube-controller-manager"
I0320 21:37:37.928930 29197 vfs_castore.go:435] Issuing new certificate:
"kubelet"
I0320 21:37:37.940619 29197 vfs_castore.go:435] Issuing new certificate:
"kops"
```

```
I0320 21:37:38.095516 29197 vfs_castore.go:435] Issuing new certificate:
"kubelet-api"
I0320 21:37:38.124966 29197 vfs_castore.go:435] Issuing new certificate:
"kube-proxy"
I0320 21:37:38.274664 29197 vfs_castore.go:435] Issuing new certificate:
"kube-scheduler"
I0320 21:37:38.344367 29197 vfs_castore.go:435] Issuing new certificate:
"apiserver-aggregator"
I0320 21:37:38.784822 29197 executor.go:91] Tasks: 54 done / 77 total; 19
can run
I0320 21:37:40.663441 29197 launchconfiguration.go:333] waiting for IAM
instance profile "nodes.gswk8s3.k8s.local" to be ready
I0320 21:37:40.889286 29197 launchconfiguration.go:333] waiting for IAM
instance profile "masters.gswk8s3.k8s.local" to be ready
I0320 21:37:51.302353 29197 executor.go:91] Tasks: 73 done / 77 total; 3
can run
I0320 21:37:52.464204 29197 vfs_castore.go:435] Issuing new certificate:
"master"
I0320 21:37:52.644756 29197 executor.go:91] Tasks: 76 done / 77 total; 1
can run
I0320 21:37:52.916042 29197 executor.go:91] Tasks: 77 done / 77 total; 0
can run
I0320 21:37:53.360796 29197 update_cluster.go:248] Exporting kubecfg for
cluster
kops has set your kubectl context to gswk8s3.k8s.local
```

As with GCE, the setup activity will take a few minutes. It will stage files in **S3** and create the appropriate instances, **Virtual Private Cloud** (**VPC**), security groups, and so on in our AWS account. Then, the Kubernetes cluster will be set up and started. Once everything is finished and started, we should see some options on what comes next:

```
Cluster is starting. It should be ready in a few minutes.

Suggestions:
 * validate cluster: kops validate cluster
 * list nodes: kubectl get nodes --show-labels
 * ssh to the master: ssh -i ~/.ssh/id_rsa admin@api.gswk8s3.k8s.local
The admin user is specific to Debian. If not using Debian please use the
appropriate user based on your OS.
 * read about installing addons:
https://github.com/kubernetes/kops/blob/master/docs/addons.md
```

You'll be able to see instances and security groups, and a VPC will be created for your cluster. The kubectl context will also be pointed at your new AWS cluster so that you can interact with it:

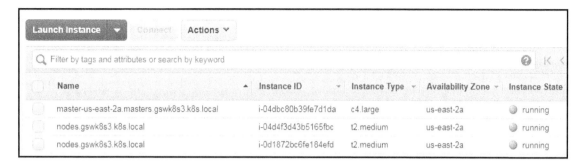

Once again, we will SSH into master. This time, we can use the native SSH client and the admin user as the AMI for Kubernetes in kops is Debian. We'll find the key files in `/home/<username>/.ssh`:

```
$ ssh -v -i /home/<username>/.ssh/<your_id_rsa_file> admin@<Your master IP>
```

If you have trouble with your SSH key, you can set it manually on the cluster by creating a secret, adding it to the cluster, and checking if the cluster requires a rolling update:

```
$ kops create secret --name gswk8s3.k8s.local sshpublickey admin -i
~/.ssh/id_rsa.pub
$ kops update cluster --yes
Using cluster from kubectl context: gswk8s3.k8s.local
I0320 22:03:42.823049 31465 apply_cluster.go:450] Gossip DNS: skipping DNS
validation
I0320 22:03:43.220675 31465 executor.go:91] Tasks: 0 done / 77 total; 30
can run
I0320 22:03:43.919989 31465 executor.go:91] Tasks: 30 done / 77 total; 24
can run
I0320 22:03:44.343478 31465 executor.go:91] Tasks: 54 done / 77 total; 19
can run
I0320 22:03:44.905293 31465 executor.go:91] Tasks: 73 done / 77 total; 3
can run
I0320 22:03:45.385288 31465 executor.go:91] Tasks: 76 done / 77 total; 1
can run
I0320 22:03:45.463711 31465 executor.go:91] Tasks: 77 done / 77 total; 0
can run
I0320 22:03:45.675720 31465 update_cluster.go:248] Exporting kubecfg for
cluster
kops has set your kubectl context to gswk8s3.k8s.local

Cluster changes have been applied to the cloud.

Changes may require instances to restart: kops rolling-update cluster

$ kops rolling-update cluster --name gswk8s3.k8s.local
```

```
NAME STATUS NEEDUPDATE READY MIN MAX NODES
master-us-east-2a Ready 0 1 1 1 1
nodes Ready 0 2 2 2 2

No rolling-update required.
$
```

Once you've gotten into the cluster master, we can look at the containers. We'll use `sudo docker ps --format 'table {{.Image}}t{{.Status}}'` to explore the running containers. We should see the following:

```
admin@ip-172-20-47-159:~$ sudo docker container ls --format 'table
{{.Image}}\t{{.Status}}'
IMAGE STATUS
kope/dns-
controller@sha256:97f80ad43ff833b254907a0341c7fe34748e007515004cf0da09727c5
442f53b Up 29 minutes
gcr.io/google_containers/pause-amd64:3.0 Up 29 minutes
gcr.io/google_containers/kube-
apiserver@sha256:71273b57d811654620dc7a0d22fd893d9852b6637616f8e7e3f4507c60
ea7357 Up 30 minutes
gcr.io/google_containers/etcd@sha256:19544a655157fb089b62d4dac02bbd095f82ca
245dd5e31dd1684d175b109947 Up 30 minutes
gcr.io/google_containers/kube-
proxy@sha256:cc94b481f168bf96bd21cb576cfaa06c55807fcba8a6620b51850e1e30febe
b4 Up 30 minutes
gcr.io/google_containers/kube-controller-
manager@sha256:5ca59252abaf231681f96d07c939e57a05799d1cf876447fe6c2e1469d58
2bde Up 30 minutes
gcr.io/google_containers/etcd@sha256:19544a655157fb089b62d4dac02bbd095f82ca
245dd5e31dd1684d175b109947 Up 30 minutes
gcr.io/google_containers/kube-
scheduler@sha256:46d215410a407b9b5a3500bf8b421778790f5123ff2f4364f99b352a2b
a62940 Up 30 minutes
gcr.io/google_containers/pause-amd64:3.0 Up 30 minutes
gcr.io/google_containers/pause-amd64:3.0 Up 30 minutes
gcr.io/google_containers/pause-amd64:3.0 Up 30 minutes
gcr.io/google_containers/pause-amd64:3.0 Up 30 minutes
gcr.io/google_containers/pause-amd64:3.0 Up 30 minutes
gcr.io/google_containers/pause-amd64:3.0 Up 30 minutes
protokube:1.8.1
```

We can see some of the same containers as our GCE cluster had. However, there are several missing. We can see the core Kubernetes components, but the `fluentd-gcp` service is missing, as well as some of the newer utilities such as `node-problem-detector`, `rescheduler`, `glbc`, `kube-addon-manager`, and `etcd-empty-dir-cleanup`. This reflects some of the subtle differences in the `kube-up` script between various public cloud providers. This is ultimately decided by the efforts of the large Kubernetes open-source community, but GCP often has many of the latest features first.

You also have a command that allows you to check on the state of the cluster in `kops validate cluster`, which allows you to make sure that the cluster is working as expected. There's also a lot of handy modes that kops provides that allow you to do various things with the output, provisioners, and configuration of the cluster.

Other modes

There are various other modes to take into consideration, including the following:

- **Build a terraform model**: `--target=terraform`. The terraform model will be built in `out/terraform`.
- **Build a cloudformation model**: `--target=cloudformation`. The Cloudformation JSON file will be built in `out/cloudformation`.
- **Specify the K8s build to run**: `--kubernetes-version=1.2.2`.
- **Run nodes in multiple zones**: `--zones=us-east-1b,us-east-1c,us-east-1d`.
- **Run with a HA master**: `--master-zones=us-east-1b,us-east-1c,us-east-1d`.
- **Specify the number of nodes**: `--node-count=4`.
- **Specify the node size**: `--node-size=m4.large`.
- **Specify the master size**: `--master-size=m4.large`.
- **Override the default DNS zone**: `--dns-zone=<my.hosted.zone>`.

The full list of CLI documentation can be found here: `https://github.com/kubernetes/kops/tree/master/docs/cli`.

Another tool for diagnosing the cluster status is the `componentstatuses` command, which will inform you of state of the major Kubernetes moving pieces:

```
$ kubectl get componentstatuses
NAME STATUS MESSAGE ERROR
scheduler Healthy ok
controller-manager Healthy ok
etcd-0 Healthy {"health": "true"}
```

Resetting the cluster

You just had a little taste of running the cluster on AWS. For the remainder of this book, I will be basing my examples on a GCE cluster. For the best experience following along, you can get back to a GCE cluster easily.

Simply tear down the AWS cluster, as follows:

```
$ kops delete cluster --name ${NAME} --yes
```

If you omit the `--yes` flag, you'll get a similar dry run output that you can confirm. Then, create a GCE cluster again using the following, and in doing so making sure that you're back in the directory where you installed the Kubernetes code:

```
$ cd ~/<kubernetes_install_dir>
$ kube-up.sh
```

Investigating other deployment automation

If you'd like to learn more about other tools for cluster automation, we recommend that you visit the kube-deploy repository, which has references to community maintained Kubernetes cluster deployment tools.

 Visit `https://github.com/kubernetes/kube-deploy` to learn more.

Local alternatives

The `kube-up.sh` script and `kops` are pretty handy ways to get started using Kubernetes on your platform of choice. However, they're not without flaws and can sometimes run aground when conditions are not just so.

Luckily, since K8's inception, a number of alternative methods for creating clusters have emerged. We'd recommend checking out Minikube in particular, as it's an extremely simple and local development environment that you can use to test out your Kubernetes configuration.

This project can be found here: `https://github.com/kubernetes/minikube`.

 It's important to mention that you're going to need a hypervisor on your machine to run Minikube. For Linux, you can use kvm/kvm2, or VirtualBox, and on macOS you can run native xhyve or VirtualBox. For Windows, Hyper-V is the default hypervisor.

The main limitation for this project is that it only runs a single node, which limits our exploration of certain advanced topics that require multiple machines. Minikube is a great resource for simple or local development however, and can be installed very simply on your Linux VM with the following:

```
$ curl -Lo minikube
https://storage.googleapis.com/minikube/releases/latest/minikube-linux-amd6
4 && chmod +x minikube && sudo mv minikube /usr/local/bin/
```

Or install it on macOS with the following:

```
$ brew cask install minikube
```

We'll cover how to get started with Minikube with the following commands:

```
$ minikube start
Starting local Kubernetes v1.7.5 cluster...
Starting VM...
SSH-ing files into VM...
Setting up certs...
Starting cluster components...
Connecting to cluster...
Setting up kubeconfig...
Kubectl is now configured to use the cluster.
```

You can create a sample deployment quite simply:

```
$ kubectl run hello-minikube --image=k8s.gcr.io/echoserver:1.4 --port=8080
deployment "hello-minikube" created
$ kubectl expose deployment hello-minikube --type=NodePort
service "hello-minikube" exposed
```

Once you have your cluster and service up and running, you can interact with it simply by using the `kubectl` tool and the `context` command. You can get to the Minikube dashboard with `minikube dashboard`.

 Minikube is powered by localkube (`https://github.com/kubernetes/minikube/tree/master/pkg/localkube`) and libmachine (`https://github.com/docker/machine/tree/master/libmachine`). Check them out!

Additionally, we've already referenced a number of managed services, including GKE, EKS, and Microsoft **Azure Container Service** (**ACS**), which provide an automated installation and some managed cluster operations.

Starting from scratch

Finally, there is the option to start from scratch. Luckily, starting in 1.4, the Kubernetes team has put a major focus on simplifying the cluster setup process. To that end, they have introduced kubeadm for Ubuntu 16.04, CentOS 7, and HypriotOS v1.0.1+.

Let's take a quick look at spinning up a cluster on AWS from scratch using the kubeadm tool.

Cluster setup

We will need to provision our cluster master and nodes beforehand. For the moment, we are limited to the operating systems and version listed earlier. Additionally, it is recommended that you have at least 1 GB of RAM. All the nodes must have network connectivity to one another.

For this walkthrough, we will need one t2.medium (master node) and three t2.mirco (nodes) sized instances on AWS. These instance have burstable CPU and come with the minimum 1 GB of RAM that's required. We will need to create one master and three worker nodes.

We will also need to create some security groups for the cluster. The following ports are needed for the master:

Type	Protocol	Port range	Source
All traffic	All	All	{This SG ID (Master SG)}
All traffic	All	All	{Node SG ID}
SSH	TCP	22	{Your Local Machine's IP}
HTTPS	TCP	443	{Range allowed to access K8s API and UI}

The following table shows the port's node security groups:

Type	Protocol	Port range	Source
All traffic	All	All	{Master SG ID}
All traffic	All	All	{This SG ID (Node SG)}
SSH	TCP	22	{Your Local Machine's IP}

Once you have these SGs, go ahead and spin up four instances (one t2.medium and three t2.mircos) using Ubuntu 16.04. If you are new to AWS, refer to the documentation on spinning up EC2 instances at the following
URL: `http://docs.aws.amazon.com/AWSEC2/latest/UserGuide/LaunchingAndUsingInstan ces.html`.

Be sure to identify the t2.medium instance as the master and associate the master security group. Name the other three as nodes and associate the node security group with those.

 These steps are adapted from the walk-through in the manual. For more information or to work with an alternative to Ubuntu, refer to `https:// kubernetes.io/docs/getting-started-guides/kubeadm/`.

Installing Kubernetes components (kubelet and kubeadm)

Next, we will need to SSH into all four of the instances and install the Kubernetes components.

As the root user, perform the following steps on all four instances:

1. Update the packages and install the `apt-transport-https` package so that we can download from sources that use HTTPS:

```
$ apt-get update
$ apt-get install -y apt-transport-https
```

2. Install the Google Cloud public key:

```
$ curl -s https://packages.cloud.google.com/apt/doc/apt-key.gpg |
apt-key add -
```

3. Next, let's set up the repository:

```
cat <<EOF >/etc/apt/sources.list.d/kubernetes.list
deb http://apt.kubernetes.io/ kubernetes-xenial main
EOF
apt-get update
apt-get install -y kubelet kubeadm kubectl docker.io kubernetes-cni
```

You'll need to make sure that the `cgroup` driver used by the `kubelet` on the master node is configured correctly to work with Docker. Make sure you're on the master node, then run the following:

```
docker info | grep -i cgroup
cat /etc/systemd/system/kubelet.service.d/10-kubeadm.conf
```

If these items don't match, you're going to need to change the kubelet configuration to match the Docker driver. Running `sed -i "s/cgroup-driver=systemd/cgroup-driver=cgroupfs/g" /etc/systemd/system/kubelet.service.d/10-kubeadm.conf` should fix the settings, or you can manually open the `systemd` file and add the correct flag to the appropriate environment. After that's complete, restart the service:

```
$ systemctl daemon-reload
$ systemctl restart kubelet
```

Setting up a master

On the instance you have previously chosen as master, we will run master initialization. Again, as the root, run the following command, and you should see the following output:

```
$ kubeadm init
[init] using Kubernetes version: v1.11.3
[preflight] running pre-flight checks
I1015 02:49:42.378355 5250 kernel_validator.go:81] Validating kernel
version
I1015 02:49:42.378609 5250 kernel_validator.go:96] Validating kernel config
[preflight/images] Pulling images required for setting up a Kubernetes
cluster
[preflight/images] This might take a minute or two, depending on the speed
of your internet connection
[preflight/images] You can also perform this action in beforehand using
'kubeadm config images pull'
[kubelet] Writing kubelet environment file with flags to file
"/var/lib/kubelet/kubeadm-flags.env"
[kubelet] Writing kubelet configuration to file
"/var/lib/kubelet/config.yaml"
[preflight] Activating the kubelet service
[certificates] Generated ca certificate and key.
[certificates] Generated apiserver certificate and key.
[certificates] apiserver serving cert is signed for DNS names [master
kubernetes kubernetes.default kubernetes.default.svc
kubernetes.default.svc.cluster.local] and IPs [10.96.0.1 172.17.0.71]
[certificates] Generated apiserver-kubelet-client certificate and key.
[certificates] Generated sa key and public key.
[certificates] Generated front-proxy-ca certificate and key.
[certificates] Generated front-proxy-client certificate and key.
[certificates] Generated etcd/ca certificate and key.
[certificates] Generated etcd/server certificate and key.
[certificates] etcd/server serving cert is signed for DNS names [master
localhost] and IPs [127.0.0.1 ::1]
[certificates] Generated etcd/peer certificate and key.
[certificates] etcd/peer serving cert is signed for DNS names [master
localhost] and IPs [172.17.0.71 127.0.0.1 ::1]
[certificates] Generated etcd/healthcheck-client certificate and key.
[certificates] Generated apiserver-etcd-client certificate and key.
[certificates] valid certificates and keys now exist in
"/etc/kubernetes/pki"
[kubeconfig] Wrote KubeConfig file to disk: "/etc/kubernetes/admin.conf"
[kubeconfig] Wrote KubeConfig file to disk: "/etc/kubernetes/kubelet.conf"
[kubeconfig] Wrote KubeConfig file to disk: "/etc/kubernetes/controller-
manager.conf"
[kubeconfig] Wrote KubeConfig file to disk:
"/etc/kubernetes/scheduler.conf"
```

```
[controlplane] wrote Static Pod manifest for component kube-apiserver to
"/etc/kubernetes/manifests/kube-apiserver.yaml"
[controlplane] wrote Static Pod manifest for component kube-controller-
manager to "/etc/kubernetes/manifests/kube-controller-manager.yaml"
[controlplane] wrote Static Pod manifest for component kube-scheduler to
"/etc/kubernetes/manifests/kube-scheduler.yaml"
[etcd] Wrote Static Pod manifest for a local etcd instance to
"/etc/kubernetes/manifests/etcd.yaml"
[init] waiting for the kubelet to boot up the control plane as Static Pods
from directory "/etc/kubernetes/manifests"
[init] this might take a minute or longer if the control plane images have
to be pulled
[apiclient] All control plane components are healthy after 43.001889
seconds
[uploadconfig] storing the configuration used in ConfigMap "kubeadm-config"
in the "kube-system" Namespace
[kubelet] Creating a ConfigMap "kubelet-config-1.11" in namespace kube-
system with the configuration for the kubelets in the cluster
[markmaster] Marking the node master as master by adding the label "node-
role.kubernetes.io/master=''"
[markmaster] Marking the node master as master by adding the taints [node-
role.kubernetes.io/master:NoSchedule]
[patchnode] Uploading the CRI Socket information "/var/run/dockershim.sock"
to the Node API object "master" as an annotation
[bootstraptoken] using token: o760dk.q4l5au0jyx4vg6hr
[bootstraptoken] configured RBAC rules to allow Node Bootstrap tokens to
post CSRs in order for nodes to get long term certificate credentials
[bootstraptoken] configured RBAC rules to allow the csrapprover controller
automatically approve CSRs from a Node Bootstrap Token
[bootstraptoken] configured RBAC rules to allow certificate rotation for
all node client certificates in the cluster
[bootstraptoken] creating the "cluster-info" ConfigMap in the "kube-public"
namespace
[addons] Applied essential addon: CoreDNS
[addons] Applied essential addon: kube-proxy

Your Kubernetes master has initialized successfully!

To start using your cluster, you need to run the following as a regular
user:

  mkdir -p $HOME/.kube
  sudo cp -i /etc/kubernetes/admin.conf $HOME/.kube/config
  sudo chown $(id -u):$(id -g) $HOME/.kube/config

You should now deploy a pod network to the cluster.
Run "kubectl apply -f [podnetwork].yaml" with one of the options listed at:
  https://kubernetes.io/docs/concepts/cluster-administration/addons/
```

You can now join any number of machines by running the following on each node
as root:

```
kubeadm join 172.17.0.71:6443 --token o760dk.q415au0jyx4vg6hr --
discovery-token-ca-cert-hash
sha256:453e2964eb9cc0cecfdb167194f60c6f7bd8894dc3913e0034bf0b33af4f40f5
```

To start using your cluster, you need to run as a regular user:

```
mkdir -p $HOME/.kube
  sudo cp -i /etc/kubernetes/admin.conf $HOME/.kube/config
  sudo chown $(id -u):$(id -g) $HOME/.kube/config
```

You should now deploy a pod network to the cluster. Run kubectl apply -f
[podnetwork].yaml with one of the options listed at https://kubernetes.io/docs/
concepts/cluster-administration/addons/.

You can now join any number of machines by running the following on each node
as root:

```
kubeadm join --token <token> <master-ip>:<master-port> --discovery-token-
ca-cert-hash sha256:<hash>
```

Note that initialization can only be run once, so if you run into problems, you'll need to
use kubeadm reset.

Joining nodes

After a successful initialization, you will get a join command that can be used by the
nodes. Copy this down for the join process later on. It should look similar to this:

```
$ kubeadm join --token=<some token> <master ip address>
```

The token is used to authenticate cluster nodes, so make sure to store it somewhere securely
for future use.

Networking

Our cluster will need a networking layer for the pods to communicate on. Note that
kubeadm requires a CNI compatible network fabric. The list of plugins currently available
can be found here: http://kubernetes.io/docs/admin/addons/.

For our example, we will use calico. We will need to create the calico components on our cluster using the following `yaml`. For convenience, you can download it here: `http://docs.projectcalico.org/v1.6/getting-started/kubernetes/installation/hosted/kubeadm/calico.yaml`.

Once you have this file on your master, create the components with the following command:

```
$ kubectl apply -f calico.yaml
```

Give this a minute to run setup and then list the `kube-system` nodes in order to check this:

```
$ kubectl get pods --namespace=kube-system
```

You should get a listing similar to the following one with three new calico pods and one completed job that is not shown:

```
NAME                                        READY   STATUS    RESTARTS   AGE
calico-etcd-7ckip                           1/1     Running   0          43s
calico-node-em917                           2/2     Running   0          43s
calico-policy-controller-i43ct              1/1     Running   0          43s
dummy-2088944543-efrgw                      1/1     Running   0          2m
etcd-ip-172-30-0-26                         1/1     Running   0          1m
kube-apiserver-ip-172-30-0-26               1/1     Running   0          2m
kube-controller-manager-ip-172-30-0-26      1/1     Running   0          2m
kube-discovery-1150918428-1kntn             1/1     Running   0          2m
kube-dns-654381707-6u52r                    2/3     Running   0          1m
kube-proxy-00wu7                            1/1     Running   0          1m
kube-scheduler-ip-172-30-0-26               1/1     Running   0          1m
   info: 1 completed object(s) was(were) not shown in pods list. Pass --show-all
to see all objects.
```

Calico setup

Joining the cluster

Now, we need to run the `join` command we copied earlier, on each of our node instances:

```
$ kubeadm join --token=<some token> <master ip address>
```

Once you've finished that, you should be able to see all nodes from the master by running the following command:

```
$ kubectl get nodes
```

If all went well, this will show three nodes and one master, as shown here:

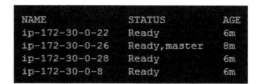

```
NAME                STATUS          AGE
ip-172-30-0-22      Ready           6m
ip-172-30-0-26      Ready,master    8m
ip-172-30-0-28      Ready           6m
ip-172-30-0-8       Ready           6m
```

Summary

We took a very brief look at how containers work and how they lend themselves to the new architecture patterns in microservices. You should now have a better understanding of how these two forces will require a variety of operations and management tasks, and how Kubernetes offers strong features to address these challenges. We created two different clusters on both GCE and AWS, and explored the startup script as well as some of the built-in features of Kubernetes. Finally, we looked at the alternatives to the kube-up script in kops, and tried our hand at manual cluster configuration with the kubeadm tool on AWS with Ubuntu 16.04.

2
Understanding Kubernetes Architecture

Kubernetes is a big open source project and ecosystem with a lot of code and a lot of functionality. Kubernetes was made by Google, but joined the **Cloud Native Computing Foundation** (**CNCF**) and became the clear leader in the field of container-based applications. In one sentence, it is a platform to orchestrate the deployment, scaling, and management of container-based applications. You have probably read about Kubernetes, and maybe even dipped your toes in and used it in a side project, or maybe even at work. But to understand what Kubernetes is all about, how to use it effectively, and what the best practices require much more. In this chapter, we will build the foundation of knowledge necessary to utilize Kubernetes to its full potential. We will start by understanding what Kubernetes is, what Kubernetes isn't, and what container orchestration means exactly. Then we will cover some important Kubernetes concepts that will form the vocabulary that we will use throughout the book. After that, we will dive into the architecture of Kubernetes in more detail and look at how it enables all the capabilities that it provides to its users. Then, we will discuss the various runtimes and container engines that Kubernetes supports (Docker is just one option) and, finally, we will discuss the role of Kubernetes in the full continuous integration and deployment pipeline.

At the end of this chapter, you will have a solid understanding of container orchestration, what problems Kubernetes addresses, the rationale for Kubernetes design and architecture, and the different runtimes it supports. You'll also be familiar with the overall structure of the open source repository and be ready to jump in and find answers to any question.

What is Kubernetes?

Kubernetes is a platform that encompasses a huge number of services and capabilities that keep growing. Its core functionality is its ability to schedule workloads in containers across your infrastructure, but it doesn't stop there. Here are some of the other capabilities Kubernetes brings to the table:

- Mounting storage systems
- Distributing secrets
- Checking application health
- Replicating application instances
- Using horizontal pod autoscaling
- Naming and discovering
- Balancing loads
- Rolling updates
- Monitoring resources
- Accessing and ingesting logs
- Debugging applications
- Providing authentication and authorization

What Kubernetes is not

Kubernetes is not a **platform as a service (PaaS)**. It doesn't dictate many of the important aspects of your desired system; instead, it leaves them up to you or to other systems built on top of Kubernetes, such as Deis, OpenShift, and Eldarion. For example:

- Kubernetes doesn't require a specific application type or framework
- Kubernetes doesn't require a specific programming language
- Kubernetes doesn't provide databases or message queues
- Kubernetes doesn't distinguish apps from services
- Kubernetes doesn't have a click-to-deploy service marketplace
- Kubernetes allows users to choose their own logging, monitoring, and alerting systems

Understanding container orchestration

The primary responsibility of Kubernetes is container orchestration. This means making sure that all the containers that execute various workloads are scheduled to run on physical or virtual machines. The containers must be packed efficiently and follow the constraints of the deployment environment and the cluster configuration. In addition, Kubernetes must keep an eye on all running containers and replace dead, unresponsive, or otherwise unhealthy containers. Kubernetes provides many more capabilities that you will learn about in the following chapters. In this section, the focus is on containers and their orchestration.

Physical machines, virtual machines, and containers

It all starts and ends with hardware. In order to run your workloads, you need some real hardware provisioned. That includes actual physical machines, with certain, compute capabilities (CPUs or cores), memory, and some local persistent storage (spinning disks or SSDs). In addition, you will need some shared persistent storage and the networking to hook up all these machines so they can find and talk to each other. At this point, you can run multiple virtual machines on the physical machines or stay at the bare-metal level (no virtual machines). Kubernetes can be deployed on a bare-metal cluster (real hardware) or on a cluster of virtual machines. Kubernetes, in turn, can orchestrate the containers it manages directly on bare-metal or virtual machines. In theory, a Kubernetes cluster can be composed of a mix of bare-metal and virtual machines, but this is not very common.

The benefits of containers

Containers represent a true paradigm shift in the development and operation of large, complicated software systems. Here are some of the benefits compared to more traditional models:

- Agile application creation and deployment
- Continuous development, integration, and deployment
- Dev and ops separation of concerns
- Environmental consistency across development, testing, and production
- Cloud- and OS-distribution portability
- Application-centric management

- Loosely coupled, distributed, elastic, liberated microservices
- Resource isolation
- Resource utilization

Containers in the cloud

Containers are ideal to package microservices because, while providing isolation to the microservice, they are very lightweight, and you don't incur a lot of overhead when deploying many microservices as you do with virtual machines. That makes containers ideal for cloud deployment, where allocating a whole virtual machine for each microservice would be cost prohibitive.

All major cloud providers, such as Amazon AWS, Google's GCE, Microsoft's Azure and even Alibaba Cloud, provide container-hosting services these days. Google's GKE has always been based on Kubernetes. AWS ECS is based on their own orchestration solution. Microsoft Azure's container service was based on Apache Mesos. Kubernetes can be deployed on all cloud platforms, but it wasn't deeply integrated with other services until today. But at the end of 2017, all cloud providers announced direct support for Kubernetes. Microsofts launched AKS, AWS released EKS, and Alibaba Cloud started working on a Kubernetes controller manager to integrate Kubernetes seamlessly.

Cattle versus pets

In the olden days, when systems were small, each server had a name. Developers and users knew exactly what software was running on each machine. I remember that, in many of the companies I worked for, we had multi-day discussions to decide on a naming theme for our servers. For example, composers and Greek mythology characters were popular choices. Everything was very cozy. You treated your servers like beloved pets. When a server died, it was a major crisis. Everybody scrambled to figure out where to get another server, what was even running on the dead server, and how to get it working on the new server. If the server stored some important data, then hopefully you had an up-to-date backup and maybe you'd even be able to recover it.

Obviously, that approach doesn't scale. When you have a few tens or hundreds of servers, you must start treating them like cattle. You think about the collective and not individuals. You may still have some pets, but your web servers are just cattle.

Kubernetes takes the cattle approach to the extreme and takes full responsibility for allocating containers to specific machines. You don't need to interact with individual machines (nodes) most of the time. This works best for stateless workloads. For stateful applications, the situation is a little different, but Kubernetes provides a solution called StatefulSet, which we'll discuss soon.

In this section, we covered the idea of container orchestration and discussed the relationships between hosts (physical or virtual) and containers, as well as the benefits of running containers in the cloud, and finished with a discussion about cattle versus pets. In the following section, we will get to know the world of Kubernetes and learn its concepts and terminology.

Kubernetes concepts

In this section, I'll briefly introduce many important Kubernetes concepts and give you some context as to why they are needed and how they interact with other concepts. The goal is to get familiar with these terms and concepts. Later, we will see how these concepts are woven together and organized into API groups and resource categories to achieve awesomeness. You can consider many of these concepts as building blocks. Some of the concepts, such as nodes and masters, are implemented as a set of Kubernetes components. These components are at a different abstraction level, and I discuss them in detail in a dedicated section, *Kubernetes components*.

Here is the famous Kubernetes architecture diagram:

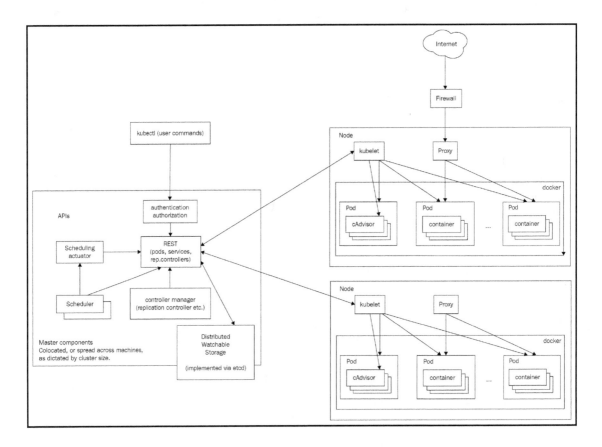

Cluster

A cluster is a collection of compute, storage, and networking resources that Kubernetes uses to run the various workloads that comprise your system. Note that your entire system may consist of multiple clusters. We will discuss this advanced use case of federation in detail later.

Node

A node is a single host. It may be a physical or virtual machine. Its job is to run pods, which we will look at in a moment. Each Kubernetes node runs several Kubernetes components, such as a kubelet and a kube proxy. Nodes are managed by a Kubernetes master. The nodes are the worker bees of Kubernetes and shoulder all the heavy lifting. In the past, they were called **minions**. If you have read some old documentation or articles, don't get confused. Minions are nodes.

Master

The master is the control plane of Kubernetes. It consists of several components, such as an API server, a scheduler, and a controller manager. The master is responsible for the global, cluster-level scheduling of pods and the handling of events. Usually, all the master components are set up on a single host. When considering high-availability scenarios or very large clusters, you will want to have master redundancy.

Pod

A pod is the unit of work in Kubernetes. Each pod contains one or more containers. Pods are always scheduled together (that is, they always run on the same machine). All the containers in a pod have the same IP address and port space; they can communicate using localhost or standard interprocess communication. In addition, all the containers in a pod can have access to shared local storage on the node hosting the pod. The shared storage can be mounted on each container. Pods are an important feature of Kubernetes. It is possible to run multiple applications inside a single Docker container by having something such as `supervisord` as the main Docker application that runs multiple processes, but this practice is often frowned upon for the following reasons:

- **Transparency**: Making the containers within the pod visible to the infrastructure enables the infrastructure to provide services to those containers, such as process management and resource monitoring. This facilitates a number of convenient functionalities for users.
- **Decoupling software dependencies**: The individual containers may be versioned, rebuilt, and redeployed independently. Kubernetes may even support live updates of individual containers someday.

- **Ease of use**: Users don't need to run their own process managers, worry about signal and exit-code propagation, and so on.
- **Efficiency**: Because the infrastructure takes on more responsibility, containers can be more lightweight.

Pods provide a great solution for managing groups of closely related containers that depend on each other and need to cooperate on the same host to accomplish their purpose. It's important to remember that pods are considered ephemeral, throwaway entities that can be discarded and replaced at will. Any pod storage is destroyed with its pod. Each pod gets a **unique ID (UID)**, so you can still distinguish between them if necessary.

Label

Labels are key-value pairs that are used to group together sets of objects, very often pods. This is important for several other concepts, such as replication controllers, replica sets, and services that operate on dynamic groups of objects and need to identify the members of the group. There is an NxN relationship between objects and labels. Each object may have multiple labels, and each label may be applied to different objects. There are certain restrictions on labels by design. Each label on an object must have a unique key. The label key must adhere to a strict syntax. It has two parts: prefix and name. The prefix is optional. If it exists, then it is separated from the name by a forward slash (/) and it must be a valid DNS subdomain. The prefix must be 253 characters long at most. The name is mandatory and must be 63 characters long at most. Names must start and end with an alphanumeric character (a-z, A-Z, 0-9) and contain only alphanumeric characters, dots, dashes, and underscores. Values follow the same restrictions as names. Note that labels are dedicated to identifying objects and not to attach arbitrary metadata to objects. This is what annotations are for (see the following section).

Annotations

Annotations let you associate arbitrary metadata with Kubernetes objects. Kubernetes just stores the annotations and makes their metadata available. Unlike labels, they don't have strict restrictions about allowed characters and size limits.

In my experience, you always need such metadata for complicated systems, and it is nice that Kubernetes recognizes this need and provides it out of the box so you don't have to come up with your own separate metadata store and map objects to their metadata.

We've covered most, if not all, of Kubernetes's concepts; there are a few more I mentioned briefly. In the next section, we will continue our journey into Kubernetes's architecture by looking into its design motivations, the internals, and its implementation, and even pick at the source code.

Label selectors

Label selectors are used to selecting objects based on their labels. Equality-based selectors specify a key name and a value. There are two operators, = (or ==) and !=, to denote equality or inequality based on the value. For example:

```
role = webserver
```

This will select all objects that have that label key and value.

Label selectors can have multiple requirements separated by a comma. For example:

```
role = webserver, application != foo
```

Set-based selectors extend the capabilities and allow selection based on multiple values:

```
role in (webserver, backend)
```

Replication controllers and replica sets

Replication controllers and replica sets both manage a group of pods identified by a label selector and ensure that a certain number is always up and running. The main difference between them is that replication controllers test for membership by name equality and replica sets can use set-based selection. Replica sets are the way to go, as they are a superset of replication controllers. I expect replication controllers to be deprecated at some point.

Kubernetes guarantees that you will always have the same number of pods running that you specified in a replication controller or a replica set. Whenever the number drops because of a problem with the hosting node or the pod itself, Kubernetes will fire up new instances. Note that if you manually start pods and exceed the specified number, the replication controller will kill the extra pods.

Replication controllers used to be central to many workflows, such as rolling updates and running one-off jobs. As Kubernetes evolved, it introduced direct support for many of these workflows, with dedicated objects such as **Deployment**, **Job**, and **DaemonSet**. We will meet them all later.

Services

Services are used to expose a certain functionality to users or other services. They usually encompass a group of pods, usually identified by—you guessed it—a label. You can have services that provide access to external resources, or to pods you control directly at the virtual IP level. Native Kubernetes services are exposed through convenient endpoints. Note that services operate at layer 3 (TCP/UDP). Kubernetes 1.2 added the `Ingress` object, which provides access to HTTP objects—more on that later. Services are published or discovered through one of two mechanisms: DNS or environment variables. Services can be load balanced by Kubernetes, but developers can choose to manage load balancing themselves in the case of services that use external resources or require special treatment.

There are many gory details associated with IP addresses, virtual IP addresses, and port spaces. We will discuss them in-depth in a future chapter.

Volume

Local storage on the pod is ephemeral and goes away with the pod. Sometimes that's all you need if the goal is just to exchange data between containers of the node, but sometimes it's important for the data to outlive the pod, or it's necessary to share data between pods. The volume concept supports that need. Note that, while Docker has a volume concept too, it is quite limited (although it is getting more powerful). Kubernetes uses its own separate volumes. Kubernetes also supports additional container types, such as rkt, so it can't rely on Docker volumes, even in principle.

There are many volume types. Kubernetes currently directly supports many volume types, but the modern approach for extending Kubernetes with more volume types is through the **Container Storage Interface** (**CSI**), which I'll discuss in detail later. The `emptyDir` volume type mounts a volume on each container that is backed by default by whatever is available on the hosting machine. You can request a memory medium if you want. This storage is deleted when the pod is terminated for any reason. There are many volume types for specific cloud environments, various networked filesystems, and even Git repositories. An interesting volume type is the `persistentDiskClaim`, which abstracts the details a little bit and uses the default persistent storage in your environment (typically in a cloud provider).

StatefulSet

Pods come and go, and if you care about their data, then you can use persistent storage. That's all good. But sometimes you might want Kubernetes to manage a distributed data store, such as Kubernetes or MySQL Galera. These clustered stores keep the data distributed across uniquely identified nodes. You can't model that with regular pods and services. Enter StatefulSet. If you remember, earlier I discussed treating servers as pets or cattle and how cattle is the way to go. Well, StatefulSet sits somewhere in the middle. StatefulSet ensures (similar to a replication set) that a given number of pets with unique identities are running at any given time. The pets have the following properties:

- A stable hostname, available in DNS
- An ordinal index
- Stable storage linked to the ordinal and hostname

StatefulSet can help with peer discovery, as well as adding or removing pets.

Secrets

Secrets are small objects that contain sensitive information, such as credentials and tokens. They are stored in etcd, are accessible by the Kubernetes API server, and can be mounted as files into pods (using dedicated secret volumes that piggyback on regular data volumes) that need access to them. The same secret can be mounted into multiple pods. Kubernetes itself creates secrets for its components, and you can create your own secrets. Another approach is to use secrets as environment variables. Note that secrets in a pod are always stored in memory (tmpfs, in the case of mounted secrets) for better security.

Names

Each object in Kubernetes is identified by a UID and a name. The name is used to refer to the object in API calls. Names should be up to 253 characters long and use lowercase alphanumeric characters, dashes (-), and dots (.). If you delete an object, you can create another object with the same name as the deleted object, but the UIDs must be unique across the life cycle of the cluster. The UIDs are generated by Kubernetes, so you don't have to worry about that.

Namespaces

A namespace is a virtual cluster. You can have a single physical cluster that contains multiple virtual clusters segregated by namespaces. Each virtual cluster is totally isolated from the other virtual clusters, and they can only communicate through public interfaces. Note that node objects and persistent volumes don't live in a namespace. Kubernetes may schedule pods from different namespaces to run on the same node. Likewise, pods from different namespaces can use the same persistent storage.

When using namespaces, you have to consider network policies and resource quotas to ensure proper access and distribution of the physical cluster resources.

Diving into Kubernetes architecture in-depth

Kubernetes has very ambitious goals. It aims to manage and simplify the orchestration, deployment, and management of distributed systems across a wide range of environments and cloud providers. It provides many capabilities and services that should work across all that diversity, while evolving and remaining simple enough for mere mortals to use. This is a tall order. Kubernetes achieves this by following a crystal-clear, high-level design and using a well-thought-out architecture that promotes extensibility and pluggability. Many parts of Kubernetes are still hard coded or environment aware, but the trend is to refactor them into plugins and keep the core generic and abstract. In this section, we will peel Kubernetes like an onion, starting with the various distributed systems design patterns and how Kubernetes supports them, then go over the mechanics of Kubernetes, including its set of APIs, and then take a look at the actual components that comprise Kubernetes. Finally, we will take a quick tour of the source-code tree to gain even better insight into the structure of Kubernetes itself.

At the end of this section, you will have a solid understanding of the Kubernetes architecture and implementation, and why certain design decisions were made.

Distributed systems design patterns

All happy (working) distributed systems are alike, to paraphrase Tolstoy in Anna Karenina. This means that, to function properly, all well-designed distributed systems must follow some best practices and principles. Kubernetes doesn't want to be just a management system. It wants to support and enable these best practices and provide high-level services to developers and administrators. Let's look at some of these design patterns.

Sidecar pattern

The sidecar pattern is about co-locating another container in a pod in addition to the main application container. The application container is unaware of the sidecar container and just goes about its business. A great example is a central logging agent. Your main container can just log to `stdout`, but the sidecar container will send all logs to a central logging service where they will be aggregated with the logs from the entire system. The benefits of using a sidecar container versus adding central logging to the main application container are enormous. First, applications are no longer burdened with central logging, which could be a nuisance. If you want to upgrade or change your central logging policy or switch to a totally new provider, you just need to update the sidecar container and deploy it. None of your application containers change, so you can't break them by accident.

Ambassador pattern

The ambassador pattern is about representing a remote service as if it were local and possibly enforcing a policy. A good example of the ambassador pattern is if you have a Redis cluster with one master for writes and many replicas for reads. A local ambassador container can serve as a proxy and expose Redis to the main application container on the localhost. The main application container simply connects to Redis on `localhost:6379` (Redis's default port), but it connects to the ambassador running in the same pod, which filters the requests, sends write requests to the real Redis master, and read requests randomly to one of the read replicas. Just as we saw with the sidecar pattern, the main application has no idea what's going on. That can help a lot when testing against a real local Redis. Also, if the Redis cluster configuration changes, only the ambassador needs to be modified; the main application remains blissfully unaware.

Adapter pattern

The adapter pattern is about standardizing output from the main application container. Consider the case of a service that is being rolled out incrementally: It may generate reports in a format that doesn't conform to the previous version. Other services and applications that consume that output haven't been upgraded yet. An adapter container can be deployed in the same pod with the new application container and can alter its output to match the old version until all consumers have been upgraded. The adapter container shares the filesystem with the main application container, so it can watch the local filesystem, and whenever the new application writes something, it immediately adapts it.

Multinode patterns

The single-node patterns are all supported directly by Kubernetes through pods. Multinode patterns, such as leader election, work queues, and scatter-gather, are not supported directly, but composing pods with standard interfaces to accomplish them is a viable approach with Kubernetes.

The Kubernetes APIs

If you want to understand the capabilities of a system and what it provides, you must pay a lot of attention to its APIs. These APIs provide a comprehensive view of what you can do with the system as a user. Kubernetes exposes several sets of REST APIs for different purposes and audiences through API groups. Some of the APIs are used primarily by tools and some can be used directly by developers. An important fact regarding the APIs is that they are under constant development. The Kubernetes developers keep it manageable by trying to extend it (by adding new objects and new fields to existing objects) and avoid renaming or dropping existing objects and fields. In addition, all API endpoints are versioned and often have an alpha or beta notation too. For example:

```
/api/v1
/api/v2alpha1
```

You can access the API through the `kubectl cli`, through client libraries, or directly through REST API calls. There are elaborate authentication and authorization mechanisms that we will explore in a later chapter. If you have the right permissions, you can list, view, create, update, and delete various Kubernetes objects. At this point, let's glimpse the surface area of the APIs. The best way to explore these APIs is through API groups. Some API groups are enabled by default. Other groups can be enabled/disabled via flags. For example, to disable the batch V1 group and enable the batch V2 alpha group, you can set the `--runtime-config` flag when running the API server as follows:

```
--runtime-config=batch/v1=false,batch/v2alpha=true
```

The following resources are enabled by default, in addition to the core resources:

- DaemonSets
- Deployments
- HorizontalPodAutoscalers
- Ingress

- Jobs
- ReplicaSets

Resource categories

In addition to API groups, another useful classification of the available APIs is functionality. The Kubernetes API is huge, and breaking it down into categories helps a lot when you're trying to find your way around. Kubernetes defines the following resource categories:

- **Workloads**: The objects you use to manage and run containers on the cluster.
- **Discovery and load balancing**: The objects you use to expose your workloads to the world as externally accessible, load-balanced services.
- **Config and storage**: The objects you use to initialize and configure your applications and to persist data that is outside the container.
- **Cluster**: The objects that define how the cluster itself is configured; these are typically used only by cluster operators.
- **Metadata**: The objects you use to configure the behavior of other resources within the cluster, such as HorizontalPodAutoscaler for scaling workloads.

In the following subsections, I'll list the resources that belong to each group, along with the API group they belong to. I will not specify the version here because APIs move rapidly from alpha to beta to **general availability (GA)**, and then from V1 to V2, and so on.

Workloads API

The workloads API contains the following resources:

- Container: Core
- CronJob: Batch
- DaemonSet: Apps
- Deployment: Apps
- Job: Batch
- Pod: Core
- ReplicaSet: Apps
- ReplicationController: Core
- StatefulSet: Apps

Containers are created by controllers using pods. Pods run containers and provide environmental dependencies, such as shared or persistent storage volumes, and configuration or secret data injected into the container.

Here is a detailed description of one of the most common operations, which gets a list of all the pods as a REST API:

GET /api/v1/pods

It accepts various query parameters (all optional):

- `pretty`: If true, the output is pretty-printed
- `labelSelector`: A selector expression to limit the result
- `watch`: If true, this watches for changes and returns a stream of events
- `resourceVersion`: Returns only events that occurred after that version
- `timeoutSeconds`: Timeout for the list or watch operation

Discovery and load balancing

By default, workloads are only accessible within the cluster, and they must be exposed externally using either a `LoadBalancer` or `NodePort` service. During development, internally accessible workloads can be accessed via a proxy through the API master using the `kubectl proxy` command:

- `Endpoints`: Core
- `Ingress`: Extensions
- `Service`: Core

Config and storage

Dynamic configuration without redeployment is a cornerstone of Kubernetes and running complex distributed applications on your Kubernetes cluster:

- `ConfigMap`: Core
- `Secret`: Core
- `PersistentVolumeClaim`: Core
- `StorageClass`: Storage
- `VolumeAttachment`: Storage

Metadata

The metadata resources typically are embedded as subresources of the resources they configure. For example, a limit range will be part of a pod configuration. You will not interact with these objects directly most of the time. There are many metadata resources. You can find the complete list at `https://kubernetes.io/docs/reference/generated/kubernetes-api/v1.10/#-strong-metadata-strong-`.

Cluster

The resources in the cluster category are designed for use by cluster operators as opposed to developers. There are many resources in this category as well. Here some of the most important resources:

- `Namespace`: Core
- `Node`: Core
- `PersistentVolume`: Core
- `ResourceQuota` : Core
- `ClusterRole`: Rbac
- `NetworkPolicy` : Networking

Kubernetes components

A Kubernetes cluster has several master components that are used to control the cluster, as well as node components that run on each cluster node. Let's get to know all these components and how they work together.

Master components

The master components typically run on one node, but in a highly available or very large cluster, they may be spread across multiple nodes.

API server

The Kube API server exposes the Kubernetes REST API. It can easily scale horizontally as it is stateless and stores all the data in the etcd cluster. The API server is the embodiment of the Kubernetes control plane.

Etcd

Etcd is a highly reliable, distributed data store. Kubernetes uses it to store the entire cluster state. In a small, transient cluster, a single instance of etcd can run on the same node as all the other master components, but for more substantial clusters, it is typical to have a three-node or even five-node etcd cluster for redundancy and high availability.

Kube controller manager

The Kube controller manager is a collection of various managers rolled up into one binary. It contains the replication controller, the pod controller, the services controller, the endpoints controller, and others. All these managers watch over the state of the cluster through the API and their job is to steer the cluster into the desired state.

Cloud controller manager

When running in the cloud, Kubernetes allows cloud providers to integrate their platform for the purpose of managing nodes, routes, services, and volumes. The cloud provider code interacts with the Kubernetes code. It replaces some of the functionality of the Kube controller manager. When running Kubernetes with a cloud controller manager, you must set the Kube controller manager flag `--cloud-provider` to *external*. This will disable the control loops that the cloud controller manager is taking over. The cloud controller manager was introduced in Kubernetes 1.6 and it is being used by multiple cloud providers already.

 A quick note about Go to help you parse the code: The method name comes first, followed by the method's parameters in parentheses. Each parameter is a pair, consisting of a name followed by its type. Finally, the return values are specified. Go allows multiple return types. It is very common to return an `error` object in addition to the actual result. If everything is OK, the `error` object will be nil.

Here is the main interface of the `cloudprovider` package:

```
package cloudprovider
import (
    "errors"
    "fmt"
    "strings"
    "k8s.io/api/core/v1"
    "k8s.io/apimachinery/pkg/types"
    "k8s.io/client-go/informers"
    "k8s.io/kubernetes/pkg/controller"
)
// Interface is an abstract, pluggable interface for cloud providers.
type Interface interface {
    Initialize(clientBuilder controller.ControllerClientBuilder)
    LoadBalancer() (LoadBalancer, bool)
    Instances() (Instances, bool)
    Zones() (Zones, bool)
    Clusters() (Clusters, bool)
    Routes() (Routes, bool)
    ProviderName() string
    HasClusterID() bool
}
```

Most of the methods return other interfaces with their own method. For example, here is the `LoadBalancer` interface:

```
type LoadBalancer interface {
    GetLoadBalancer(clusterName string,
                              service *v1.Service) (status
    *v1.LoadBalancerStatus,
                                                          exists
    bool,
                                                          err
    error)
    EnsureLoadBalancer(clusterName string,
                                    service *v1.Service,
                                    nodes []*v1.Node)
    (*v1.LoadBalancerStatus, error)
        UpdateLoadBalancer(clusterName string, service *v1.Service, nodes
    []*v1.Node) error
        EnsureLoadBalancerDeleted(clusterName string, service *v1.Service)
    error
}
```

Kube-scheduler

`kube-scheduler` is responsible for scheduling pods into nodes. This is a very complicated task as it requires considering multiple interacting factors, such as the following:

- Resource requirements
- Service requirements
- Hardware/software policy constraints
- Node affinity and antiaffinity specifications
- Pod affinity and antiaffinity specifications
- Taints and tolerations
- Data locality
- Deadlines

If you need some special scheduling logic not covered by the default Kube scheduler, you can replace it with your own custom scheduler. You can also run your custom scheduler side by side with the default scheduler and have your custom scheduler schedule only a subset of the pods.

DNS

Since Kubernetes 1.3, a DNS service has been part of the standard Kubernetes cluster. It is scheduled as a regular pod. Every service (except headless services) receives a DNS name. Pods can receive a DNS name too. This is very useful for automatic discovery.

Node components

Nodes in the cluster need a couple of components to interact with the cluster master components and to receive workloads to execute and update the cluster on their status.

Proxy

The Kube proxy does low-level, network housekeeping on each node. It reflects the Kubernetes services locally and can do TCP and UDP forwarding. It finds cluster IPs through environment variables or DNS.

Kubelet

The kubelet is the Kubernetes representative on the node. It oversees communicating with the master components and manages the running pods. This includes the following actions:

- Downloading pod secrets from the API server
- Mounting volumes
- Running the pod's container (through the CRI or rkt)
- Reporting the status of the node and each pod
- Running container liveness probes

In this section, we dug into the guts of Kubernetes, explored its architecture (from a very high-level perspective), and supported design patterns, through its APIs and the components used to control and manage the cluster. In the next section, we will take a quick look at the various runtimes that Kubernetes supports.

Kubernetes runtimes

Kubernetes originally only supported Docker as a container runtime engine. But that is no longer the case. Kubernetes now supports several different runtimes:

- `Docker` (through a CRI shim)
- `Rkt` (direct integration to be replaced with rktlet)
- `Cri-o`
- `Frakti` (Kubernetes on the hypervisor, previously Hypernetes)
- `Rktlet` (CRI implementation for rkt)
- `cri-containerd`

A major design policy is that Kubernetes itself should be completely decoupled from specific runtimes. The **Container Runtime Interface** (**CRI**) enables this.

In this section, you'll get a closer look at the CRI and get to know the individual runtime engines. At the end of this section, you'll be able to make a well-informed decision about which runtime engine is appropriate for your use case and under what circumstances you may switch or even combine multiple runtimes in the same system.

The Container Runtime Interface (CRI)

The CRI is a gRPC API, containing specifications/requirements and libraries for container runtimes to integrate with kubelet on a node. In Kubernetes 1.7, the internal Docker integration in Kubernetes was replaced with a CRI-based integration. This is a big deal. It opened the door to multiple implementations that take advantage of advances in the field of container. The Kubelet doesn't need to interface directly with multiple runtimes. Instead, it can talk to any CRI-compliant container runtime. The following diagram illustrates the flow:

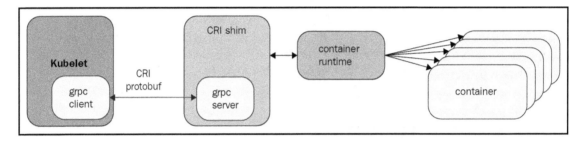

There are two gRPC service interfaces—`ImageService` and `RuntimeService`—that CRI container runtimes (or shims) must implement. The `ImageService` is responsible for managing images. Here is the gRPC/protobuf interface (this is not Go):

```
service ImageService {
    rpc ListImages(ListImagesRequest) returns (ListImagesResponse) {}
    rpc ImageStatus(ImageStatusRequest) returns (ImageStatusResponse) {}
    rpc PullImage(PullImageRequest) returns (PullImageResponse) {}
    rpc RemoveImage(RemoveImageRequest) returns (RemoveImageResponse) {}
    rpc ImageFsInfo(ImageFsInfoRequest) returns (ImageFsInfoResponse) {}
}
```

The `RuntimeService` is responsible for managing pods and containers. Here is the gRPC/profobug interface:

```
service RuntimeService {
    rpc Version(VersionRequest) returns (VersionResponse) {}
    rpc RunPodSandbox(RunPodSandboxRequest) returns (RunPodSandboxResponse)
{}
    rpc StopPodSandbox(StopPodSandboxRequest) returns
(StopPodSandboxResponse) {}
    rpc RemovePodSandbox(RemovePodSandboxRequest) returns
(RemovePodSandboxResponse) {}
    rpc PodSandboxStatus(PodSandboxStatusRequest) returns
(PodSandboxStatusResponse) {}
```

```
    rpc ListPodSandbox(ListPodSandboxRequest) returns
(ListPodSandboxResponse) {}
    rpc CreateContainer(CreateContainerRequest) returns
(CreateContainerResponse) {}
    rpc StartContainer(StartContainerRequest) returns
(StartContainerResponse) {}
    rpc StopContainer(StopContainerRequest) returns (StopContainerResponse)
{}
    rpc RemoveContainer(RemoveContainerRequest) returns
(RemoveContainerResponse) {}
    rpc ListContainers(ListContainersRequest) returns
(ListContainersResponse) {}
    rpc ContainerStatus(ContainerStatusRequest) returns
(ContainerStatusResponse) {}
    rpc UpdateContainerResources(UpdateContainerResourcesRequest) returns
(UpdateContainerResourcesResponse) {}
    rpc ExecSync(ExecSyncRequest) returns (ExecSyncResponse) {}
    rpc Exec(ExecRequest) returns (ExecResponse) {}
    rpc Attach(AttachRequest) returns (AttachResponse) {}
    rpc PortForward(PortForwardRequest) returns (PortForwardResponse) {}
    rpc ContainerStats(ContainerStatsRequest) returns
(ContainerStatsResponse) {}
    rpc ListContainerStats(ListContainerStatsRequest) returns
(ListContainerStatsResponse) {}
    rpc UpdateRuntimeConfig(UpdateRuntimeConfigRequest) returns
(UpdateRuntimeConfigResponse) {}
    rpc Status(StatusRequest) returns (StatusResponse) {}
}
```

The data types used as arguments and return types are called messages, and are also defined as part of the API. Here is one of them:

```
message CreateContainerRequest {
    string pod_sandbox_id = 1;
    ContainerConfig config = 2;
    PodSandboxConfig sandbox_config = 3;
}
```

As you can see, messages can be embedded inside each other. The CreateContainerRequest message has one string field and two other fields, which are themselves messages: ContainerConfig and PodSandboxConfig.

Now that you are familiar at the code level with the Kubernetes runtime engine, let's look at the individual runtime engines briefly.

Docker

Docker is, of course, the 800-pound gorilla of containers. Kubernetes was originally designed to manage only Docker containers. The multi-runtime capability was first introduced in Kubernetes 1.3 and the CRI in Kubernetes 1.5. Until then, Kubernetes could only manage Docker containers.

If you are reading this book, I assume you're very familiar with Docker and what it brings to the table. Docker is enjoying tremendous popularity and growth, but there is also a lot of criticism being directed toward it. Critics often mention the following concerns:

- Security
- Difficulty setting up multi-container applications (in particular, networking)
- Development, monitoring, and logging
- Limitations of Docker containers running one command
- Releasing half-baked features too fast

Docker is aware of the criticisms and has addressed some of these concerns. In particular, Docker has invested in its Docker Swarm product. Docker swarm is a Docker-native orchestration solution that competes with Kubernetes. It is simpler to use than Kubernetes, but it's not as powerful or mature.

 Since Docker 1.12, swarm mode has been included in the Docker daemon natively, which upset some people because of its bloat and scope creep. That in turn made more people turn to CoreOS rkt as an alternative solution.

Since Docker 1.11, released in April 2016, Docker has changed the way it runs containers. The runtime now uses `containerd` and `runC` to run **Open Container Initiative (OCI)** images in containers:

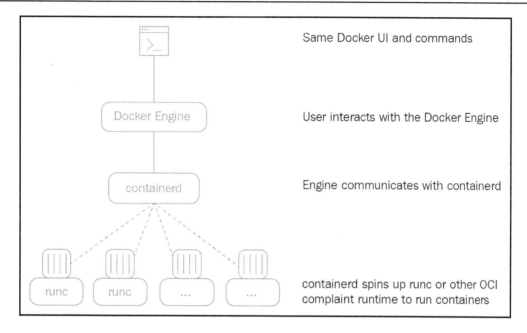

Rkt

Rkt is a container manager from CoreOS (the developers of the CoreOS Linux distro, etcd, flannel, and more). The rkt runtime prides itself on its simplicity and strong emphasis on security and isolation. It doesn't have a daemon like the Docker engine, and relies on the OS init system, such as `systemd`, to launch the rkt executable. Rkt can download images (both **app container** (**appc**) images and OCI images), verify them, and run them in containers. Its architecture is much simpler.

App container

CoreOS started a standardization effort in December 2014 called appc. This included the standard image format (ACI), runtime, signing, and discovery. A few months later, Docker started its own standardization effort with OCI. At this point, it seems these efforts will converge. This is a great thing as tools, images, and runtime will be able to interoperate freely. We're not there yet.

Cri-O

Cri-o is a Kubernetes incubator project. It is designed to provide an integration path between Kubernetes and OCI-compliant container runtimes, such as Docker. The idea is that Cri-O will provide the following capabilities:

- Support multiple image formats, including the existing Docker image format
- Support multiple means of downloading images, including trust and image verification
- Container image management (managing image layers, overlaying filesystems, and so on)
- Container process life cycle management
- The monitoring and logging required to satisfy the CRI
- Resource isolation as required by the CRI

Then any OCI-compliant container runtime can be plugged in and will be integrated with Kubernetes.

Rktnetes

Rktnetes is Kubernetes plus rkt as the runtime engine. Kubernetes is still in the process of abstracting away the runtime engine. Rktnetes is not really a separate product. From the outside, all it takes is running the Kubelet on each node with a couple of command-line switches.

Is rkt ready for use in production?

I don't have a lot of hands-on experience with rkt. However, it is used by Tectonic—the commercial CoreOS-based Kubernetes distribution. If you run a different type of cluster, I would suggest that you wait until rkt is integrated with Kubernetes through the CRI/rktlet. There are some known issues you need to be aware of when using rkt as opposed to Docker with Kubernetes—for example, missing volumes are not created automatically, Kubectl's attach and get logs don't work, and `init` containers are not supported, among other issues.

Hyper containers

Hyper containers are another option. A Hyper container has a lightweight VM (its own guest kernel) and it runs on bare metal. Instead of relying on Linux cgroups for isolation, it relies on a hypervisor. This approach presents an interesting mix compared to standard, bare-metal clusters that are difficult to set up and public clouds where containers are deployed on heavyweight VMs.

Stackube

Stackube (previously called Hypernetes) is a multitenant distribution that uses Hyper containers as well as some OpenStack components for authentication, persistent storage, and networking. Since containers don't share the host kernel, it is safe to run containers of different tenants on the same physical host. Stackube uses Frakti as its container runtime, of course.

In this section, we've covered the various runtime engines that Kubernetes supports, as well as the trend toward standardization and convergence. In the next section, we'll take a step back and look at the big picture, as well as how Kubernetes fits into the CI/CD pipeline.

Continuous integration and deployment

Kubernetes is a great platform for running your microservice-based applications. But, at the end of the day, it is an implementation detail. Users, and often most developers, may not be aware that the system is deployed on Kubernetes. But Kubernetes can change the game and make things that were too difficult before possible.

In this section, we'll explore the CI/CD pipeline and what Kubernetes brings to the table. At the end of this section, you'll be able to design CI/CD pipelines that take advantage of Kubernetes properties, such as easy-scaling and development-production parity, to improve the productivity and robustness of your day-to-day development and deployment.

What is a CI/CD pipeline?

A CI/CD pipeline is a set of steps implemented by developers or operators that modify the code, data, or configuration of a system, test it, and deploy it to production. Some pipelines are fully automated and some are semiautomated with human checks. In large organizations, there may be test and staging environments that changes are deployed to automatically, but release to production requires manual intervention. The following diagram describes a typical pipeline.

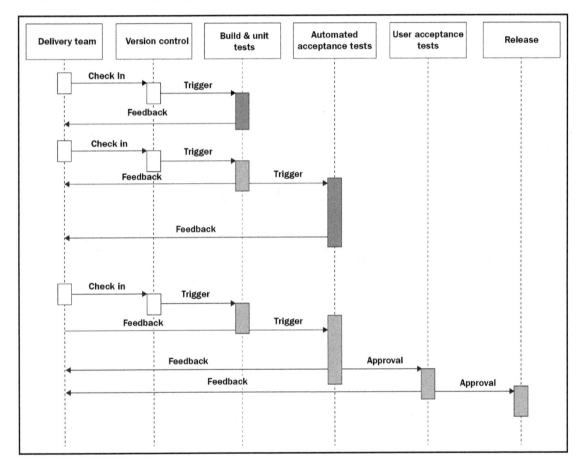

It may be worth mentioning that developers can be completely isolated from the production infrastructure. Their interface is just a Git workflow—a good example of this is the Deis workflow (PaaS on Kubernetes; similar to Heroku).

Designing a CI/CD pipeline for Kubernetes

When your deployment target is a Kubernetes cluster, you should rethink some traditional practices. For starters, the packaging is different. You need to bake images for your containers. Reverting code changes is super easy and instantaneous using smart labeling. It gives you a lot of confidence that, if a bad change slips through the testing net, somehow, you'll be able to revert to the previous version immediately. But you want to be careful there. Schema changes and data migrations can't be automatically rolled back.

Another unique capability of Kubernetes is that developers can run a whole cluster locally. That takes some work when you design your cluster, but since the microservices that comprise your system run in containers, and those containers interact through APIs, it is possible and practical to do. As always, if your system is very data-driven, you will need to accommodate for that and provide data snapshots and synthetic data that your developers can use.

Summary

In this chapter, we covered a lot of ground, and you got to understand the design and architecture of Kubernetes. Kubernetes is an orchestration platform for microservice-based applications running as containers. Kubernetes clusters have master and worker nodes. Containers run within pods. Each pod runs on a single physical or virtual machine. Kubernetes directly supports many concepts, such as services, labels, and persistent storage. You can implement various distributed system design patterns on Kubernetes. Container runtimes just need to implement the CRI. Docker, rkt, Hyper containers, and more are supported.

In Chapter 10, *Creating Kubernetes Clusters*, we will explore the various ways to create Kubernetes clusters, discuss when to use different options, and build a multi-node cluster.

3
Building a Foundation with Core Kubernetes Constructs

This chapter will cover the core Kubernetes constructs, namely pods, services, replication controllers, replica sets, and labels. We will describe Kubernetes components, dimensions of the API, and Kubernetes objects. We will also dig into the major Kubernetes cluster components. A few simple application examples will be included to demonstrate each construct. This chapter will also cover basic operations for your cluster. Finally, health checks and scheduling will be introduced with a few examples.

The following topics will be covered in this chapter:

- Kubernetes' overall architecture
- The context of Kubernetes architecture within system theory
- Introduction to core Kubernetes constructs, architecture, and components
- How labels can simplify the management of a Kubernetes cluster
- Monitoring services and container health
- Setting up scheduling constraints based on available cluster resources

Technical requirements

You'll need to have your Google Cloud Platform account enabled and logged in or you can use a local Minikube instance of Kubernetes. You can also use Play with Kubernetes over the web: `https://labs.play-with-k8s.com/`.

Here's the GitHub repository for this chapter: `https://github.com/PacktPublishing/The-Complete-Kubernetes-Guide/tree/master/Chapter03`.

The Kubernetes system

To understand the complex architecture and components of Kubernetes, we should take a step back and look at the landscape of the overall system in order to understand the context and place of each moving piece. This book focuses mainly on the technical pieces and processes of the Kubernetes software, but let's examine the system from a top-down perspective. In the following diagram, you can see the major parts of the Kubernetes system, which is a great way to think about the classification of the parts we'll describe and utilize in this book:

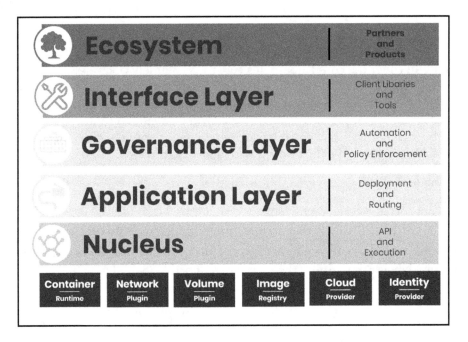

Let's take a look at each piece, starting from the bottom.

Nucleus

The nucleus of the Kubernetes system is devoted to providing a standard API and manner in which operators and/or software can execute work on the cluster. The nucleus is the bare minimum set of functionality that should be considered absolutely stable in order to build up the layers above. Each piece of this layer is clearly documented, and these pieces are required to build higher-order concepts at other layers of the system. You can consider the APIs here to make up the core bits of the Kubernetes control plane.

The cluster control plane is the first half of the Kubernetes nucleus, and it provides the RESTful APIs that allow operators to utilized the mostly CRUD-based operations of the cluster. It is important to note that the Kubernetes nucleus and consequently the cluster control plane was built with multi-tenancy in mind, so the layer must be flexible enough to provide logical separation of teams or workloads within a single cluster. The cluster control plane follows API conventions that allow it to take advantage of shared services such as identity and auditing, and has access to the namespaces and events of the cluster.

The second half of the nucleus is execution. While there are a number of controllers in Kubernetes, such as the replication controller, replica set, and deployments, the kubelet is the most important controller and it forms the basis of the node and pod APIs that allow us to interact with the container execution layer. Kubernetes builds upon the kubelet with the concept of pods, which allow us to manage many containers and their constituent storage as a core capability of the system. We'll dig more into pods later.

Below the nucleus, we can see the various pieces that the kubelet depends on in order to manage the container, network, container storage, image storage, cloud provider, and identity. We've left these intentionally vague as there are several options for each box, and you can pick and choose from standard and popular implementations or experiment with emerging tech. To give you an idea of how many options there are in the base layer, we'll outline container runtime and network plugin options here.

Container Runtime options: You'll use the Kubernetes **Container Runtime Interface (CRI)** to interact with the two main container runtimes:

- containerd
- rkt

You're still able to run Docker containers on Kubernetes at this point, and as containerd is the default runtime, it's going to be transparent to the operator at this point due to the defaults. You'll be able to run all of the same `docker <action>` commands on the cluster to introspect and gather information about your clusters.

There are also several competing, emerging formats:

- `cri-containerd`: https://github.com/containerd/cri-containerd
- `runv` and `clear` containers, which are hypervisor-based solutions: https://github.com/hyperhq/runv and https://github.com/clearcontainers/runtime
- `kata` containers, which are a combination of `runv` and clear containers: https://katacontainers.io/
- `frakti` containers, which combine `runv` and Docker: https://github.com/kubernetes/frakti

You can read more about the CRI here: `http://blog.kubernetes.io/2016/12/container-runtime-interface-cri-in-kubernetes.html`.

Network plugin: You can use the CNI to leverage any of the following plugins or the simple Kubenet networking implementation if you're going to rely on a cloud provider's network segmentation, or if you're going to be running a single node cluster:

- Cilium
- Contiv
- Contrail
- Flannel
- Kube-router
- Multus
- Calico
- Romana
- Weave net

Application layer

The application layer, often referred to as the service fabric or orchestration layer, does all of the fun things we've come to value so highly in Kubernetes: basic deployment and routing, service discovery, load balancing, and self-healing. In order for a cluster operator to manage the life cycle of the cluster, these primitives must be present and functional in this layer. Most containerized applications will depend on the full functionality of this layer, and will interact with these functions in order to provide "orchestration" of the application across multiple cluster hosts. When an application scales up or changes a configuration setting, the application layer will be managed by this layer. The application layer cares about the desired state of the cluster, the application composition, service discovery, load balancing, and routing, and utilizes all of these pieces to keep data flowing from the correct point A to the correct point B.

Governance layer

The governance layer consists of high-level automation and policy enforcement. This layer can be thought of as an opinionated version of the application management layer, as it provides the ability to enforce tenancy, gather metrics, and do intelligent provisioning and autoscaling of containers. The APIs at this layer should be considered options for running containerized applications.

The governance layer allows operators to control methods used for authorization, as well as quotas and control around network and storage. At this layer, functionality should be applicable to scenarios that large enterprises care about, such as operations, security, and compliance scenarios.

Interface layer

The interface layer is made up of commonly used tools, systems, user interfaces, and libraries that other custom Kubernetes distributions might use. The `kubectl` library is a great example of the interface layer, and importantly it's not seen as a privileged part of the Kubernetes system; it's considered a client tool in order to provide maximum flexibility for the Kubernetes API. If you run `$ kubectl -h`, you will get a clear picture of the functionality exposed to the interface layer.

Other pieces at this layer include cluster federation tools, dashboards, Helm, and client libraries such as `client-node`, `KubernetesClient`, and `python`. These tools provide common tasks for you, so you don't have to worry about writing code for authentication, for example. These libraries use the Kubernetes Service Account to authenticate to the cluster.

Ecosystem

The last layer of the Kubernetes system is the ecosystem, and it's by far the busiest and most hectic part of the picture. Kubernetes approach to container orchestration and management is to present the user with the options of a complementary choice; there are plug-in and general purpose APIs available for external systems to utilize. You can consider three types of ecosystem pieces in the Kubernetes system:

- **Above Kubernetes:** All of the glue software and infrastructure that's needed to "make things go" sits at this level, and includes operational ethos such as ChatOps and DevOps, logging and monitoring, Continuous Integration and Delivery, big data systems, and Functions as a Service.

- **Inside Kubernetes:** In short, what's inside a container is outside of Kubernetes. Kubernetes, or **K8s**, cares not at all what you run inside of a container.
- **Below Kubernetes**: These are the gray squares detailed at the bottom of the diagram. You'll need a technology for each piece of foundational technology to make Kubernetes function, and the ecosystem is where you get them. The cluster state store is probably the most famous example of an ecosystem component: `etcd`. Cluster bootstrapping tools such as `minikube`, `bootkube`, `kops`, `kube-aws`, and `kubernetes-anywhere` are other examples of community-provided ecosystem tools.

Let's move on to the architecture of the Kubernetes system, now that we understand the larger context.

The architecture

Although containers bring a helpful layer of abstraction and tooling for application management, Kubernetes brings additional to schedule and orchestrate containers at scale, while managing the full application life cycle.

K8s moves up the stack, giving us constructs to deal with management at the application- or service- level. This gives us automation and tooling to ensure high availability, application stack, and service-wide portability. K8s also allows finer control of resource usage, such as CPU, memory, and disk space across our infrastructure.

Kubernetes architecture is comprised of three main pieces:

- The cluster control plane (the **master**)
- The cluster state (a distributed storage system called etcd)
- Cluster nodes (individual servers running agents called **kubelets**)

The Master

The **cluster control plane**, otherwise known as the **Master**, makes global decisions based on the current and desired state of the cluster, detecting and responding to events as they propagate across the cluster. This includes starting and stopping pods if the replication factor of a replication controller is unsatisfied or running a scheduled cron job.

The overarching goal of the control plane is to report on and work towards a desired state. The API that the master runs depends on the persistent state store, `etcd`, and utilizes the `watch` strategy for minimizing change latency while enabling decentralized component coordination.

Components of the Master can be realistically run on any machine in the cluster, but best practices and production-ready systems dictate that master components should be co-located on a single machine (or a multi-master high availability setup). Running all of the Master components on a single machine allows operators to exclude running user containers on those machines, which is recommended for more reliable control plane operations. The less you have running on your Master node, the better!

We'll dig into the Master components, including `kube-apiserver`, etcd, `kube-scheduler`, `kube-controller-manager`, and `cloud-controller-manager` when we get into more detail on the Master node. It is important to note that the Kubernetes goal with these components is to provide a RESTful API against mostly persistent storage resources and a CRUD (Create, Read, Update, and Delete) strategy. We'll explore the basic primitives around container-specific orchestration and scheduling later in this chapter when we read about services, ingress, pods, deployments, StatefulSet, CronJobs, and ReplicaSets.

Cluster state

The second major piece of the Kubernetes architecture, the cluster state, is the `etcd` key value store. `etcd` is consistent and highly available, and is designed to quickly and reliably provide Kubernetes access to critical cluster current and desired state. etcd is able to provide this distributed coordination of data through such core concepts as leader election and distributed locks. The Kubernetes API, via its API server, is in charge of updating objects in etcd that correspond to the RESTful operations of the cluster. This is very important to remember: the API server is responsible for managing what's stuck into Kubernetes' picture of the world. Other components in this ecosystem watch etcd for changes in order to modify themselves and enter into the desired state.

This is of particular important because every component we've described in the Kubernetes Master and those that we'll investigate in the nodes below are stateless, which means their state is stored elsewhere, and that elsewhere is etcd.

Kubernetes doesn't take specific action to make things happen on the cluster; the Kubernetes API, via the API server, writes into etcd what should be true, and then the various pieces of Kubernetes make it so. etcd provides this interface via a simple HTTP/JSON API, which makes interacting with it quite simple.

etcd is also important in considerations of the Kubernetes security model due to it existing at a very low layer of the Kubernetes system, which means that any component that can write data to etcd has `root` to the cluster. Later on, we'll look into how the Kubernetes system is divided into layers in order to minimize this exposure. You can consider etcd to underlay Kubernetes with other parts of the ecosystem such as the container runtime, an image registry, a file storage, a cloud provider interface, and other dependencies that Kubernetes manages but does not have an opinionated perspective on.

In non-production Kubernetes clusters, you'll see single-node instantiations of etcd to save money on compute, simplify operations, or otherwise reduce complexity. It is essential to note however that a multi-master strategy of *2n+1* nodes is essential for production-ready clusters, in order to replicate data effectively across masters and ensure fault tolerance. It is recommended that you check the etcd documentation for more information.

Check out the etcd documentation here: `https://github.com/coreos/` `etcd/blob/master/Documentation/docs.md`.

If you're in front of your cluster, you can check to see the status of etcd by checking `componentstatuses` or `cs`:

```
[node3 /]$ kubectl get componentstatuses
NAME                    STATUS MESSAGE           ERROR
scheduler               Healthy ok
controller-manager      Healthy ok
etcd-0                  Healthy {"health": "true"}
```

Due to a bug in the AKS ecosystem, this will currently not work on Azure. You can track this issue here to see when it is resolved:

`https://github.com/Azure/AKS/issues/173`: `kubectl get` `componentstatus fails for scheduler and controller-` `manager #173`

If you were to see an unhealthy `etcd` service, it'd look something like so:

```
[node3 /]$ kubectl get cs

NAME                    STATUS       MESSAGE       ERROR
etcd-0                  Unhealthy                  Get
http://127.0.0.1:2379/health: dial tcp 127.0.0.1:2379: getsockopt:
connection refused
controller-manager      Healthy      ok
scheduler               Healthy      ok
```

Cluster nodes

The third and final major Kubernetes component are the cluster nodes. While the master node components only run on a subset of the Kubernetes cluster, the node components run everywhere; they manage the maintenance of running pods, containers, and other primitives and provide the runtime environment. There are three node components:

- Kubelet
- Kube-proxy
- Container runtime

We'll dig into the specifics of these components later, but it's important to note several things about node componentry first. The kubelet can be considered the primary controller within Kubernetes, and providers the pod/node APIs that are used by the container runtime to execute container functionality. This functionality is grouped by container and their corresponding storage volumes into the concept of pods. The concept of a pod gives application developers a straightforward packaging paradigm from which to design their application, and allows us to take maximum advantage of the portability of containers, while realizing the power of orchestration and scheduling across many instances of a cluster.

It's interesting to note that a number of Kubernetes components run on Kubernetes itself (in other words, powered by the kubelets), including DNS, ingress, the Dashboard, and the resource monitoring of Heapster:

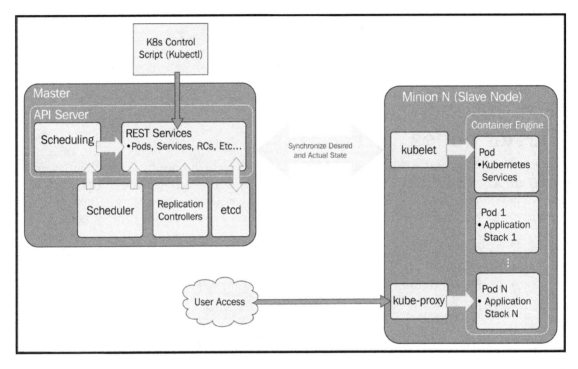

Kubernetes core architecture

In the preceding diagram, we see the core architecture of Kubernetes. Most administrative interactions are done via the `kubectl` script and/or RESTful service calls to the API.

As mentioned, note the ideas of the desired state and actual state carefully. This is the key to how Kubernetes manages the cluster and its workloads. All the pieces of K8s are constantly working to monitor the current actual state and synchronize it with the desired state defined by the administrators via the API server or `kubectl` script. There will be times when these states do not match up, but the system is always working to reconcile the two.

Let's dig into more detail on the Master and node instances.

Master

We know now that the **Master** is the brain of our cluster. We have the core API server, which maintains RESTful web services for querying and defining our desired cluster and workload state. It's important to note that the control pane only accesses the master to initiate changes and not the nodes directly.

Additionally, the master includes the **scheduler.** The replication controller/replica set works with the API server to ensure that the correct number of pod replicas are running at any given time. This is exemplary of the desired state concept. If our replication controller/replica set is defining three replicas and our actual state is two copies of the pod running, then the scheduler will be invoked to add a third pod somewhere in our cluster. The same is true if there are too many pods running in the cluster at any given time. In this way, K8s is always pushing toward that desired state.

As discussed previously, we'll look more closely into each of the Master components. `kube-apiserver` has the job of providing the API for the cluster as the front end of the control plane that the Master is providing. In fact, the apiserver is exposed through a service specifically called `kubernetes`, and we install the API server using the kubelet. This service is configured via the `kube-apiserver.yaml` file, which lives in `/etc/kubernetes/manifests/` on every manage node within your cluster.

`kube-apiserver` is a key portion of high availability in Kubernetes and, as such, it's designed to scale horizontally. We'll discuss how to construct highly available clusters later in this book, but suffice to say that you'll need to spread the `kube-apiserver` container across several Master nodes and provide a load balancer in the front.

Since we've gone into some detail about the cluster state store, it will suffice to say that an `etcd` agent is running on all of the Master nodes.

The next piece of the puzzle is `kube-scheduler`, which makes sure that all pods are associated and assigned to a node for operation. The schedulers works with the API server to schedule workloads in the form of pods on the actual minion nodes. These pods include the various containers that make up our application stacks. By default, the basic Kubernetes scheduler spreads pods across the cluster and uses different nodes for matching pod replicas. Kubernetes also allows specifying necessary resources, hardware and software policy constraints, affinity or anti-affinity as required, and data volume locality for each container, so scheduling can be altered by these additional factors.

The last two main pieces of the Master nodes are `kube-controller-manager` and `cloud-controller-manager`. As you might have guessed based on their names, while both of these services play an important part in container orchestration and scheduling, `kube-controller-manager` helps to orchestrate core internal components of Kubernetes, while `cloud-controller-manager` interacts with different vendors and their cloud provider APIs.

`kube-controller-manager` is actually a Kubernetes daemon that embeds the core control loops, otherwise known as controllers, that are included with Kubernetes:

- The **Node** controller, which manages pod availability and manages pods when they go down
- The **Replication** controller, which ensures that each replication controller object in the system has the correct number of pods
- The **Endpoints** controller, which controls endpoint records in the API, thereby managing DNS resolution of a pod or set of pods backing a service that defines selectors

In order to reduce the complexity of the controller components, they're all packed and shipped within this single daemon as `kube-controller-manager`.

`cloud-controller-manager`, on the other hand, pays attention to external components, and runs controller loops that are specific to the cloud provider that your cluster is using. The original intent of this design was to decouple the internal development of Kubernetes from cloud-specific vendor code. This was accomplished through the use of plugins, which prevents Kubernetes from relying on code that is not inherent to its value proposition. We can expect over time that future releases of Kubernetes will move vendor-specific code completely out of the Kubernetes code base, and that vendor-specific code will be maintained by the vendor themselves, and then called on by the Kubernetes `cloud-controller-manager`. This design prevents the need for several pieces of Kubernetes to communicate with the cloud provider, namely the kubelet, Kubernetes controller manager, and the API server.

Nodes (formerly minions)

In each node, we have several components as mentioned already. Let's look at each of them in detail.

The `kubelet` interacts with the API server to update the state and to start new workloads that have been invoked by the scheduler. As previously mentioned, this agent runs on every node of the cluster. The primary interface of the kubelet is one or more PodSpecs, which ensure that the containers and configurations are healthy.

The `kube-proxy` provides basic load balancing and directs the traffic destined for specific services to the proper pod on the backend. It maintains these network rules to enable the service abstraction through connection forwarding.

The last major component of the node is the container runtime, which is responsible for initiating, running, and stopping containers. The Kubernetes ecosystem has introduced the OCI runtime specification to democratize the container scheduler/orchestrator interface. While Docker, rkt, and runc are the current major implementations, the OCI aims to provide a common interface so you can bring your own runtime. At this point, Docker is the overwhelmingly dominant runtime.

Read more about the OCI runtime specifications here: `https://github.com/opencontainers/runtime-spec`.

In your cluster, the nodes may be virtual machines or bare metal hardware. Compared to other items such as controllers and pods, the node is not an abstraction that is created by Kubernetes. Rather, Kubernetes leverages `cloud-controller-manager` to interact with the cloud provider API, which owns the life cycle of the nodes. That means that when we instantiate a node in Kubernetes, we're simply creating an object that represents a machine in your given infrastructure. It's up to Kubernetes to determine if the node has converged with the object definition. Kubernetes validates the node's availability through its IP address, which is gathered via the `metadata.name` field. The status of these nodes can be discovered through the following status keys.

The addresses are where we'll find information such as the hostname and private and public IPs. This will be specific to your cloud provider's implementation. The condition field will give you a view into the state of your node's status in terms of disk, memory, network, and basic configuration.

Here's a table with the available node conditions:

Node Condition	Description
OutOfDisk	**True** if there is insufficient free space on the node for adding new pods, otherwise **False**
Ready	**True** if the node is healthy and ready to accept pods, **False** if the node is not healthy and is not accepting pods, and **Unknown** if the node controller has not heard from the node in the last 40 seconds
MemoryPressure	**True** if pressure exists on the node memory – that is, if the node memory is low; otherwise **False**
DiskPressure	**True** if pressure exists on the disk size – that is, if the disk capacity is low; otherwise **False**
NetworkUnavailable	**True** if the network for the node is not correctly configured, otherwise **False**
ConfigOK	**True** if the kubelet is correctly configured, otherwise **False**

A healthy node will have a status that looks similar to the following if you run it, you'll see the following output in the code:

```
$ kubectl get nodes -o json

"conditions": [
  {
    "type": "Ready",
    "status": "True"
  }
]
```

Capacity is simple: it's the available CPU, memory, and resulting number of pods that can be run on a given node. Nodes self-report their capacity and leave the responsibility for scheduling the appropriate number of resources to Kubernetes. The `Info` key is similarly straightforward and provides version information for Docker, OS, and Kubernetes.

It's important to note that the major component of the Kubernetes and node relationship is the **node controller**, which we called out previously as one of the core system controllers. There are three strategic pieces to this relationship:

- **Node health**: When you run large clusters in private, public, or hybrid cloud scenarios, you're bound to lose machines from time to time. Even within the data center, given a large enough cluster, you're bound to see regular failures at scale. The node controller is responsible for updating the node's `NodeStatus` to either `NodeReady` or `ConditionUnknown`, depending on the instance's availability. This management is key as Kubernetes will need to migrate pods (and therefore containers) to available nodes if `ConditionUnknown` occurs. You can set the health check interval for nodes in your cluster with `--node-monitor-period`.
- **IP assignment**: Every node needs some IP addresses, so it can distribute IPs to services and or containers.
- **Node list**: In order to manage pods across a number of machines, we need to keep an up-to-date list of available machines. Based on the aforementioned `NodeStatus`, the node controller will keep this list current.

We'll look into node controller specifics when investigating highly available clusters that span **Availability Zones** (**AZs**), which requires the spreading of nodes across AZs in order to provide availability.

Finally, we have some default pods, which run various infrastructure services for the node. As we explored briefly in the previous chapter, the pods include services for the **Domain Name System** (**DNS**), logging, and pod health checks. The default pod will run alongside our scheduled pods on every node.

 In v1.0, minion was renamed to node, but there are still remnants of the term minion in some of the machine naming scripts and documentation that exists on the web. For clarity, I've added the term minion in addition to node in a few places throughout this book.

Core constructs

Now, let's dive a little deeper and explore some of the core abstractions Kubernetes provides. These abstractions will make it easier to think about our applications and ease the burden of life cycle management, high availability, and scheduling.

Pods

Pods allow you to keep related containers close in terms of the network and hardware infrastructure. Data can live near the application, so processing can be done without incurring a high latency from network traversal. Similarly, common data can be stored on volumes that are shared between a number of containers. Pods essentially allow you to logically group containers and pieces of our application stacks together.

While pods may run one or more containers inside, the pod itself may be one of many that is running on a Kubernetes node (minion). As we'll see, pods give us a logical group of containers across which we can then replicate, schedule, and balance service endpoints.

Pod example

Let's take a quick look at a pod in action. We'll spin up a Node.js application on the cluster. You'll need a GCE cluster running for this; if you don't already have one started, refer to the *Our first cluster* section in `Chapter 1`, *Introduction to Kubernetes*.

Now, let's make a directory for our definitions. In this example, I'll create a folder in the `/book-examples` subfolder under our home directory:

```
$ mkdir book-examples
$ cd book-examples
$ mkdir 02_example
$ cd 02_example
```

 You can download the example code files from your account at `http://www.packtpub.com` for all of the Packt Publishing books you have purchased. If you purchased this book elsewhere, you can visit `http://www.packtpub.com/support` and register to have the files emailed directly to you.

Use your favorite editor to create the following file and name it as `nodejs-pod.yaml`:

```
apiVersion: v1
kind: Pod
metadata:
  name: node-js-pod
spec:
  containers:
  - name: node-js-pod
    image: bitnami/apache:latest
    ports:
    - containerPort: 80
```

This file creates a pod named `node-js-pod` with the latest `bitnami/apache` container running on port `80`. We can check this using the following command:

```
$ kubectl create -f nodejs-pod.yaml
pod "node-js-pod" created
```

This gives us a pod running the specified container. We can see more information on the pod by running the following command:

```
$ kubectl describe pods/node-js-pod
```

You'll see a good deal of information, such as the pod's status, IP address, and even relevant log events. You'll note the pod IP address is a private IP address, so we cannot access it directly from our local machine. Not to worry, as the `kubectl exec` command mirrors Docker's `exec` functionality. You can get the pod IP address in a number of ways. A simple `get` of the pod will show you the IP where we use a template output that looks up the IP address in the status output:

```
$ kubectl get pod node-js-pod --template={{.status.podIP}}
```

You can use that IP address directly, or execute that command within backticks to `exec` into the pod. Once the pod shows it's in a running state, we can use this feature to run a command inside a pod:

```
$ kubectl exec node-js-pod -- curl <private ip address>

--or--

$ kubectl exec node-js-pod -- curl `kubectl get pod node-js-pod --template={{.status.podIP}}`
```

> By default, this runs a command in the first container it finds, but you can select a specific one using the `-c` argument.

After running the command, you should see some HTML code. We'll have a prettier view later in this chapter, but for now, we can see that our pod is indeed running as expected.

If you have experience with containers, you've probably also exec 'd into a container. You can do something very similar with Kubernetes:

```
master $ kubectl exec -it node-js-pod -- /bin/bash
root@node-js-pod:/opt/bitnami/apache/htdocs# exit
master $
```

You can also run other command directly into the container with the `exec` command. Note that you'll need to use two dashes to separate your command's argument in case it has the same in `kubectl`:

```
$ kubectl exec node-js-pod ls /
$ kubectl exec node-js-pod ps aux
$ kubectl exec node-js-pod -- uname -a
```

Labels

Labels give us another level of categorization, which becomes very helpful in terms of everyday operations and management. Similar to tags, labels can be used as the basis of service discovery as well as a useful grouping tool for day-to-day operations and management tasks. Labels are attached to Kubernetes objects and are simple key-value pairs. You will see them on pods, replication controllers, replica sets, services, and so on. Labels themselves and the keys/values inside of them are based on a constrained set of variables, so that queries against them can be evaluated efficiently using optimized algorithms and data structures.

The label indicates to Kubernetes which resources to work with for a variety of operations. Think of it as a filtering option. It is important to note that labels are meant to be meaningful and usable to the operators and application developers, but do not imply any semantic definitions to the cluster. Labels are used for organization and selection of subsets of objects, and can be added to objects at creation time and/or modified at any time during cluster operations. Labels are leveraged for management purposes, an example of which is when you want to know all of the backing containers for a particular service, you can normally get them via the labels on the container which correspond to the service at hand. With this type of management, you often end up with multiple labels on an object.

Kubernetes cluster management is often a cross-cutting operation, involving scaling up of different resources and services, management of multiple storage devices and dozens of nodes and is therefore a highly multi-dimensional operation.

Labels allow horizontal, vertical, and diagonal encapsulation of Kubernetes objects. You'll often see labels such as the following:

- `environment: dev`, `environment: integration`, `environment: staging`, `environment: UAT`, `environment: production`
- `tier: web`, `tier: stateless`, `tier: stateful`, `tier: protected`
- `tenancy: org1`, `tenancy: org2`

Once you've mastered labels, you can use selectors to identify a novel group of objects based on a particular set of label combination. There are currently equality-based and set-based selectors. Equality-based selectors allow operators to filter by keys/value pairs, and in order to `select (or)` an object, it must match all specified constraints. This kind of selector is often used to choose a particular node, perhaps to run against particularly speedy storage. Set-based selectors are more complex, and allow the operator to filter keys according to a specific value. This kind of selector is often used to determine where a object belongs, such as a tier, tenancy zone, or environment.

In short, an object may have many labels attached to it, but a selector can provide uniqueness to an object or set of objects.

We will take a look at labels in more depth later in this chapter, but first we will explore the remaining three constructs: services, replication controllers, and replica sets.

The container's afterlife

As Werner Vogels, CTO of AWS, famously said, *everything fails all the time;* containers and pods can and will crash, become corrupted, or maybe even just get accidentally shut off by a clumsy administrator poking around on one of the nodes. Strong policy and security practices such as enforcing least privilege curtail some of these incidents, but involuntary workload slaughter happens and is simply a fact of operations.

Luckily, Kubernetes provides two very valuable constructs to keep this somber affair all tidied up behind the curtains. Services and replication controllers/replica sets give us the ability to keep our applications running with little interruption and graceful recovery.

Services

Services allow us to abstract access away from the consumers of our applications. Using a reliable endpoint, users and other programs can access pods running on your cluster seamlessly. This is in direct contradiction to one of our core Kubernetes constructs: pods.

Pods by definition are ephemeral and when they die they are not resurrected. If we trust that replication controllers will do their job to create and destroy pods as necessary, we'll need another construct to create a logical separation and policy for access.

Here we have services, which use a label selector to target a group of ever-changing pods. Services are important because we want frontend services that don't care about the specifics of backend services, and vice versa. While the pods that compose those tiers are fungible, the service via `ReplicationControllers` manages the relationships between objects and therefore decouples different types of applications.

For applications that require an IP address, there's a **Virtual IP** (VIP) available which can send round robin traffic to a backend pod. With cloud-native applications or microservices, Kubernetes provides the Endpoints API for simple communication between services.

K8s achieves this by making sure that every node in the cluster runs a proxy named `kube-proxy`. As the name suggests, the job of `kube-proxy` is to proxy communication from a service endpoint back to the corresponding pod that is running the actual application:

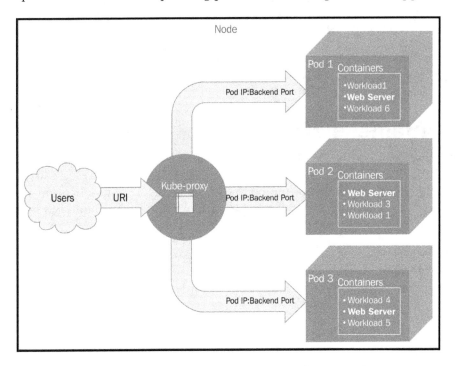

The kube-proxy architecture

Membership of the service load balancing pool is determined by the use of selectors and labels. Pods with matching labels are added to the list of candidates where the service forwards traffic. A virtual IP address and port are used as the entry points for the service, and the traffic is then forwarded to a random pod on a target port defined by either K8s or your definition file.

Updates to service definitions are monitored and coordinated from the K8s cluster Master and propagated to the `kube-proxy daemons` running on each node.

At the moment, `kube-proxy` is running on the node host itself. There are plans to containerize this and the kubelet by default in the future.

A service is a RESTful object, which relies on a `POST` transaction to the apiserver to create a new instance of the Kubernetes object. Here's an example of a simple service named `service-example.yaml`:

```
kind: Service
apiVersion: v1
metadata:
  name: gsw-k8s-3-service
spec:
  selector:
    app: gswk8sApp
  ports:
  - protocol: TCP
    port: 80
    targetPort: 8080
```

This creates a service named `gsw-k8s-3-service`, which opens up a target port of `8080` with the key/value label of `app:gswk8sApp`. While the selector is continuously evaluated by a controller, the results of the IP address assignment (also called a cluster IP) will be posted to the endpoints object of `gsw-k8s-3-service`. The `kind` field is required, as is `ports`, while `selector` and `type` are optional.

Kube-proxy runs a number of other forms of virtual IP for services aside from the strategy outlined previously. There are three different types of proxy modes that we'll mention here, but will investigate in later chapters:

- Userspace
- Iptables
- Ipvs

Replication controllers and replica sets

Replication controllers have been deprecated in favor of using Deployments, which configure ReplicaSets. This method is a more robust manner of application replication and has been developed as a response to the feedback of the container running community.

Replication controllers (**RCs**), as the name suggests, manage the number of nodes that a pod and included container images run on. They ensure that an instance of an image is being run with the specific number of copies. RCs ensure that a pod or many same pods are always up and available to serve application traffic.

As you start to operationalize your containers and pods, you'll need a way to roll out updates, scale the number of copies running (both up and down), or simply ensure that at least one instance of your stack is always running. RCs create a high-level mechanism to make sure that things are operating correctly across the entire application and cluster. Pods created by RCs are replaced if they fail, and are deleted when terminated. RCs are recommended for use even if you only have a single pod in your application.

RCs are simply charged with ensuring that you have the desired scale for your application. You define the number of pod replicas you want running and give it a template for how to create new pods. Just like services, we'll use selectors and labels to define a pod's membership in an RC.

Kubernetes doesn't require the strict behavior of the replication controller, which is ideal for long-running processes. In fact, job controllers can be used for short-lived workloads, which allow jobs to be run to a completion state and are well suited for batch work.

Replica sets are a new type, currently in beta, that represent an improved version of replication controllers. Currently, the main difference consists of being able to use the new set-based label selectors, as we will see in the following examples.

Our first Kubernetes application

Before we move on, let's take a look at these three concepts in action. Kubernetes ships with a number of examples installed, but we'll create a new example from scratch to illustrate some of the concepts.

We already created a pod definition file but, as you learned, there are many advantages to running our pods via replication controllers. Again, using the `book-examples/02_example` folder we made earlier, we'll create some definition files and start a cluster of Node.js servers using a replication controller approach. Additionally, we'll add a public face to it with a load-balanced service.

Use your favorite editor to create the following file and name it as `nodejs-controller.yaml`:

```
apiVersion: v1
kind: ReplicationController
metadata:
  name: node-js
  labels:
    name: node-js
spec:
  replicas: 3
  selector:
    name: node-js
  template:
    metadata:
      labels:
        name: node-js
    spec:
      containers:
      - name: node-js
        image: jonbaier/node-express-info:latest
        ports:
        - containerPort: 80
```

This is the first resource definition file for our cluster, so let's take a closer look. You'll note that it has four first-level elements (`kind`, `apiVersion`, `metadata`, and `spec`). These are common among all top-level Kubernetes resource definitions:

- `Kind`: This tells K8s the type of resource we are creating. In this case, the type is `ReplicationController`. The `kubectl` script uses a single `create` command for all types of resources. The benefit here is that you can easily create a number of resources of various types without the need for specifying individual parameters for each type. However, it requires that the definition files can identify what it is they are specifying.
- `apiVersion`: This simply tells Kubernetes which version of the schema we are using.

- `Metadata`: This is where we will give the resource a name and also specify labels that will be used to search and select resources for a given operation. The metadata element also allows you to create annotations, which are for the non-identifying information that might be useful for client tools and libraries.
- Finally, we have `spec`, which will vary based on the `kind` or `type` of resource we are creating. In this case, it's `ReplicationController`, which ensures the desired number of pods are running. The `replicas` element defines the desired number of pods, the `selector` element tells the controller which pods to watch, and finally, the `template` element defines a template to launch a new pod. The `template` section contains the same pieces we saw in our pod definition earlier. An important thing to note is that the `selector` values need to match the `labels` values specified in the pod template. Remember that this matching is used to select the pods being managed.

Now, let's take a look at the service definition named `nodejs-rc-service.yaml`:

```
apiVersion: v1
kind: Service
metadata:
  name: node-js
  labels:
    name: node-js
spec:
  type: LoadBalancer
  ports:
  - port: 80
  selector:
    name: node-js
```

If you are using the free trial for Google Cloud Platform, you may have issues with the `LoadBalancer` type services. This type creates an external IP addresses, but trial accounts are limited to only one static address.

For this example, you won't be able to access the example from the external IP address using Minikube. In Kubernetes versions above 1.5, you can use Ingress to expose services but that is outside of the scope of this chapter.

The YAML here is similar to `ReplicationController`. The main difference is seen in the service `spec` element. Here, we define the `Service` type, listening `port`, and `selector`, which tell the `Service` proxy which pods can answer the service.

> Kubernetes supports both YAML and JSON formats for definition files.

Create the Node.js express replication controller:

```
$ kubectl create -f nodejs-controller.yaml
```

The output is as follows:

```
replicationcontroller "node-js" created
```

This gives us a replication controller that ensures that three copies of the container are always running:

```
$ kubectl create -f nodejs-rc-service.yaml
```

The output is as follows:

```
service "node-js" created
```

On GCE, this will create an external load balancer and forwarding rules, but you may need to add additional firewall rules. In my case, the firewall was already open for port `80`. However, you may need to open this port, especially if you deploy a service with ports other than `80` and `443`.

OK, now we have a running service, which means that we can access the Node.js servers from a reliable URL. Let's take a look at our running services:

```
$ kubectl get services
```

The following screenshot is the result of the preceding command:

NAME	CLUSTER-IP	EXTERNAL-IP	PORT(S)	AGE
kubernetes	10.0.0.1	<none>	443/TCP	11m
node-js	10.0.200.192	35.184.181.18	80:30874/TCP	4m

Services listing

In the preceding screenshot (services listing), we should note that the `node-js` service is running, and in the `IP(S)` column, we should have both a private and a public (`130.211.186.84` in the screenshot) IP address. If you don't see the external IP, you may need to wait a minute for the IP to be allocated from GCE. Let's see if we can connect by opening up the public address in a browser:

Host: node-js-u26fd
Running OS: linux
Uptime: 525274
Network Information: 10.244.1.17, fe80::42:aff:fef4:111
DNS Servers: 10.0.0.10,169.254.169.254,10.240.0.1

Container information application

You should see something like the previous screenshot. If we visit multiple times, you should note that the container name changes. Essentially, the service load balancer is rotating between available pods on the backend.

 Browsers usually cache web pages, so to really see the container name change, you may need to clear your cache or use a proxy like this one: `https://hide.me/en/proxy`.

Let's try playing chaos monkey a bit and kill off a few containers to see what Kubernetes does. In order to do this, we need to see where the pods are actually running. First, let's list our pods:

```
$ kubectl get pods
```

The following screenshot is the result of the preceding command:

NAME	READY	STATUS	RESTARTS	AGE
node-js-1fxoy	1/1	Running	0	1d
node-js-m4w4a	1/1	Running	0	1d
node-js-sjc03	1/1	Running	0	1d

Currently running pods

Now, let's get some more details on one of the pods running a `node-js` container. You can do this with the `describe` command and one of the pod names listed in the last command:

```
$ kubectl describe pod/node-js-sjc03
```

The following screenshot is the result of the preceding command:

```
Name:                           node-js-sjc03
Namespace:                      default
Image(s):                       petegoo/node-express-sample:latest
Node:                           kubernetes-minion-aqdf/10.240.142.178
Labels:                         name=node-js
Status:                         Running
Reason:
Message:
IP:                             10.244.0.10
Replication Controllers:        node-js (3/3 replicas created)
Containers:
  node-js:
    Image:        petegoo/node-express-sample:latest
    Limits:
      cpu:                      100m
    State:                      Running
      Started:                 Tue, 28 Jul 2015 16:57:33 -0400
    Ready:                      True
      Restart Count:           0
Conditions:
  Type              Status
  Ready             True
No events.
```

Pod description

You should see the preceding output. The information we need is the `Node:` section. Let's use the node name to **SSH** (short for **Secure Shell**) into the node (minion) running this workload:

```
$ gcloud compute --project "<Your project ID>" ssh --zone "<your gce zone>"
"<Node from
pod describe>"
```

Once SSHed into the node, if we run the `sudo docker ps` command, we should see at least two containers: one running the `pause` image and one running the actual `node-express-info` image. You may see more if K8s scheduled more than one replica on this node. Let's grab the container ID of the `jonbaier/node-express-info` image (not `gcr.io/google_containers/pause`) and kill it off to see what happens. Save this container ID somewhere for later:

```
$ sudo docker ps --filter="name=node-js"
$ sudo docker stop <node-express container id>
$ sudo docker rm <container id>
$ sudo docker ps --filter="name=node-js"
```

Unless you are really quick, you'll probably note that there is still a `node-express-info` container running, but look closely and you'll note that `container id` is different and the creation timestamp shows only a few seconds ago. If you go back to the service URL, it is functioning as normal. Go ahead and exit the SSH session for now.

Here, we are already seeing Kubernetes playing the role of on-call operations, ensuring that our application is always running.

Let's see if we can find any evidence of the outage. Go to the **Events** page in the Kubernetes UI. You can find it by navigating to the **Nodes** page on the main K8s dashboard. Select a node from the list (the same one that we SSHed into) and scroll down to **Events** on the node details page.

You'll see a screen similar to the following screenshot:

Message	Source	Sub-object	Count	First seen	Last seen
Starting kubelet.	kubelet gke-cluster-1-default-pool-3185750f-q6sx	-	1	22/12/16 21:42 UTC	22/12/16 21:42 UTC
Node gke-cluster-1-default-pool-3185750f-q6sx status is now: NodeHasSufficientDisk	kubelet gke-cluster-1-default-pool-3185750f-q6sx	-	17	22/12/16 21:42 UTC	22/12/16 21:44 UTC
Node gke-cluster-1-default-pool-3185750f-q6sx status is now: NodeHasSufficientMemory	kubelet gke-cluster-1-default-pool-3185750f-q6sx	-	17	22/12/16 21:42 UTC	22/12/16 21:44 UTC
Node gke-cluster-1-default-pool-3185750f-q6sx status is now: NodeHasNoDiskPressure	kubelet gke-cluster-1-default-pool-3185750f-q6sx	-	17	22/12/16 21:42 UTC	22/12/16 21:44 UTC

Kubernetes UI event page

You should see three recent events. First, Kubernetes pulls the image. Second, it creates a new container with the pulled image. Finally, it starts that container again. You'll note that, from the timestamps, this all happens in less than a second. Time taken may vary based on the cluster size and image pulls, but the recovery is very quick.

More on labels

As mentioned previously, labels are just simple key-value pairs. They are available on pods, replication controllers, replica sets, services, and more. If you recall our service YAML `nodejs-rc-service.yaml`, there was a `selector` attribute. The `selector` attribute tells Kubernetes which labels to use in finding pods to forward traffic for that service.

K8s allows users to work with labels directly on replication controllers, replica sets, and services. Let's modify our replicas and services to include a few more labels. Once again, use your favorite editor to create these two files and name it as `nodejs-labels-controller.yaml` and `nodejs-labels-service.yaml`, as follows:

```
apiVersion: v1
kind: ReplicationController
metadata:
  name: node-js-labels
  labels:
    name: node-js-labels
    app: node-js-express
    deployment: test
spec:
  replicas: 3
  selector:
    name: node-js-labels
    app: node-js-express
    deployment: test
  template:
    metadata:
      labels:
        name: node-js-labels
        app: node-js-express
        deployment: test
    spec:
      containers:
      - name: node-js-labels
        image: jonbaier/node-express-info:latest
        ports:
        - containerPort: 80
```

```
apiVersion: v1
kind: Service
metadata:
  name: node-js-labels
  labels:
    name: node-js-labels
    app: node-js-express
    deployment: test
spec:
  type: LoadBalancer
  ports:
  - port: 80
  selector:
    name: node-js-labels
    app: node-js-express
    deployment: test
```

Create the replication controller and service as follows:

```
$ kubectl create -f nodejs-labels-controller.yaml
$ kubectl create -f nodejs-labels-service.yaml
```

Let's take a look at how we can use labels in everyday management. The following table shows us the options to select labels:

Operators	Description	Example
= or ==	You can use either style to select keys with values equal to the string on the right	name = apache
!=	Select keys with values that do not equal the string on the right	Environment != test
in	Select resources whose labels have keys with values in this set	tier in (web, app)
notin	Select resources whose labels have keys with values not in this set	tier notin (lb, app)
<Key name>	Use a key name only to select resources whose labels contain this key	tier

Label selectors

Let's try looking for replicas with `test` deployments:

```
$ kubectl get rc -l deployment=test
```

The following screenshot is the result of the preceding command:

NAME	DESIRED	CURRENT	READY	AGE
node-js-labels	3	3	3	46s

Replication controller listing

You'll notice that it only returns the replication controller we just started. How about services with a label named `component`? Use the following command:

```
$ kubectl get services -l component
```

The following screenshot is the result of the preceding command:

NAME	CLUSTER-IP	EXTERNAL-IP	PORT(S)	AGE
kubernetes	10.0.0.1	<none>	443/TCP	5d

Listing of services with a label named component

Here, we see the core Kubernetes service only. Finally, let's just get the `node-js` servers we started in this chapter. See the following command:

```
$ kubectl get services -l "name in (node-js,node-js-labels)"
```

The following screenshot is the result of the preceding command:

NAME	CLUSTER-IP	EXTERNAL-IP	PORT(S)	AGE
node-js	10.0.13.62	104.197.124.230	80:30798/TCP	14h
node-js-labels	10.0.207.25	104.154.54.104	80:31315/TCP	1m

Listing of services with a label name and a value of node-js or node-js-labels

Additionally, we can perform management tasks across a number of pods and services. For example, we can kill all replication controllers that are part of the `demo` deployment (if we had any running), as follows:

```
$ kubectl delete rc -l deployment=demo
```

Otherwise, kill all services that are part of a `production` or `test` deployment (again, if we have any running), as follows:

```
$ kubectl delete service -l "deployment in (test, production)"
```

It's important to note that, while label selection is quite helpful in day-to-day management tasks, it does require proper deployment hygiene on our part. We need to make sure that we have a tagging standard and that it is actively followed in the resource definition files for everything we run on Kubernetes.

> While we used service definition YAML files to create our services so far, you can actually create them using a `kubectl` command only. To try this out, first run the `get pods` command and get one of the `node-js` pod names. Next, use the following `expose` command to create a service endpoint for just that pod:
> ```
> $ kubectl expose pods node-js-gxkix --port=80 --
> name=testing-vip --type=LoadBalancer
> ```
> This will create a service named `testing-vip` and also a public `vip` (load balancer IP) that can be used to access this pod over port `80`.
> There are number of other optional parameters that can be used. These can be found with the following command: `kubectl expose --help`.

Replica sets

As discussed earlier, replica sets are the new and improved version of replication controllers. Here is an example of `ReplicaSet` based on and similar to the `ReplicationController`. Name this file as `nodejs-labels-replicaset.yaml`:

```
apiVersion: extensions/v1beta1
kind: ReplicaSet
metadata:
  name: node-js-rs
spec:
  replicas: 3
  selector:
    matchLabels:
      app: node-js-express
      deployment: test
    matchExpressions:
      - {key: name, operator: In, values: [node-js-rs]}
  template:
    metadata:
      labels:
```

```
        name: node-js-rs
        app: node-js-express
        deployment: test
    spec:
      containers:
      - name: node-js-rs
        image: jonbaier/node-express-info:latest
        ports:
        - containerPort: 80
```

Health checks

Kubernetes provides three layers of health checking. First, in the form of HTTP or TCP checks, K8s can attempt to connect to a particular endpoint and give a status of healthy on a successful connection. Second, application-specific health checks can be performed using command-line scripts. We also use the exec container to run a health check from within your container. Anything that exits with a 0 status will be considered healthy.

Let's take a look at a few health checks in action. First, we'll create a new controller named nodejs-health-controller.yaml with a health check:

```
apiVersion: v1
kind: ReplicationController
metadata:
  name: node-js
  labels:
    name: node-js
spec:
  replicas: 3
  selector:
    name: node-js
  template:
    metadata:
      labels:
        name: node-js
    spec:
      containers:
      - name: node-js
        image: jonbaier/node-express-info:latest
        ports:
        - containerPort: 80
        livenessProbe:
          # An HTTP health check
          httpGet:
            path: /status/
```

```
            port: 80
      initialDelaySeconds: 30
      timeoutSeconds: 1
```

Note the addition of the livenessprobe element. This is our core health check element. From here, we can specify httpGet, tcpScoket, or exec. In this example, we use httpGet to perform a simple check for a URI on our container. The probe will check the path and port specified and restart the pod if it doesn't successfully return.

 Status codes between 200 and 399 are all considered healthy by the probe.

Finally, initialDelaySeconds gives us the flexibility to delay health checks until the pod has finished initializing. The timeoutSeconds value is simply the timeout value for the probe.

Let's use our new health check-enabled controller to replace the old node-js RC. We can do this using the replace command, which will replace the replication controller definition:

```
$ kubectl replace -f nodejs-health-controller.yaml
```

Replacing the RC on its own won't replace our containers because it still has three healthy pods from our first run. Let's kill off those pods and let the updated ReplicationController replace them with containers that have health checks:

```
$ kubectl delete pods -l name=node-js
```

Now, after waiting a minute or two, we can list the pods in an RC and grab one of the pod IDs to inspect it a bit deeper with the `describe` command:

```
$ kubectl describe rc/node-js
```

The following screenshot is the result of the preceding command:

```
Name:           node-js
Namespace:      default
Image(s):       jonbaier/node-express-info:latest
Selector:       name=node-js
Labels:         name=node-js
Replicas:       3 current / 3 desired
Pods Status:    3 Running / 0 Waiting / 0 Succeeded / 0 Failed
No volumes.
Events:
  FirstSeen     LastSeen        Count   From                            SubobjectPath   Type
  Reason                        Message
  ---------     --------        -----   ----                            -------------   ------
  --            ------                  -------
  42s           42s             1       {replication-controller }                       Normal
SuccessfulCreate                Created pod: node-js-7esbp
  42s           42s             1       {replication-controller }                       Normal
SuccessfulCreate                Created pod: node-js-istu0
  42s           42s             1       {replication-controller }                       Normal
SuccessfulCreate                Created pod: node-js-im7jw
```

Description of node-js replication controller

Now, use the following command for one of the pods:

```
$ kubectl describe pods/node-js-7esbp
```

The following screenshot is the result of the preceding command:

```
Name:              node-js-7esbp
Namespace:         default
Node:              kubernetes-minion-group-k0rn/10.128.0.3
Start Time:        Mon, 02 Jan 2017 13:54:22 -0500
Labels:            name=node-js
Status:            Running
IP:                10.244.1.18
Controllers:       ReplicationController/node-js
Containers:
  node-js:
    Container ID:    docker://ce35e1fba7c3464cc89607ebd335250a7b52bebd5e03683e3f6313f
35fe68244
    Image:           jonbaier/node-express-info:latest
    Image ID:        docker://sha256:6a276384568844d1840049552f79c69311c3132d3a2b884a
3e9c4e51087a436b
    Port:            80/TCP
    Requests:
      cpu:           100m
    State:           Waiting
      Reason:        CrashLoopBackOff
    Last State:      Terminated
      Reason:        Error
      Exit Code:     137
      Started:       Mon, 02 Jan 2017 14:13:42 -0500
      Finished:      Mon, 02 Jan 2017 14:14:42 -0500
    Ready:           False
    Restart Count:   9
    Liveness:        http-get http://:80/status/ delay=30s timeout=1s period=10s #suc
cess=1 #failure=3
    Volume Mounts:
      /var/run/secrets/kubernetes.io/serviceaccount from default-token-7z353 (ro)
    Environment Variables:        <none>
Conditions:
  Type            Status
  Initialized     True
  Ready           False
  PodScheduled    True
Volumes:
  default-token-7z353:
    Type:          Secret (a volume populated by a Secret)
    SecretName:    default-token-7z353
QoS Class:         Burstable
Tolerations:       <none>
Events:
  FirstSeen    LastSeen        Count   From              Reason        Message                       Subobjec
tPath
  ---------    --------        -----   ----              ------        -------                       --------
  -----
  22m          22m             1       {default-scheduler }                                         N
ormal        Scheduled       Successfully assigned node-js-7esbp to kubernetes-minion
-group-k0rn
  21m          21m             1       {kubelet kubernetes-minion-group-k0rn}   spec.con
tainers{node-js}         Normal          Created         Created container with docker id
4b2b5587a119; Security:[seccomp=unconfined]
  21m          21m             1       {kubelet kubernetes-minion-group-k0rn}   spec.con
tainers{node-js}         Normal          Started         Started container with docker id
4b2b5587a119
  20m          20m             1       {kubelet kubernetes-minion-group-k0rn}   spec.con
tainers{node-js}         Normal          Killing         Killing container with docker id
4b2b5587a119: pod "node-js-7esbp_default(df9e1d36-d11c-11e6-9141-42010a800002)" contain
er "node-js" is unhealthy, it will be killed and re-created.
  20m          20m             1       {kubelet kubernetes-minion-group-k0rn}   spec.con
tainers{node-js}         Normal          Created         Created container with docker id
53e4c1ec9e20; Security:[seccomp=unconfined]
  20m          20m             1       {kubelet kubernetes-minion-group-k0rn}   spec.con
tainers{node-js}         Normal          Started         Started container with docker id
53e4c1ec9e20
```

Description of node-js-1m3cs pod

At the top, we'll see the overall pod details. Depending on your timing, under `State`, it will either show `Running` or `Waiting` with a `CrashLoopBackOff` reason and some error information. A bit below that, we can see information on our `Liveness` probe and we will likely see a failure count above 0. Further down, we have the pod events. Again, depending on your timing, you are likely to have a number of events for the pod. Within a minute or two, you'll note a pattern of killing, started, and created events repeating over and over again. You should also see a note in the `Killing` entry that the container is unhealthy. This is our health check failing because we don't have a page responding at /status.

You may note that if you open a browser to the service load balancer address, it still responds with a page. You can find the load balancer IP with a `kubectl get services` command.

This is happening for a number of reasons. First, the health check is simply failing because /status doesn't exist, but the page where the service is pointed is still functioning normally between restarts. Second, the `livenessProbe` is only charged with restarting the container on a health check fail. There is a separate `readinessProbe` that will remove a container from the pool of pods answering service endpoints.

Let's modify the health check for a page that does exist in our container, so we have a proper health check. We'll also add a readiness check and point it to the nonexistent status page. Open the `nodejs-health-controller.yaml` file and modify the `spec` section to match the following listing and save it as `nodejs-health-controller-2.yaml`:

```
apiVersion: v1
kind: ReplicationController
metadata:
  name: node-js
  labels:
    name: node-js
spec:
  replicas: 3
  selector:
    name: node-js
  template:
    metadata:
      labels:
        name: node-js
    spec:
      containers:
      - name: node-js
        image: jonbaier/node-express-info:latest
        ports:
        - containerPort: 80
        livenessProbe:
```

```
      # An HTTP health check
      httpGet:
        path: /
        port: 80
      initialDelaySeconds: 30
      timeoutSeconds: 1
    readinessProbe:
      # An HTTP health check
      httpGet:
        path: /status/
        port: 80
      initialDelaySeconds: 30
      timeoutSeconds: 1
```

This time, we'll delete the old RC, which will kill the pods with it, and create a new RC with our updated YAML file:

```
$ kubectl delete rc -l name=node-js-health
$ kubectl create -f nodejs-health-controller-2.yaml
```

Now, when we describe one of the pods, we only see the creation of the pod and the container. However, you'll note that the service load balancer IP no longer works. If we run the describe command on one of the new nodes, we'll note a Readiness probe failed error message, but the pod itself continues running. If we change the readiness probe path to path: /, we'll again be able to fulfill requests from the main service. Open up nodejs-health-controller-2.yaml in an editor and make that update now. Then, once again remove and recreate the replication controller:

```
$ kubectl delete rc -l name=node-js
$ kubectl create -f nodejs-health-controller-2.yaml
```

Now the load balancer IP should work once again. Keep these pods around as we will use them again in Chapter 4, *Working with Networking, Load Balancers, and Ingress*.

TCP checks

Kubernetes also supports health checks via simple TCP socket checks and also with custom command-line scripts.

The following snippets are examples of what both use cases look like in the YAML file.

Health check using command-line script:

```
livenessProbe:
  exec:
    command:
    -/usr/bin/health/checkHttpServce.sh
  initialDelaySeconds:90
  timeoutSeconds: 1
```

Health check using simple TCP Socket connection:

```
livenessProbe:
  tcpSocket:
    port: 80
  initialDelaySeconds: 15
  timeoutSeconds: 1
```

Life cycle hooks or graceful shutdown

As you run into failures in real-life scenarios, you may find that you want to take additional action before containers are shut down or right after they are started. Kubernetes actually provides life cycle hooks for just this kind of use case.

The following example controller definition, `apache-hooks-controller.yaml`, defines both a `postStart` action and a `preStop` action to take place before Kubernetes moves the container into the next stage of its life cycle:

```
apiVersion: v1
kind: ReplicationController
metadata:
  name: apache-hook
  labels:
    name: apache-hook
spec:
  replicas: 3
  selector:
    name: apache-hook
  template:
    metadata:
      labels:
        name: apache-hook
    spec:
      containers:
      - name: apache-hook
```

```
image: bitnami/apache:latest
ports:
- containerPort: 80
lifecycle:
  postStart:
    httpGet:
      path: http://my.registration-server.com/register/
      port: 80
  preStop:
    exec:
      command: ["/usr/local/bin/apachectl","-k","graceful-
      stop"]
```

You'll note that, for the `postStart` hook, we define an `httpGet` action, but for the `preStop` hook, we define an `exec` action. Just as with our health checks, the `httpGet` action attempts to make an HTTP call to the specific endpoint and port combination, while the `exec` action runs a local command in the container.

The `httpGet` and `exec` actions are both supported for the `postStart` and `preStop` hooks. In the case of `preStop`, a parameter named `reason` will be sent to the handler as a parameter. See the following table for valid values:

Reason parameter	Failure description
Delete	Delete command issued via `kubectl` or the API
Health	Health check fails
Dependency	Dependency failure such as a disk mount failure or a default infrastructure pod crash

Valid preStop reasons

 Check out the references section here: `https://github.com/kubernetes/kubernetes/blob/release-1.0/docs/user-guide/container-environment.md#container-hooks`.

It's important to note that hook calls are delivered at least once. Therefore, any logic in the action should gracefully handle multiple calls. Another important note is that `postStart` runs before a pod enters its ready state. If the hook itself fails, the pod will be considered unhealthy.

Application scheduling

Now that we understand how to run containers in pods and even recover from failure, it may be useful to understand how new containers are scheduled on our cluster nodes.

As mentioned earlier, the default behavior for the Kubernetes scheduler is to spread container replicas across the nodes in our cluster. In the absence of all other constraints, the scheduler will place new pods on nodes with the least number of other pods belonging to matching services or replication controllers.

Additionally, the scheduler provides the ability to add constraints based on resources available to the node. Today, this includes minimum CPU and memory allocations. In terms of Docker, these use the CPU-shares and memory limit flags under the covers.

When additional constraints are defined, Kubernetes will check a node for available resources. If a node does not meet all the constraints, it will move to the next. If no nodes can be found that meet the criteria, then we will see a scheduling error in the logs.

The Kubernetes road map also has plans to support networking and storage. Because scheduling is such an important piece of overall operations and management for containers, we should expect to see many additions in this area as the project grows.

Scheduling example

Let's take a look at a quick example of setting some resource limits. If we look at our K8s dashboard, we can get a quick snapshot of the current state of resource usage on our cluster using `https://<your master ip>/api/v1/proxy/namespaces/kube-system/services/kubernetes-dashboard` and clicking on **Nodes** on the left-hand side menu.

We'll see a dashboard, as shown in the following screenshot:

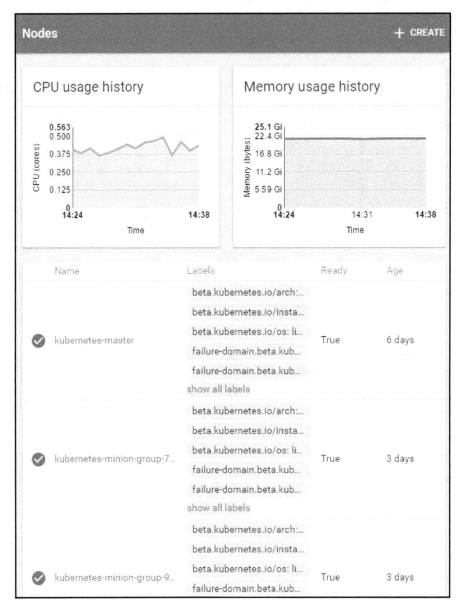

Kube node dashboard

This view shows the aggregate CPU and memory across the whole cluster, nodes, and Master. In this case, we have fairly low CPU utilization, but a decent chunk of memory in use.

Let's see what happens when I try to spin up a few more pods, but this time, we'll request 512 Mi for memory and 1500 m for the CPU. We'll use 1500 m to specify 1.5 CPUs; since each node only has 1 CPU, this should result in failure. Here's an example of the RC definition. Save this file as nodejs-constraints-controller.yaml:

```
apiVersion: v1
kind: ReplicationController
metadata:
  name: node-js-constraints
  labels:
    name: node-js-constraints
spec:
  replicas: 3
  selector:
    name: node-js-constraints
  template:
    metadata:
      labels:
        name: node-js-constraints
    spec:
      containers:
      - name: node-js-constraints
        image: jonbaier/node-express-info:latest
        ports:
        - containerPort: 80
        resources:
          limits:
            memory: "512Mi"
            cpu: "1500m"
```

To open the preceding file, use the following command:

```
$ kubectl create -f nodejs-constraints-controller.yaml
```

The replication controller completes successfully, but if we run a get pods command, we'll note the node-js-constraints pods are stuck in a pending state. If we look a little closer with the describe pods/<pod-id> command, we'll note a scheduling error (for pod-id use one of the pod names from the first command):

```
$ kubectl get pods
$ kubectl describe pods/<pod-id>
```

The following screenshot is the result of the preceding command:

```
Name:               node-js-constraints-n9dlx
Namespace:          default
Node:               /
Labels:             name=node-js-constraints
Status:             Pending
IP:
Controllers:        ReplicationController/node-js-constraints
Containers:
  node-js-constraints:
    Image:          jonbaier/node-express-info:latest
    Port:           80/TCP
    Limits:
      cpu:          1500m
      memory:       512Mi
    Requests:
      cpu:          1500m
      memory:       512Mi
    Volume Mounts:
      /var/run/secrets/kubernetes.io/serviceaccount from default-token-7z353 (ro)
    Environment Variables:        <none>
Conditions:
  Type          Status
  PodScheduled  False
Volumes:
  default-token-7z353:
    Type:         Secret (a volume populated by a Secret)
    SecretName:   default-token-7z353
QoS Class:        Guaranteed
Tolerations:      <none>
Events:
  FirstSeen     LastSeen        Count   From                            SubobjectPath   Type    R
eason                           Message
  ---------     ---------       -----   ----                            -------------   -------
  1m            1m              3       {default-scheduler }                            WarningF
ailedScheduling pod (node-js-constraints-n9dlx) failed to fit in any node
fit failure on node (kubernetes-minion-group-9zf7): Insufficient cpu
fit failure on node (kubernetes-minion-group-k0rn): Insufficient cpu
fit failure on node (kubernetes-minion-group-7th4): Insufficient cpu

  1m    1m      3       {default-scheduler }                    Warning FailedScheduling        p
od (node-js-constraints-n9dlx) failed to fit in any node
fit failure on node (kubernetes-minion-group-7th4): Insufficient cpu
fit failure on node (kubernetes-minion-group-9zf7): Insufficient cpu
fit failure on node (kubernetes-minion-group-k0rn): Insufficient cpu

  1m    41s     2       {default-scheduler }                    Warning FailedScheduling        p
od (node-js-constraints-n9dlx) failed to fit in any node
fit failure on node (kubernetes-minion-group-k0rn): Insufficient cpu
fit failure on node (kubernetes-minion-group-7th4): Insufficient cpu
fit failure on node (kubernetes-minion-group-9zf7): Insufficient cpu
```

Pod description

Note, in the bottom events section, that the `WarningFailedScheduling pod` error listed in `Events` is accompanied by `fit failure on node....Insufficient cpu` after the error. As you can see, Kuberneftes could not find a fit in the cluster that met all the constraints we defined.

If we now modify our CPU constraint down to `500 m`, and then recreate our replication controller, we should have all three pods running within a few moments.

Summary

We took a look at the overall architecture for Kubernetes, as well as the core constructs provided to build your services and application stacks. You should have a better understanding of how these abstractions make it easier to manage the life cycle of your stack and/or services as a whole and not just the individual components. Additionally, we took a first-hand look at how to manage some simple day-to-day tasks using pods, services, and replication controllers. We also looked at how to use Kubernetes to automatically respond to outages via health checks. Finally, we explored the Kubernetes scheduler and some of the constraints users can specify to influence scheduling placement.

4
Working with Networking, Load Balancers, and Ingress

In this chapter, we will discuss Kubernetes' approach to cluster networking and how it differs from other approaches. We will describe key requirements for Kubernetes networking solutions and explore why these are essential for simplifying cluster operations. We will investigate DNS in the Kubernetes cluster, dig into the **Container Network Interface** (**CNI**) and plugin ecosystems, and will take a deeper dive into services and how the Kubernetes proxy works on each node. Finishing up, we will look at a brief overview of some higher level isolation features for multitenancy.

In this chapter, we will cover the following topics:

- Kubernetes networking
- Advanced services concepts
- Service discovery
- DNS, CNI, and ingress
- Namespace limits and quotas

Technical requirements

You'll need a running Kubernetes cluster like the one we created in the previous chapters. You'll also need access to deploy the cluster through the `kubectl` command.

The GitHub repository for this chapter can be found at `https://github.com/PacktPublishing/The-Complete-Kubernetes-Guide/tree/master/Chapter04`.

Container networking

Networking is a vital concern for production-level operations. At a service level, we need a reliable way for our application components to find and communicate with each other. Introducing containers and clustering into the mix makes things more complex as we now have multiple networking namespaces to bear in mind. Communication and discovery now becomes a feat that must navigate container IP space, host networking, and sometimes even multiple data center network topologies.

Kubernetes benefits here from getting its ancestry from the clustering tools used by Google for the past decade. Networking is one area where Google has outpaced the competition with one of the largest networks on the planet. Earlier, Google built its own hardware switches and **Software-defined Networking** (**SDN**) to give them more control, redundancy, and efficiency in their day-to-day network operations. Many of the lessons learned from running and networking two billion containers per week have been distilled into Kubernetes, and informed how K8s networking is done.

The Docker approach

In order to understand the motivation behind the K8s networking model, let's review Docker's approach to container networking.

Docker default networks

The following are some of Docker's default networks:

- **Bridge network**: In a nonswarm scenario, Docker will use the bridge network driver (called `bridge`) to allow standalone containers to speak to each other. You can think of the bridge as a link layer device that forwards network traffic between segments. If containers are connected to the same bridge network, they can communicate; if they're not connected, they can't. The bridged network is the default choice unless otherwise specified. In this mode, the container has its own networking namespace and is then bridged via virtual interfaces to the host (or node, in the case of K8s) network. In the bridged network, two containers can use the same IP range because they are completely isolated. Therefore, service communication requires some additional port mapping through the host side of network interfaces.

- **Host based**: Docker also offers host-based networking for standalone containers, which creates a virtual bridge called `docker0` that allocates private IP address space for the containers using that bridge. Each container gets a virtual Ethernet (`veth`) device that you can see in the container as `eth0`. Performance is greatly benefited since it removes a level of network virtualization; however, you lose the security of having an isolated network namespace. Additionally, port usage must be managed more carefully since all containers share an IP.

There's also a none network, which creates a container with no external interface. Only a `loopback` device is shown if you inspect the network interfaces.

In all of these scenarios, we are still on a single machine, and outside of host mode, the container IP space is not available outside that machine. Connecting containers across two machines requires NAT and port mapping for communication.

Docker user-defined networks

In order to address the cross-machine communication issue and allow greater flexibility, Docker also supports user-defined networks via network plugins. These networks exist independent of the containers themselves. In this way, containers can join the same existing networks. Through the new plugin architecture, various drivers can be provided for different network use cases such as the following:

- **Swarm**: In a clustered situation with Swarm, the default behavior is an overlay network, which allows you to connect multiple Docker daemons running on multiple machines. In order to coordinate across multiple hosts, all containers and daemons must all agree on the available networks and their topologies. Overlay networking introduces a significant amount of complexity with dynamic port mapping that Kubernetes avoids.

You can read more about overlay networks here: `https://docs.docker.com/network/overlay/`.

- **Macvlan**: Docker also provides macvlan addressing, which is most similar to the networking model that Kubernetes provides, as it assigns each Docker container a MAC address that makes it appear as a physical device on your network. Macvlan offers a more efficient network virtualization and isolation as it bypasses the Linux bridge. It is important to note that as of this book's publishing, Macvlan isn't supported in most cloud providers.

As a result of these options, Docker must manage complex port allocation on a per-machine basis for each host IP, and that information must be maintained and propagated to all other machines in the cluster. Docker users a gossip protocol to manage the forwarding and proxying of ports to other containers.

The Kubernetes approach

Kubernetes' approach to networking differs from the Docker's, so let's see how. We can learn about Kubernetes while considering four major topics in cluster scheduling and orchestration:

- Decoupling container-to-container communication by providing pods, not containers, with an IP address space
- Pod-to-pod communication and service as the dominant communication paradigm within the Kubernetes networking model
- Pod-to-service and external-to-service communications, which are provided by the `services` object

These considerations are a meaningful simplification for the Kubernetes networking model, as there's no dynamic port mapping to track. Again, IP addressing is scoped at the pod level, which means that networking in Kubernetes requires that each pod has its own IP address. This means that all containers in a given pod share that IP address, and are considered to be in the same network namespace. We'll explore how to manage this shared IP resource when we discuss internal and external services later in this chapter. Kubernetes facilitates the pod-to-pod communication by not allowing the use of **network address translation** (**NAT**) for container-to-container or container-to-node (minion) traffic. Furthermore, the internal container IP address must match the IP address that is used to communicate with it. This underlines the Kubernetes assumption that all pods are able to communicate with all other pods regardless of the host they've landed on, and that communication then informs routing within pods to a local IP address space that is provided to containers. All containers within a given host can communicate with each other on their reserved ports via localhost. This unNATed, flat IP space simplifies networking changes when you begin scaling to thousands of pods.

These rules keep much of the complexity out of our networking stack and ease the design of the applications. Furthermore, they eliminate the need to redesign network communication in legacy applications that are migrated from existing infrastructure. In greenfield applications, they allow for a greater scale in handling hundreds, or even thousands of services and application communications.

Astute readers may have also noticed that this creates a model that's backward compatible with VMs and physical hosts that have a similar IP architecture as pods, with a single address per VM or physical host. This means you don't have to change your approach to service discovery, load balancing, application configuration, and port management, and can port over your application management workflows when working with Kubernetes.

K8s achieves this pod-wide IP magic using a pod container placeholder. Remember that the pause container that we saw in Chapter 1, *Introduction to Kubernetes*, in the *Services running on the master* section, is often referred to as a pod infrastructure container, and it has the important job of reserving the network resources for our application containers that will be started later on. Essentially, the pause container holds the networking namespace and IP address for the entire pod, and can be used by all the containers running within. The pause container joins first and holds the namespace while the subsequent containers in the pod join it when they start up using Docker's `--net=container:%ID%` function.

If you'd like to look over the code in the pause container, it's right here: `https://github.com/kubernetes/kubernetes/blob/master/build/pause/pause.c`.

Kubernetes can achieve the preceding feature set using either CNI plugins for production workloads or kubenet networking for simplified cluster communication. Kubernetes can also be used when your cluster is going to rely on logical partitioning provided by a cloud service provider's security groups or **network access control lists** (**NACLs**). Let's dig into the specific networking options now.

Networking options

There are two approaches to the networking model that we have suggested. First, you can use one of the CNI plugins that exist in the ecosystem. This involves solutions that work with native networking layers of AWS, GCP, and Azure. There are also overlay-friendly plugins, which we'll cover in the next section. CNI is meant to be a common plugin architecture for containers. It's currently supported by several orchestration tools such as Kubernetes, Mesos, and CloudFoundry.

Network plugins are considered in alpha and therefore their capabilities, content, and configuration will change rapidly.

If you're looking for a simpler alternative for testing and using smaller clusters, you can use the kubenet plugin, which uses `bridge` and `host-local` CNI plugs with a straightforward implementation of `cbr0`. This plugin is only available on Linux, and doesn't provide any advanced features. As it's often used with the supplementation of a cloud provider's networking stance, it does not handle policies or cross-node networking.

Just as with CPU, memory, and storage, Kubernetes takes advantage of network namespaces, each with their own iptables rules, interfaces, and route tables. Kubernetes uses iptables and NAT to manage multiple logical addresses that sit behind a single physical address, though you have the option to provide your cluster with multiple physical interfaces (NICs). Most people will find themselves generating multiple logical interfaces and using technologies such as multiplexing, virtual bridges, and hardware switching using SR-IOV in order to create multiple devices.

 You can find out more information at `https://github.com/` `containernetworking/cni`.

Always refer to the Kubernetes documentation for the latest and full list of supported networking options.

Networking comparisons

To get a better understanding of networking in containers, it can be instructive to look at the popular choices for container networking. The following approaches do not make an exhaustive list, but should give a taste of the options available.

Weave

Weave provides an overlay network for Docker containers. It can be used as a plugin with the new Docker network plugin interface, and it is also compatible with Kubernetes through a CNI plugin. Like many overlay networks, many criticize the performance impact of the encapsulation overhead. Note that they have recently added a preview release with **Virtual Extensible LAN** (**VXLAN**) encapsulation support, which greatly improves performance. For more information, visit `http://blog.weave.works/2015/06/12/weave-fast-datapath/`.

Flannel

Flannel comes from CoreOS and is an etcd-backed overlay. Flannel gives a full subnet to each host/node, enabling a similar pattern to the Kubernetes practice of a routable IP per pod or group of containers. Flannel includes an in-kernel VXLAN encapsulation mode for better performance and has an experimental multi-network mode similar to the overlay Docker plugin. For more information, visit `https://github.com/coreos/flannel`.

Project Calico

Project Calico is a layer 3-based networking model that uses the built-in routing functions of the Linux kernel. Routes are propagated to virtual routers on each host via **Border Gateway Protocol** (**BGP**). Calico can be used for anything from small-scale deploys to large internet-scale installations. Because it works at a lower level on the network stack, there is no need for additional NAT, tunneling, or overlays. It can interact directly with the underlying network infrastructure. Additionally, it has a support for network-level ACLs to provide additional isolation and security. For more information,
visit `http://www.projectcalico.org/`.

Canal

Canal merges both Calico for the network policy and Flannel for the overlay into one solution. It supports both Calico and Flannel type overlays and uses the Calico policy enforcement logic. Users can choose from overlay and non-overlay options with this setup as it combines the features of the preceding two projects. For more information,
visit `https://github.com/tigera/canal`.

Kube-router

Kube-router option is a purpose-built networking solution that aims to provide high performance that's easy to use. It's based on the Linux LVS/IPVS kernel load balancing technologies as proxy. It also uses kernel-based networking and uses iptables as a network policy enforcer. Since it doesn't use an overlay technology, it's potentially a high-performance option for the future. For more information, visit the following URL: `https://github.com/cloudnativelabs/kube-router`.

Balanced design

It's important to point out the balance that Kubernetes is trying to achieve by placing the IP at the pod level. Using unique IP addresses at the host level is problematic as the number of containers grows. Ports must be used to expose services on specific containers and allow external communication. In addition to this, the complexity of running multiple services that may or may not know about each other (and their custom ports) and managing the port space becomes a big issue.

However, assigning an IP address to each container can be overkill. In cases of sizable scale, overlay networks and NATs are needed in order to address each container. Overlay networks add latency, and IP addresses would be taken up by backend services as well since they need to communicate with their frontend counterparts.

Here, we really see an advantage in the abstractions that Kubernetes provides at the application and service level. If I have a web server and a database, we can keep them on the same pod and use a single IP address. The web server and database can use the local interface and standard ports to communicate, and no custom setup is required. Furthermore, services on the backend are not needlessly exposed to other application stacks running elsewhere in the cluster (but possibly on the same host). Since the pod sees the same IP address that the applications running within it see, service discovery does not require any additional translation.

If you need the flexibility of an overlay network, you can still use an overlay at the pod level. Weave, Flannel, and Project Calico can be used with Kubernetes as well as a plethora of other plugins and overlays that are available.

This is also very helpful in the context of scheduling the workloads. It is key to have a simple and standard structure for the scheduler to match constraints and understand where space exists on the cluster's network at any given time. This is a dynamic environment with a variety of applications and tasks running, so any additional complexity here will have rippling effects.

There are also implications for service discovery. New services coming online must determine and register an IP address on which the rest of the world, or at least a cluster, can reach them. If NAT is used, the services will need an additional mechanism to learn their externally facing IP.

Advanced services

Let's explore the IP strategy as it relates to services and communication between containers. If you recall, in the *Services* section of `Chapter 3`, *Building a Foundation with Core Kubernetes Constructs*, you learned that Kubernetes is using `kube-proxy` to determine the proper pod IP address and port serving each request. Behind the scenes, `kube-proxy` is actually using virtual IPs and iptables to make all this magic work.

`kube-proxy` now has two modes—*userspace* and *iptables*. As of now, 1.2 iptables is the default mode. In both modes, `kube-proxy` is running on every host. Its first duty is to monitor the API from the Kubernetes master. Any updates to services will trigger an update to iptables from `kube-proxy`. For example, when a new service is created, a virtual IP address is chosen and a rule in iptables is set, which will direct its traffic to `kube-proxy` via a random port. Thus, we now have a way to capture service-destined traffic on this node. Since `kube-proxy` is running on all nodes, we have cluster-wide resolution for the service **VIP** (short for **virtual IP**). Additionally, DNS records can point to this VIP as well.

In the userspace mode, we have a hook created in iptables, but the proxying of traffic is still handled by `kube-proxy`. The iptables rule is only sending traffic to the service entry in `kube-proxy` at this point. Once `kube-proxy` receives the traffic for a particular service, it must then forward it to a pod in the service's pool of candidates. It does this using a random port that was selected during service creation.

Refer to the following diagram for an overview of the flow:

Kube-proxy communication

> **TIP**
>
> It is also possible to always forward traffic from the same client IP to the same backend pod/container using the `sessionAffinity` element in your service definition.

In the iptables mode, the pods are coded directly in the iptable rules. This removes the dependency on `kube-proxy` for actually proxying the traffic. The request will go straight to iptables and then on to the pod. This is faster and removes a possible point of failure. Readiness probe, as we discussed in the *Health Check* section of `Chapter 3`, *Building a Foundation with Core Kubernetes Constructs*, is your friend here as this mode also loses the ability to retry pods.

External services

In the previous chapter, we saw a few service examples. For testing and demonstration purposes, we wanted all the services to be externally accessible. This was configured by the `type: LoadBalancer` element in our service definition. The `LoadBalancer` type creates an external load balancer on the cloud provider. We should note that support for external load balancers varies by provider, as does the implementation. In our case, we are using GCE, so integration is pretty smooth. The only additional setup needed is to open firewall rules for the external service ports.

Let's dig a little deeper and do a `describe` command on one of the services from the *More on labels* section in `Chapter 3`, *Building a Foundation with Core Kubernetes Constructs*:

```
$ kubectl describe service/node-js-labels
```

The following screenshot is the result of the preceding command:

```
Name:               node-js-labels
Namespace:          default
Labels:             app=node-js-express,deployment=test,name=node-js-labels
Selector:           app=node-js-express,name=node-js-labels
Type:               LoadBalancer
IP:                 10.0.115.200
LoadBalancer Ingress:  146.148.56.25
Port:               <unnamed>        80/TCP
NodePort:           <unnamed>        30237/TCP
Endpoints:          10.244.0.29:80,10.244.2.34:80,10.244.2.35:80
Session Affinity:   None
No events.
```

Service description

In the output of the preceding screenshot, you'll note several key elements. Our `Namespace:` is set to `default`, the `Type:` is `LoadBalancer`, and we have the external IP listed under `LoadBalancer Ingress:`. Furthermore, we can see `Endpoints:`, which shows us the IPs of the pods that are available to answer service requests.

Internal services

Let's explore the other types of services that we can deploy. First, by default, services are only internally facing. You can specify a type of `clusterIP` to achieve this, but, if no type is defined, `clusterIP` is the assumed type. Let's take a look at an example, `nodejs-service-internal.yaml`; note the lack of the `type` element:

```
apiVersion: v1
kind: Service
```

```
metadata:
  name: node-js-internal
  labels:
    name: node-js-internal
spec:
  ports:
  - port: 80
  selector:
    name: node-js
```

Use this listing to create the service definition file. You'll need a healthy version of the `node-js` RC (Listing `nodejs-health-controller-2.yaml`). As you can see, the selector matches on the pods named `node-js` that our RC launched in the previous chapter. We will create the service and then list the currently running services with a filter as follows:

```
$ kubectl create -f nodejs-service-internal.yaml
$ kubectl get services -l name=node-js-internal
```

The following screenshot is the result of the preceding command:

NAME	LABELS	SELECTOR	IP(S)	PORT(S)
node-js-internal	name=node-js-internal	name=node-js	10.0.5.134	80/TCP

Internal service listing

As you can see, we have a new service, but only one IP. Furthermore, the IP address is not externally accessible. We won't be able to test the service from a web browser this time. However, we can use the handy `kubectl exec` command and attempt to connect from one of the other pods. You will need `node-js-pod` (`nodejs-pod.yaml`) running. Then, you can execute the following command:

```
$ kubectl exec node-js-pod -- curl <node-js-internal IP>
```

This allows us to run a `docker exec` command as if we had a shell in the `node-js-pod` container. It then hits the internal service URL, which forwards to any pods with the `node-js` label.

If all is well, you should get the raw HTML output back. You have successfully created an internal-only service. This can be useful for backend services that you want to make available to other containers running in your cluster, but not open to the world at large.

Custom load balancing

A third type of service that K8s allows is the `NodePort` type. This type allows us to expose a service through the host or node (minion) on a specific port. In this way, we can use the IP address of any node (minion) and access our service on the assigned node port. Kubernetes will assign a node port by default in the range of `3000-32767`, but you can also specify your own custom port. In the example in the following listing `nodejs-service-nodeport.yaml`, we choose port `30001`, as follows:

```
apiVersion: v1
kind: Service
metadata:
  name: node-js-nodeport
  labels:
    name: node-js-nodeport
spec:
  ports:
  - port: 80
    nodePort: 30001
  selector:
    name: node-js
  type: NodePort
```

Once again, create this YAML definition file and create your service, as follows:

```
$ kubectl create -f nodejs-service-nodeport.yaml
```

The output should have a message like this:

```
You have exposed your service on an external port on all nodes in your
cluster.  If you want to expose this service to the external internet,
you may
need to set up firewall rules for the service port(s) (tcp:30001) to se
rve traffic.

See http://releases.k8s.io/HEAD/docs/user-guide/services-firewalls.md f
or more details.
services/node-js-nodeport
```

New GCP firewall rule

Note message about opening firewall ports. Similar to the external load balancer type, `NodePort` is exposing your service externally using ports on the nodes. This could be useful if, for example, you want to use your own load balancer in front of the nodes. Let's make sure that we open those ports on GCP before we test our new service.

From the GCE VM instance console, click on the details for any of your nodes (minions). Then, click on the network, which is usually the default unless otherwise specified during creation. In **Firewall rules**, we can add a rule by clicking on **Add firewall rule**.

Create a rule like the one shown in the following screenshot (`tcp:30001` on the `0.0.0.0/0` IP range):

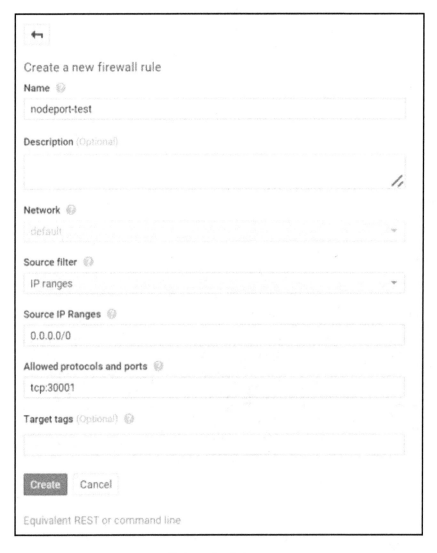

Create a new firewall rule page

We can now test our new service by opening a browser and using an IP address of any node (minion) in your cluster. The format to test the new service is as follows:

```
http://<Minoion IP Address>:<NodePort>/
```

Finally, the latest version has added an `ExternalName` type, which maps a `CNAME` to the service.

Cross-node proxy

Remember that `kube-proxy` is running on all the nodes, so even if the pod is not running there, the traffic will be given a proxy to the appropriate host. Refer to the *Cross-node traffic* screenshot for a visual on how the traffic flows. A user makes a request to an external IP or URL. The request is serviced by **Node** in this case. However, the pod does not happen to run on this node. This is not a problem because the pod IP addresses are routable. So, `kube-proxy` or **iptables** simply passes traffic onto the pod IP for this service. The network routing then completes on **Node 2**, where the requested application lives:

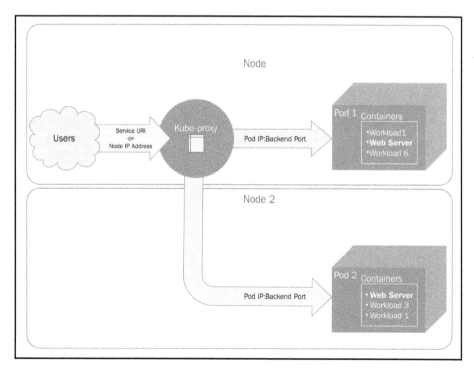

Cross-node traffic

Custom ports

Services also allow you to map your traffic to different ports; then, the containers and pods expose themselves. We will create a service that exposes port 90 and forwards traffic to port 80 on the pods. We will call the `node-js-90` pod to reflect the custom port number. Create the following two definition files, `nodejs-customPort-controller.yaml` and `nodejs-customPort-service.yaml`:

```
apiVersion: v1
kind: ReplicationController
metadata:
  name: node-js-90
  labels:
    name: node-js-90
spec:
  replicas: 3
  selector:
    name: node-js-90
  template:
    metadata:
      labels:
        name: node-js-90
    spec:
      containers:
      - name: node-js-90
        image: jonbaier/node-express-info:latest
        ports:
        - containerPort: 80
```

```
apiVersion: v1
kind: Service
metadata:
  name: node-js-90
  labels:
    name: node-js-90
spec:
  type: LoadBalancer
  ports:
  - port: 90
    targetPort: 80
  selector:
    name: node-js-90
```

> If you are using the free trial for Google Cloud Platform, you may have issues with the `LoadBalancer` type services. This type creates multiple external IP addresses, but trial accounts are limited to only one static address.

You'll note that in the service definition, we have a `targetPort` element. This element tells the service the port to use for pods/containers in the pool. As we saw in previous examples, if you do not specify `targetPort`, it assumes that it's the same port as the service. This port is still used as the service port, but, in this case, we are going to expose the service on port `90` while the containers serve content on port `80`.

Create this RC and service and open the appropriate firewall rules, as we did in the last example. It may take a moment for the external load balancer IP to propagate to the `get service` command. Once it does, you should be able to open and see our familiar web application in a browser using the following format:

```
http://<external service IP>:90/
```

Multiple ports

Another custom port use case is that of multiple ports. Many applications expose multiple ports, such as HTTP on port `80` and port `8888` for web servers. The following example shows our app responding on both ports. Once again, we'll also need to add a firewall rule for this port, as we did for the list `nodejs-service-nodeport.yaml` previously. Save the listing as `nodejs-multi-controller.yaml` and `nodejs-multi-service.yaml`:

```
apiVersion: v1
kind: ReplicationController
metadata:
  name: node-js-multi
  labels:
    name: node-js-multi
spec:
  replicas: 3
  selector:
    name: node-js-multi
  template:
    metadata:
      labels:
        name: node-js-multi
    spec:
```

```
    containers:
    - name: node-js-multi
      image: jonbaier/node-express-multi:latest
      ports:
      - containerPort: 80
      - containerPort: 8888

apiVersion: v1
kind: Service
metadata:
  name: node-js-multi
  labels:
    name: node-js-multi
spec:
  type: LoadBalancer
  ports:
  - name: http
    protocol: TCP
    port: 80
  - name: fake-admin-http
    protocol: TCP
    port: 8888
  selector:
    name: node-js-multi
```

 The application and container itself must be listening on both ports for this to work. In this example, port 8888 is used to represent a fake admin interface. If, for example, you want to listen on port 443, you would need a proper SSL socket listening on the server.

Ingress

We previously discussed how Kubernetes uses the service abstract as a means to proxy traffic to a backing pod that's distributed throughout our cluster. While this is helpful in both scaling and pod recovery, there are more advanced routing scenarios that are not addressed by this design.

To that end, Kubernetes has added an ingress resource, which allows for custom proxying and load balancing to a back service. Think of it as an extra layer or hop in the routing path before traffic hits our service. Just as an application has a service and backing pods, the ingress resource needs both an Ingress entry point and an ingress controller that perform the custom logic. The entry point defines the routes and the controller actually handles the routing. This is helpful for picking up traffic that would normally be dropped by an edge router or forwarded elsewhere outside of the cluster.

Ingress itself can be configured to offer externally addressable URLs for internal services, to terminate SSL, offer name-based virtual hosting as you'd see in a traditional web server, or load balance traffic. Ingress on its own cannot service requests, but requires an additional ingress controller to fulfill the capabilities outlined in the object. You'll see nginx and other load balancing or proxying technology involved as part of the controller framework. In the following examples, we'll be using GCE, but you'll need to deploy a controller yourself in order to take advantage of this feature. A popular option at the moment is the nginx-based ingress-nginx controller.

 You can check it out here: `https://github.com/kubernetes/ingress-gce/blob/master/BETA_LIMITATIONS.md#glbc-beta-limitations`.

An ingress controller is deployed as a pod which runs a daemon. This pod watches the Kubernetes apiserver/ingresses endpoint for changes to the ingress resource. For our examples, we will use the default GCE backend.

Types of ingress

There are a couple different types of ingress, such as the following:

- **Single service ingress**: This strategy exposes a single service via creating an ingress with a default backend that has no rules. You can alternatively use `Service.Type=LoadBalancer` or `Service.Type=NodePort`, or a port proxy to accomplish something similar.
- **Fanout**: Given that od IP addressing is only available internally to the Kubernetes network, you'll need to use a simple fanout strategy in order to accommodate edge traffic and provide ingress to the correct endpoints in your cluster. This will resemble a load balancer in practice.
- **Name-based hosting**: This approach is similar to **service name indication (SNI)**, which allows a web server to present multiple HTTPS websites with different certificates on the same TCP port and IP address.

Kubernetes uses host headers to route requests with this approach. The following example snippet `ingress-example.yaml` shows what name-based virtual hosting would look like:

```
apiVersion: extensions/v1beta1
kind: Ingress
metadata:
  name: name-based-hosting
spec:
  rules:
  - host: example01.foo.com
    http:
      paths:
      - backend:
          serviceName: sevice01
          servicePort: 8080
  - host: example02.foo.com
    http:
      paths:
      - backend:
          serviceName: sevice02
          servicePort: 8080
```

As you may recall, in Chapter 1, *Introduction to Kubernetes*, we saw that a GCE cluster comes with a default back which provides Layer 7 load balancing capability. We can see this controller running if we look at the `kube-system` namespace:

$ kubectl get rc --namespace=kube-system

We should see an RC listed with the `17-default-backend-v1.0` name, as shown here:

NAME	DESIRED	CURRENT	READY	AGE
kube-dns-v20	1	1	1	8d
kubernetes-dashboard-v1.4.0	1	1	1	8d
17-default-backend-v1.0	1	1	1	8d
monitoring-influxdb-grafana-v4	1	1	1	8d

GCE Layer 7 Ingress controller

This provides the ingress controller piece that actually routes the traffic defined in our ingress entry points. Let's create some resources for an Ingress.

First, we will create a few new replication controllers with the `httpwhalesay` image. This is a remix of the original whalesay that was displayed in a browser. The following listing, `whale-rcs.yaml`, shows the YAML. Note the three dashes that let us combine several resources into one YAML file:

```yaml
apiVersion: v1
kind: ReplicationController
metadata:
  name: whale-ingress-a
spec:
  replicas: 1
  template:
    metadata:
      labels:
        app: whale-ingress-a
    spec:
      containers:
      - name: sayhey
        image: jonbaier/httpwhalesay:0.1
        command: ["node", "index.js", "Whale Type A, Here."]
        ports:
        - containerPort: 80
---
apiVersion: v1
kind: ReplicationController
metadata:
  name: whale-ingress-b
spec:
  replicas: 1
  template:
    metadata:
      labels:
        app: whale-ingress-b
    spec:
      containers:
      - name: sayhey
        image: jonbaier/httpwhalesay:0.1
        command: ["node", "index.js", "Hey man, It's Whale B, Just
        Chillin'."]
        ports:
        - containerPort: 80
```

Note that we are creating pods with the same container, but different startup parameters. Take note of these parameters for later. We will also create Service endpoints for each of these RCs as shown in the whale-svcs.yaml listing:

```
apiVersion: v1
kind: Service
metadata:
  name: whale-svc-a
  labels:
    app: whale-ingress-a
spec:
  type: NodePort
  ports:
  - port: 80
    nodePort: 30301
    protocol: TCP
    name: http
  selector:
    app: whale-ingress-a
---
apiVersion: v1
kind: Service
metadata:
  name: whale-svc-b
  labels:
    app: whale-ingress-b
spec:
  type: NodePort
  ports:
  - port: 80
    nodePort: 30284
    protocol: TCP
    name: http
  selector:
    app: whale-ingress-b
---
apiVersion: v1
kind: Service
metadata:
 name: whale-svc-default
 labels:
   app: whale-ingress-a
spec:
  type: NodePort
  ports:
  - port: 80
    nodePort: 30302
    protocol: TCP
```

```
      name: http
   selector:
      app: whale-ingress-a
```

Again, create these with the `kubectl create -f` command, as follows:

```
$ kubectl create -f whale-rcs.yaml
$ kubectl create -f whale-svcs.yaml
```

We should see messages about the successful creation of the RCs and Services. Next, we need to define the Ingress entry point. We will use `http://a.whale.hey` and `http://b.whale.hey` as our demo entry points as shown in the following listing `whale-ingress.yaml`:

```
apiVersion: extensions/v1beta1
kind: Ingress
metadata:
  name: whale-ingress
spec:
  rules:
  - host: a.whale.hey
    http:
      paths:
      - path: /
        backend:
          serviceName: whale-svc-a
          servicePort: 80
  - host: b.whale.hey
    http:
      paths:
      - path: /
        backend:
          serviceName: whale-svc-b
          servicePort: 80
```

Again, use `kubectl create -f` to create this ingress. Once this is successfully created, we will need to wait a few moments for GCE to give the ingress a static IP address. Use the following command to watch the Ingress resource:

```
$ kubectl get ingress
```

Once the Ingress has an IP, we should see an entry in ADDRESS, like the one shown here:

```
NAME             HOSTS                       ADDRESS          PORTS   AGE
whale-ingress    a.whale.hey,b.whale.hey     130.211.24.177   80      3h
```

Ingress description

Since this is not a registered domain name, we will need to specify the resolution in the curl command, like this:

```
$ curl --resolve a.whale.hey:80:130.211.24.177 http://a.whale.hey/
```

This should display the following:

```
<html>
    <head>
        <title>HTTP Whalesay</title>
    </head>
    <body>
        <pre>
            <code>
    Whale Type A, Here.
         \
          \
           \
                                                ##        .
                                          ## ## ##       ==
                                       ## ## ## ##      ===
                                   /""""""""""""""""___/ ===
                              ~~~ {~~ ~~~~ ~~~ ~~~~ ~~ ~ /  ===- ~~~
                                   _____ o          __/
                                    \    \        __/
                                     _____/
            </code>
        </pre>
        <body/>
</html>
```

Whalesay A

We can also try the second URL. Doing this, we will get our second RC:

```
$ curl --resolve b.whale.hey:80:130.211.24.177 http://b.whale.hey/
```

```
<html>
    <head>
        <title>HTTP Whalesay</title>
    </head>
    <body>
        <pre>
            <code>
        Hey man, It's Whale B, Just Chillin'.
            \
             \
              \
                                            ##
                              ## ## ##            ==
                           ## ## ## ##          ===
                       /""""""""""""""""___/ ===
                  ~~~ {~~ ~~~~ ~~~ ~~~~ ~~ ~ /  ===- ~~~
                       _____ o          __/
                        \    \        __/
                         _____/
            </code>
        </pre>
        <body/>
</html>
```

Whalesay B

Note that the images are almost the same, except that the words from each whale reflect the startup parameters from each RC we started earlier. Thus, our two Ingress points are directing traffic to different backends.

In this example, we used the default GCE backend for an Ingress controller. Kubernetes allows us to build our own, and nginx actually has a few versions available as well.

Migrations, multicluster, and more

As we've already seen so far, Kubernetes offers a high level of flexibility and customization to create a service abstraction around your containers running in the cluster. However, there may be times where you want to point to something outside your cluster.

An example of this would be working with legacy systems or even applications running on another cluster. In the case of the former, this is a perfectly good strategy in order to migrate to Kubernetes and containers in general. We can begin by managing the service endpoints in Kubernetes while stitching the stack together using the K8s orchestration concepts. Additionally, we can even start bringing over pieces of the stack, as the frontend, one at a time as the organization refactors applications for microservices and/or containerization.

To allow access to non pod-based applications, the services construct allows you to use endpoints that are outside the cluster. Kubernetes is actually creating an endpoint resource every time you create a service that uses selectors. The `endpoints` object keeps track of the pod IPs in the load balancing pool. You can see this by running the `get endpoints` command, as follows:

```
$ kubectl get endpoints
```

You should see something similar to the following:

```
NAME            ENDPOINTS
http-pd         10.244.2.29:80,10.244.2.30:80,10.244.3.16:80
kubernetes      10.240.0.2:443
node-js         10.244.0.12:80,10.244.2.24:80,10.244.3.13:80
```

You'll note the entry for all the services we currently have running on our cluster. For most services, the endpoints are just the IP of each pod running in an RC. As I mentioned previously, Kubernetes does this automatically based on the selector. As we scale the replicas in a controller with matching labels, Kubernetes will update the endpoints automatically.

If we want to create a service for something that is not a pod and therefore has no labels to select, we can easily do this with both a service definition `nodejs-custom-service.yaml` and endpoint definition `nodejs-custom-endpoint.yaml`, as follows:

```
apiVersion: v1
kind: Service
metadata:
  name: custom-service
spec:
  type: LoadBalancer
  ports:
  - name: http
    protocol: TCP
    port: 80
```

```
apiVersion: v1
kind: Endpoints
metadata:
  name: custom-service
subsets:
- addresses:
  - ip: <X.X.X.X>
  ports:
    - name: http
      port: 80
      protocol: TCP
```

In the preceding example, you'll need to replace <X.X.X.X> with a real IP address, where the new service can point to. In my case, I used the public load balancer IP from the node-js-multi service we created earlier in listing ingress-example.yaml. Go ahead and create these resources now.

If we now run a get endpoints command, we will see this IP address at port 80, which is associated with the custom-service endpoint. Furthermore, if we look at the service details, we will see the IP listed in the Endpoints section:

```
$ kubectl describe service/custom-service
```

We can test out this new service by opening the custom-service external IP from a browser.

Custom addressing

Another option to customize services is with the clusterIP element. In our examples so far, we've not specified an IP address, which means that it chooses the internal address of the service for us. However, we can add this element and choose the IP address in advance with something like clusterip: 10.0.125.105.

There may be times when you don't want to load balance and would rather have DNS with *A* records for each pod. For example, software that needs to replicate data evenly to all nodes may rely on *A* records to distribute data. In this case, we can use an example like the following one and set clusterip to None.

Kubernetes will not assign an IP address and instead only assign *A* records in DNS for each of the pods. If you are using DNS, the service should be available at `node-js-none` or `node-js-none.default.cluster.local` from within the cluster. For this, we will use the following listing `nodejs-headless-service.yaml`:

```
apiVersion: v1
kind: Service
metadata:
  name: node-js-none
  labels:
    name: node-js-none
spec:
  clusterIP: None
  ports:
  - port: 80
  selector:
    name: node-js
```

Test it out after you create this service with the trusty `exec` command:

```
$ kubectl exec node-js-pod -- curl node-js-none
```

Service discovery

As we discussed earlier, the Kubernetes master keeps track of all service definitions and updates. Discovery can occur in one of three ways. The first two methods use Linux environment variables. There is support for the Docker link style of environment variables, but Kubernetes also has its own naming convention. Here is an example of what our `node-js` service example might look like using K8s environment variables (note that IPs will vary):

```
NODE_JS_PORT_80_TCP=tcp://10.0.103.215:80
NODE_JS_PORT=tcp://10.0.103.215:80
NODE_JS_PORT_80_TCP_PROTO=tcp
NODE_JS_PORT_80_TCP_PORT=80
NODE_JS_SERVICE_HOST=10.0.103.215
NODE_JS_PORT_80_TCP_ADDR=10.0.103.215
NODE_JS_SERVICE_PORT=80
```

Another option for discovery is through DNS. While environment variables can be useful when DNS is not available, it has drawbacks. The system only creates variables at creation time, so services that come online later will not be discovered or will require some additional tooling to update all the system environments.

DNS

DNS solves the issues seen with environment variables by allowing us to reference the services by their name. As services restart, scale out, or appear anew, the DNS entries will be updating and ensuring that the service name always points to the latest infrastructure. DNS is set up by default in most of the supported providers. You can add DNS support for your cluster via a cluster add on (`https://kubernetes.io/docs/concepts/cluster-administration/addons/`).

> If DNS is supported by your provider, but is not set up, you can configure the following variables in your default provider config when you create your Kubernetes cluster:
> `ENABLE_CLUSTER_DNS="${KUBE_ENABLE_CLUSTER_DNS:-true}"`
> `DNS_SERVER_IP="10.0.0.10"`
> `DNS_DOMAIN="cluster.local"`
> `DNS_REPLICAS=1.`

With DNS active, services can be accessed in one of two forms—either the service name itself, `<service-name>`, or a fully qualified name that includes the namespace, `<service-name>.<namespace-name>.cluster.local`. In our examples, it would look similar to `node-js-90` or `node-js-90.default.cluster.local`.

The DNS server create DNS records based on new services that are created through the API. Pods in shared DNS namespaces will be able to see each other, and can use DNS SRV records to record ports as well.

Kubernetes DNS is comprised of a DNS pod and Service on the cluster which communicates directly with kubelets and containers in order to translate DNS names to IP. Services with clusterIPs are given `my-service.my-namespace.svc.cluster.local` addresses. If the service does not have a clusterIP (otherwise called headless) it gets the same address format, but this resolves in a round-robin fashion to a number of IPs that point to the pods of a service. There a number of DNS policies that can also be set.

One of the Kubernetes incubator projects, `CoreDNS` can also be used for service discovery. This replaces the native `kube-dns` DNS services and requires Kubernetes v1.9 or later. You'll need to leverage `kubeadm` during the initialization process in order to try CoreDNS out. You can install this on your cluster with the following command:

```
$ kubeadm init --feature-gates=CoreDNS=true
```

If you'd like more information on an example use case of CoreDNS, check out this blog post: `https://coredns.io/2017/05/08/custom-dns-entries-for-kubernetes/`.

Multitenancy

Kubernetes also has an additional construct for isolation at the cluster level. In most cases, you can run Kubernetes and never worry about namespaces; everything will run in the default namespace if not specified. However, in cases where you run multitenancy communities or want broad-scale segregation and isolation of the cluster resources, namespaces can be used to this end. True, end-to-end multitenancy is not yet feature complete in Kubernetes, but you can get very close using RBAC, container permissions, ingress rules, and clear network policing. If you're interested in enterprise-strength multitenancy right now, Red Hat's **Openshift Origin (OO)** would be a good place to learn.

You can check out OO at `https://github.com/openshift/origin`.

To start, Kubernetes has two namespaces—`default` and `kube-system`. The `kube-system` namespace is used for all the system-level containers we saw in *Chapter 1, Introduction to Kubernetes*, in the *Services running on the minions* section. UI, logging, DNS, and so on are all run in `kube-system`. Everything else the user creates runs in the default namespace. However, our resource definition files can optionally specify a custom namespace. For the sake of experimenting, let's take a look at how to build a new namespace.

First, we'll need to create a namespace definition file `test-ns.yaml` like the one in the following lines of code:

```
apiVersion: v1
kind: Namespace
metadata:
  name: test
```

We can go ahead and create this file with our handy `create` command:

```
$ kubectl create -f test-ns.yaml
```

Now, we can create resources that use the `test` namespace. The following listing, `ns-pod.yaml`, is an example of a pod using this new namespace:

```
apiVersion: v1
kind: Pod
metadata:
  name: utility
  namespace: test
spec:
  containers:
  - image: debian:latest
    command:
      - sleep
      - "3600"
    name: utility
```

While the pod can still access services in other namespaces, it will need to use the long DNS form of `<service-name>.<namespace-name>.cluster.local`. For example, if you were to run a command from inside the container in listing `ns-pod.yaml`, you could use `node-js.default.cluster.local` to access the Node.js example from `Chapter 3`, *Building a Foundation with Core Kubernetes Constructs*.

Here is a note about resource utilization. At some point in this book, you may run out of space on your cluster to create new Kubernetes resources. The timing will vary based on cluster size, but it's good to keep this in mind and do some cleanup from time to time. Use the following commands to remove old examples:

```
$ kubectl delete pod <pod name>
$ kubectl delete svc <service name>
$ kubectl delete rc <replication controller name>
$ kubectl delete rs <replicaset name>.
```

Limits

Let's inspect our new namespace a bit more. Run the `describe` command as follows:

```
$ kubectl describe namespace/test
```

The following screenshot is the result of the preceding command:

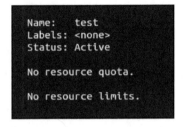

The describe namespace

Kubernetes allows you to both limit the resources used by individual pods or containers and the resources used by the overall namespace using quotas. You'll note that there are no resource limits or quotas currently set on the `test` namespace.

Suppose we want to limit the footprint of this new namespace; we can set quotas as shown in the following listing `quota.yaml`:

```
apiVersion: v1
kind: ResourceQuota
metadata:
  name: test-quotas
  namespace: test
spec:
  hard:
    pods: 3
    services: 1
    replicationcontrollers: 1
```

In reality, namespaces would be for larger application communities and would probably never have quotas this low. I am using this for ease of illustration of the capability in this example.

Here, we will create a quota of 3 pods, 1 RC, and 1 service for the test namespace. As you have probably guessed, this is executed once again by our trusty `create` command, as follows:

```
$ kubectl create -f quota.yaml
```

Now that we have that in place, let's use `describe` on the namespace, as follows:

```
$ kubectl describe namespace/test
```

The following screenshot is the result of the preceding command:

```
Name:   test
Labels: <none>
Status: Active

Resource Quotas
  Resource                 Used   Hard
  - - -                    - - -  - - -
  pods                     0      3
  replicationcontrollers   0      1
  services                 0      1

No resource limits.
```

The describe namespace after the quota is set

You'll note that we now have some values listed in the quota section, and that the limits section is still blank. We also have a `Used` column, which lets us know how close to the limits we are at the moment. Let's try to spin up a few pods using the following definition `busybox-ns.yaml`:

```
apiVersion: v1
kind: ReplicationController
metadata:
  name: busybox-ns
  namespace: test
  labels:
    name: busybox-ns
spec:
  replicas: 4
  selector:
    name: busybox-ns
```

```
template:
  metadata:
    labels:
      name: busybox-ns
  spec:
    containers:
    - name: busybox-ns
      image: busybox
      command:
        - sleep
        - "3600"
```

You'll note that we are creating four replicas of this basic pod. After using `create` to build this RC, run the `describe` command on the `test` namespace once more. You'll notice that the `Used` values for pods and RCs are at their max. However, we asked for four replicas and can only see three pods in use.

Let's see what's happening with our RC. You might attempt to do that with the following command:

kubectl describe rc/busybox-ns

However, if you try, you'll be discouraged by being met with a `not found` message from the server. This is because we created this RC in a new namespace and `kubectl` assumes the default namespace if not specified. This means that we need to specify `--namepsace=test` with every command when we wish to access resources in the `test` namespace.

We can also set the current namespace by working with the context settings. First, we need to find our current context, which is found with the following command:
$ kubectl config view | grep current-context
Next, we can take that context and set the namespace variable like in the following code:
$ kubectl config set-context <Current Context> --namespace=test
Now, you can run the `kubectl` command without the need to specify the namespace. Just remember to switch back when you want to look at the resources running in your default namespace.

Run the command with the namespace specified as shown in the following command. If you've set your current namespace as demonstrated in the tip box, you can leave off the `--namespace` argument:

```
$ kubectl describe rc/busybox-ns --namespace=test
```

The following screenshot is the result of the preceding command:

```
Name:               busybox-ns
Namespace:          test
Image(s):           busybox
Selector:           name=busybox-ns
Labels:             name=busybox-ns
Replicas:           3 current / 4 desired
Pods Status:        3 Running / 0 Waiting / 0 Succeeded / 0 Failed
Events:
  FirstSeen                              LastSeen                          Count    F
rom                         SubobjectPath   Reason                        Message
  Mon, 17 Aug 2015 16:29:43 -0400        Mon, 17 Aug 2015 16:29:43 -0400  1        {
replication-controller }                       successfulCreate           Created p
od: busybox-ns-spfrn
  Mon, 17 Aug 2015 16:29:43 -0400        Mon, 17 Aug 2015 16:29:43 -0400  1        {
replication-controller }                       successfulCreate           Created p
od: busybox-ns-xjf6q
  Mon, 17 Aug 2015 16:29:43 -0400        Mon, 17 Aug 2015 16:29:43 -0400  1        {
replication-controller }                       successfulCreate           Created p
od: busybox-ns-zeuuy
  Mon, 17 Aug 2015 16:29:44 -0400        Mon, 17 Aug 2015 16:33:01 -0400  18       {
replication-controller }                       failedCreate               Error cre
ating: Pod "busybox-ns-" is forbidden: Limited to 3 pods
```

Namespace quotas

As you can see in the preceding image, the first three pods were successfully created, but our final one fails with a `Limited to 3 pods` error.

This is an easy way to set limits for resources partitioned out at a community scale. It's worth noting that you can also set quotas for CPU, memory, persistent volumes, and secrets. Additionally, limits work in a similar way to quota, but they set the limit for each pod or container within the namespace.

A note on resource usage

As most of the examples in this book utilize GCP or AWS, it can be costly to keep everything running. It's also easy to run out of resources using the default cluster size, especially if you keep every example running. Therefore, you may want to delete older pods, replication controllers, replica sets, and services periodically. You can also destroy the cluster and recreate it using `Chapter 1`, *Introduction to Kubernetes*, as a way to lower your cloud provider bill.

Summary

In this chapter, we took a deeper look into networking and services in Kubernetes. You should now understand how networking communications are designed in K8s and feel comfortable accessing your services internally and externally. We saw how `kube-proxy` balances traffic both locally and across the cluster. Additionally, we explored the new Ingress resources that allow us finer control of incoming traffic. We also looked briefly at how DNS and service discovery is achieved in Kubernetes. We finished off with a quick look at namespaces and isolation for multitenancy.

5
Using Critical Kubernetes Resources

In this chapter, we will design a massive-scale platform that will challenge Kubernetes' capabilities and scalability. The Hue platform is all about creating an omniscient and omnipotent digital assistant. Hue is a digital extension of you. It will help you do anything, find anything, and, in many cases, will do a lot on your behalf. It will obviously need to store a lot of information, integrate with many external services, respond to notifications and events, and be smart about interacting with you.

We will take the opportunity in this chapter to get to know Kubectl and other related tools a little better, and will explore in detail resources that we've seen before, such as pods, as well as new resources, such as **jobs**. At the end of this chapter, you will have a clear picture of how impressive Kubernetes is and how it can be used as the foundation for hugely complex systems.

Designing the Hue platform

In this section, we will set the stage and define the scope of the amazing Hue platform. Hue is not Big Brother, Hue is Little Brother! Hue will do whatever you allow it to do. It will be able to do a lot, but some people might be concerned, so you get to pick how much or how little Hue can help you with. Get ready for a wild ride!

Defining the scope of Hue

Hue will manage your digital persona. It will know you better than you know yourself. Here is a list of some of the services which Hue can manage and help you with:

- Search and content aggregation
- Medical
- Smart home
- Finance-bank, savings, retirement, investing
- Office
- Social
- Travel
- Wellbeing
- Family
- **Smart reminders and notifications**: Let's think of the possibilities. Hue will know you, but also know your friends and the aggregate of other users across all domains. Hue will update its models in real time. It will not be confused by stale data. It will act on your behalf, present relevant information, and learn your preferences continuously. It can recommend new shows or books that you may like, make restaurant reservations based on your schedule and your family or friends, and control your home automation.
- **Security, identity, and privacy**: Hue is your proxy online. The ramifications of someone stealing your Hue identity, or even just eavesdropping on your Hue interaction, are devastating. Potential users may even be reluctant to trust the Hue organization with their identity. Let's devise a non-trust system where users have the power to pull the plug on Hue at any time. Here are a few ideas in the right direction:
    - Strong identity through a dedicated device with multi-factor authorization, including multiple biometric reasons
    - Frequently rotating credentials
    - Quick service pause and identity re-verification of all external services (will require original proof of identity to each provider)
    - The Hue backend will interact with all external services through short-lived tokens
    - Architecting Hue as a collection of loosely-coupled microservices

Hue's architecture will need to support enormous variation and flexibility. It will also need to be very extensible where existing capabilities and external services are constantly upgraded, and new capabilities and external services are integrated into the platform. That level of scale calls for microservices, where each capability or service is totally independent of other services except for well-defined interfaces through standard and/or discoverable APIs.

Hue components

Before embarking on our microservice journey, let's review the types of component we need to construct for Hue.

- **User profile**:

  The user profile is a major component, with lots of sub-components. It is the essence of the user, their preferences, history across every area, and everything that Hue knows about them.

- **User graph**:

  The user graph component models networks of interactions between users across multiple domains. Each user participates in multiple networks: social networks such as Facebook and Twitter, professional networks, hobby networks, and volunteering communities. Some of these networks are ad hoc, and Hue will be able to structure them to benefit users. Hue can take advantage of the rich profiles it has of user connections to improve interactions even without exposing private information.

- **Identity**:

  Identity management is critical, as mentioned previously, so it deserves a separate component. A user may prefer to manage multiple mutually exclusive profiles with separate identities. For example, maybe users are not comfortable with mixing their health profile with their social profile because of the risk of inadvertently exposing personal health information to their friends.

- **Authorizer**:

  The authorizer is a critical component where the user explicitly authorizes Hue to perform certain actions or collect various data on its behalf. This includes access to physical devices, accounts of external services, and level of initiative.

- **External service**:

Hue is an aggregator of external services. It is not designed to replace your bank, your health provider, or your social network. It will keep a lot of metadata about your activities, but the content will remain with your external services. Each external service will require a dedicated component to interact with the external service API and policies. When no API is available, Hue emulates the user by automating the browser or native apps.

- **Generic sensor**:

A big part of Hue's value proposition is to act on the user's behalf. In order to do that effectively, Hue needs to be aware of various events. For example, if Hue reserved a vacation for you but it senses that a cheaper flight is available, it can either automatically change your flight or ask you for confirmation. There is an infinite number of things to sense. To reign in sensing, a generic sensor is needed. A generic sensor will be extensible, but exposes a generic interface that the other parts of Hue can utilize uniformly even as more and more sensors are added.

- **Generic actuator**:

This is the counterpart of the generic sensor. Hue needs to perform actions on your behalf, such as reserving a flight. To do that, Hue needs a generic actuator that can be extended to support particular functions but can interact with other components, such as the identity manager and the authorizer, in a uniform fashion.

- **User learner**:

This is the brain of Hue. It will constantly monitor all of your interactions (that you authorize) and update its model of you. This will allow Hue to become more and more useful over time, predict what you need and what will interest you, provide better choices, surface more relevant information at the right time, and avoid being annoying and overbearing.

Hue microservices

The complexity of each of the components is enormous. Some of the components, such as the external service, the generic sensor, and generic actuator, will need to operate across hundreds, thousands, or more external services that constantly change outside the control of Hue. Even the user learner needs to learn the user's preferences across many areas and domains. Microservices address this need by allowing Hue to evolve gradually and grow more isolated capabilities without collapsing under its own complexity. Each microservice interacts with generic Hue infrastructure services through standard interfaces and, optionally, with a few other services through well-defined and versioned interfaces. The surface area of each microservice is manageable, and the orchestration between microservices is based on standard best practices:

- **Plugins**:

  Plugins are the key to extending Hue without a proliferation of interfaces. The thing about plugins is that you often need plugin chains that cross multiple abstraction layers. For example, if we want to add a new integration for Hue with YouTube, then you can collect a lot of YouTube-specific information: your channels, favorite videos, recommendations, and videos you have watched. To display this information to users and allow them to act on it, you need plugins across multiple components and eventually in the user interface as well. Smart design will help by aggregating categories of actions such as recommendations, selections, and delayed notifications to many different services.

  The great thing about plugins is that they can be developed by anyone. Initially, the Hue development team will have to develop the plugins, but as Hue becomes more popular, external services will want to integrate with Hue and build Hue plugins to enable their service.

  That will lead, of course, to a whole ecosystem of plugin registration, approval, and curation.

- **Data stores**:

  Hue will need several types of data store, and multiple instances of each type, to manage its data and metadata:

    - Relational database
    - Graph database
    - Time-series database
    - In-memory caching

Due to the scope of Hue, each one of these databases will have to be clustered and distributed.

- **Stateless microservices**:

The microservices should be mostly stateless. This will allow specific instances to be started and killed quickly, and migrated across the infrastructure as necessary. The state will be managed by the stores and accessed by the microservices with short-lived access tokens.

- **Queue-based interactions**:

All these microservices need to talk to each other. Users will ask Hue to perform tasks on their behalf. External services will notify Hue of various events. Queues coupled with stateless microservices provide the perfect solution. Multiple instances of each microservice will listen to various queues and respond when relevant events or requests are popped from the queue. This arrangement is very robust and easy to scale. Every component can be redundant and highly available. While each component is fallible, the system is very fault-tolerant.

A queue can be used for asynchronous RPC or request-response style interactions too, where the calling instance provides a private queue name and the callee posts the response to the private queue.

Planning workflows

Hue often needs to support workflows. A typical workflow will get a high-level task, such as making a dentist appointment; it will extract the user's dentist details and schedule, match it with the user's schedule, choose between multiple options, potentially confirm with the user, make the appointment, and set up a reminder. We can classify workflows into fully automatic and human workflows where humans are involved. Then there are workflows that involve spending money.

Automatic workflows

Automatic workflows don't require human intervention. Hue has full authority to execute all the steps from start to finish. The more autonomy the user allocates to Hue, the more effective it will be. The user should be able to view and audit all workflows, past and present.

Human workflows

Human workflows require interaction with a human. Most often it will be the user that needs to make a choice from multiple options or approve an action, but it may involve a person on another service. For example, to make an appointment with a dentist, you may have to get a list of available times from the secretary.

Budget-aware workflows

Some workflows, such as paying bills or purchasing a gift, require spending money. While, in theory, Hue can be granted unlimited access to the user's bank account, most users will probably be more comfortable with setting budgets for different workflows or just making spending a human-approved activity.

Using Kubernetes to build the Hue platform

In this section, we will look at various Kubernetes resources and how they can help us build Hue. First, we'll get to know the versatile Kubectl a little better, then we will look at running long-running processes in Kubernetes, exposing services internally and externally, using namespaces to limit access, launching ad hoc jobs, and mixing in non-cluster components. Obviously, Hue is a huge project, so we will demonstrate the ideas on a local Minikube cluster and not actually build a real Hue Kubernetes cluster.

Using Kubectl effectively

Kubectl is your Swiss Army knife. It can do pretty much anything around the cluster. Under the hood, Kubectl connects to your cluster through the API. It reads your `.kube/config` file, which contains information necessary to connect to your cluster or clusters. The commands are divided into multiple categories:

- **Generic commands**: Deal with resources in a generic way: `create`, `get`, `delete`, `run`, `apply`, `patch`, `replace`, and so on
- **Cluster management commands**: Deal with nodes and the cluster at large: `cluster-info`, `certificate`, `drain`, and so on
- **Troubleshooting commands**: `describe`, `logs`, `attach`, `exec`, and so on
- **Deployment commands**: Deal with deployment and scaling: `rollout`, `scale`, `auto-scale`, and so on

- **Settings commands**: Deal with labels and annotations: `label`, `annotate`, and so on

  `Misc commands: help, config, and version`

You can view the configuration with Kubernetes `config view`.

Here is the configuration for a Minikube cluster:

```
~/.minikube > k config view
apiVersion: v1
clusters:
- cluster:
    certificate-authority: /Users/gigi.sayfan/.minikube/ca.crt
    server: https://192.168.99.100:8443
  name: minikube
contexts:
- context:
    cluster: minikube
    user: minikube
  name: minikube
current-context: minikube
kind: Config
preferences: {}
users:
- name: minikube
  user:
    client-certificate: /Users/gigi.sayfan/.minikube/client.crt
    client-key: /Users/gigi.sayfan/.minikube/client.key
```

Understanding Kubectl resource configuration files

Many Kubectl operations, such as `create`, require complicated hierarchical output (since the API requires this output). Kubectl uses YAML or JSON configuration files. Here is a JSON configuration file for creating a pod:

```
apiVersion: v1
kind: Pod
metadata:
  name: ""
  labels:
    name: ""
  namespace: ""
  annotations: []
```

```
generateName: ""
spec:
    . . .
```

- apiVersion: The very important Kubernetes API keeps evolving and can support different versions of the same resource through different versions of the API.
- kind: kind tells Kubernetes what type of resource it is dealing with, in this case, pod. This is always required.
- metadata: This is a lot of information that describes the pod and where it operates:
  - name: Identifies the pod uniquely within its namespace
  - labels: Multiple labels can be applied
  - namespace: The namespace the pod belongs to
  - annotations: A list of annotations available for query
- spec: spec is a pod template that contains all of the information necessary to launch a pod. It can be quite elaborate, so we'll explore it in multiple parts:

```
"spec": {
  "containers": [
  ],
  "restartPolicy": "",
  "volumes": [
  ]
}
```

- Container spec: The pod spec's container is a list of container specs. Each container spec has the following structure:

```
{
  "name": "",
  "image": "",
  "command": [
    ""
  ],
  "args": [
    ""
  ],
  "env": [
    {
      "name": "",
      "value": ""
    }
  ],
```

```
        "imagePullPolicy": "",
        "ports": [
          {
            "containerPort": 0,
            "name": "",
            "protocol": ""
          }
        ],
        "resources": {
          "cpu": ""
          "memory": ""
        }
      }
    }
```

Each container has an image, a command that, if specified, replaces the Docker image command. It also has arguments and environment variables. Then, there are, of course, the image pull policy, ports, and resource limits. We covered those in earlier chapters.

Deploying long-running microservices in pods

Long-running microservices should run in pods and be stateless. Let's look at how to create pods for one of Hue's microservices. Later, we will raise the level of abstraction and use a deployment.

Creating pods

Let's start with a regular pod configuration file for creating a Hue learner internal service. This service doesn't need to be exposed as a public service, and it will listen to a queue for notifications and store its insights in some persistent storage.

We need a simple container that the pod will run in. Here is possibly the simplest Docker file ever, which will simulate the Hue learner:

```
FROM busybox
CMD ash -c "echo 'Started...'; while true ; do sleep 10 ; done"
```

It uses the busybox base image, prints to standard output Started... and then goes into an infinite loop, which is, by all accounts, long-running.

I have built two Docker images tagged as `g1g1/hue-learn:v3.0` and `g1g1/hue-learn:v4.0` and pushed them to the Docker Hub registry (`g1g1` is my user name).

```
docker build . -t g1g1/hue-learn:v3.0
docker build . -t g1g1/hue-learn:v4.0
docker push g1g1/hue-learn:v3.0
docker push g1g1/hue-learn:v4.0
```

Now, these images are available to be pulled into containers inside of Hue's pods.

We'll use YAML here because it's more concise and human-readable. Here are the boilerplate and `metadata` labels:

```
apiVersion: v1
kind: Pod
metadata:
  name: hue-learner
  labels:
    app: hue
    runtime-environment: production
    tier: internal-service
  annotations:
    version: "3.0"
```

The reason I use an annotation for the version and not a label is that labels are used to identify the set of pods in the deployment. Modifying labels is not allowed.

Next comes the important `containers` spec, which defines for each container the mandatory `name` and `image`:

```
spec: containers: - name: hue-learner image: g1g1/hue-learn:v3.0
```

The resources section tells Kubernetes the resource requirements of the container, which allows for more efficient and compact scheduling and allocations. Here, the container requests 200 milli-cpu units (0.2 core) and 256 MiB:

```
resources:
  requests:
    cpu: 200m
    memory: 256Mi
```

The environment section allows the cluster administrator to provide environment variables that will be available to the container. Here it tells it to discover the queue and the store through `dns`. In a testing environment, it may use a different discovery method:

```
env:
- name: DISCOVER_QUEUE
  value: dns
- name: DISCOVER_STORE
  value: dns
```

Decorating pods with labels

Labeling pods wisely is key for flexible operations. It lets you evolve your cluster live, organize your microservices into groups that you can operate on uniformly, and drill down in an ad hoc manner to observe different subsets.

For example, our Hue learner pod has the following labels:

- **Runtime-environment**: Production
- **Tier**: Internal-service

The version annotation can be used to support running multiple versions at the same time. If both version 2 and version 3 need to run at the same time, either to provide backward compatibility or just temporarily during the migration from v2 to v3, then having a version annotation or label allows both scaling pods of different versions independently and exposing services independently. The `runtime-environment` label allows performing global operations on all pods that belong to a certain environment. The `tier` label can be used to query all pods that belong to a particular tier. These are just examples; your imagination is the limit here.

Deploying long-running processes with deployments

In a large-scale system, pods should never be just created and let loose. If a pod dies unexpectedly for whatever reason, you want another one to replace it to maintain overall capacity. You can create replication controllers or replica sets yourself, but that leaves the door open to mistakes as well as the possibility of partial failure. It makes much more sense to specify how many replicas you want when you launch your pods.

Let's deploy three instances of our Hue learner microservice with a Kubernetes deployment resource. Note that deployment objects became stable at Kubernetes 1.9:

```
apiVersion: apps/v1 (use apps/v1beta2 before 1.9)
 kind: Deployment
 metadata:
   name: hue-learn
   labels:
     app: hue
 spec:
   replicas: 3
   selector:
     matchLabels:
       app: hue
   template:
     metadata:
       labels:
         app: hue
     spec:
             <same spec as in the pod template>
```

The `pod spec` is identical to the `spec` section from the pod configuration file that we used previously.

Let's create the deployment and check its status:

```
> kubectl create -f .\deployment.yaml
deployment "hue-learn" created
> kubectl get deployment hue-learn
NAME          DESIRED   CURRENT   UP-TO-DATE   AVAILABLE   AGE
hue-learn     3         3         3            3           4m
> kubectl get pods | grep hue-learn
NAME                         READY     STATUS    RESTARTS   AGE
hue-learn-237202748-d770r    1/1       Running   0          2m
hue-learn-237202748-fwv2t    1/1       Running   0          2m
hue-learn-237202748-tpr4s    1/1       Running   0          2m
```

You can get a lot more information about the deployment using the `kubectl describe` command.

Updating a deployment

The Hue platform is a large and ever-evolving system. You need to upgrade constantly. Deployments can be updated to roll out updates in a painless manner. You change the pod template to trigger a rolling update which is fully managed by Kubernetes.

Currently, all the pods are running with version 3.0:

```
> kubectl get pods -o json | jq .items[0].spec.containers[0].image
"3.0"
```

Let's update the deployment to upgrade to version 4.0. Modify the image version in the deployment file. Don't modify labels; it will cause an error. Typically, you modify the image and some related metadata in annotations. Then we can use the `apply` command to upgrade the version:

```
> kubectl apply -f hue-learn-deployment.yaml
deployment "hue-learn" updated
> kubectl get pods -o json | jq .items[0].spec.containers[0].image
"4.0"
```

Separating internal and external services

Internal services are services that are accessed directly only by other services or jobs in the cluster (or administrators that log in and run ad hoc tools). In some cases, internal services are not accessed at all, and just perform their function and store their results in a persistent store that other services access in a decoupled way.

But some services need to be exposed to users or external programs. Let's look at a fake Hue service that manages a list of reminders for a user. It doesn't really do anything, but we'll use it to illustrate how to expose services. I pushed a dummy `hue-reminders` image (the same as `hue-learn`) to Docker Hub:

```
docker push g1g1/hue-reminders:v2.2
```

Deploying an internal service

Here is the deployment, which is very similar to the Hue-learner deployment, except that I dropped the `annotations`, `env`, and `resources` sections, kept just one label to save space, and added a `ports` section to the container. That's crucial, because a service must expose a port through which other services can access it:

```
apiVersion: apps/v1a1
kind: Deployment
metadata:
  name: hue-reminders
spec:
  replicas: 2
```

```
template:
  metadata:
    name: hue-reminders
    labels:
      app: hue-reminders
  spec:
    containers:
    - name: hue-reminders
      image: g1g1/hue-reminders:v2.2
      ports:
      - containerPort: 80
```

When we run the deployment, two Hue `reminders` pods are added to the cluster:

```
> kubectl create -f hue-reminders-deployment.yaml
> kubectl get pods
NAME                              READY   STATUS    RESTARTS   AGE
hue-learn-56886758d8-h7vm7        1/1     Running   0          49m
hue-learn-56886758d8-lqptj        1/1     Running   0          49m
hue-learn-56886758d8-zwkqt        1/1     Running   0          49m
hue-reminders-75c88cdfcf-5xqtp    1/1     Running   0          50s
hue-reminders-75c88cdfcf-r6jsx    1/1     Running   0          50s
```

OK, the pods are running. In theory, other services can look up or be configured with their internal IP address and just access them directly because they are all in the same network space. But this doesn't scale. Every time a reminders pod dies and is replaced by a new one, or when we just scale up the number of pods, all the services that access these pods must know about it. Services solve this issue by providing a single access point to all the pods. The service is as follows:

```
apiVersion: v1
kind: Service
metadata:
  name: hue-reminders
  labels:
    app: hue-reminders
spec:
  ports:
  - port: 80
    protocol: TCP
  selector:
    app: hue-reminders
```

The service has a selector that selects all the pods that have labels that match it. It also exposes a port, which other services will use to access it (it doesn't have to be the same port as the container's port).

Creating the hue-reminders service

Let's create the service and explore it a little bit:

```
> kubectl create -f hue-reminders-service.yaml
service "hue-reminders" created
> kubectl describe svc hue-reminders
Name:              hue-reminders
Namespace:         default
Labels:            app=hue-reminders
Annotations:       <none>
Selector:          app=hue-reminders
Type:              ClusterIP
IP:                10.108.163.209
Port:              <unset>   80/TCP
TargetPort:        80/TCP
Endpoints:         172.17.0.4:80,172.17.0.6:80
Session Affinity:  None
Events:            <none>
```

The service is up and running. Other pods can find it through environment variables or DNS. The environment variables for all services are set at pod creation time. That means that if a pod is already running when you create your service, you'll have to kill it and let Kubernetes recreate it with the environment variables (you create your pods through a deployment, right?):

```
> kubectl exec hue-learn-56886758d8-fjzdd -- printenv | grep
HUE_REMINDERS_SERVICE
HUE_REMINDERS_SERVICE_PORT=80
HUE_REMINDERS_SERVICE_HOST=10.108.163.209
```

But using DNS is much simpler. Your service DNS name is:

```
<service name>.<namespace>.svc.cluster.local
> kubectl exec hue-learn-56886758d8-fjzdd -- nslookup hue-reminders
Server:     10.96.0.10
Address 1: 10.96.0.10 kube-dns.kube-system.svc.cluster.local
Name:       hue-reminders
Address 1: 10.108.163.209 hue-reminders.default.svc.cluster.local
```

Exposing a service externally

The service is accessible inside the cluster. If you want to expose it to the world, Kubernetes provides two ways to do it:

- Configure `NodePort` for direct access
- Configure a cloud load balancer if you run it in a cloud environment

Before you configure a service for external access, you should make sure it is secure. The Kubernetes documentation has a good example that covers all the gory details here:

`https://github.com/kubernetes/examples/blob/master/staging/https-nginx/README.md`.

Here is the `spec` section of the Hue-reminders service when exposed to the world through `NodePort`:

```
spec:
  type: NodePort
  ports:
  - port: 8080
    targetPort: 80
    protocol: TCP
    name: http
  - port: 443
    protocol: TCP
    name: https
  selector:
    app: hue-reminders
```

Ingress

`Ingress` is a Kubernetes configuration object that lets you expose a service to the outside world and take care of a lot of details. It can do the following:

- Provide an externally visible URL to your service
- Load-balance traffic
- Terminate SSL
- Provide name-based virtual hosting

To use `Ingress`, you must have an `Ingress` controller running in your cluster. Note that Ingress is still in beta and has many limitations. If you're running your cluster on GKE, you're probably OK. Otherwise, proceed with caution. One of the current limitations of the `Ingress` controller is that it isn't built for scale. As such, it is not a good option for the Hue platform yet. We'll cover the `Ingress` controller in greater detail in Chapter 15, *Advanced Kubernetes Networking*.

Here is what an `Ingress` resource looks like:

```
apiVersion: extensions/v1beta1
kind: Ingress
metadata:
  name: test
spec:
  rules:
  - host: foo.bar.com
    http:
      paths:
      - path: /foo
        backend:
          serviceName: fooSvc
          servicePort: 80
  - host: bar.baz.com
    http:
      paths:
      - path: /bar
        backend:
          serviceName: barSvc
          servicePort: 80
```

The Nginx `Ingress` controller will interpret this `Ingress` request and create a corresponding configuration file for the Nginx web server:

```
http {
  server {
    listen 80;
    server_name foo.bar.com;

    location /foo {
      proxy_pass http://fooSvc;
    }
  }
  server {
    listen 80;
    server_name bar.baz.com;

    location /bar {
```

```
        proxy_pass http://barSvc;
    }
  }
}
```

It is possible to create other controllers.

Using namespace to limit access

The Hue project is moving along nicely, and we have a few hundred microservices and about 100 developers and DevOps engineers working on it. Groups of related microservices emerge, and you notice that many of these groups are pretty autonomous. They are completely oblivious to the other groups. Also, there are some sensitive areas, such as health and finance, that you will want to control access to more effectively. Enter namespaces.

Let's create a new service, Hue-finance, and put it in a new namespace called restricted.

Here is the YAML file for the new restricted namespace:

```
kind: Namespace
 apiVersion: v1
 metadata:
    name: restricted
    labels:
      name: restricted
> kubectl create -f restricted-namespace.yaml
namespace "restricted" created
```

Once the namespace has been created, we need to configure a context for the namespace. This will allow restricting access just to this namespace:

```
> kubectl config set-context restricted --namespace=restricted --
cluster=minikube --user=minikube
Context "restricted" set.
> kubectl config use-context restricted
Switched to context "restricted".
```

Let's check our `cluster` configuration:

```
> kubectl config view
apiVersion: v1
clusters:
- cluster:
    certificate-authority: /Users/gigi.sayfan/.minikube/ca.crt
    server: https://192.168.99.100:8443
  name: minikube
contexts:
- context:
    cluster: minikube
    user: minikube
  name: minikube
- context:
    cluster: minikube
    namespace: restricted
    user: minikube
  name: restricted
current-context: restricted
kind: Config
preferences: {}
users:
- name: minikube
  user:
    client-certificate: /Users/gigi.sayfan/.minikube/client.crt
    client-key: /Users/gigi.sayfan/.minikube/client.key
```

As you can see, the current context is `restricted`.

Now, in this empty namespace, we can create our `hue-finance` service, and it will be on its own:

```
> kubectl create -f hue-finance-deployment.yaml
deployment "hue-finance" created
> kubectl get pods
NAME                          READY   STATUS    RESTARTS   AGE
hue-finance-7d4b84cc8d-gcjnz  1/1     Running   0          6s
hue-finance-7d4b84cc8d-tqvr9  1/1     Running   0          6s
hue-finance-7d4b84cc8d-zthdr  1/1     Running   0          6s
```

You don't have to switch contexts. You can also use the `--namespace=<namespace>` and `--all-namespaces` command-line switches.

Launching jobs

Hue has a lot of long-running processes deployed as microservices, but it also has a lot of tasks that run, accomplish some goal, and exit. Kubernetes supports this functionality through the job resource. A Kubernetes job manages one or more pods and ensures that they run until success. If one of the pods managed by the job fails or is deleted, then the job will run a new pod until it succeeds.

Here is a job that runs a Python process to compute the factorial of 5 (hint: it's 120):

```
apiVersion: batch/v1
kind: Job
metadata:
  name: factorial5
spec:
  template:
    metadata:
      name: factorial5
    spec:
      containers:
      - name: factorial5
        image: python:3.6
        command: ["python",
                  "-c",
                  "import math; print(math.factorial(5))"]
      restartPolicy: Never
```

Note that the `restartPolicy` must be either `Never` or `OnFailure`. The default `Always` value is invalid because a job shouldn't restart after successful completion.

Let's start the job and check its status:

```
> kubectl create -f .\job.yaml
job "factorial5" created
> kubectl get jobs
NAME          DESIRED     SUCCESSFUL    AGE
factorial5    1           1             25s
```

The pods of completed tasks are not displayed by default. You must use the `--show-all` option:

```
> kubectl get pods --show-all
NAME                            READY    STATUS      RESTARTS   AGE
factorial5-ntp22                0/1      Completed   0          2m
hue-finance-7d4b84cc8d-gcjnz    1/1      Running     0          9m
hue-finance-7d4b84cc8d-tqvr9    1/1      Running     0          8m
hue-finance-7d4b84cc8d-zthdr    1/1      Running     0          9m
```

The `factorial5` pod has a status of `Completed`. Let's check out its output:

```
> kubectl logs factorial5-ntp22
120
```

Running jobs in parallel

You can also run a job with parallelism. There are two fields in the spec, called `completions` and `parallelism`. The `completions` are set to 1 by default. If you want more than one successful completion, then increase this value. `parallelism` determines how many pods to launch. A job will not launch more pods than needed for successful completions, even if the parallelism number is greater.

Let's run another job that just sleeps for 20 seconds until it has three successful completions. We'll use a `parallelism` factor of 6, but only three pods will be launched:

```
apiVersion: batch/v1
kind: Job
metadata:
  name: sleep20
spec:
  completions: 3
  parallelism: 6
  template:
    metadata:
      name: sleep20
    spec:
      containers:
      - name: sleep20
        image: python:3.6
        command: ["python",
                  "-c",
                  "import time; print('started...');
                  time.sleep(20); print('done.')"]
      restartPolicy: Never
```

```
> Kubectl get pods
NAME            READY   STATUS    RESTARTS  AGE
sleep20-1t8sd    1/1    Running   0         10s
sleep20-sdjb4    1/1    Running   0         10s
sleep20-wv4jc    1/1    Running   0         10s
```

Cleaning up completed jobs

When a job completes, it sticks around - and its pods do, too. This is by design, so you can look at logs or connect to pods and explore. But normally, when a job has completed successfully, it is not needed anymore. It's your responsibility to clean up completed jobs and their pods. The easiest way is to simply delete the job object, which will delete all the pods too:

```
> kubectl delete jobs/factroial5
job "factorial5" deleted
> kubectl delete jobs/sleep20
job "sleep20" deleted
```

Scheduling cron jobs

Kubernetes cron jobs are jobs that run for a specified time, once or repeatedly. They behave as regular Unix cron jobs, specified in the /etc/crontab file.

In Kubernetes 1.4 they were known as a ScheduledJob. But, in Kubernetes 1.5, the name was changed to CronJob. Starting with Kubernetes 1.8, the CronJob resource is enabled by default in the API server and there no need to pass a --runtime-config flag anymore, but it's still in beta. Here is the configuration to launch a cron job every minute to remind you to stretch. In the schedule, you may replace the * with ?:

```
apiVersion: batch/v1beta1
kind: CronJob
metadata:
  name: stretch
spec:
  schedule: "*/1 * * * *"
  jobTemplate:
    spec:
      template:
        metadata:
          labels:
            name: stretch
        spec:
```

```
        containers:
        - name: stretch
          image: python
          args:
          - python
          - -c
          - from datetime import datetime; print('[{}]
Stretch'.format(datetime.now()))
          restartPolicy: OnFailure
```

In the pod spec, under the job template, I added a label called `name`. The reason is that cron jobs and their pods are assigned names with a random prefix by Kubernetes. The label allows you to easily discover all the pods of a particular cron job. See the following command lines:

```
> kubectl get pods
NAME                          READY       STATUS               RESTARTS    AGE
stretch-1482165720-qm5bj      0/1         ImagePullBackOff     0           1m
stretch-1482165780-bkqjd      0/1         ContainerCreating    0           6s
```

Note that each invocation of a cron job launches a new `job` object with a new pod:

```
> kubectl get jobs
NAME                  DESIRED    SUCCESSFUL    AGE
stretch-1482165300    1          1             11m
stretch-1482165360    1          1             10m
stretch-1482165420    1          1             9m
stretch-1482165480    1          1             8m
```

When a cron job invocation completes, its pod gets into a `Completed` state and will not be visible without the `-show-all` or `-a` flags:

```
> Kubectl get pods --show-all
NAME                          READY      STATUS        RESTARTS    AGE
stretch-1482165300-g5ps6      0/1        Completed     0           15m
stretch-1482165360-cln08      0/1        Completed     0           14m
stretch-1482165420-n8nzd      0/1        Completed     0           13m
stretch-1482165480-0jq31      0/1        Completed     0           12m
```

As usual, you can check the output of the pod of a completed cron job using the `logs` command:

```
> kubectl logs stretch-1482165300-g5ps6
[2016-12-19 16:35:15.325283] Stretch
```

When you delete a cron job, it stops scheduling new jobs and deletes all the existing job objects along with all the pods it created.

You can use the designated label (the name is equal to `STRETCH` in this case) to locate all the job objects launched by the cron job. You can also suspend a cron job so it doesn't create more jobs without deleting completed jobs and pods. You can also manage previous jobs by setting in the spec history limits: `spec.successfulJobsHistoryLimit` and `.spec.failedJobsHistoryLimit`.

Mixing non-cluster components

Most real-time system components in the Kubernetes cluster will communicate with out-of-cluster components. These could be completely external third-party services which are accessible through some API, but could also be internal services running in the same local network that, for various reasons, are not part of the Kubernetes cluster.

There are two categories here: inside-the-cluster-network and outside-the-cluster-network. Why is the distinction important?

Outside-the-cluster-network components

These components have no direct access to the cluster. They can only access it through APIs, externally visible URLs, and exposed services. These components are treated just like any external user. Often, cluster components will just use external services, which pose no security issue. For example, in my previous job we had a Kubernetes cluster that reported exceptions to a third-party service (`https://sentry.io/welcome/`). It was one-way communication from the Kubernetes cluster to the third-party service.

Inside-the-cluster-network components

These are components that run inside-the-network but are not managed by Kubernetes. There are many reasons to run such components. They could be legacy applications that have not be Kubernetized yet, or some distributed data store that is not easy to run inside Kubernetes. The reason to run these components inside-the-network is for performance, and to have isolation from the outside world so that traffic between these components and pods can be more secure. Being part of the same network ensures low-latency, and the reduced need for authentication is both convenient and can avoid authentication overhead.

Managing the Hue platform with Kubernetes

In this section, we will look at how Kubernetes can help operate a huge platform such as Hue. Kubernetes itself provides a lot of capabilities to orchestrate pods and manage quotas and limits, detecting and recovering from certain types of generic failures (hardware malfunctions, process crashes, and unreachable services). But, in a complicated system such as Hue, pods and services may be up and running but in an invalid state or waiting for other dependencies in order to perform their duties. This is tricky because if a service or pod is not ready yet, but is already receiving requests, then you need to manage it somehow: fail (puts responsibility on the caller), retry (*how many times? for how long? how often?*), and queue for later (*who will manage this queue?*).

It is often better if the system at large can be aware of the readiness state of different components, or if components are visible only when they are truly ready. Kubernetes doesn't know Hue, but it provides several mechanisms, such as liveness probes, readiness probes, and Init Containers, to support the application-specific management of your cluster.

Using liveness probes to ensure your containers are alive

Kubectl watches over your containers. If a container process crashes, Kubelet will take care of it based on the restart policy. But this is not always enough. Your process may not crash, but instead run into an infinite loop or a deadlock. The restart policy might not be nuanced enough. With a liveness probe, you get to decide when a container is considered alive. Here is a pod template for the Hue music service. It has a livenessProbe section, which uses the httpGet probe. An HTTP probe requires a scheme (HTTP or HTTPS, default to HTTP, a host (which defaults to PodIp), a path, and a port). The probe is considered successful if the HTTP status is between 200 and 399. Your container may need some time to initialize, so you can specify an initialDelayInSeconds. The Kubelet will not hit the liveness check during this period:

```
apiVersion: v1
kind: Pod
metadata:
  labels:
    app: hue-music
  name: hue-music
spec:
  containers:
    image: the_g1g1/hue-music
    livenessProbe:
```

```
      httpGet:
        path: /pulse
        port: 8888
        httpHeaders:
          - name: X-Custom-Header
            value: ItsAlive
      initialDelaySeconds: 30
      timeoutSeconds: 1
    name: hue-music
```

If a liveness probe fails for any container, then the pod's restart policy goes into effect. Make sure your restart policy is not *Never*, because that will make the probe useless.

There are two other types of probe:

- `TcpSocket`: Just check that a port is open
- `Exec`: Run a command that returns 0 for success

Using readiness probes to manage dependencies

Readiness probes are used for different purpose. Your container may be up and running, but it may depend on other services that are unavailable at the moment. For example, Hue-music may depend on access to a data service that contains your listening history. Without access, it is unable to perform its duties. In this case, other services or external clients should not send requests to the Hue music service, but there is no need to restart it. Readiness probes address this use case. When a readiness probe fails for a container, the container's pod will be removed from any service endpoint it is registered with. This ensures that requests don't flood services that can't process them. Note that you can also use readiness probes to temporarily remove pods that are overbooked until they drain some internal queue.

Here is a sample readiness probe. I use the exec probe here to execute a `custom` command. If the command exits a non-zero exit code, the container will be torn down:

```
readinessProbe:
  exec:
    command:
        - /usr/local/bin/checker
        - --full-check
        - --data-service=hue-multimedia-service
    initialDelaySeconds: 60
    timeoutSeconds: 5
```

It is fine to have both a readiness probe and a liveness probe on the same container as they serve different purposes.

Employing Init Containers for orderly pod bring-up

Liveness and readiness probes are great. They recognize that, at startup, there may be a period where the container is not ready yet, but shouldn't be considered failed. To accommodate that there is the `initialDelayInSeconds` setting where containers will not be considered failed. But what if this initial delay is potentially very long? Maybe, in most cases, a container is ready after a couple of seconds and ready to process requests, but because the initial delay is set to five minutes just in case, we waste a lot of time when the container is idle. If the container is part of a high-traffic service, then many instances can all sit idle for five minutes after each upgrade and pretty much make the service unavailable.

Init Containers address this problem. A pod may have a set of Init Containers that run to completion before other containers are started. An Init Container can take care of all the non-deterministic initialization and let application containers with their readiness probe have minimal delay.

Init Containers came out of beta in Kubernetes 1.6. You specify them in the pod spec as the `initContainers` field, which is very similar to the `containers` field. Here is an example:

```
apiVersion: v1
kind: Pod
metadata:
  name: hue-fitness
spec:
  containers:
    name: hue-fitness
    Image: hue-fitness:v4.4
  InitContainers:
    name: install
    Image: busybox
    command: /support/safe_init
    volumeMounts:
    - name: workdir
      mountPath: /workdir
```

Sharing with DaemonSet pods

DaemonSet pods are pods that are deployed automatically, one per node (or a designated subset of the nodes). They are typically used for keeping an eye on nodes and ensuring that they are operational. This is a very important function that we covered in Chapter 8, *Monitoring, Logging, and Troubleshooting*, when we discussed the node problem detector. But they can be used for much more. The nature of the default Kubernetes scheduler is that it schedules pods based on resource availability and requests. If you have lots of pods that don't require a lot of resources, many pods will be scheduled on the same node. Let's consider a pod that performs a small task and then, every second, sends a summary of all its activities to a remote service. Imagine that, on average, 50 of these pods are scheduled on the same node. This means that, every second, 50 pods make 50 network requests with very little data. How about we cut it down by 50 times to just a single network request? With a DaemonSet pod, all the other 50 pods can communicate with it instead of talking directly to the remote service. The DaemonSet pod will collect all the data from the 50 pods and, once a second, will report it in aggregate to the remote service. Of course, that requires the remote service API to support aggregate reporting. The nice thing is that the pods themselves don't have to be modified; they will just be configured to talk to the DaemonSet pod on localhost instead of the remote service. The DaemonSet pod serves as an aggregating proxy.

The interesting part about this configuration file is that the hostNetwork, hostPID, and hostIPC options are set to true. This enables the pods to communicate efficiently with the proxy, utilizing the fact that they are running on the same physical host:

```
apiVersion: apps/v1
kind: DaemonSet
metadata:
  name: hue-collect-proxy
  labels:
    tier: stats
    app: hue-collect-proxy
spec:
  template:
    metadata:
      labels:
        hue-collect-proxy
    spec:
      hostPID: true
      hostIPC: true
      hostNetwork: true
      containers:
          image: the_g1g1/hue-collect-proxy
          name: hue-collect-proxy
```

Evolving the Hue platform with Kubernetes

In this section, we'll discuss other ways to extend the Hue platform and service additional markets and communities. The question is always, *What Kubernetes features and capabilities can we use to address new challenges or requirements?*

Utilizing Hue in enterprises

Enterprises often can't run in the cloud, either due to security and compliance reasons, or for performance reasons because the system has work with data and legacy systems that are not cost-effective to move to the cloud. Either way, Hue for enterprise must support on-premise clusters and/or bare-metal clusters.

While Kubernetes is most often deployed on the cloud, and even has a special cloud-provider interface, it doesn't depend on the cloud and can be deployed anywhere. It does require more expertise, but enterprise organizations that already run systems on their own datacenters have that expertise.

CoreOS provides a lot of material regarding deploying Kubernetes clusters on bare-metal lusters.

Advancing science with Hue

Hue is so great at integrating information from multiple sources that it would be a boon for the scientific community. Consider how Hue can help multi-disciplinary collaborations between scientists from different areas.

A network of scientific communities might require deployment across multiple geographically-distributed clusters. Enter cluster federation. Kubernetes has this use case in mind and evolves its support. We will discuss it at length in a later chapter.

Educating the kids of the future with Hue

Hue can be utilized for education and provide many services to online education systems. But privacy concerns may prevent deploying Hue for kids as a single, centralized system. One possibility is to have a single cluster, with namespaces for different schools. Another deployment option is that each school or county has its own Hue Kubernetes cluster. In the second case, Hue for education must be extremely easy to operate to cater for schools without a lot of technical expertise. Kubernetes can help a lot by providing self-healing and auto-scaling features and capabilities for Hue, to be as close to zero-administration as possible.

Summary

In this chapter, we designed and planned the development, deployment, and management of the Hue platform - an imaginary omniscient and omnipotent service - built on microservices architecture. We used Kubernetes as the underlying orchestration platform, of course, and delved into many of its concepts and resources. In particular, we focused on deploying pods for long-running services, as opposed to jobs for launching short-term or cron jobs, explored internal services versus external services, and also used namespaces to segment a Kubernetes cluster. Then we looked at the management of a large system such as Hue with liveness and readiness probes, Init Containers, and DaemonSets.

You should now feel comfortable architecting web-scale systems composed of microservices, and understand how to deploy and manage them in a Kubernetes cluster.

In the next chapter, we will look into the super-important area of storage. Data is king, but often the least-flexible element of the system. Kubernetes provides a storage model, and many options for integrating with various storage solutions.

6
Exploring Kubernetes Storage Concepts

In order to power modern microservices and other stateless applications, Kubernetes operators need to have a way to manage stateful data storage on the cluster. While it's advantageous to maintain as much state as possible outside of the cluster in dedicated database clusters as a part of cloud-native service offerings, there's often a need to keep a statement of record or state cluster for stateless and ephemeral services. We'll explore what's considered a more difficult problem in the container orchestration and scheduling world: managing locality-specific, mutable data in a world that relies on declarative state, decoupling physical devices from logical objects, and immutable approaches to system updates. We'll explore strategies for setting up reliable, replicated storage for modern database engines.

In this chapter, we will discuss how to attach persistent volumes and create storage for stateful applications and data. We will walk through storage concerns and how we can persist data across pods and the container life cycle. We will explore the `PersistentVolumes` types, as well as `PersistentVolumeClaim`. Finally, we will take a look at StatefulSets and how to use dynamic volume provisioning.

The following topics will be covered in the chapter:

- Persistent storage
- `PersistentVolumes`
- `PersistentVolumeClaim`
- Storage Classes
- Dynamic volume provisioning
- StatefulSets

Technical requirements

You'll need to have a running Kubernetes cluster to go through these examples. Please start your cluster up on your cloud provider of choice, or a local Minikube instance.

The code for this repository can be found here: `https://github.com/PacktPublishing/The-Complete-Kubernetes-Guide/tree/master/Chapter06`.

Persistent storage

So far, we only worked with workloads that we could start and stop at will, with no issue. However, real-world applications often carry state and record data that we prefer (even insist) not to lose. The transient nature of containers themselves can be a big challenge. If you recall our discussion of layered filesystems in `Chapter 1`, *Introduction to Kubernetes*, the top layer is writable. (It's also frosting, which is delicious.) However, when the container dies, the data goes with it. The same is true for crashed containers that Kubernetes restarts.

This is where volumes or disks come into play. Volumes exist outside the container and are coupled to the pod, which allows us to save our important data across containers outages. Further more, if we have a volume at the pod level, data can be shared between containers in the same application stack and within the same pod. A volume itself on Kubernetes is a directory, which the Pod provides to the containers running on it. There are a number of different volume types available at `spec.volumes`, which we'll explore, and they're mounted into containers with the `spec.containers.volumeMounts` parameter.

 To see all the types of volumes available, visit `https://kubernetes.io/docs/concepts/storage/volumes/#types-of-volumes`.

Docker itself has some support for volumes, but Kubernetes gives us persistent storage that lasts beyond the lifetime of a single container. The volumes are tied to pods and live and die with those pods. Additionally, a pod can have multiple volumes from a variety of sources. Let's take a look at some of these sources.

Temporary disks

One of the easiest ways to achieve improved persistence amid container crashes and data sharing within a pod is to use the `emptydir` volume. This volume type can be used with either the storage volumes of the node machine itself or an optional RAM disk for higher performance.

Again, we improve our persistence beyond a single container, but when a pod is removed, the data will be lost. A machine reboot will also clear any data from RAM-type disks. There may be times when we just need some shared temporary space or have containers that process data and hand it off to another container before they die. Whatever the case, here is a quick example of using this temporary disk with the RAM-backed option.

Open your favorite editor and create a `storage-memory.yaml` file and type the following code:

```
apiVersion: v1
kind: Pod
metadata:
  name: memory-pd
spec:
  containers:
  - image: nginx:latest
    ports:
    - containerPort: 80
    name: memory-pd
    volumeMounts:
    - mountPath: /memory-pd
      name: memory-volume
  volumes:
  - name: memory-volume
    emptyDir:
      medium: Memory
```

The preceding example is probably second nature by now, but we will once again issue a `create` command followed by an `exec` command to see the folders in the container:

```
$ kubectl create -f storage-memory.yaml
$ kubectl exec memory-pd -- ls -lh | grep memory-pd
```

This will give us a Bash shell in the container itself. The `ls` command shows us a `memory-pd` folder at the top level. We use `grep` to filter the output, but you can run the command without `| grep memory-pd` to see all folders:

```
/home/k8s/nodejs# kubectl.sh exec memory-pd -- ls -lh | grep memory
drwxrwxrwt 2 root root   40 Oct 24 15:21 memory-pd
```

Temporary storage inside a container

Again, this folder is temporary as everything is stored in the node's (minion's) RAM. When the node gets restarted, all the files will be erased. We will look at a more permanent example next.

Cloud volumes

Let's move on to something more robust. There are two types of PersistentVolumes that we'll touch base with in order to explain how you can use AWS's and GCE's block storage engines to provide stateful storage for your Kubernetes cluster. Given that many companies have already made significant investment in cloud infrastructure, we'll get you up and running with two key examples. You can consider these types of volumes or persistent volumes as storage classes. These are different from the `emptyDir` that we created before, as the contents of a GCE persistent disk or AWS EBS volume will persist even if a pod is removed. Looking ahead, this provides operators with the clever feature of being able to pre-populate data in these drives and can also be switched between pods.

GCE Persistent Disks

Let's mount a `gcePersistentDisk` first. You can see more information about these drives here: `https://cloud.google.com/compute/docs/disks/`.

Google Persistent Disk is durable and high performance block storage for the Google Cloud Platform. Persistent Disk provides SSD and HDD storage, which can be attached to instances running in either Google Compute Engine or Google Container Engine. Storage volumes can be transparently resized, quickly backed up, and offer the ability to support simultaneous readers.

You'll need to create a Persistent Disk using the GCE GUI, API, or CLI before we're able to use it in our cluster, so let's get started:

1. From the console, in **Compute Engine**, go to **Disks**. On this new screen, click on the **Create Disk** button. We'll be presented with a screen similar to the following **GCE new persistent disk** screenshot:

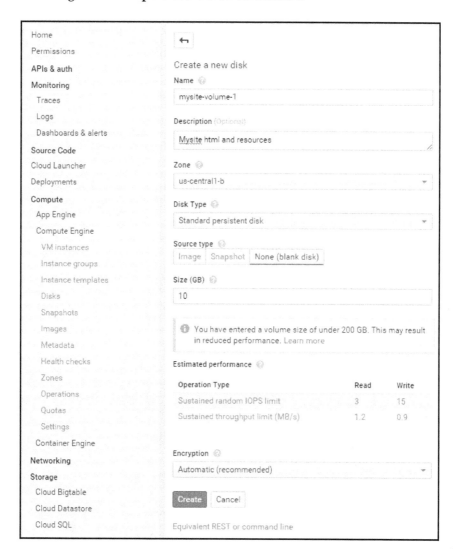

GCE new persistent disk

2. Choose a name for this volume and give it a brief description. Make sure that **Zone** is the same as the nodes in your cluster. GCE Persistent Disks can only be attached to machines in the same zone.

3. Enter `mysite-volume-1` in the **Name** field. Choose a zone matching at least one node in your cluster. Choose **None (blank disk)** for **Source type** and give 10 (10 GB) as the value in **Size (GB)**. Finally, click on **Create**:

The nice thing about Persistent Disks on GCE is that they allow for mounting to multiple machines (nodes in our case). However, when mounting to multiple machines, the volume must be in read-only mode. So, let's first mount this to a single pod, so we can create some files. Use the following code to make a `storage-gce.yaml` file to create a pod that will mount the disk in read/write mode:

```
apiVersion: v1
kind: Pod
metadata:
  name: test-gce
spec:
  containers:
  - image: nginx:latest
    ports:
    - containerPort: 80
    name: test-gce
    volumeMounts:
    - mountPath: /usr/share/nginx/html
      name: gce-pd
  volumes:
  - name: gce-pd
    gcePersistentDisk:
      pdName: mysite-volume-1
      fsType: ext4
```

First, let's issue a `create` command followed by a `describe` command to find out which node it is running on:

```
$ kubectl create -f storage-gce.yaml
$ kubectl describe pod/test-gce
```

Note the node and save the pod IP address for later. Then, open an SSH session into that node:

```
Name:               test-gce
Namespace:          default
Node:               kubernetes-minion-group-zwpm/10.128.0.4
Start Time:         Sun, 15 Jan 2017 16:51:02 -0500
Labels:             <none>
Status:             Running
IP:                 10.244.4.5
Controllers:        <none>
Containers:
  test-gce:
    Container ID:   docker://15871d81eb72557cc230df70a5c724617289d710a550da66e4dfaf7083
    Image:          nginx:latest
    Image ID:       docker://sha256:01f818af747d88b4ebca7cdabd0c581e406e0e790be72678d25
    Port:           80/TCP
    Requests:
      cpu:          100m
    State:          Running
      Started:      Sun, 15 Jan 2017 16:53:00 -0500
    Ready:          True
    Restart Count:  0
    Volume Mounts:
      /usr/share/nginx/html from gce-pd (rw)
      /var/run/secrets/kubernetes.io/serviceaccount from default-token-728d1 (ro)
    Environment Variables:      <none>
Conditions:
  Type          Status
  Initialized   True
  Ready         True
  PodScheduled  True
Volumes:
  gce-pd:
    Type:         GCEPersistentDisk (a Persistent Disk resource in Google Compute Engine)
    PDName:       mysite-volume-1
    FSType:       ext4
    Partition:    0
    ReadOnly:     false
  default-token-728d1:
    Type:         Secret (a volume populated by a Secret)
    SecretName:   default-token-728d1
QoS Class:        Burstable
Tolerations:      <none>
```

Pod described with persistent disk

Type the following command:

```
$ gcloud compute --project "<Your project ID>" ssh --zone "<your gce zone>"
"<Node running test-gce pod>"
```

Since we've already looked at the volume from inside the running container, let's access it directly from the node (minion) itself this time. We will run a df command to see where it is mounted, but we will need to switch to root first:

```
$ sudo su -
$ df -h | grep mysite-volume-1
```

As you can see, the GCE volume is mounted directly to the node itself. We can use the mount path listed in the output of the earlier df command. Use cd to change to the folder now. Then, create a new file named index.html with your favorite editor:

```
$ cd /var/lib/kubelet/plugins/kubernetes.io/gce-pd/mounts/mysite-volume-1
$ vi index.html
```

Enter a quaint message, such as Hello from my GCE PD!. Now, save the file and exit the editor. If you recall from the storage-gce.yaml file, the Persistent Disk is mounted directly to the nginx HTML directory. So, let's test this out while we still have the SSH session open on the node. Do a simple curl command to the pod IP we wrote down earlier:

```
$ curl <Pod IP from Describe>
```

You should see Hello from my GCE PD! or whatever message you saved in the index.html file. In a real-world scenario, we can use the volume for an entire website or any other central storage. Let's take a look at running a set of load balanced web servers all pointing to the same volume.

First, leave the SSH session with two exit commands. Before we proceed, we will need to remove our test-gce pod so that the volume can be mounted read-only across a number of nodes:

```
$ kubectl delete pod/test-gce
```

Now, we can create an ReplicationController that will run three web servers, all mounting the same Persistent Disk, as follows. Save the following code as the http-pd-controller.yaml file:

```
apiVersion: v1
kind: ReplicationController
metadata:
  name: http-pd
  labels:
    name: http-pd
spec:
  replicas: 3
```

```
selector:
  name: http-pd
template:
  metadata:
    name: http-pd
    labels:
      name: http-pd
  spec:
    containers:
    - image: nginx:latest
      ports:
      - containerPort: 80
      name: http-pd
      volumeMounts:
      - mountPath: /usr/share/nginx/html
        name: gce-pd
    volumes:
    - name: gce-pd
      gcePersistentDisk:
        pdName: mysite-volume-1
        fsType: ext4
        readOnly: true
```

Let's also create an external service and save it as the `http-pd-service.yaml` file, so we can see it from outside the cluster:

```
apiVersion: v1
kind: Service
metadata:
  name: http-pd
  labels:
    name: http-pd
spec:
  type: LoadBalancer
  ports:
  - name: http
    protocol: TCP
    port: 80
  selector:
    name: http-pd
```

Go ahead and create these two resources now. Wait a few moments for the external IP to get assigned. After this, a `describe` command will give us the IP we can use in a browser:

```
$ kubectl describe service/http-pd
```

The following screenshot is the result of the preceding command:

```
Name:                    http-pd
Namespace:               default
Labels:                  name=http-pd
Selector:                name=http-pd
Type:                    LoadBalancer
IP:                      10.0.118.195
LoadBalancer Ingress:    130.211.186.84
Port:                    http      80/TCP
NodePort:                http      32429/TCP
Endpoints:               10.244.2.15:80,10.244.2.16:80,10.244.3.5:80
Session Affinity:        None
No events.
```

K8s service with GCE PD shared across three pods

If you don't see the `LoadBalancer Ingress` field yet, it probably needs more time to get assigned. Type the IP address from `LoadBalancer Ingress` into a browser, and you should see your familiar `index.html` file show up with the text we entered previously!

AWS Elastic Block Store

K8s also supports AWS **Elastic Block Store** (**EBS**) volumes. Like the GCE Persistent Disks, EBS volumes are required to be attached to an instance running in the same availability zone. A further limitation is that EBS can only be mounted to a single instance at one time. Similarly to before, you'll need to create an EBS volume using API calls, the CLI, or you'll need to log in to the GUI manually and create the volume referenced by `volumeID`. If you're authorized in the AWS CLI, you can use the following command to create a volume:

```
$ aws ec2 create-volume --availability-zone=us-west-1a eu-west-1a --size=20
--volume-type=gp2
```

Make sure that your volume is created in the same region as your Kubernetes cluster!

For brevity, we will not walk through an AWS example, but a sample YAML file is included to get you started. Again, remember to create the EBS volume before your pod. Save the following code as the `storage-aws.yaml` file:

```
apiVersion: v1
kind: Pod
metadata:
  name: test-aws
spec:
  containers:
  - image: nginx:latest
```

```
  ports:
  - containerPort: 80
  name: test-aws
  volumeMounts:
  - mountPath: /usr/share/nginx/html
    name: aws-pd
volumes:
- name: aws-pd
  awsElasticBlockStore:
    volumeID: aws://<availability-zone>/<volume-id>
    fsType: ext4
```

Other storage options

Kubernetes supports a variety of other types of storage volumes. A full list can be found here: https://kubernetes.io/docs/concepts/storage/volumes/#types-of-volumes.

Here are a few that may be of particular interest:

- nfs: This type allows us to mount a **Network File Share** (**NFS**), which can be very useful for both persisting the data and sharing it across the infrastructure
- gitrepo: As you might have guessed, this option clones a Git repository into a new and empty folder

PersistentVolumes and Storage Classes

Thus far, we've seen examples of directly provisioning the storage within our pod definitions. This works quite well if you have full control over your cluster and infrastructure, but at larger scales, application owners will want to use storage that is managed separately. Typically, a central IT team or the cloud provider will take care of the details behind provisioning storage and leave the application owners to worry about their primary concern, the application itself. This separation of concerns and duties in Kubernetes allows you to structure your engineering focus around a storage subsystem that can be managed by a distinct group of engineers.

In order to accommodate this, we need some way for the application to specify and request storage without being concerned with how that storage is provided. This is where PersistentVolumes and PersistentVolumeClaim come into play.

PersistentVolumes are similar to the volumes we created earlier, but they are provided by the cluster administrator and are not dependent on a particular pod. PersistentVolumes are a resource that's provided to the cluster just like any other object. The Kubernetes API provides an interface for this object in the form of NFS, EBS Persistent Disks, or any other volume type described before. Once the volume has been created, you can use PersistentVolumeClaims to request storage for your applications.

PersistentVolumeClaims is an abstraction that allows users to specify the details of the storage needed. We can defined the amount of storage, as well as the access type, such as ReadWriteOnce (read and write by one node), ReadOnlyMany (read-only by multiple nodes), and ReadWriteMany (read and write by many nodes). The cluster operators are in charge of providing a wide variety of storage options for application operators in order to meet requirements across a number of different access modes, sizes, speeds, and durability without requiring the end users to know the details of that implementation. The modes supported by cluster operators is dependent on the backing storage provider. For example, we saw in the AWS aws-ebs example that mounting to multiple nodes was not an option, while with GCP Persistent Disks could be shared among several nodes in read-only mode.

Additionally, Kubernetes provides two other methods for specifying certain groupings or types of storage volumes. The first is the use of selectors, as we have seen previously for pod selection. Here, labels can be applied to storage volumes and then claims can reference these labels to further filter the volume they are provided. Second, Kubernetes has the concept of StorageClass, which allows us specify a storage provisioner and parameters for the types of volumes it provisions.

PersistentVolumes and PersistentVolumeClaims have a life cycle that involves the following phases:

- Provisioning
- Static or dynamic
- Binding
- Using
- Reclaiming
- Delete, retain, or recycle

We will dive into Storage Classes in the next section, but here is a quick example of a PersistentVolumeClaim for illustration purposes. You can see in the annotations that we request 1Gi of storage in ReadWriteOnce mode with a StorageClass of solidstate and a label of aws-storage. Save the following code as the pvc-example.yaml file:

```
kind: PersistentVolumeClaim
apiVersion: v1
```

```
metadata:
  name: demo-claim
spec:
  accessModes:
  - ReadWriteOnce
  volumeMode: Filesystem
  resources:
    requests:
      storage: 1Gi
  storageClassName: ssd
  selector:
    matchLabels:
      release: "aws-storage"
  matchExpressions:
    - {key: environment, operator: In, values: [dev, stag, uat]}
```

As of Kubernetes version 1.8, there's also alpha support for expanding `PersistentVolumeClaim` for `gcePersistentDisk`, `awsElasticBlockStore`, `Cinder`, `glusterfs`, and `rbd` volume claim types. These are similar to the thin provisioning that you may have seen with systems such as VMware, and they allow for resizing of a storage class via the `allowVolumeExpansion` field as long as you're running either XFS or Ext3/Ext4 filesystems. Here's a quick example of what that looks like:

```
kind: StorageClass
apiVersion: storage.k8s.io/v1
metadata:
 name: Cinder-volume-01
provisioner: kubernetes.io/cinder
parameters:
 resturl: "http://192.168.10.10:8080"
 restuser: ""
 secretNamespace: ""
 secretName: ""
allowVolumeExpansion: true
```

Dynamic volume provisioning

Now that we've explored how to build from volumes, storage classes, persistent volumes, and persistent volume claims, let's take a look at how to make that all dynamic and take advantage of the built-in scaling of the cloud! Dynamic provisioning removes the need for pre-crafted storage; it relies on requests from application users instead. You use the `StorageClass` API object to create dynamic resources.

First, we can create a manifest that will define the type of storage class that we'll use for our dynamic storage. We'll use a vSphere example here to try out another storage class:

```
apiVersion: storage.k8s.io/v1
kind: StorageClass
metadata:
  name: durable-medium
provisioner: kubernetes.io/vsphere-volume
parameters:
  type: thin
```

Once we have the manifest, we can use this storage by including it as a class in a new `PersistentVolumeClaim`. You may remember this as `volume.beta.kubernetes.io/storage-class` in earlier, pre-1.6 versions of Kubernetes, but now you can simply include this property in the `PersistentVolumeClaim` object. Keep in mind that the value of `storageClassName` must match the available, dynamic `StorageClass` that the cluster operators have provided. Here's an example of that:

```
apiVersion: v1
kind: PersistentVolumeClaim
metadata:
 name: webtier-vclaim-01
spec:
 accessModes:
    - ReadWriteMany
 storageClassName: durable-medium
 resources:
   requests:
     storage: 20Gi
```

When this claim is removed, the storage is dynamically deleted. You can make this a cluster default by ensuring that the `DefaultStorageClass` admission controller is turned on, and after you ensure that one `StorageClass` object is set to default.

StatefulSets

The purpose of StatefulSets is to provide some consistency and predictability to application deployments with stateful data. Thus far, we have deployed applications to the cluster, defining loose requirements around required resources such as compute and storage. The cluster has scheduled our workload on any node that can meet these requirements. While we can use some of these constraints to deploy in a more predictable manner, it will be helpful if we had a construct built to help us provide this consistency.

StatefulSets were set to GA in 1.6 as we went to press. There were previously beta in version 1.5 and were known as Pet Sets prior to that (alpha in 1.3 and 1.4).

This is where StatefulSets come in. StatefulSets provide us first with numbered and reliable naming for both network access and storage claims. The pods themselves are named with the following convention, where N is from 0 to the number of replicas:

```
"Name of Set"-N
```

This means that a StatefulSet called db with three replicas will create the following pods:

```
db-0
db-1
db-2
```

This gives Kubernetes a way to associate network names and PersistentVolumes with specific pods. Additionally, it also serves to order the creation and termination of pods. Pod will be started from 0 to N and terminated from N to 0.

A stateful example

Let's take a look at an example of a stateful application. First, we will want to create and use a StorageClass, as we discussed earlier. This will allow us to hook into the Google Cloud Persistent Disk provisioner. The Kubernetes community is building provisioners for a variety of StorageClasses, including GCP and AWS. Each provisioner has its own set of parameters available. Both GCP and AWS providers let you choose the type of disk (solid-state, standard, and so on) as well as the fault zone that is needed to match the pod attaching to it. AWS additionally allows you to specify encryption parameters as well as IOPs for provisioned IOPs volumes. There are a number of other provisioners in the works, including Azure and a variety of non-cloud options. Save the following code as solidstate-sc.yaml file:

```yaml
kind: StorageClass
apiVersion: storage.k8s.io/v1
metadata:
  name: solidstate
provisioner: kubernetes.io/gce-pd
parameters:
  type: pd-ssd
  zone: us-central1-b
```

Use the following command with the preceding listing to create a `StorageClass` kind of SSD drive in `us-central1-b`:

```
$ kubectl create -f solidstate.yaml
```

Next, we will create a `StatefulSet` kind with our trusty `httpwhalesay` demo. While this application does include any real state, we can see the storage claims and explore the communication path as shown in the listing `sayhey-statefulset.yaml`:

```
apiVersion: apps/v1
kind: StatefulSet
metadata:
  name: whaleset
spec:
  serviceName: sayhey-svc
  replicas: 3
  template:
    metadata:
      labels:
        app: sayhey
    spec:
      terminationGracePeriodSeconds: 10
      containers:
      - name: sayhey
        image: jonbaier/httpwhalesay:0.2
        command: ["node", "index.js", "Whale it up!."]
        ports:
        - containerPort: 80
          name: web
        volumeMounts:
        - name: www
          mountPath: /usr/share/nginx/html
  volumeClaimTemplates:
  - metadata:
      name: www
      annotations:
        volume.beta.kubernetes.io/storage-class: solidstate
    spec:
      accessModes: [ "ReadWriteOnce" ]
      resources:
        requests:
          storage: 1Gi
```

Use the following command to start the creation of this StatefulSet. If you observe pod creation closely, you will see it create `whaleset-0`, `whaleset-1`, and `whaleset-2` in succession:

```
$ kubectl create -f sayhey-statefulset.yaml
```

Immediately after this, we can see our StatefulSet and the corresponding pods using the familiar `get` subcommand:

```
$ kubectl get statefulsets
$ kubectl get pods
```

These pods should create an output similar to the following images:

```
NAME        DESIRED    CURRENT    AGE
whaleset    3          3          46s
```

StatefulSet listing

The `get pods` output will show the following:

```
NAME         READY    STATUS              RESTARTS    AGE
whaleset-0   1/1      Running             0           54s
whaleset-1   1/1      Running             0           29s
whaleset-2   0/1      ContainerCreating   0           11s
```

Pods created by StatefulSet

Depending on your timing, the pods may still be being created. As you can see in the preceding screenshot, the third container is still being spun up.

We can also see the volumes the set has created and claimed for each pod. First are the `PersistentVolumes` themselves:

```
$ kubectl get pv
```

The preceding command should show the three `PersistentVolumes` named www-whaleset-N. We notice the size is 1Gi and the access mode is set to **ReadWriteOnce (RWO)**, just as we defined in our `StorageClass`:

NAME AGE	STATUS	VOLUME	CAPACITY	ACCESSMODES
www-whaleset-0 4m	Bound	pvc-43346a3d-e024-11e6-af6d-42010a800002	1Gi	RWO
www-whaleset-1 4m	Bound	pvc-43381dc9-e024-11e6-af6d-42010a800002	1Gi	RWO
www-whaleset-2 4m	Bound	pvc-433a3864-e024-11e6-af6d-42010a800002	1Gi	RWO

The PersistentVolumes listing

Next, we can look at the `PersistentVolumeClaim` that reserves the volumes for each pod:

```
$ kubectl get pvc
```

The following is the output of the preceding command:

NAME CLAIM	REASON	AGE	CAPACITY	ACCESSMODES	RECLAIMPOLICY	STATUS
pvc-43346a3d-e024-11e6-af6d-42010a800002 default/www-whaleset-0		4m	1Gi	RWO	Delete	Bound
pvc-43381dc9-e024-11e6-af6d-42010a800002 default/www-whaleset-1		4m	1Gi	RWO	Delete	Bound
pvc-433a3864-e024-11e6-af6d-42010a800002 default/www-whaleset-2		4m	1Gi	RWO	Delete	Bound

The PersistentVolumeClaim listing

You'll notice many of the same settings here as with the `PersistentVolumes` themselves. You might also notice the end of the claim name (or `PersistentVolumeClaim` name in the previous listing) looks like www-whaleset-N. www is the mount name we specified in the preceding YAML definition. This is then appended to the pod name to create the actual `PersistentVolume` and `PersistentVolumeClaim` name. One more area we can ensure that the proper disk is linked with it's matching pod.

Another area where this alignment is important is in network communication. StatefulSets also provide consistent naming here. Before we can do this, let's create a service endpoint `sayhey-svc.yaml`, so we have a common entry point for incoming requests:

```yaml
apiVersion: v1
kind: Service
metadata:
  name: sayhey-svc
  labels:
    app: sayhey
spec:
  ports:
  - port: 80
    name: web
  clusterIP: None
  selector:
    app: sayhey
```

```
$ kubectl create -f sayhey-svc.yaml
```

Now, let's open a shell in one of the pods and see if we can communicate with another in the set:

```
$ kubectl exec whaleset-0 -i -t bash
```

The preceding command gives us a bash shell in the first `whaleset` pod. We can now use the service name to make a simple HTTP request. We can use both the short name, `sayhey-svc`, and the fully qualified name, `sayhey-svc.default.svc.cluster.local`:

```
$ curl sayhey-svc
$ curl sayhey-svc.default.svc.cluster.local
```

You'll see an output similar to the following screenshot. The service endpoint acts as a common communication point for all three pods:

```
<html>
    <head>
        <title>HTTP Whalesay</title>
    </head>
    <body>
        <pre>
            <code>
------------------------------------------------
| Whale it up!. --Sent from whaleset-0 |
------------------------------------------------
        \
         \
          \
                                               ##
                                 ## ## ##         ==
                              ## ## ## ##       ===
                          /"""""""""""""""""___/ ===
                     ~~~ {~~ ~~~~ ~~~ ~~~~ ~~ ~ /  ===- ~~~
                          _____ o          __/
                           \    \        __/
                            _____/
        </code>
        </pre>
    <body/>
</html>
```

HTTP whalesay curl output (whalesay-0 Pod)

Now, let's see if we can communicate with a specific pod in the StatefulSet. As we noticed earlier, the StatefulSet named the pods in an orderly manner. It also gives them hostnames in a similar fashion so that there is a specific DNS entry for each pod in the set. Again, we will see the convention of `"Name of Set"`-N and then add the fully qualified service URL. The following example shows this for `whaleset-1`, which is the second pod in our set:

```
$ curl whaleset-1.sayhey-svc.default.svc.cluster.local
```

Running this command from our existing Bash shell in `whaleset-0` will show us the output from `whaleset-1`:

```
<html>
    <head>
        <title>HTTP Whalesay</title>
    </head>
    <body>
        <pre>
            <code>
- - - - - - - - - - - - - - - - - - - - - - - - - - - - - - - - - - - -
| Whale it up!. --Sent from whaleset-1 |
- - - - - - - - - - - - - - - - - - - - - - - - - - - - - - - - - - - -
          \
           \
            \
                                                            ##        .
                                                    ## ## ##       ==
                                                 ## ## ## ##      ===
                                             /""""""""""""""""___/ ===
                                        ~~~ {~~ ~~~~ ~~~ ~~~~ ~~ ~ /  ===- ~~~
                                             _____ o          __/
                                              \    \        __/
                                               _____/
            </code>
        </pre>
    <body/>
</html>
```

HTTP whalesay curl output (whalesay-1 Pod)

You can exit out of this shell now with `exit`.

For learning purposes, it may also be instructive to describe some of the items from this section in more detail. For example, `kubectl describe svc sayhey-svc` will show us all three pod IP address in the service endpoints.

Summary

In this chapter, we explored a variety of persistent storage options and how to implement them with our pods. We looked at `PersistentVolumes` and also `PersistentVolumeClaim`, which allow us to separate storage provisioning and application storage requests. Additionally, we looked at `StorageClasses` for provisioning groups of storage according to a specification. We also explored the new StatefulSets abstraction and learned how we can deploy stateful applications in a consistent and ordered manner.

Monitoring and Logging

7

This chapter will cover the use and customization of both built-in and third-party monitoring tools on our Kubernetes cluster. We will cover how to use the tools to monitor the health and performance of our cluster. In addition, we will look at built-in logging, the Google Cloud Logging service, and Sysdig.

The following topics will be covered in this chapter:

- How Kuberentes uses cAdvisor, Heapster, InfluxDB, and Grafana
- Customizing the default Grafana dashboard
- Using Fluentd and Grafana
- Installing and using logging tools
- Working with popular third-party tools, such as Stackdriver and Sysdig, to extend our monitoring capabilities

Technical requirements

You'll need to have your Google Cloud Platform account enabled and logged in to it, or you can use a local Minikube instance of Kubernetes. You can also use Play with Kubernetes over the web: `https://labs.play-with-k8s.com/`.

Monitoring operations

Real-world monitoring goes far beyond checking whether a system is up and running. Although health checks like those you learned in `Chapter 3`, *Building a Foundation with Core Kubernetes Constructs*, in the *Health checks* section can help us isolate problem applications, operations teams can best serve the business when they can anticipate the issues and mitigate them before a system goes offline.

The best practices in monitoring are to measure the performance and usage of core resources and watch for trends that stray from the normal baseline. Containers are not different here, and a key component to managing our Kubernetes cluster is having a clear view of the performance and availability of the OS, network, system (CPU and memory), and storage resources across all nodes.

In this chapter, we will examine several options to monitor and measure the performance and availability of all our cluster resources. In addition, we will look at a few options for alerting and notifications when irregular trends start to emerge.

Built-in monitoring

If you recall from Chapter 1, *Introduction to Kubernetes*, we noted that our nodes were already running a number of monitoring services. We can see these once again by running the get pods command with the kube-system namespace specified as follows:

```
$ kubectl get pods --namespace=kube-system
```

The following screenshot is the result of the preceding command:

NAME	READY	STATUS	RESTARTS	AGE
etcd-empty-dir-cleanup-kubernetes-master	1/1	Running	2	2d
etcd-server-events-kubernetes-master	1/1	Running	2	2d
etcd-server-kubernetes-master	1/1	Running	2	2d
fluentd-cloud-logging-kubernetes-master	1/1	Running	2	2d
fluentd-cloud-logging-kubernetes-minion-group-rh7t	1/1	Running	0	3m
fluentd-cloud-logging-kubernetes-minion-group-s345	1/1	Running	0	3m
fluentd-cloud-logging-kubernetes-minion-group-tp2h	1/1	Running	0	3m
heapster-v1.2.0-2805816975-80mjc	4/4	Running	0	20h
kube-addon-manager-kubernetes-master	1/1	Running	2	2d
kube-apiserver-kubernetes-master	1/1	Running	4	2d
kube-controller-manager-kubernetes-master	1/1	Running	2	2d
kube-dns-4101612645-bwsd4	4/4	Running	0	20h
kube-dns-autoscaler-2715466192-gt3r7	1/1	Running	0	20h
kube-proxy-kubernetes-minion-group-rh7t	1/1	Running	0	4m
kube-proxy-kubernetes-minion-group-s345	1/1	Running	0	4m
kube-proxy-kubernetes-minion-group-tp2h	1/1	Running	0	3m
kube-scheduler-kubernetes-master	1/1	Running	2	2d
kubernetes-dashboard-3543765157-65g1m	1/1	Running	0	20h
l7-default-backend-2234341178-g4wct	1/1	Running	0	20h
l7-lb-controller-v0.8.0-kubernetes-master	1/1	Running	2	2d
monitoring-influxdb-grafana-v4-7x0n0	2/2	Running	0	20h
node-problem-detector-v0.1-1zfml	1/1	Running	0	4m
node-problem-detector-v0.1-cjrtz	1/1	Running	0	4m
node-problem-detector-v0.1-f87pp	1/1	Running	2	2d
node-problem-detector-v0.1-vj001	1/1	Running	0	4m
rescheduler-v0.2.1-kubernetes-master	1/1	Running	2	2d

System pod listing

Again, we see a variety of services, but how does this all fit together? If you recall, the node (formerly minions) section from `Chapter 3`, *Building a Foundation with Core Kubernetes Constructs*, each node is running a `kubelet`. The `kubelet` is the main interface for nodes to interact with and update the API server. One such update is the metrics of the node resources. The actual reporting of resource usage is performed by a program named cAdvisor.

The cAdvisor program is another open source project from Google, which provides various metrics on container resource use. Metrics include CPU, memory, and network statistics. There is no need to tell cAdvisor about individual containers; it collects the metrics for all containers on a node and reports this back to the `kubelet`, which in turn reports to Heapster.

>
>
> **Google's open source projects**: Google has a variety of open source projects related to Kubernetes. Check them out, use them, and even contribute your own code!
>
> Both cAdvisor and Heapster are mentioned in the following sections of GitHub:
>
> - **cAdvisor**: `https://github.com/google/cadvisor`
> - **Heapster**: `https://github.com/kubernetes/heapster`
>
> Contrib is a catch-all term for a variety of components that are not part of core Kubernetes. It can be found at `https://github.com/kubernetes/contrib`. LevelDB is a key store library that was used in the creation of InfluxDB. It can be found at `https://github.com/google/leveldb`.

Heapster is yet another open source project from Google; you may start to see a theme emerging here (see the preceding information box). Heapster runs in a container on one of the minion nodes and aggregates the data from a `kubelet`. A simple REST interface is provided to query the data.

When using the GCE setup, a few additional packages are set up for us, which saves us time and gives us a complete package to monitor our container workloads. As we can see from the preceding *System pod listing* screenshot, there is another pod with `influx-grafana` in the title.

InfluxDB is described on its official website as follows:

An open-source distributed time series database with no external dependencies.

InfluxDB is based on a key store package (refer to the previous *Google's open source projects* information box) and is perfect to store and query event- or time-based statistics such as those provided by Heapster.

Finally, we have Grafana, which provides a dashboard and graphing interface for the data stored in InfluxDB. Using Grafana, users can create a custom monitoring dashboard and get immediate visibility into the health of their Kubernetes cluster, and therefore their entire container infrastructure.

Exploring Heapster

Let's quickly look at the REST interface by running SSH to the node that is running the Heapster pod. First, we can list the pods to find the one that is running Heapster, as follows:

```
$ kubectl get pods --namespace=kube-system
```

The name of the pod should start with `monitoring-heapster`. Run a `describe` command to see which node it is running on, as follows:

```
$ kubectl describe pods/<Heapster monitoring Pod> --namespace=kube-system
```

From the output in the following screenshot, we can see that the pod is running in `kubernetes-minion-merd`. Also note the IP for the pod, a few lines down, as we will need that in a moment:

Heapster pod details

Next, we can SSH to this box with the familiar `gcloud ssh` command, as follows:

```
$ gcloud compute --project "<Your project ID>" ssh --zone "<your gce zone>" "<kubernetes minion from describe>"
```

From here, we can access the Heapster REST API directly using the pod's IP address. Remember that pod IPs are routable not only in the containers but also on the nodes themselves. The `Heapster` API is listening on port `8082`, and we can get a full list of metrics at `/api/v1/metric-export-schema/`.

Let's look at the list now by issuing a `curl` command to the pod IP address we saved from the `describe` command, as follows:

```
$ curl -G <Heapster IP from describe>:8082/api/v1/metric-export-schema/
```

We will see a listing that is quite long. The first section shows all the metrics available. The last two sections list fields by which we can filter and group. For your convenience, I've added the following tables which are a little bit easier to read:

Metric	Description	Unit	Type
uptime	The number of milliseconds since the container was started	ms	Cumulative
cpu/usage	The cumulative CPU usage on all cores	ns	Cumulative
cpu/limit	The CPU limit in millicores	-	Gauge
memory/usage	Total memory usage	Bytes	Gauge
memory/working_set	Total working set usage; the working set is the memory that is being used, and is not easily dropped by the kernel	Bytes	Gauge
memory/limit	The memory limit	Bytes	Gauge
memory/page_faults	The number of page faults	-	Cumulative
memory/major_page_faults	The number of major page faults	-	Cumulative
network/rx	The cumulative number of bytes received over the network	Bytes	Cumulative
network/rx_errors	The cumulative number of errors while receiving over the network	-	Cumulative
network/tx	The cumulative number of bytes sent over the network	Bytes	Cumulative
network/tx_errors	The cumulative number of errors while sending over the network	-	Cumulative
filesystem/usage	The total number of bytes consumed on a filesystem	Bytes	Gauge
filesystem/limit	The total size of filesystem in bytes	Bytes	Gauge
filesystem/available	The number of available bytes remaining in a the filesystem	Bytes	Gauge

Table 6.1. Available Heapster metrics

Field	Description	Label type
nodename	The node name where the container ran	Common
hostname	The host name where the container ran	Common

host_id	An identifier specific to a host, which is set by the cloud provider or user	Common
container_base_image	The user-defined image name that is run inside the container	Common
container_name	The user-provided name of the container or full container name for system containers	Common
pod_name	The name of the pod	Pod
pod_id	The unique ID of the pod	Pod
pod_namespace	The namespace of the pod	Pod
namespace_id	The unique ID of the namespace of the pod	Pod
labels	A comma-separated list of user-provided labels	Pod

Table 6.2. Available Heapster fields

Customizing our dashboards

Now that we have the fields, we can have some fun. Recall the Grafana page that we looked at in Chapter 1, *Introduction to Kubernetes*. Let's pull that up again by going to our cluster's monitoring URL. Note that you may need to log in with your cluster credentials. Refer to the following format of the link you need to use: https://<your master IP>/api/v1/proxy/namespaces/kube-system/services/monitoring-grafana

We'll see the default **Home** dashboard. Click on the down arrow next to **Home** and select **Cluster**. This shows the Kubernetes cluster dashboard, and now we can add our own statistics to the board. Scroll all the way to the bottom and click on **Add a Row**. This should create a space for a new row and present a green tab on the left-hand side of the screen.

Let's start by adding a view into the filesystem usage for each node (minion). Click on the green tab to expand, and then select **Add Panel** and then **Graph**. An empty graph should appear on the screen, along with a query panel for our custom graph.

The first field in this panel should show a query that starts with **SELECT mean("value") FROM**. Click on the **A** character next to this field to expand it. Leave the first field next to **FROM** as **default** and then click on the next field with the **select measurement** value. A drop-down menu will appear with the Heapster metrics we saw in the previous tables. Select filesystem/usage_bytes_gauge. Now, in the **SELECT** row, click on **mean()** and then on the **x** symbol to remove it. Next, click on the + symbol on the end of the row and add **selectors** and **max**. Then, you'll see a **GROUP BY** row with **time($interval)** and **fill(none)**. Carefully click on **fill** and not on the **(none)** portion, and again on **x** to remove it.

Then, click on the + symbol at the end of the row and select **tag(hostname)**.Finally, at the bottom of the screen we should see a **Group by time interval.** Enter 5 s there and you should have something similar to the following screenshot:

Heapster pod details

Next, let's click on the **Axes** tab, so that we can set the units and legend. Under **Left Y Axis**, click on the field next to **Unit** and set it to **data | bytes** and **Label** to **Disk Space Used**. Under **Right Y Axis**, set **Unit** to **none | none**. Next, on the **Legend** tab, make sure to check **Show** in **Options** and **Max** in **Values**.

Now, let's quickly go to the **General** tab and choose a title. In my case, I named mine `Filesystem Disk Usage by Node (max)`.

We don't want to lose this nice new graph we've created, so let's click on the save icon in the top-right corner. It looks like a floppy disk (you can do a Google image search if you don't know what this is).

After we click on the save icon, we will see a green dialog box that verifies that the dashboard was saved. We can now click the **x** symbol above the graph details panel and below the graph itself.

This will return us to the dashboard page. If we scroll all the way down, we will see our new graph. Let's add another panel to this row. Again, use the *green* tab and then select **Add Panel | singlestat**. Once again, an empty panel will appear with a setting form below it.

Let's say we want to watch a particular node and monitor network usage. We can easily do this by first going to the **Metrics** tab. Then, expand the query field and set the second value in the **FROM** field to **network/rx.** Now, we can specify the **WHERE** clause by clicking the + symbol at the end of the row and choosing **hostname** from the drop-down. After **hostname =**, click on **select tag value** and choose one of the minion nodes from the list.

Finally, leave **mean()** for the second **SELECT** field shown as follows:

Singlestat		General	Metrics	Options	Value Mappings	Time range

Big value	Prefix		Value	avg ▾	Postfix	
Font size	Prefix	50% ▾	Value	80% ▾	Postfix	50% ▾
Unit	bytes			Decimals	auto	

Coloring	Background	Value	Thresholds ❷	184907710, 190907710
			Colors	invert order

Spark lines	Show ✔	Background mode ✔	Line Color	Fill Color

Gauge	Show	Min	0	Max	100
Threshold labels		Threshold markers ✔			

Singlestat options

In the **Options** tab, make sure that **Unit format** is set to **data | bytes** and check the **Show** box next to **Spark lines**. The spark line gives us a quick historical view of the recent variations in the value. We can use **Background mode** to take up the entire background; by default, it uses the area below the value.

In **Coloring**, we can optionally check the **Value** or **Background** box and choose **Thresholds** and **Colors.** This will allow us to choose different colors for the value based on the threshold tier we specify. Note that an unformatted version of the number must be used for threshold values.

Now, let's go back to the **General** tab and set the title as Network bytes received (Node35ao). Use the identifier for your minion node.

Once again, let's save our work and return to the dashboard. We should now have a row that looks like the following screenshot:

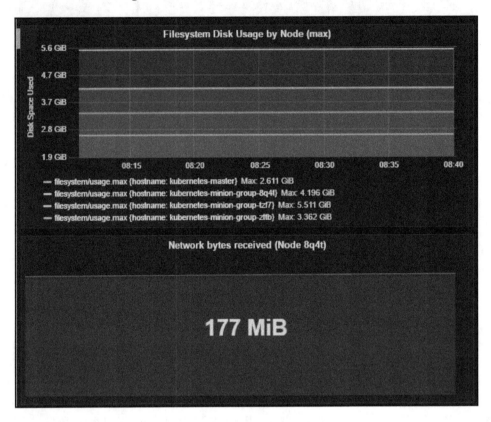

Custom dashboard panels

Grafana has a number of other panel types that you can play with, such as **Dashboard list**, **Plugin list**, **Table**, and **Text**.

As we can see, it is pretty easy to build a custom dashboard and monitor the health of our cluster at a glance.

FluentD and Google Cloud Logging

Looking back at the *System pod listing* screenshot at the beginning of the chapter, you may have noted a number of pods starting with the words `fluentd-cloud-logging-kubernetes`. These pods appear when using the GCE provider for your K8s cluster.

A pod like this exists on every node in our cluster, and its sole purpose is to handle the processing of Kubernetes logs. If we log in to our Google Cloud Platform account, we can see some of the logs processed there. Simply use the left side, and under **Stackdriver**, select **Logging**. This will take us to a log listing page with a number of drop-down menus on the top. If this is your first time visiting the page, the first drop-down will likely be set to **Cloud HTTP Load Balancer**.

In this drop-down menu, we'll see a number of GCE types of entries. Select GCE VM instances and then the Kubernetes master or one of the nodes. In the second drop-down, we can choose various log groups, including **kubelet.** We can also filter by the event log level and date. Additionally, we can use the play button to watch events stream in live shown as follows:

The Google Cloud Logging filter

FluentD

Now we know that the `fluentd-cloud-logging-kubernetes` pods are sending the data to the Google Cloud, but why do we need FluentD? Simply put, FluentD is a collector.

It can be configured to have multiple sources to collect and tag logs, which are then sent to various output points for analysis, alerting, or archiving. We can even transform data using plugins before it is passed on to its destination.

Not all provider setups have FluentD installed by default, but it is one of the recommended approaches to give us greater flexibility for future monitoring operations. The AWS Kubernetes setup also uses FluentD, but instead forwards events to Elasticsearch.

> **Exploring FluentD**: If you are curious about the inner workings of the FluentD setup or just want to customize the log collection, we can explore quite easily using the `kubectl exec` command and one of the pod names from the command we ran earlier in the chapter. First, let's see if we can find the FluentD `config` file: **$ kubectl exec fluentd-cloud-logging-kubernetes-minion-group-r4qt --namespace=kube-system -- ls /etc/td-agent**.
> We will look in the `etc` folder and then `td-agent`, which is the `fluent` sub folder. While searching in this directory, we should see a `td-agent.conf` file. We can view that file with a simple `cat` command, as follows: **$ kubectl exec fluentd-cloud-logging-kubernetes-minion-group-r4qt --namespace=kube-system -- cat /etc/td-agent/td-agent.conf**.
>
> We should see a number of sources, including the various Kubernetes components, Docker, and some GCP elements. While we can make changes here, remember that it is a running container and our changes won't be saved if the pod dies or is restarted. If we really want to customize, it's best to use this container as a base and build a new container, which we can push to a repository for later use.

Maturing our monitoring operations

While Grafana gives us a great start to monitoring our container operations, it is still a work in progress. In the real world of operations, having a complete dashboard view is great once we know there is a problem. However, in everyday scenarios, we'd prefer to be proactive and actually receive notifications when issues arise. This kind of alerting capability is a must to keep the operations team ahead of the curve and out of reactive mode.

There are many solutions available in this space, and we will take a look at two in particular: GCE monitoring (Stackdriver) and Sysdig.

GCE (Stackdriver)

Stackdriver is a great place to start for infrastructure in the public cloud. It is actually owned by Google, so it's integrated as the Google Cloud Platform monitoring service. Before your lock-in alarm bells start ringing, Stackdriver also has solid integration with AWS. In addition, Stackdriver has alerting capability with support for notification to a variety of platforms and webhooks for anything else.

Signing up for GCE monitoring

In the GCE console, in the **Stackdriver** section, click on **Monitoring.** This will open a new window, where we can sign up for a free trial of Stackdriver. We can then add our GCP project and optionally an AWS account as well. This requires a few more steps, but instructions are included on the page. Finally, we'll be given instructions on how to install the agents on our cluster nodes. We can skip this for now, but will come back to it in a minute.

Click on **Continue**, set up your daily alerts, and click on **Continue** again.

Click on **Launch Monitoring** to proceed. We'll be taken to the main dashboard page, where we will see some basic statistics on our node in the cluster. If we select **Resources** from the side menu and then **Instances**, we'll be taken to a page with all our nodes listed. By clicking on the individual node, we can again see some basic information even without an agent installed.

 Stackdriver also offers monitoring and logging agents that can be installed on the nodes. However, it currently does not support the container OS that is used by default in the GCE `kube-up` script. You can still see the basic metrics for any nodes in GCE or AWS, but will need to use another OS if you want a detailed agent installation.

Alerts

Next, we can look at the alerting policies available as part of the monitoring service. From the instance details page, click on the **Create Alerting Policy** button in the **Incidents** section at the top of the page.

We will click on **Add Condition** and select a **Metric Threshold**. In the **Target** section, set **RESOURCE TYPE** to **Instance (GCE)**. Then, set **APPLIES TO** to **Group** and **kubernetes**. Leave **CONDITION TRIGGERS IF** set to **Any Member Violates**.

In the **Configuration** section, leave **IF METRIC** as **CPU Usage (GCE Monitoring)** and **CONDITION** as **above**. Now, set **THRESHOLD** to `80` and set the time in **FOR** to **5 minutes**.

Then click on **Save Condition**:

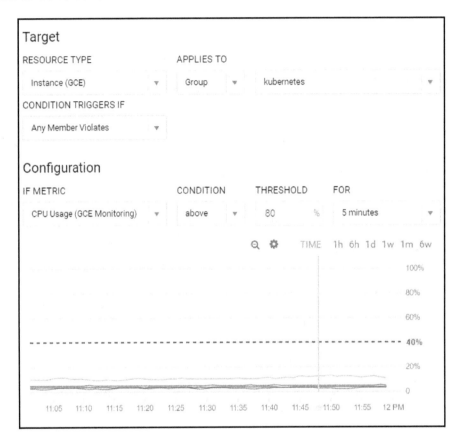

Google Cloud Monitoring alert policy

Next, we will add a notification. In the **Notification** section, leave **Method** as **Email** and enter your email address.

We can skip the **Documentation** section, but this is where we can add text and formatting to alert messages.

Finally, name the policy `Excessive CPU Load` and click on **Save Policy**.

Now, whenever the CPU from one of our instances goes above 80 percent, we will receive an email notification. If we ever need to review our policies, we can find them in the **Alerting** drop-down and then in **Policies Overview** in the menu on the left-hand side of the screen.

Beyond system monitoring with Sysdig

Monitoring our cloud systems is a great start, but what about the visibility of the containers themselves? Although there are a variety of cloud monitoring and visibility tools, Sysdig stands out for its ability to dive deep, not only into system operations, but specifically containers.

Sysdig is open source and is billed as a universal system visibility tool with native support for containers. It is a command line tool that provides insight into the areas we looked at earlier, such as storage, network, and system processes. What sets it apart is the level of detail and visibility it offers for these process and system activities. Furthermore, it has native support for containers, which gives us a full picture of our container operations. This is a highly recommended tool for your container operations arsenal. The main website of Sysdig is `http://www.sysdig.org/`.

Sysdig Cloud

We will take a look at the Sysdig tool and some of the useful command line-based UIs in a moment. However, the team at Sysdig has also built a commercial product, named **Sysdig Cloud**, which provides the advanced dashboard, alerting, and notification services we discussed earlier in the chapter. Also, the differentiator here has high visibility into containers, including some nice visualizations of our application topology.

 If you'd rather skip the *Sysdig Cloud* section and just try out the command-line tool, simply skip to *The Sysdig command line* section later in this chapter.

If you have not done so already, sign up for Sysdig Cloud at `http://www.sysdigcloud.com`.

After activating and logging in for the first time, we'll be taken to a welcome page. Clicking on **Next**, we are shown a page with various options to install the Sysdig agents. For our example environment, we will use the Kubernetes setup. Selecting Kubernetes will give you a page with your API key and a link to instructions. The instructions will walk you through how to create a Sysdig agent DaemonSet on your cluster. Don't forget to add the API key from the install page.

We will not be able to continue on the install page until the agents connect. After creating the DaemonSet and waiting a moment, the page should continue to the AWS integration page. You can fill this out if you like, but for this walk-through, we will click on **Skip**. Then, click on **Let's Get Started**.

 As of this writing, Sysdig and Sysdig Cloud were not fully compatible with the latest container OS deployed by default in the GCE `kube-up` script, Container-optimized OS from Google: `https://cloud.google.com/container-optimized-os/docs`.

We'll be taken to the main **Sysdig Cloud** dashboard screen. We should see at least two minion nodes appear under the **Explore** tab. We should see something similar to the following screenshot with our minion nodes:

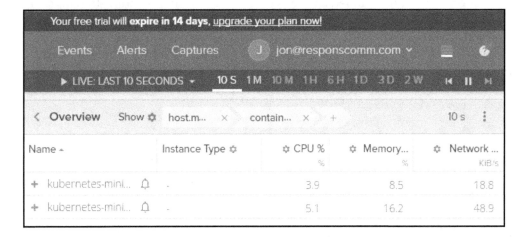

Sysdig Cloud Explore page

This page shows us a table view, and the links on the left let us explore some key metrics for CPU, memory, networking, and so on. Although this is a great start, the detailed views will give us a much deeper look at each node.

Detailed views

Let's take a look at these views. Select one of the minion nodes and then scroll down to the detail section that appears below. By default, we should see the **System: Overview by Process** view (if it's not selected, just click on it from the list on the left-hand side). If the chart is hard to read, simply use the maximize icon in the top-left corner of each graph for a larger view.

There are a variety of interesting views to explore. Just to call out a few others, **Services | HTTP Overview** and **Hosts & Containers | Overview by Container** give us some great charts for inspection. In the latter view, we can see stats for CPU, memory, network, and file usage by container.

Topology views

In addition, there are three topology views at the bottom. These views are perfect for helping us understand how our application is communicating. Click on **Topology | Network Traffic** and wait a few seconds for the view to fully populate. It should look similar to the following screenshot:

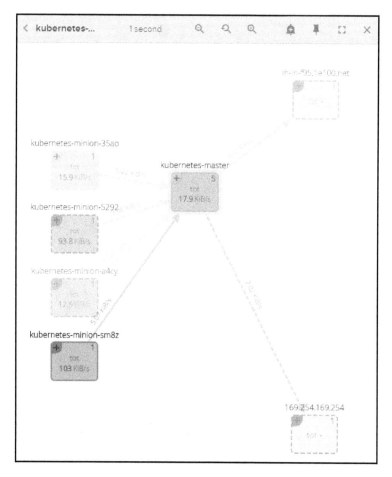

Sysdig Cloud network topology view

Note that the view maps out the flow of communication between the minion nodes and the master in the cluster. You may also note a + symbol in the top corner of the node boxes. Click on that in one of the minion nodes and use the zoom tools at the top of the view area to zoom into the details, as shown in the following screenshot:

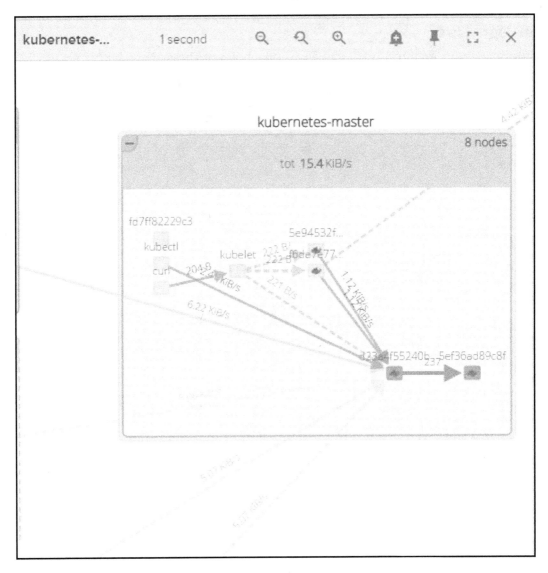

The Sysdig Cloud network topology detailed view

Note that we can now see all the components of Kubernetes running inside the master. We can see how the various components work together. We can see `kube-proxy` and the `kubelet` process running, as well as a number of boxes with the Docker whale, which indicate that they are containers. If we zoom in and use the plus icon, we can see that these are the containers for our pods and core Kubernetes processes, as we saw in the services running on the master section in `Chapter 1`, *Introduction to Kubernetes*.

Also, if you have the master included in your monitored nodes, you can watch `kubelet` initiate communication from a minion and follow it all the way through the `kube-apiserver` container in the master.

We can even sometimes see the instance communicating with the GCE infrastructure to update metadata. This view is great in order to get a mental picture of how our infrastructure and underlying containers are talking to one another.

Metrics

Next, let's switch over to the **Metrics** tab in the left-hand menu next to **Views**. Here, there are also a variety of helpful views.

Let's look at **capacity.estimated.request.total.count** in **System**. This view shows us an estimate of how many requests a node is capable of handling when fully loaded. This can be really useful for infrastructure planning:

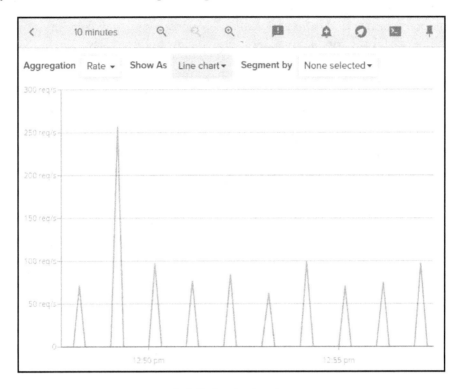

Sysdig Cloud capacity estimate view

Alerting

Now that we have all this great information, let's create some notifications. Scroll back up to the top of the page and find the bell icon next to one of your minion entries. This will open a **Create Alert** dialog. Here, we can set manual alerts similar to what we did earlier in the chapter. However, there is also the option to use **BASELINE** and **HOST COMPARISON**.

Using the **BASELINE** option is extremely helpful, as Sysdig will watch the historical patterns of the node and alert us whenever one of the metrics strays outside the expected metric thresholds. No manual settings are required, so this can really save time for the notification setup and help our operations team to be proactive before issues arise. Refer to the following screenshot:

Name alert

Insert alert description

warning ▾

1 Define Condition

MANUAL	BASELINE	HOST COMPARISON
☑ cpu.idle.percent	☑ cpu.iowait.percent	☑ cpu.nice.percent
☑ cpu.stolen.percent	☑ cpu.system.percent	☑ cpu.used.percent
☑ cpu.user.percent	☑ file.bytes.total	☑ fs.used.percent
☑ memory.bytes.used	☑ memory.swap.bytes.available	☑ memory.swap.bytes.total
☑ memory.swap.bytes.used	☑ memory.swap.used.percent	☑ net.bytes.total
☑ net.request.count.in	☑ net.request.time.in	☑ net.tcp.queue.len

Aggregated across everywhere ▾

Segmented by none ▾

2 Set Notifications

Configure your notification channels here. Each alert you create can route notifications to any combination of these channels.

✉ **Email to jon@responscomm.com (Globally disabled)**

This notification channel is globally disabled. Go to Notification Settings page to review settings.

3 Activate Sysdig Capture

Sysdig Capture lets you analyze a record of every system call executed on a host to troubleshoot containers, even after they have been deleted.

CANCEL   **CREATE**

Sysdig Cloud new alert

The **HOST COMPARISON** option is also a great help as it allows us to compare metrics with other hosts and alert whenever one host has a metric that differs significantly from the group. A great use case for this is monitoring resource usage across minion nodes to ensure that our scheduling constraints are not creating a bottleneck somewhere in the cluster.

You can choose whichever option you like and give it a name and warning level. Enable the notification method. Sysdig supports email, **SNS** (short for **Simple Notification Service**), and **PagerDuty** as notification methods. You can optionally enable **Sysdig Capture** to gain deeper insight into issues. Once you have everything set, just click on **Create** and you will start to receive alerts as issues come up.

The Sysdig command line

Whether you only use the open source tool or you are trying out the full Sysdig Cloud package, the command line utility is a great companion to have to track down issues or get a deeper understanding of your system.

In the core tool, there is the main `sysdig` utility and also a command line-style UI named `csysdig`. Let's take a look at a few useful commands.

Find the relevant installation instructions for your OS here: `http://www.sysdig.org/install/`.

Once installed, let's first look at the process with the most network activity by issuing the following command:

```
$ sudo sysdig -pc -c topprocs_net
```

The following screenshot is the result of the preceding command:

Bytes	Process	Host_pid	Container_pid	container.name
79.06KB	kube-apise	5152	15	host
58.10KB	etcd	5211	10	host
6.29KB	dragent	19284	19292	host
4.52KB	kube-contr	5164	11	host
4.11KB	etcd	5211	11	host
1.95KB	kube-sched	5227	13	host
1.72KB	sshd	18963	18963	host

A Sysdig top process by network activity

This is an interactive view that will show us a top process in terms of network activity. Also, there are a plethora of commands to use with `sysdig`. A few other useful commands to try out include the following:

```
$ sudo sysdig -pc -c topprocs_cpu
$ sudo sysdig -pc -c topprocs_file
$ sudo sysdig -pc -c topprocs_cpu container.name=<Container Name NOT ID>
```

More examples can be found at http://www.sysdig.org/wiki/sysdig-examples/.

The Csysdig command-line UI

Just because we are in a shell on one of our nodes doesn't mean we can't have a UI. Csysdig is a customizable UI for exploring all the metrics and insight that Sysdig provides. Simply type `csysdig` in the prompt:

```
$ csysdig
```

After entering `csysdig`, we will see a real-time listing of all processes on the machine. At the bottom of the screen, you'll note a menu with various options. Click on **Views** or press *F2* if you love to use your keyboard. In the left-hand menu, there are a variety of options, but we'll look at threads. Double-click on **Threads**.

On some operating systems and with some SSH clients, you may have issues with the function keys. Check the settings on your terminal and make sure that the function keys are using the VT100+ sequences.

We can see all the threads currently running on the system and some information about the resource usage. By default, we see a big list that is updated often. If we click on the **Filter**, *F4* for the mouse-challenged, we can slim down the list.

Type `kube-apiserver`, if you are on the master, or `kube-proxy`, if you are on a node (minion), in the filter box and press *Enter*. The view now filters for only the threads in that command:

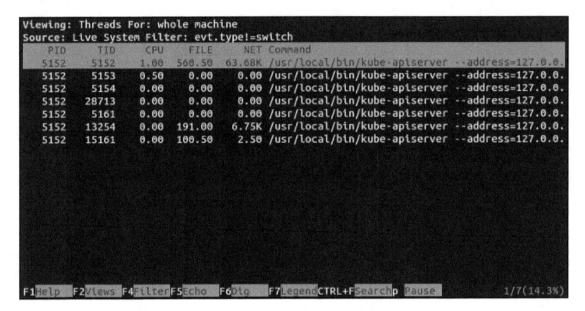

```
Viewing: Threads For: whole machine
Source: Live System Filter: evt.type!=switch
   PID     TID     CPU     FILE     NET  Command
  5152    5152    1.00   560.50  63.68K  /usr/local/bin/kube-apiserver --address=127.0.0.
  5152    5153    0.50     0.00   0.00   /usr/local/bin/kube-apiserver --address=127.0.0.
  5152    5154    0.00     0.00   0.00   /usr/local/bin/kube-apiserver --address=127.0.0.
  5152   28713    0.00     0.00   0.00   /usr/local/bin/kube-apiserver --address=127.0.0.
  5152    5161    0.00     0.00   0.00   /usr/local/bin/kube-apiserver --address=127.0.0.
  5152   13254    0.00   191.00  6.75K   /usr/local/bin/kube-apiserver --address=127.0.0.
  5152   15161    0.00   100.50   2.50   /usr/local/bin/kube-apiserver --address=127.0.0.




F1Help  F2Views F4Filter F5Echo  F6Dig   F7Legend CTRL+F Search p Pause              1/7(14.3%)
```

Csysdig threads

If we want to inspect this a little further, we can simply select one of the threads in the list and click on **Dig** or press *F6*. Now, we see a detailed listing of system calls from the command in real time. This can be a really useful tool to gain deep insight into the containers and processes running on our cluster.

Click on **Back** or press the *Backspace* key to go back to the previous screen. Then, go to **Views** once more. This time, we will look at the **Containers** view. Once again, we can filter and also use the **Dig** view to get more in-depth visibility into what is happening at the system call level.

Another menu item you might note here is **Actions**, which is available in the newest release. These features allow us to go from process monitoring to action and response. It gives us the ability to perform a variety of actions from the various process views in Csysdig. For example, the container view has actions to drop into a Bash shell, kill containers, inspect logs, and more. It's worth getting to know the various actions and hotkeys, and even add your own custom hotkeys for common operations.

Prometheus

A newcomer to the monitoring scene is an open source tool called Prometheus. Prometheus is an open source monitoring tool that was built by a team at SoundCloud. You can find more about the project at `https://prometheus.io`.

Their website offers the following features:

- A multi-dimensional data model (`https://prometheus.io/docs/concepts/data_model/`) (the time series are identified by their metric name and key/value pairs)
- A flexible query language (`https://prometheus.io/docs/prometheus/latest/querying/basics/`) to leverage this dimensionality
- No reliance on distributed storage; single-server nodes are autonomous
- Time series collection happens via a pull model over HTTP
- Pushing time series (`https://prometheus.io/docs/instrumenting/pushing/`) is supported via an intermediary gateway
- Targets are discovered via service discovery or static configuration
- Multiple modes of graphing and dashboard support

Prometheus summary

Prometheus offers a lot of value to the operators of a Kubernetes cluster. Let's look at some of the more important dimensions of the software:

- **Simple to operate**: It was built to run as individual servers using local storage for reliability
- **It's precise**: You can use a query language similar to JQL, DDL, DCL, or SQL queries to define alerts and provide a multi-dimensional view of status
- **Lots of libraries**: You can use more than ten languages and numerous client libraries in order to introspect your services and software
- **Efficient**: With data stored in an efficient, custom format both in memory and on disk, you can scale out easily with sharding and federation, creating a strong platform from which to issue powerful queries that can construct powerful data models and ad hoc tables, graphs, and alerts

Also, Promethus is 100% open source and is (as of July 2018) currently an incubating project in the CNCF. You can install it with Helm as we did with other software, or do a manual installation as we'll detail here. Part of the reason that we're going to look at Prometheus today is due to the overall complexity of the Kubernetes system. With lots of moving parts, many servers, and potentially differing geographic regions, we need a system that can cope with all of that complexity.

A nice part about Prometheus is the pull nature, which allows you to focus on exposing metrics on your nodes as plain text via HTTP, which Prometheus can then pull back to a central monitoring and logging location. It's also written in Go and inspired by the closed source Borgmon system, which makes it a perfect match for our Kubernetes cluster. Let's get started with an install!

Prometheus installation choices

As with previous examples, we'll need to either use our local Minikube install or the GCP cluster that we've spun up. Log in to your cluster of choice, and then let's get Prometheus set up. There's actually lots of options for installing Prometheus due to the fast moving nature of the software:

- The simplest, manual method; if you'd like to build the software from the getting started documents, you can jump in with `https://prometheus.io/docs/prometheus/latest/getting_started/` and get Prometheus monitoring itself.
- The middle ground, with Helm; if you'd like to take the middle road, you can install Prometheus on your cluster with Helm (`https://github.com/helm/charts/tree/master/stable/prometheus`).
- The advanced `Operator` method; if you want to use the latest and greatest, let's take a look at the Kubernetes `Operator` class of software, and use it to install Prometheus. The `Operator` was created by CoreOS, who have recently been acquired by Red Hat. That should mean interesting things for Project Atomic and Container Linux. We'll talk more about that later, however! We'll use the Operator model here.

 The Operator is designed to build upon the Helm-style management of software in order to build additional human operational knowledge into the installation, maintenance, and recovery of applications. You can think of the Operator software just like an SRE Operator: someone who's an expert in running a piece of software.

An Operator is an application-specific controller that extends the Kubernetes API in order to manage complex stateful applications such as caches, monitoring systems, and relational or non-relational databases. The Operator uses the API in order to create, configure, and manage these stateful systems on behalf of the user. While Deployments are excellent in dealing with seamless management of stateless web applications, the Deployment object in Kubernetes struggles to orchestrate all of the moving pieces in a stateful application when it comes to scaling, upgrading, recovering from failure, and reconfiguring these systems.

 You can read more about extending the Kubernetes API here: `https://kubernetes.io/docs/concepts/extend-kubernetes/api-extension/`.

Operators leverage some core Kubernetes concepts that we've discussed in other chapters. Resources (ReplicaSets) and Controllers (for example Deployments, Services, and DaemonSets) are leverage with additional operational knowledge of the manual steps that are encoded in the Operator software. For example, when you scale up an etcd cluster manually, one of the key steps in the process is to create a DNS name for the new etcd member that can be used to route to the new member once it's been added to the cluster. With the Operator pattern being used, that systematized knowledge is built into the `Operator` class to provide the cluster administrator with seamless updates to the etcd software.

The difficulty in creating operators is understanding the underlying functionality of the stateful software in question, and then encoding that into a resource configuration and control loop. Keep in mind that Kubernetes can be thought of as simply being a large distributed messaging queue, with messages that exist in the form of a YAML blob of declarative state that the cluster operator defines, which the Kubernetes system puts into place.

Tips for creating an Operator

If you want to create your own `Operator` in the future, you can keep the following tips from CoreOS in mind. Given the nature of their application-specific domain, you'll need to keep a few things in mind when managing complex applications. First, you'll have a set of system flow activities that your `Operator` should be able to perform. This will be actions such as creating a user, creating a database, modifying user permissions and passwords, and deleting users (such as the default user installed when creating many systems).

You'll also need to manage your installation dependencies, which are the items that need to be present and configured for your system to work in the first place. CoreOS also recommends the following principles be followed when creating an `Operator`:

- **Single step to deploy**: Make sure your `Operator` can be initialized and run with a single command that takes no additional work to get running.
- **New third-party type**: Your `Operator` should leverage the third-party API types, which users will take advantage of when creating applications that use your software.
- **Use the basics**: Make sure that your `Operator` uses the core Kubernetes objects such as ReplicaSets, Services, and StatefulSets, in order to leverage all of the hard work being poured into the open source Kubernetes project.
- **Compatible and default working**: Make sure you build your `Operators` so that they exist in harmony with older versions, and design your system so that it still continues to run unaffected if the `Operator` is stopped or accidentally deleted from your cluster.
- **Version**: Make sure to facilitate the ability to version instances of your `Operator`, so cluster administrators don't shy away from updating your software.
- **Test**: Also, make sure to test your `Operator` against a destructive force such as a Chaos Monkey! Your `Operator` should be able to survive the failure of nodes, pods, storage, configuration, and networking outages.

Installing Prometheus

Let's run through an install of Prometheus using the new pattern that we've discovered. First, let's use the Prometheus definition file to create the deployment. We'll use Helm here to install the Operator!

Make sure you have Helm installed, and then make sure you've initialized it:

```
$ helm init
master $ helm init
Creating /root/.helm
. . .
Adding stable repo with URL:
https://kubernetes-charts.storage.googleapis.com
Adding local repo with URL: http://127.0.0.1:8879/charts
$HELM_HOME has been configured at /root/.helm.
. . .
Happy Helming!
$
```

Next, we can install the various `Operator` packages required for this demo:

```
$ helm repo add coreos
https://s3-eu-west-1.amazonaws.com/coreos-charts/stable/
"coreos" has been added to your repositories
```

Now, install the `Operator`:

```
$ helm install coreos/prometheus-operator --name prometheus-operator
```

You can see that it's installed and running by first checking the installation:

```
$ helm ls prometheus-operator
NAME                     REVISION UPDATED                     STATUS
CHART NAMESPACE
prometheus-operator     1 Mon Jul 23 02:10:18 2018          DEPLOYED
prometheus-operator-0.0.28 default
```

Then, look at the pods:

```
$ kubectl get pods
NAME READY STATUS RESTARTS AGE
prometheus-operator-d75587d6-bmmvx 1/1 Running 0 2m
```

Now, we can install `kube-prometheus` to get all of our dependencies up and running:

```
$ helm install coreos/kube-prometheus --name kube-prometheus --set
global.rbacEnable=true
NAME:   kube-prometheus
LAST DEPLOYED: Mon Jul 23 02:15:59 2018
NAMESPACE: default
STATUS: DEPLOYED

RESOURCES:
==> v1/Alertmanager
NAME            AGE
kube-prometheus  1s

==> v1/Pod(related)
NAME                                              READY STATUS RESTARTS
AGE
kube-prometheus-exporter-node-45rwl               0/1 ContainerCreating
0 1s
kube-prometheus-exporter-node-d84mp               0/1 ContainerCreating
0 1s
kube-prometheus-exporter-kube-state-844bb6f589-z58b6 0/2 ContainerCreating
0 1s
kube-prometheus-grafana-57d5b4d79f-mgqw5          0/2 ContainerCreating
0 1s
```

```
==> v1beta1/ClusterRoleBinding
NAME                                          AGE
psp-kube-prometheus-alertmanager              1s
kube-prometheus-exporter-kube-state           1s
psp-kube-prometheus-exporter-kube-state       1s
psp-kube-prometheus-exporter-node             1s
psp-kube-prometheus-grafana                   1s
kube-prometheus                               1s
psp-kube-prometheus                           1s
...
```

We've truncated the output here as there's a lot of information. Let's look at the pods again:

```
$ kubectl get pods
NAME                                                        READY STATUS
RESTARTS AGE
alertmanager-kube-prometheus-0                              2/2 Running 0 3m
kube-prometheus-exporter-kube-state-85975c8577-vf16t        2/2
Running 0 2m
kube-prometheus-exporter-node-45rwl                         1/1 Running 0 3m
kube-prometheus-exporter-node-d84mp                         1/1 Running 0 3m
kube-prometheus-grafana-57d5b4d79f-mgqw5                    2/2 Running 0 3m
prometheus-kube-prometheus-0                                3/3 Running 1 3m
prometheus-operator-d75587d6-bmmvx                          1/1 Running 0 8m
```

Nicely done!

If you forward the port for `prometheus-kube-prometheus-0` to `8448`, you should be able to see the Prometheus dashboard, which we'll revisit in later chapters as we explore high availability and the productionalization of your Kubernetes cluster. You can check this out at `http://localhost:8449/alerts`.

Summary

We took a quick look at monitoring and logging with Kubernetes. You should now be familiar with how Kubernetes uses cAdvisor and Heapster to collect metrics on all the resources in a given cluster. Furthermore, we saw how Kubernetes saves us time by providing InfluxDB and Grafana set up and configured out of the box. Dashboards are easily customizable for our everyday operational needs.

In addition, we looked at the built-in logging capabilities with FluentD and the Google Cloud Logging service. Also, Kubernetes gives us great time savings by setting up the basics for us.

Finally, you learned about the various third-party options available to monitor our containers and clusters. Using these tools will allow us to gain even more insight into the health and status of our applications. All these tools combine to give us a solid toolset to manage day-to-day operations. Lastly, we explored different methods of installing Prometheus, with an eye on building more robust production systems.

8
Monitoring, Logging, and Troubleshooting

In `Chapter 10`, *Creating Kubernetes Clusters,* you learned how to create Kubernetes clusters in different environments, experimented with different tools, and created a couple of clusters.

Creating a Kubernetes cluster is just the beginning of the story. Once the cluster is up and running, you need to make sure that it is operational, all the necessary components are in place and properly configured, and enough resources are deployed to satisfy the requirements. Responding to failures, debugging, and troubleshooting is a major part of managing any complicated system, and Kubernetes is no exception.

The following topics will be covered in this chapter:

- Monitoring with Heapster
- Performance analytics with Kubernetes dashboard
- Central logging
- Detecting problems at the node level
- Troubleshooting scenarios
- Using Prometheus

At the end of this chapter, you will have a solid understanding of the various options available to monitor Kubernetes clusters, how to access logs, and how to analyze them. You will be able to look at a healthy Kubernetes cluster and verify that everything is OK. You will also be able to look at an unhealthy Kubernetes cluster and methodically diagnose it, locate the problems, and address them.

Monitoring Kubernetes with Heapster

Heapster is a Kubernetes project that provides a robust monitoring solution for Kubernetes clusters. It runs as a pod (of course), so it can be managed by Kubernetes itself. Heapster supports Kubernetes and CoreOS clusters. It has a very modular and flexible design. Heapster collects both operational metrics and events from every node in the cluster, stores them in a persistent backend (with a well-defined schema), and allows visualization and programmatic access. Heapster can be configured to use different backends (or sinks, in Heapster's parlance) and their corresponding visualization frontends. The most common combination is InfluxDB as the backend and Grafana as the frontend. The Google Cloud Platform integrates Heapster with the Google monitoring service. There are many other less common backends, as follows:

- Log
- Google Cloud monitoring
- Google Cloud logging
- Hawkular-Metrics (metrics only)
- OpenTSDB
- Monasca (metrics only)
- Kafka (metrics only)
- Riemann (metrics only)
- Elasticsearch

You can use multiple backends by specifying sinks on the command line:

```
--sink=log --sink=influxdb:http://monitoring-influxdb:80/
```

cAdvisor

cAdvisor is part of the kubelet, which runs on every node. It collects information about the CPU/cores' usage, memory, network, and filesystems of each container. It provides a basic UI on port 4194, but, most importantly for Heapster, it provides all this information through the Kubelet. Heapster records the information collected by cAdvisor on each node and stores it in its backend for analysis and visualization.

The cAdvisor UI is useful if you want to quickly verify that a particular node is set up correctly, for example, while creating a new cluster when Heapster is not hooked up yet.

Here is what it looks like:

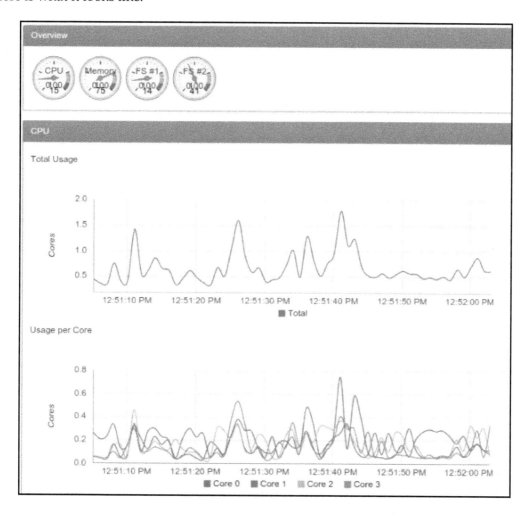

Installing Heapster

Heapster components may or may not be installed in your Kubernetes cluster. If Heapster is not installed, you can install it with a few simple commands. First, let's clone the Heapster repo:

```
> git clone https://github.com/kubernetes/heapster.git
> cd heapster
```

In earlier versions of Kubernetes, Heapster exposed the services as `NodePort` by default. Now, they are exposed by default as `ClusterIP`, which means that they are available only inside the cluster. To make them available locally, I added type: `NodePort` to the spec of each service in `deploy/kube-config/influxdb`. For example, for `deploy/kube-config/influxdb/influxdb.yaml`:

```
> git diff deploy/kube-config/influxdb/influxdb.yaml
diff --git a/deploy/kube-config/influxdb/influxdb.yaml b/deploy/kube-config/influxdb/influxdb.yaml
index 29408b81..70f52d2c 100644
--- a/deploy/kube-config/influxdb/influxdb.yaml
+++ b/deploy/kube-config/influxdb/influxdb.yaml
@@ -33,6 +33,7 @@ metadata:
   name: monitoring-influxdb
   namespace: kube-system
 spec:
+ type: NodePort
 ports:
 - port: 8086
   targetPort: 8086
```

I made a similar change to `deploy/kube-config/influxdb/grafana.yaml`, which has + type: `NodePort` this line commented out, so I just uncommented it. Now, we can actually install InfluxDB and Grafana:

```
> kubectl create -f deploy/kube-config/influxdb
```

You should see the following output:

```
deployment "monitoring-grafana" created
service "monitoring-grafana" created
serviceaccount "heapster" created
deployment "heapster" created
service "heapster" created
deployment "monitoring-influxdb" created
service "monitoring-influxdb" created
```

InfluxDB backend

InfluxDB is a modern and robust distributed time-series database. It is very well-suited and used broadly for centralized metrics and logging. It is also the preferred Heapster backend (outside the Google Cloud Platform). The only thing is InfluxDB clustering; high availability is part of enterprise offering.

The storage schema

The InfluxDB storage schema defines the information that Heapster stores in InfluxDB, and it is available for querying and graphing later. The metrics are divided into multiple categories, named measurements. You can treat and query each metric separately, or you can query a whole category as one measurement and receive the individual metrics as fields. The naming convention is <category>/<metrics name> (except for uptime, which has a single metric). If you have an SQL background, you can think of measurements as tables. Each metric is stored per container. Each metric is labeled with the following information:

- pod_id: A unique ID of a pod
- pod_name: A user-provided name of a pod
- pod_namespace: The namespace of a pod
- container_base_image: A base image for the container
- container_name: A user-provided name of the container or full cgroup name for system containers
- host_id: A cloud-provider-specified or user-specified identifier of a node
- hostname: The hostname where the container ran
- labels: The comma-separated list of user-provided labels; format is key:value
- namespace_id: The UID of the namespace of a pod
- resource_id: A unique identifier used to differentiate multiple metrics of the same type, for example, FS partitions under filesystem/usage

Here are all the metrics grouped by category, as you can see, it is quite extensive.

CPU

The CPU metrics are:

- cpu/limit: CPU hard limit in millicores
- cpu/node_capacity: CPU capacity of a node
- cpu/node_allocatable: CPU allocatable of a node
- cpu/node_reservation: Share of CPU that is reserved on the node allocatable
- cpu/node_utilization: CPU utilization as a share of node allocatable

- `cpu/request`: CPU request (the guaranteed amount of resources) in millicores
- `cpu/usage`: Cumulative CPU usage on all cores
- `cpu/usage_rate`: CPU usage on all cores in millicores

Filesystem

The Filesystem metrics are:

- `filesystem/usage`: The total number of bytes consumed on a filesystem
- `filesystem/limit`: The total size of the filesystem in bytes
- `filesystem/available`: The number of available bytes remaining in the filesystem

Memory

The memory metrics are:

- `memory/limit`: Memory hard limit in bytes
- `memory/major_page_faults`: The number of major page faults
- `memory/major_page_faults_rate`: The number of major page faults per second
- `memory/node_capacity`: Memory capacity of a node
- `memory/node_allocatable`: Memory allocatable of a node
- `memory/node_reservation`: Share of memory that is reserved on the node allocatable
- `memory/node_utilization`: Memory utilization as a share of memory allocatable
- `memory/page_faults`: The number of page faults
- `memory/page_faults_rate`: The number of page faults per second
- `memory/request`: Memory request (the guaranteed amount of resources) in bytes
- `memory/usage`: Total memory usage
- `memory/working_set`: Total working set usage; working set is the memory being used and is not easily dropped by the kernel

Network

The network metrics are:

- `network/rx`: Cumulative number of bytes received over the network
- `network/rx_errors`: Cumulative number of errors while receiving over the network
- `network/rx_errors_rate`: The number of errors per second while receiving over the network
- `network/rx_rate`: The number of bytes received over the network per second
- `network/tx`: Cumulative number of bytes sent over the network
- `network/tx_errors`: Cumulative number of errors while sending over the network
- `network/tx_errors_rate`: The number of errors while sending over the network
- `network/tx_rate`: The number of bytes sent over the network per second

Uptime

Uptime is the number of milliseconds since the container was started.

You can work with InfluxDB directly if you're familiar with it. You can either connect to it using its own API or use its web interface. Type the following command to find its port and endpoint:

```
> k describe service monitoring-influxdb --namespace=kube-system | grep
NodePort
Type:              NodePort
NodePort:          <unset>   32699/TCP
```

Now, you can browse the InfluxDB web interface using the HTTP port. You'll need to configure it to point to the API port. The `Username` and `Password` are `root` and `root` by default:

Once you're set up, you can select what database to use (see the top-right corner). The Kubernetes database is named `k8s`. You can now query the metrics using the InfluxDB query language.

Grafana visualization

Grafana runs in its own container and serves a sophisticated dashboard that works well with InfluxDB as a data source. To locate the port, type the following command:

```
k describe service monitoring-influxdb --namespace=kube-system | grep
NodePort
Type:             NodePort
NodePort:         <unset> 30763/TCP
```

Now, you can access the Grafana web interface on that port. The first thing you need to do is set up the data source to point to the InfluxDB backend:

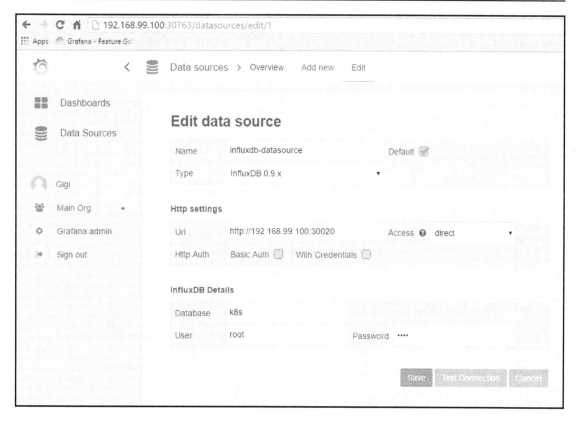

Make sure to test the connection and then go explore the various options in the dashboards. There are several default dashboards, but you should be able to customize them to your preferences. Grafana is designed to let you adapt it to your needs.

Performance analysis with the dashboard

My favorite tool by far, when I just want to know what's going on in the cluster, is the Kubernetes dashboard. There are a couple of reasons for this, as follows:

- It is built-in (always in sync and tested with Kubernetes)
- It's fast
- It provides an intuitive drill-down interface, from the cluster level all the way down to individual container
- It doesn't require any customization or configuration

Although Heapster, InfluxDB, and Grafana are better for customized and heavy-duty views and queries, the Kubernetes dashboard's predefined views can probably answer all your questions 80-90% of the time.

You can also deploy applications and create any Kubernetes resource using the dashboard by uploading the proper YAML or JSON file, but I will not cover this because it is an anti-pattern for manageable infrastructure. It may be useful when playing around with a test cluster, but for actually modifying the state of the cluster, I prefer the command line. Your mileage may vary.

Let's find the port first:

```
k describe service kubernetes-dashboard --namespace=kube-system | grep
NodePort
Type:                    NodePort
NodePort:                <unset> 30000/TCP
```

Top-level view

The dashboard is organized with a hierarchical view on the left (it can be hidden by clicking the hamburger menu) and dynamic, context-based content on the right. You can drill down into the hierarchical view to get deeper into the information that's relevant.

There are several top-level categories:

- Cluster
- Overview
- Workloads
- Discovery and load balancing
- Config and storage

You can also filter everything by a particular namespace or choose all namespaces.

Cluster

The Cluster view has five sections: **Namespaces**, **Nodes**, **PersistentVolumes**, **Roles**, and **Storage Classes**. It is mostly about observing the physical resources of the cluster:

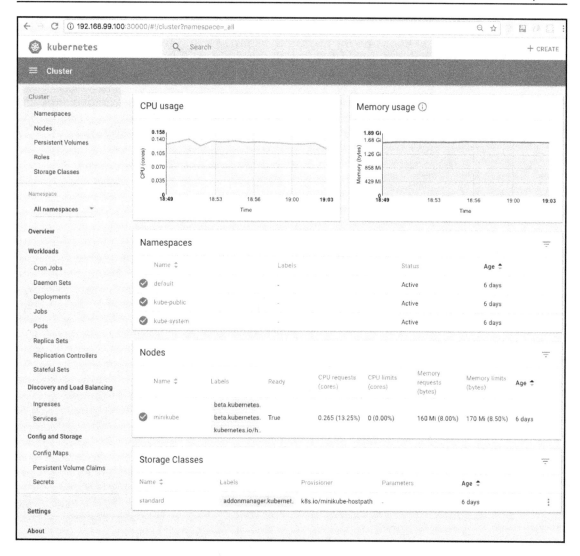

You get, in a glance, a lot of information: CPU and memory usage of all the nodes, what namespaces are available, their **Status**, and **Age**. For each node, you can see its **Age**, **Labels**, and if it's ready or not. If there were persistent volumes and roles, you would see them as well, then the storage classes (just host path in this case).

If we drill down the nodes and click on the **minikube** node itself, we get a detailed screen of information about that node and the allocated resources in a nice pie chart. This is critical for dealing with performance issues. If a node doesn't have enough resources, then it might not be able to satisfy the needs of its pods:

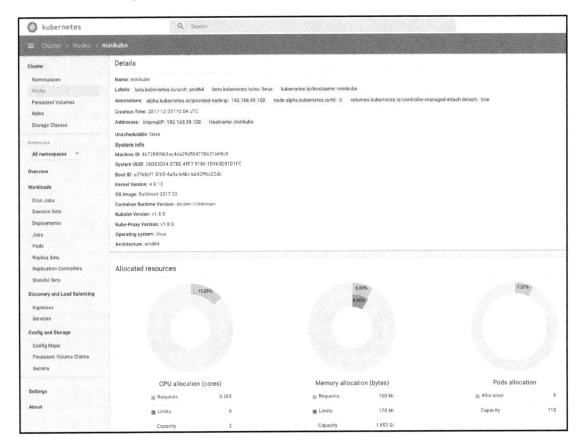

If you scroll down, you'll see even more interesting information. The **Conditions** pane is where it's at. You get a great, concise view of memory and disk pressure at the individual node level:

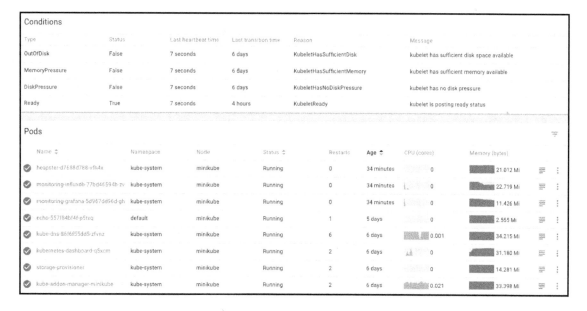

There are also **Pods** and **Events** panes. We'll talk about pods in the next section.

Workloads

The Workloads category is the main one. It organizes many types of Kubernetes resources, such as **CronJobs**, **Daemon Sets**, **Deployments**, **Jobs**, **Pods**, **Replica Sets**, **Replication Controllers**, and **Stateful Sets**. You can drill down along any of these dimensions. Here is the top-level Workloads view for the default namespace that currently has only the echo service deployed. You can see the **Deployments**, **Replica Sets**, and **Pods**:

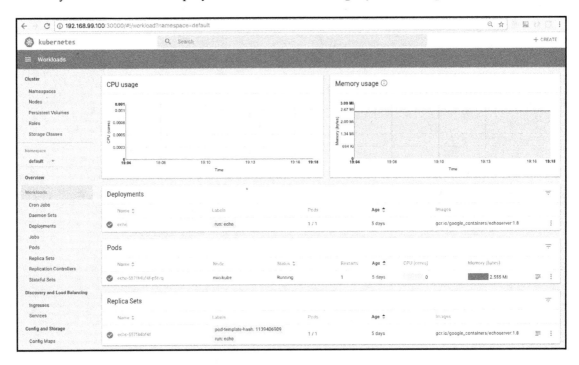

Let's switch to all namespaces and dive into the **Pods** subcategory. This is a very useful view. In each row, you can tell if the pod is running or not, how many times it restarted, its IP, and the CPU and memory usage histories are even embedded as nice little graphs:

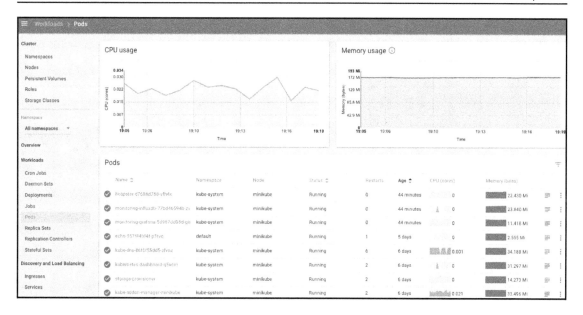

You can also view the **Logs** for any pod by clicking the text symbol (second from the right). Let's check the **Logs** of the InfluxDB pod. It looks like everything is in order and Heapster is successfully writing to it:

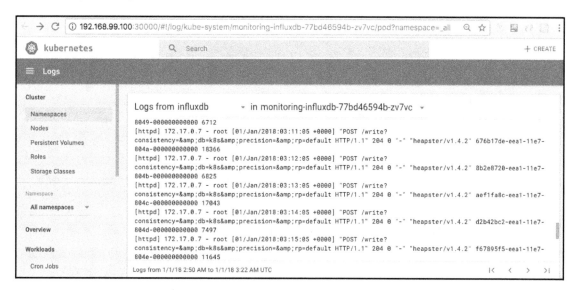

There is one more level of detail that we haven't explored yet. We can go down to the container level. Let's click on the **kubedns** pod. We get the following screen, which shows the individual containers and their `run` command; we can also view their logs:

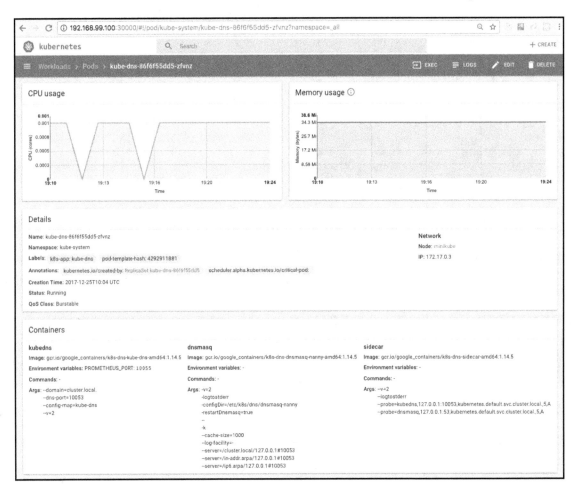

Discovery and load balancing

The discovery and load balancing category is often where you start from. **Services** are the public interface to your Kubernetes cluster. Serious problems will affect your services, which will affect your users:

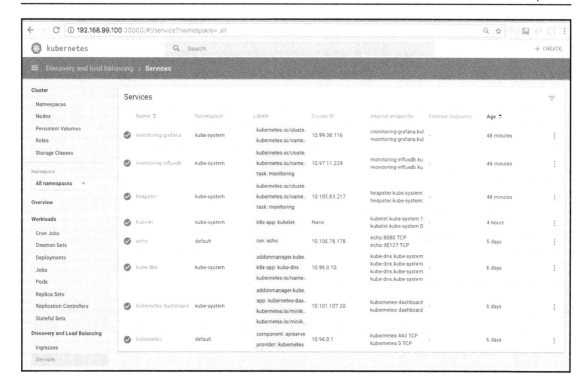

When you drill down by clicking on a service, you get some information about the service (most important is the label selector) and a pods view.

Adding central logging

Central logging or cluster-level logging is a fundamental requirement for any cluster with more than a couple of nodes, pods, or containers. First, it is impractical to view the logs of each pod or container independently. You can't get a global picture of the system, and there will be just too many messages to sift through. You need a solution that aggregates the log messages and lets you slice and dice them easily. The second reason is that containers are ephemeral. Problematic pods will often just die, and their replication controller or replica set will just start a new instance, losing all the important log info. By logging to a central logging service, you preserve this critical troubleshooting information.

Planning central logging

Conceptually, central logging is very simple. On each node, you run a dedicated agent that intercepts all log messages from all the pods and containers on the node, and sends them, along with enough metadata, to a central repository where they are stored safely.

As usual, if you run on the Google platform, then GKE's got you covered, and there is a Google central-logging service integrated nicely. For other platforms, a popular solution is fluentd, Elasticsearch, and Kibana. There is an official add-on to set up the proper services for each component. The `fluentd-elasticsearch` add-on is at `http://bit.ly/2f6MF5b`.

It is installed as a set of services for Elasticsearch and Kibana, and the fluentd agent is installed on each node.

Fluentd

Fluentd is a unified logging layer that sits between arbitrary data sources and arbitrary data sinks and makes sure that log messages can stream from A to B. Kubernetes comes with an add-on that has a Docker image that deploys the fluentd agent, which knows how to read various logs that are relevant to Kubernetes, such as `Docker` logs, `etcd` logs, and `Kube` logs. It also adds labels to each log message to make it easy for users to filter later by label. Here is a snippet from the `fluentd-es-configmap.yaml` file:

```
# Example:
# 2016/02/04 06:52:38 filePurge: successfully removed file
/var/etcd/data/member/wal/00000000000006d0-00000000010a23d1.wal
<source>
  type tail
  # Not parsing this, because it doesn't have anything particularly
useful to
  # parse out of it (like severities).
  format none
  path /var/log/etcd.log
  pos_file /var/log/es-etcd.log.pos
  tag etcd
</source>
```

Elasticsearch

Elasticsearch is a great document store and full-text search engine. It is a favorite in the enterprise because it is very fast, reliable, and scalable. It is used in the Kubernetes central logging add-on as a Docker image, and it is deployed as a service. Note that a fully-fledged production cluster of Elasticsearch (which will be deployed on a Kubernetes cluster) requires its own master, client, and data nodes. For large-scale and highly-available Kubernetes clusters, the central logging itself will be clustered. Elasticsearch can use self-discovery. Here is an enterprise grade solution: `https://github.com/pires/kubernetes-elasticsearch-cluster`.

Kibana

Kibana is Elasticsearch's partner in crime. It is used to visualize and interact with the data stored and indexed by Elasticsearch. It is also installed as a service by the add-on. Here is the Kibana Dockerfile template (`http://bit.ly/2lwmtpc`).

Detecting node problems

In Kubernetes' conceptual model, the unit of work is the pod. However, pods are scheduled on nodes. When it comes to monitoring and reliability, the nodes are what require the most attention, because Kubernetes itself (the scheduler and replication controllers) takes care of the pods. Nodes can suffer from a variety of problems that Kubernetes is unaware of. As a result, it will keep scheduling pods to the bad nodes and the pods might fail to function properly. Here are some of the problems that nodes may suffer while still appearing functional:

- Bad CPU
- Bad memory
- Bad disk
- Kernel deadlock
- Corrupt filesystem
- Problems with the Docker daemon

The kubelet and cAdvisor don't detect these issues, another solution is needed. Enter the node problem detector.

Node problem detector

The node problem detector is a pod that runs on every node. It needs to solve a difficult problem. It needs to detect various problems across different environments, different hardware, and different OSes. It needs to be reliable enough not to be affected itself (otherwise, it can't report the problem), and it needs to have relatively-low overhead to avoid spamming the master. In addition, it needs to run on every node. Kubernetes recently received a new capability named DaemonSet that addresses that last concern.

The source code is at `https://github.com/kubernetes/node-problem-detector`.

DaemonSet

DaemonSet is a pod for every node. Once you define DaemonSet, every node that's added to the cluster automatically gets a pod. If that pod dies, Kubernetes will start another instance of that pod on that node. Think about it as a fancy replication controller with 1:1 node-pod affinity. Node problem detector is defined as a DaemonSet, which is a perfect match for its requirements. It is possible to use affinity, anti-affinity, and taints to have more fine-grained control over DaemonSet scheduling.

Problem daemons

The problem with node problem detector (pun intended) is that there are too many problems which it needs to handle. Trying to cram all of them into a single codebase can lead to a complex, bloated, and never-stabilizing codebase. The design of the node problem detector calls for separation of the core functionality of reporting node problems to the master from the specific problem detection. The reporting API is based on generic conditions and events. The problem detection should be done by separate problem daemons (each in its own container). This way, it is possible to add and evolve new problem detectors without impacting the core node problem detector. In addition, the control plane may have a remedy controller that can resolve some node problems automatically, therefore implementing self-healing.

 At this stage (Kubernetes 1.10), problem daemons are baked into the node problem detector binary, and they execute as Goroutines, so you don't get the benefits of the loosely-coupled design just yet.

In this section, we covered the important topic of node problems, which can get in the way of successful scheduling of workloads, and how the node problem detector can help. In the next section, we'll talk about various failure scenarios and how to troubleshoot them using Heapster, central logging, the Kubernetes dashboard, and node problem detector.

Troubleshooting scenarios

There are so many things that can go wrong in a large Kubernetes cluster, and they will, this is expected. You can employ best practices and minimize some of them (mostly human errors) using stricter processes. However, some issues such as hardware failures and networking issues can't be totally avoided. Even human errors should not always be minimized if it means slower development time. In this section, we'll discuss various categories of failures, how to detect them, how to evaluate their impact, and consider the proper response.

Designing robust systems

When you want to design a robust system, you first need to understand the possible failure modes, the risk/probability of each failure, and the impact/cost of each failure. Then, you can consider various prevention and mitigation measures, loss-cutting strategies, incident-management strategies, and recovery procedures. Finally, you can come up with a plan that matches risks to mitigation profiles, including cost. A comprehensive design is important and needs to be updated as the system evolves. The higher the stakes, the more thorough your plan should be. This process has to be tailored for each organization. A corner of error recovery and robustness is detecting failures and being able to troubleshoot. The following subsections describe common failure categories, how to detect them, and where to collect additional information.

Hardware failure

Hardware failures in Kubernetes can be divided into two groups:

- The node is unresponsive
- The node is responsive

When the node is not responsive, it can be difficult sometimes to determine if it's a networking issue, a configuration issue, or actual hardware failure. You obviously can't use any information like logs or run diagnostics on the node itself. What can you do? First, consider if the node was ever responsive. If it's a node that was just added to the cluster, it is more likely a configuration issue. If it's a node that was part of the cluster then you can look at historical data from the node on Heapster or central logging and see if you detect any errors in the logs or degradation in performance that may indicate failing hardware.

When the node is responsive, it may still suffer from the failure of redundant hardware, such as non-OS disk or some cores. You can detect the hardware failure if the node problem detector is running on the node and raises some event or node condition to the attention of master. Alternatively, you may note that pods keep getting restarted or jobs take longer to complete. All of these may be signs of hardware failure. Another strong hint for hardware failure is if the problems are isolated to a single node and standard maintenance operations such as reboot don't alleviate the symptoms.

If your cluster is deployed in the cloud, replacing a node which you suspect as having hardware problems is trivial. It is simple to just manually provision a new VM and remove the bad VM. In some cases, you may want to employ a more automated process and employ a remedy controller, as suggested by the node problem detector design. Your remedy controller will listen to problems (or missing health checks) and can automatically replace bad nodes. This approach can work even for private hosting or bare metal if you keep a pool of extra nodes ready to kick in. Large-scale clusters can function just fine, even with reduced capacity most of the time. Either you can tolerate slightly reduced capacity when a small number of nodes are down, or you can over-provision a little bit. This way, you have some headway when a node goes down.

Quotas, shares, and limits

Kubernetes is a multitenant system. It is designed to use resources efficiently, but it schedules pods and allocates resources based on a system of checks and balances between available quotas and limits per namespace, and requests for guaranteed resources from pods and containers. We will dive into the details later in the book. Here, we'll just consider what can go wrong and how to detect it. There are several bad outcomes you can run into:

- **Insufficient resources**: If a pod requires a certain amount of CPU or memory, and there is no node with available capacity, then the pod can't be scheduled.
- **Under-utilization**: A pod may declare that it requires a certain amount of CPU or memory, and Kubernetes will oblige, but then the pod may only use a small percentage of its requested resources. This is just wasteful.

- **Mismatched node configuration**: A pod that requires a lot of CPU but very little memory may be scheduled to a high-memory node and use all its CPU resources, thereby hogging the node, so no other pod can be scheduled but the unused memory is wasted.

Checking out the dashboard is a great way to look for suspects visually. Nodes and pods that are either over-subscribed or under-utilized are candidates for quota and resource request mismatches:

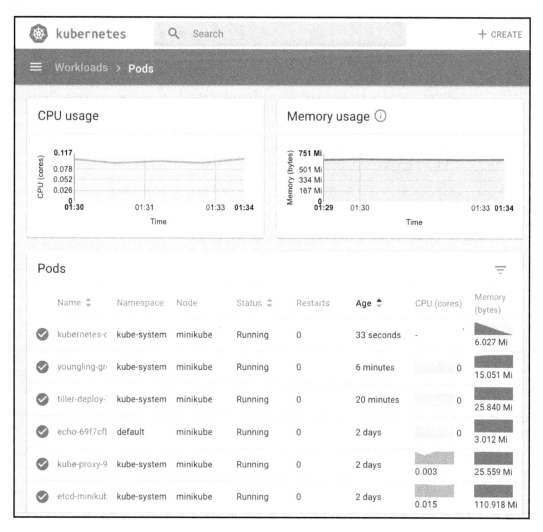

Once you detect a candidate, you can dive into using the `describe` command at the node or pod level. In a large-scale cluster, you should have automated checks that compare the utilization against capacity planning. This is important because most large systems have some level of fluctuation and a uniform load is not expected. Make sure that you understand the demands on your system and that your cluster's capacity is within the normal range or can adjust elastically, as needed.

Bad configuration

Bad configuration is an umbrella term. Your Kubernetes cluster state is configuration; your containers' command-line arguments are configuration; all the environment variables used by Kubernetes, your application services, and any third-party services are configuration; and all the configuration files are configuration. In some data-driven systems, configuration is stored in various data stores. Configuration issues are very common because, usually, there aren't any established good practices to test them. They often have various fallbacks (for example, search path for configuration files) and defaults, and the production-environment configuration is different to the development or staging environment.

At the Kubernetes cluster level, there are many possible configuration problems, as follows:

- Incorrect labeling of nodes, pods, or containers
- Scheduling pods without a replication controller
- Incorrect specification of ports for services
- Incorrect ConfigMap

Most of these problems can be addressed by having a proper automated deployment process, but you must have a deep understanding of your cluster architecture and how Kubernetes resources fit together.

Configuration problems typically occur after you change something. It is critical, after each deployment or manual change to the cluster, to verify its state.

Heapster and the dashboard are great options here. I suggest starting from the services and verifying that they are available, responsive, and functional. Then, you can dive deeper and verify that the system also operates within the expected performance parameters.

The logs also provide helpful hints and can pinpoint specific configuration options.

Cost versus performance

Large clusters are not cheap. This is especially true if you run in the cloud. A major part of operating massive-scale systems is keeping track of the expense.

Managing cost on the cloud

One of the greatest benefits of the cloud is that it can satisfy elastic demand that caters for systems that expand and contract automatically by allocating and deallocating resources as needed. Kubernetes fits this model very well and can be extended to provision more nodes as necessary. The risk here is that, if not constrained properly, a denial-of-service attack (malicious, accidental, or self-inflicted) can lead to arbitrary provisioning of expensive resources. This needs to be monitored carefully, so it can be caught early on. Quotas on namespaces can avoid it, but you still need to be able to dive in and pinpoint the core issue. The root cause can be external (a botnet attack), misconfiguration, an internal test gone awry, or a bug in the code that detects or allocate resources.

Managing cost on bare metal

On bare metal, you typically don't have to worry about runaway allocation, but you can easily run into a wall if you need extra capacity and can't provision more resources fast enough. Capacity planning and monitoring your system's performance to detect the need early are primary concerns for OPS. Heapster can show historical trends and help identify both peak times and overall growth in demand.

Managing cost on hybrid clusters

Hybrid clusters run on both bare metal and the cloud (and possibly on private hosting services too). The considerations are similar, but you may need to aggregate your analysis. We will discuss hybrid clusters in more detail later.

Using Prometheus

Heapster and the default monitoring and logging that come in the box with Kubernetes are a great starting point. However, the Kubernetes community is bursting with innovation and several alternative solutions are available. One of the most popular solutions is Prometheus. In this section, we will explore the new world of operators, the Prometheus Operator, how to install it, and how to use it to monitor your cluster.

What are operators?

Operators are a new class of software that encapsulates the operational knowledge needed to develop, manage, and maintain applications on top of Kubernetes. The term was introduced by CoreOS in late 2016. An operator is an application-specific controller that extends the Kubernetes API to create, configure, and manage instances of complex stateful applications on behalf of a Kubernetes user. It builds upon the basic Kubernetes resource and controller concepts, but includes domain or application-specific knowledge to automate common tasks.

The Prometheus Operator

Prometheus (`https://prometheus.io`) is an open source systems monitoring and alerting toolkit for monitoring applications in clusters. It was inspired by Google's Borgmon and designed for the Kubernetes model of assigning and scheduling units of work. It joined CNCF in 2016, and it has been adopted widely across the industry. The primary differences between InfluxDB and Prometheus is that Prometheus uses a pull model where anyone can hit the /metrics endpoint, and its query language is very expressive, but simpler than the SQL-like query language of InfluxDB.

Kubernetes has built-in features to support Prometheus metrics, and Prometheus awareness of Kuberneres keeps improving. The Prometheus Operator packages all that monitoring goodness into an easy to install and use bundle.

Installing Prometheus with kube-prometheus

The easiest way to install Prometheus is using kube-prometheus. It uses the Prometheus Operator as well as Grafana for dashboarding and `AlertManager` for managing alerts. To get started, clone the repo and run the `deploy` script:

```
> git clone https://github.com/coreos/prometheus-operator.git
> cd contrib/kube-prometheus
> hack/cluster-monitoring/deploy
```

The script creates a monitoring namespace and lots of Kubernetes entities and supporting components:

- The Prometheus Operator itself
- The Prometheus node_exporter
- kube-state metrics
- A Prometheus configuration covering monitoring of all Kubernetes core components and exporters
- A default set of alerting rules on the cluster components' health
- A Grafana instance serving dashboards on cluster metrics
- A three node highly available Alertmanager cluster

Let's verify that everything is in order:

```
> kg po --namespace=monitoring
NAME                                    READY   STATUS    RESTARTS   AGE
alertmanager-main-0                     2/2     Running   0          1h
alertmanager-main-1                     2/2     Running   0          1h
alertmanager-main-2                     0/2     Pending   0          1h
grafana-7d966ff57-rvpwk                 2/2     Running   0          1h
kube-state-metrics-5dc6c89cd7-s9n4m     2/2     Running   0          1h
node-exporter-vfbhq                     1/1     Running   0          1h
prometheus-k8s-0                        2/2     Running   0          1h
prometheus-k8s-1                        2/2     Running   0          1h
prometheus-operator-66578f9cd9-5t6xw    1/1     Running   0          1h
```

Note that `alertmanager-main-2` is pending. I suspect that this is due to Minikube running on two cores. It is not causing any problem in practice in my setup.

Monitoring your cluster with Prometheus

Once the Prometheus Operator is up and running along with Grafana and the Alertmanager, you can access their UIs and interact with the different components:

- Prometheus UI on node port 30900
- Alertmanager UI on node port 30903
- Grafana on node port 30902

Prometheus supports a dizzying array of metrics to choose from. Here is a screenshot that shows the duration of HTTP requests in microseconds broken down by container:

To limit the view to only the 0.99 quantile for the `prometheus-k8s` service, use the following query:

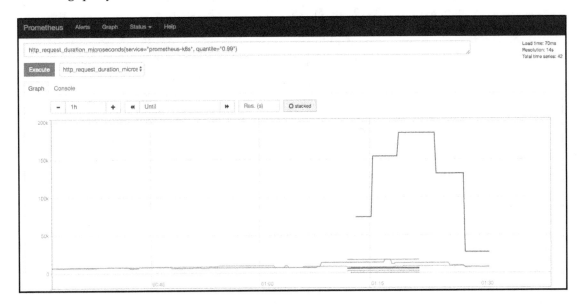

```
http_request_duration_microseconds{service="prometheus-k8s",
quantile="0.99"}
```

The **Alertmanager** is another important part of the Prometheus monitoring story. Here is a screenshot of the web UI that lets you define and configure alerts based on arbitrary metrics.

Summary

In this chapter, we looked at monitoring, logging, and troubleshooting. This is a crucial aspect of operating any system and, in particular, a platform such as Kubernetes with so many moving pieces. My greatest worry, whenever I'm responsible for something, is that something will go wrong and I will have no systematic way to figure out what's wrong and how to fix it. Kubernetes has ample tools and facilities built in, such as Heapster, logging, DaemonSets, and node problem detector. You can also deploy any kind of monitoring solution you prefer.

9
Operating Systems, Platforms, and Cloud and Local Providers

The first half of this chapter will cover how open standards encourage a diverse ecosystem of container implementations. We'll look at the **Open Container Initiative** (**OCI**) and its mission to provide an open container specification as well. The second half of this chapter will cover the various operating systems available for running containerized workloads, such as CoreOS. We'll also look at its advantages as a host OS, including performance and support for various container implementations. Additionally, we'll take a brief look at the Tectonic Enterprise offering from CoreOS. We'll look at the various hosted platforms offered by the major **cloud service providers** (**CSPs**) and see how they stack up.

This chapter will discuss the following topics:

- Why do standards matter?
- The OCI and the **Cloud Native Computing Foundation** (**CNCF**)
- Container specifications versus implementations
- Various container-oriented operating systems
- Tectonic
- The CSP platforms available that can run Kubernetes workloads

Technical requirements

You'll need to have your Google Cloud Platform account enabled and logged in, or you can use a local Minikube instance of Kubernetes. You can also use Play with Kubernetes online at https://labs.play-with-k8s.com/.

You'll also need GitHub credentials, which we'll go over setting up later in the chapter.

The GitHub repository for this chapter can be found at `https://github.com/PacktPublishing/The-Complete-Kubernetes-Guide/tree/master/Chapter09`.

The importance of standards

Over the past two years, containerization technology has had tremendous growth in popularity. While Docker has been at the center of this ecosystem, there is an increasing number of players in the container space. There are already a number of alternatives to the containerization and Docker implementation itself (rkt, Garden, and so on). In addition, there is a rich ecosystem of third-party tools that enhance and complement your container infrastructure. While Kubernetes is designed to manage the state of a container and the orchestration, scheduling, and networking side of this ecosystem, the bottom line is that all of these tools form the basis to build cloud-native applications.

As we mentioned at the very beginning of this book, one of the most attractive things about containers is their ability to package our application for deployment across various environment tiers (that is, development, testing, and production) and various infrastructure providers (GCP, AWS, on-premises, and so on).

To truly support this type of deployment agility, we need not only the containers themselves to have a common platform, but also the underlying specifications to follow a common set of ground rules. This will allow for implementations that are both flexible and highly specialized. For example, some workloads may need to be run on a highly secure implementation. To provide this, the implementation will have to make more intentional decisions about some aspects of the implementation. In either case, we will have more agility and freedom if our containers are built on some common structures that all implementations agree on and support.

In the following pages, we'll explore the building blocks of the many competing standards in the Kubernetes ecosystem. We'll explain how they're changing and developing and what part they may play in the future.

One of the examples that we'll explore more deeply in this third edition is the CRI-O project, which came to be after the creation of the OCI Charter. Let's make sure we understand the importance of that mission.

The OCI Charter

The mission of the OCI Charter is to ensure that the open source community has a stable platform from which industry participants can contribute the portable, open, and vendor-neutral runtimes required to build container-powered applications. The Linux Foundation is the holder of the charter, which is a sister organization to the CNCF.

 If you'd like to read more about these foundations, you can check out their websites here: `https://www.linuxfoundation.org/` and `https://www.cncf.io/`.

While the OCI Charter tries to standardize the building blocks of the ecosystem, it does not attempt to define the system at the macroscopic level, nor does it market a particular pathway or solution. There's also a process defined that helps technology mature in a responsible way through these foundations, to ensure that the best possible technology is reaching the end user. These are defined as the following stages:

1. Sandbox
2. Incubating
3. Graduated

For the specifics of this chapter as regards the OCI, let's look at what else they're trying to accomplish. Firstly, we're attempting to create a format specification. This specification will call out a few important dimensions in order to create a consensus:

- **Provide a format**: In order to ensure a specification that can be used across multiple runtimes, you need a standard container format and runtime specification. The container format is represented by the root filesystem that sits on the disk, with the necessary additional configuration that allows a given container to be run on the system. There is a push to categorize the standardization into the following layers: base, optional, and out of scope.
- **Provide a runtime**: This is more straightforward, as it's designed to provide an executable that can directly run a container via consumption of the aforementioned container format and runtime specification.

The Charter also incentivizes a number of projects, the first two of which are the runc projects, and the third of which involves the definition of its own specifications in the OCI Specification project. New projects are added by members through a review process that needs two-thirds approval from the current **Technical Oversight Board** (**TOB**). If we look deeper into the principles that govern the OCI, the website names six guiding principles:

- Technology leadership
- Influence through contribution
- Limited scope, limited politics
- Minimalist structure
- Representative leadership
- Adherence to anti-trust regulations

These items are a blend of philosophical and logical frameworks that encourage competition, collaboration, meritocracy, and the continuous improvement cycles that many Agile and DevOps practitioners have long utilized.

Let's dig more into the initiative itself now.

The OCI

One of the first initiatives to gain widespread industry engagement is the OCI. Among the 36 industry collaborators are Docker, Red Hat, VMware, IBM, Google, and AWS, as listed on the OCI website at `https://www.opencontainers.org/`.

The purpose of the OCI is to split implementations, such as Docker and rkt, from a standard specification for the format and runtime of containerized workloads. According to their own terms, the goal of the OCI specifications has three basic tenets (you can refer to more details about this in the *Further reading* section at the end of the chapter):

- Creating a formal specification for container image formats and runtime, which will allow a compliant container to be portable across all major, compliant operating systems and platforms without artificial technical barriers.
- Accepting, maintaining, and advancing the projects associated with these standards. It will look to agree on a standard set of container actions (start, exec, pause, and so on), as well as a runtime environment associated with a container runtime.
- Harmonizing the previously referenced standard with other proposed standards, including the appc specification.

By following these principals, the OCI hopes to bolster a collaborative and inclusive ecosystem that provides a rich and evolving toolset to meet the needs of today's complex application workloads, be they cloud-native or traditional.

There are additionally some guiding principles for the development of standards in this space. These principles were integrated from the founding beliefs of the folks who created appc, and are as follows:

- **Security**: Isolate containers via pluggable interfaces using secure cryptographic principles, and a chain of custody for both images and application code.
- **Portability**: Ensure that containers continue to be portable across a wide variety software, clouds, and hardware.
- **Decentralized**: Container images should be straightforward and should take advantage of federation and namespacing.
- **Open**: The runtime and formats should be community-built, with multiple interchangeable parts.
- **Backward compatible**: Given the popularity of Docker and containers with nearly 9 billion downloads, backward compatibility should be given high priority.
- **Composable**: Tools for the operation of containers should be well integrated, but modular.
- **Code**: Consensus should be built from running, working code that follows principles of minimalism that adhere to domain-driven design. It should be stable and extensible.

Container Runtime Interface

Let's look at one of the newer and Kubernetes-specific OCI-based initiatives, CRI-O. CRI-O is currently part of the Kubernetes incubator, but it may move out to its own project as it matures. One of the compelling parts of the CRI-O design is that it never breaks Kubernetes. This is different because other runtimes are designed to do many things, such as building images, managing security, orchestration, and inspecting images. CRI-O is only designed to help Kubernetes orchestrate and schedule containers.

> You can get the code for the CRI-O project and read the documentation at `https://github.com/kubernetes-incubator/cri-o/`.

To this end, CRI-O is developed congruently with the CRI itself, and aligns itself with upstream releases of the Kubernetes system. The following diagram shows how the CRI-O works with the OCI:

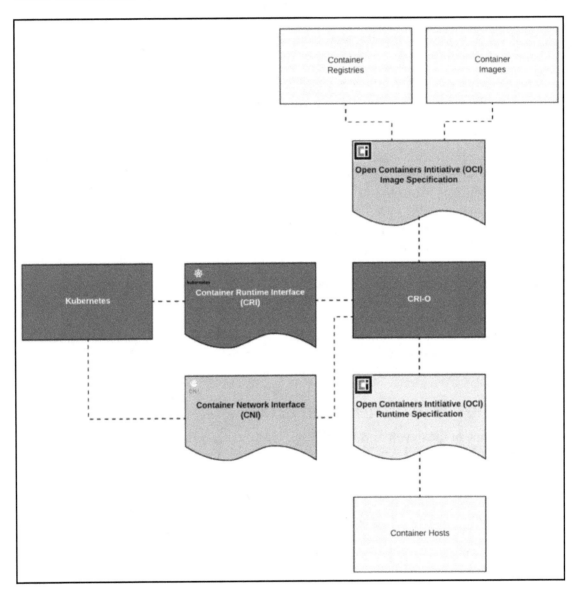

In order to achieve this workflow, the following happens:

1. The operator decides to start a pod, which causes Kubernetes to use the `kubelet` to start a pod. That `kubelet` talks through the CRI to the CRI-O daemon.
2. CRI-O then uses several libraries, built with the OCI standard, to pull and unpack the given container image from a registry. From these operations, CRI-O generates a JSON blob that is used in the next step to run the container.
3. CRI-O kicks off an OCI-compatible runtime, which then runs the container process. This could be runc or the new Kata Container runtime (which has absorbed Intel's clear containers initiative).

You'll notice here that the CRI-O is acting as an interleaving layer between the libraries and runtimes, such that it's using standard formats to accomplish most its goals. This ensures the goal is making Kubernetes work at all times. Here's a diagram showing the system of the flow that was described in this section:

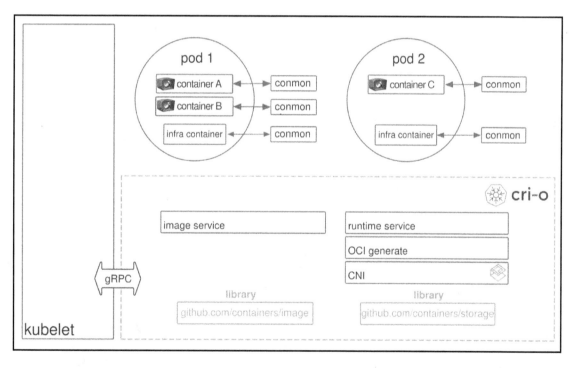

For networking, CRI-O would leverage the **Container Networking Interface (CNI)**, which is similar to the CRI, but deals with the networking stack. You should begin to see a pattern emerge here.

CRI-O is an implementation that helps to implement the OCI specification. This allows users to take for granted the container runtime being used as an implementation detail, and to focus instead on how the application is interacting with the objects and abstractions of the Kubernetes system.

Trying out CRI-O

Let's look at some installation methods so you can give CRI-O a try on your own. In order to get started, you'll need a few things, including runc or another OCI compatible runtime, as well as socat, iproute, and iptables. There's a few options for running CRI-O in Kubernetes:

- In a full-scale cluster, using `kube-adm` and `systemd` to leverage the CRI-O socket with `--container-runtime-endpoint /var/run/crio/crio.sock`
- With Minikube, by starting it up with specific command-line options
- On atomic with atomic install `--system-package=no -n cri-o --storage ostree registry.centos.org/projectatomic/cri-o:latest`

If you'd like to build CRI-O from source, you can run the following on your laptop. You need some dependencies installed in order to make this build phase work. First, run the following commands to get your dependencies installed.

The following commands are for Fedora, CentOS, and RHEL distributions:

```
yum install -y \
  btrfs-progs-devel \
  device-mapper-devel \
  git \
  glib2-devel \
  glibc-devel \
  glibc-static \
  go \
  golang-github-cpuguy83-go-md2man \
  gpgme-devel \
  libassuan-devel \
  libgpg-error-devel \
  libseccomp-devel \
  libselinux-devel \
  ostree-devel \
  pkgconfig \
  runc \
  skopeo-containers
```

These commands are to be used for Debian, Ubuntu, and related distributions:

```
apt-get install -y \
  btrfs-tools \
  git \
  golang-go \
  libassuan-dev \
  libdevmapper-dev \
  libglib2.0-dev \
  libc6-dev \
  libgpgme11-dev \
  libgpg-error-dev \
  libseccomp-dev \
  libselinux1-dev \
  pkg-config \
  go-md2man \
  runc \
  skopeo-containers
```

Secondly, you'll need to grab the source code like so:

```
git clone https://github.com/kubernetes-incubator/cri-o # or your fork
cd cri-o
```

Once you have the code, go ahead and build it:

```
make install.tools
make
sudo make install
```

You can use additional build flags to add thing such as `seccomp`, SELinux, and `apparmor` with this format: `make BUILDTAGS='seccomp apparmor'`.

You can run Kubernetes locally with the `local-up-cluster.sh` script in Kubernetes. I'll also show you how to run this on Minikube.

First, clone the Kubernetes repository:

```
git clone https://github.com/kubernetes/kubernetes.git
```

Next, you'll need to start the CRI-O daemon and run the following command to get spin up your cluster using CRI-O:

```
CGROUP_DRIVER=systemd \
 CONTAINER_RUNTIME=remote \
 CONTAINER_RUNTIME_ENDPOINT='unix:///var/run/crio/crio.sock  --runtime-
request-timeout=15m' \
 ./hack/local-up-cluster.sh
```

TIP If you have a running cluster, you can also use the instructions, available at the following URL, to switch the runtime from Docker to CRI-O: `https://github.com/kubernetes-incubator/cri-o/blob/master/kubernetes.md/`.

Let's also check how to use CRI-O on Minikube, which is one of the easiest ways to get experimenting:

```
minikube start \
  --network-plugin=cni \
  --extra-config=kubelet.container-runtime=remote \
  --extra-config=kubelet.container-runtime-endpoint=/var/run/crio/crio.sock \
  --extra-config=kubelet.image-service-endpoint=/var/run/crio/crio.sock \
  --bootstrapper=kubeadm
```

Lastly, we can use our GCP platform to spin up a cluster with CRI-O and start experimenting:

```
gcloud compute instances create cri-o \
  --machine-type n1-standard-2 \
  --image-family ubuntu-1610 \
  --image-project ubuntu-os-cloud
```

Let's use these machines to run through a quick tutorial. SSH into the machine using `gcloud compute ssh cri-o`.

Once you're on the server, we'll need to install the `cri-o`, `crioctl`, `cni`, and `runc` programs. Grab the `runc` binary first:

```
wget
https://github.com/opencontainers/runc/releases/download/v1.0.0-rc4/runc.am
d64
```

Set it executable and move it to your path as follows:

```
chmod +x runc.amd64
sudo mv runc.amd64 /usr/bin/runc
```

You can see it's working by checking the version:

```
$ runc -version
runc version 1.0.0-rc4
commit: 2e7cfe036e2c6dc51ccca6eb7fa3ee6b63976dcd
spec: 1.0.0
```

You'll need to install the CRI-O binary from source, as it's not currently shipping any binaries.

First, download the latest binary release and install Go:

```
wget https://storage.googleapis.com/golang/go1.8.5.linux-amd64.tar.gz
sudo tar -xvf go1.8.5.linux-amd64.tar.gz -C /usr/local/
mkdir -p $HOME/go/src
export GOPATH=$HOME/go
export PATH=$PATH:/usr/local/go/bin:$GOPATH/bin
```

This should feel familiar, as you would install Go the same way for any other project. Check your version:

```
go version
go version go1.8.5 linux/amd64
```

Next up, get `crictl` using the following commands:

```
go get github.com/kubernetes-incubator/cri-tools/cmd/crictl
cd $GOPATH/src/github.com/kubernetes-incubator/cri-tools
make
make install
```

After that's downloaded, you'll need to build CRI-O from source:

```
sudo apt-get update && apt-get install -y libglib2.0-dev \
  libseccomp-dev \
  libgpgme11-dev \
  libdevmapper-dev \
  make \
  git
```

Now, get CRI-O and install it:

```
go get -d github.com/kubernetes-incubator/cri-o
cd $GOPATH/src/github.com/kubernetes-incubator/cri-o
make install.tools
Make
sudo make install
```

After this is complete, you'll need to create configuration files with `sudo make install.config`. You need to ensure that you're using a valid registry option in the `/etc/crio/cirio.conf` file. An example of this looks like the following:

```
registries = ['registry.access..com', 'registry.fedoraproject.org',
'docker.io']
```

At this point, we're ready to start the CRI-O system daemon, which we can do by leveraging `systemctl`. Let's create a `crio.service`:

```
$ vim /etc/systemd/system/crio.service
```

Add the following text:

```
[Unit]
Description=OCI-based implementation of Kubernetes Container Runtime
Interface
Documentation=https://github.com/kubernetes-incubator/cri-o

[Service]
ExecStart=/usr/local/bin/crio
Restart=on-failure
RestartSec=5

[Install]
WantedBy=multi-user.target
```

Once that's complete, we can reload `systemctl` and enable CRI-O:

```
$ sudo systemctl daemon-reload && \
  sudo systemctl enable crio && \
  sudo systemctl start crio
```

After this is complete, we can validate whether or not we have a working install of CRI-O by checking the version of the endpoint as follows:

```
$ sudo crictl --runtime-endpoint unix:///var/run/crio/crio.sock version
Version:   0.1.0
RuntimeName:  cri-o
RuntimeVersion:   1.10.0-dev
RuntimeApiVersion:   v1alpha1
```

Next up, we'll need to grab the latest version of the CNI plugin, so we can build and use it from source. Let's use Go to grab our source code:

```
go get -d github.com/containernetworking/plugins
cd $GOPATH/src/github.com/containernetworking/plugins
./build.sh
```

Next, install the CNI plugins into your cluster:

```
sudo mkdir -p /opt/cni/bin
sudo cp bin/* /opt/cni/bin/
```

Now, we can configure the CNI so that CRI-O can use it. First, make a directory to store the configuration, then we'll set two configuration files as follows:

```
sudo mkdir -p /etc/cni/net.d
```

Next, you'll want to create and compose 10-mynet.conf:

```
sudo sh -c 'cat >/etc/cni/net.d/10-mynet.conf <<-EOF
{
"cniVersion": "0.2.0",
    "name": "mynet",
    "type": "bridge",
    "bridge": "cni0",
    "isGateway": true,
    "ipMasq": true,
    "ipam": {
        "type": "host-local",
        "subnet": "10.88.0.0/16",
        "routes": [
            { "dst": "0.0.0.0/0"  }
        ]
    }
}
EOF'
```

And then, compose the loopback interface as follows:

```
sudo sh -c 'cat >/etc/cni/net.d/99-loopback.conf <<-EOF
{
    "cniVersion": "0.2.0",
    "type": "loopback"
}
EOF'
```

Next up, we'll need some special containers from Project Atomic to get this working. skopeo is a command-line utility that is OCI-compliant and can perform various operations on container images and image repositories. Install the containers as follows:

```
sudo add-apt-repository ppa:projectatomic/ppa
sudo apt-get update
sudo apt-get install skopeo-containers -y
```

Restart CRI-O to pick up the CNI configuration with sudo systemctl restart crio. Great! Now that we have these components installed, let's build something!

First off, we'll create a sandbox using a template policy from the Kubernetes incubator.

This template is NOT production ready!

Change first to the CRI-O source tree with the template, as follows:

```
cd $GOPATH/src/github.com/kubernetes-incubator/cri-o
```

Next, you'll need to create and capture the pod ID:

```
sudo mkdir /etc/containers/
sudo cp test/policy.json /etc/containers
```

You can use `critcl` to get the status of the pod as follows:

```
sudo crictl inspectp --output table $POD_ID
ID: cd6c0883663c6f4f99697aaa15af8219e351e03696bd866bc3ac055ef289702a
Name: podsandbox1
UID: redhat-test-crio
Namespace: redhat.test.crio
Attempt: 1
Status: SANDBOX_READY
Created: 2016-12-14 15:59:04.373680832 +0000 UTC
Network namespace: /var/run/netns/cni-bc37b858-fb4d-41e6-58b0-9905d0ba23f8
IP Address: 10.88.0.2
Labels:
group -> test
Annotations:
owner -> jwhite
security.alpha.kubernetes.io/seccomp/pod -> unconfined
security.alpha.kubernetes.io/sysctls ->
kernel.shm_rmid_forced=1,net.ipv4.ip_local_port_range=1024 65000
security.alpha.kubernetes.io/unsafe-sysctls -> kernel.msgmax=8192
```

We'll use the `crictl` tool again to pull a container image for a Redis server:

```
sudo crictl pull quay.io/crio/redis:alpine
CONTAINER_ID=$(sudo crictl create $POD_ID
test/testdata/container_redis.json test/testdata/sandbox_config.json)
```

Next, we'll start and check the status of the Redis container as follows:

```
sudo crictl start $CONTAINER_ID
sudo crictl inspect $CONTAINER_ID
```

At this point, you should be able to `telnet` into the Redis container to test its functionality:

```
telnet 10.88.0.2 6379
Trying 10.88.0.2...
Connected to 10.88.0.2.
Escape character is '^]'.
```

Nicely done—you've now created a pod and container manually, using some of the core abstractions of the Kubernetes system! You can stop the container and shut down the pod with the following commands:

```
sudo crictl stop $CONTAINER_ID
sudo crictl rm $CONTAINER_ID
sudo crictl stopp $POD_ID
sudo crictl rmp $POD_ID
sudo crictl pods
sudo crictl ps
```

More on container runtimes

There's a number of container- and VM-based options for OCI-compliant implementations. We know of runc, which is the standard reference implementation of the OCI runtime. This is what the container uses. There's also the following available:

- `projectatomic/bwrap-oci` (`https://github.com/projectatomic/bwrap-oci`): Converts the OCI spec file to a command line for `projectatomic/bubblewrap` (`https://github.com/projectatomic/bubblewrap`)
- `giuseppe/crun` (`https://github.com/giuseppe/crun`): Runtime implementation in C

There are also VM-based implementations that take a different path towards security:

- `hyperhq/runv` (`https://github.com/hyperhq/runv`)—hypervisor-based runtime for OCI
- `clearcontainers/runtime` (`https://github.com/clearcontainers/runtime`)—hypervisor-based OCI runtime utilizing `containers/virtcontainers` (`https://github.com/containers/virtcontainers`) by Intel
- `google/gvisor` (`https://github.com/google/gvisor`)—gVisor is a user-space kernel, which contains runsc to run sandboxed containers

- `kata-containers/runtime` (`https://github.com/kata-containers/runtime`)—hypervisor-based OCI runtime combining technology from `clearcontainers/runtime` (`https://github.com/clearcontainers/runtime`) and `hyperhq/runv` (`https://github.com/hyperhq/runv`)

The most interesting project of these is the last in the list, Kata containers, which combines clear container and runV into a cohesive package. These foundational pieces are already in production use at scale in the enterprises, and Kata is looking to provide a secure, lightweight VM for containerized environments. By utilizing runV, Kata containers can run inside of any KVM-compatible VM, such as Xen, KVM, and vSphere, while still remaining compatible with CRI-O, which is important! Kata hopes to offer the speed of a container with the security surface of a VM.

Here's a diagram from Kata's site, explaining the architecture in visual detail:

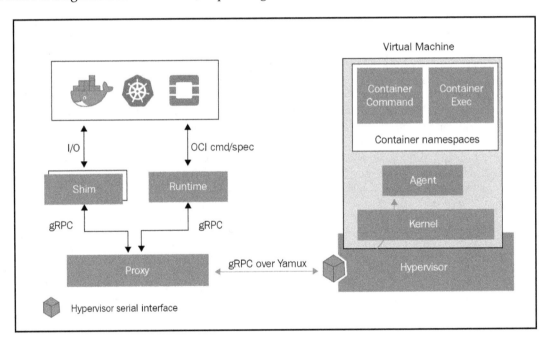

CNCF

A second initiative that also has widespread industry acceptance is the CNCF. While still focused on containerized workloads, the CNCF operates a bit higher up the stack, at the application design level.

Its purpose is to provide a standard set of tools and technologies to build, operate, and orchestrate cloud-native application stacks. Cloud has given us access to a variety of new technologies and practices that can improve and evolve our classic software designs. The CNCF is also particularly focused on the new paradigm of microservice-oriented development.

As a founding participant in the CNCF, Google has donated the Kubernetes open source project. The goal will be to increase interoperability in the ecosystem and support better integration with projects. The CNCF already hosts a variety of projects on orchestration, logging, monitoring, tracing, and application resilience.

For more information on CNCF, refer to `https://cncf.io/`.

We'll talk more about the CNCF, **Special Interest Groups** (**SIGs**), and the landscape therein in the following chapters.

For now, here's a landscape and trail map to consider: `https://www.cncf.io/blog/2018/03/08/introducing-the-cloud-native-landscape-2-0-interactive-edition/`.

Standard container specification

A core result of the OCI effort is the creation and development of the overarching container specification. The specification has five core principles that all containers should follow, which I will briefly paraphrase:

- The container must have *standard operations* to create, start, and stop containers across all implementations.
- The container must be *content-agnostic*, which means that type of application inside the container does not alter the standard operations or publishing of the container itself.
- The container must be *infrastructure-agnostic* as well. Portability is paramount; therefore, the container must be able to operate just as easily in GCE as in your company's data center or on a developer's laptop.

- A container must also be *designed for automation,* which allows us to automate across the build, as well as for updates and the deployment pipelines. While this rule is a bit vague, the container implementation should not require onerous manual steps for creation and release.
- Finally, the implementation must support *industrial-grade delivery.* Once again, this means speaking to the build and deployment pipelines and requiring streamlined efficiency in the portability and transit of the containers between infrastructure and deployment tiers.

The specification also defines core principles for container formats and runtimes. You can read more about the specifications on the open containers GitHub page at `https://github.com/opencontainers/specs`.

While the core specification can be a bit abstract, the runc implementation is a concrete example of the OCI specs, in the form of a container runtime and image format. Again, you can read more of the technical details on GitHub at `https://github.com/opencontainers/runc`.

The backing format and runtime for a variety of popular container tools is runc. It was donated to OCI by Docker and was created from the same plumbing work used in the Docker platform. Since its release, it has received a welcome uptake by numerous projects.

Even the popular open source PaaS Cloud Foundry announced that it will use runc in Garden. Garden provides the containerization plumbing for Diego, which acts as an orchestration layer similar to Kubernetes.

The rkt implementation was originally based on the appc specification. The appc specification was actually an earlier attempt by the folks at CoreOS to form a common specification around containerization. Now that CoreOS is participating in OCI, they are working to help merge the appc specification into OCI; this should result in a higher level of compatibility across the container ecosystem.

CoreOS

While the specifications provide us with a common ground, there are also some trends evolving around the choice of OS for our containers. There are several tailored-fit OSes that are being developed specifically to run container workloads. Although implementations vary, they all have similar characteristics. The focus is on a slim installation base, atomic OS updating, and signed applications for efficient and secure operations.

One OS that is gaining popularity is CoreOS. CoreOS offers major benefits for both security and resource utilization. It provides resource utilization by completely removing package dependencies from the picture. Instead, CoreOS runs all applications and services in containers. By providing only a small set of services required to support running containers and bypassing the need for hypervisor usage, CoreOS lets us use a larger portion of the resource pool to run our containerized applications. This allows users to gain higher performance from their infrastructure and better container-to-node (server) usage ratios.

Recently, CoreOS was purchased by Red Hat, which means that the current version of container Linux will evolve against Red Hat's container OS offering, Project Atomic. These two products will eventually turn into Red Hat CoreOS. If you consider the upstream community approach that Fedora takes to Red Hat Enterprise Linux, it seems likely that there will be something similar for Red Hat CoreOS.

This also means that Red Hat will be integration Tectonic, which we'll explore later in the chapter, and the Quay, the enterprise container registry that CoreOS acquired. It's important to note that the rkt container standard will not be part of the acquisition, and will instead become a community supported project.

> If you'd like to see the relevant official announcements for the news discussed in the preceding section, you can check out these posts:
>
> - **Press release**: https://www.redhat.com/en/about/press-releases/red-hat-acquire-coreos-expanding-its-kubernetes-and-containers-leadership
> - **Red Hat blog**: https://www.redhat.com/en/blog/coreos-bet
> - **CoreOS blog**: https://coreos.com/blog/coreos-agrees-to-join-red-hat/

Here's a brief overview of the various container OSes. There are several other container-optimized OSes that have emerged recently:

- *Red Hat Enterprise Linux Atomic Host* focuses on security with SELinux enabled by default and atomic updates to the OS similar to what we saw with CoreOS. Refer to the following link: https://access.redhat.com/articles/rhel-atomic-getting-started.
- *Ubuntu Snappy* also capitalizes on the efficiency and security gains of separating the OS components from the frameworks and applications. Using application images and verification signatures, we get an efficient Ubuntu-based OS for our container workloads at http://www.ubuntu.com/cloud/tools/snappy.

- *Ubuntu LXD* runs a container hypervisor and provides a path for migrating Linux-based VMs to containers with ease: `https://www.ubuntu.com/cloud/lxd`.
- *VMware Photon* is another lightweight container OS that is optimized specifically for vSphere and the VMware platform. It runs Docker, rkt, and Garden and also has some images that you can run on the popular public cloud providers. Refer to the following link: `https://vmware.github.io/photon/`.

Using the isolated nature of containers, we increase reliability and decrease the complexity of updates for each application. Now, applications can be updated along with supporting libraries whenever a new container release is ready, as shown in the following diagram:

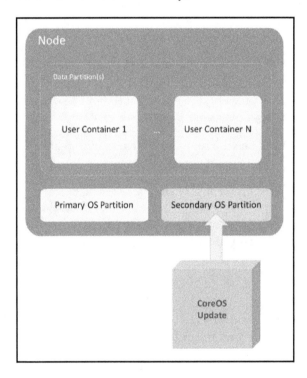

CoreOS update procedure

Finally, CoreOS has some added advantages in the realm of security. For starters, the OS can be updated as one whole unit, instead of via individual packages (refer to the preceding diagram). This avoids many issues that arise from partial updates. To achieve this, CoreOS uses two partitions: one as the active OS partition, and a secondary one to receive a full update. Once updates are completed successfully, a reboot promotes the secondary partition. If anything goes wrong, the original partition is available as a fallback.

The system owners can also control when those updates are applied. This gives us the flexibility to prioritize critical updates, while working with real-world scheduling for the more common updates. In addition, the entire update is signed and transmitted via SSL for added security across the entire process.

rkt

As mentioned previously, rkt will be continuing on as a community driven project. rkt is another implementation with a specific focus on security. The main advantage of rkt is that it runs the engine without a daemon as root, the way Docker does today. Initially, rkt also had an advantage in the establishment of trust for container images. However, recent updates to Docker have made great strides, especially the new content trust feature.

The bottom line is that rkt is still an implementation, with a focus on security, for running containers in production. rkt uses an image format named ACI, but it also supports Docker-based images. Over the past year, rkt has undergone significant updates and is now at version 1.24.0. It has gained much momentum as a means to run Docker images securely in production.

Here's a diagram showing how the rkt execution chain works:

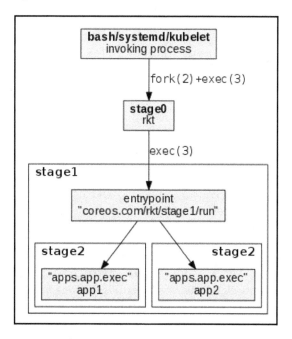

In addition, CoreOS is working with Intel® to integrate the new Intel® Virtualization Technology, which allows containers to run in higher levels of isolation. This hardware-enhanced security allows the containers to be run inside a **Kernel-based Virtual Machine (KVM)** process, providing isolation from the kernel in a similar fashion to what we see with hypervisors today.

etcd

Another central piece in the CoreOS ecosystem worth mentioning is their open source etcd project. etcd is a distributed and consistent key-value store. A RESTful API is used to interface with etcd, so it's easy to integrate with your project.

If it sounds familiar, it's because we saw this process running in `Chapter 1`, *Introduction to Kubernetes*, in the section entitled *Services running on the master*. Kubernetes actually utilizes etcd to keep track of cluster configuration and current state. K8s uses it for its service discovery capabilities as well. For more details, refer to `https://github.com/coreos/etcd`.

Kubernetes with CoreOS

Now that we understand the benefits, let's take a look at a Kubernetes cluster using CoreOS. The documentation supports a number of platforms, but one of the easiest to spin up is AWS with the CoreOS CloudFormation and CLI scripts.

If you are interested in running Kubernetes with CoreOS on other platforms, you can find more details in the CoreOS documentation at `https://coreos.com/kubernetes/docs/latest/`. You can find the latest instructions for AWS at `https://coreos.com/kubernetes/docs/latest/kubernetes-on-aws.html`.

You can follow the instructions covered previously in this chapter to spin up Kubernetes on CoreOS. You'll need to create a key pair on AWS, and also specify a region, cluster name, cluster size, and DNS to proceed.

In addition, we will need to create a DNS entry, and will require a service such as Route 53 or a production DNS service. When following the instructions, you'll want to set the DNS to a domain or sub-domain on which you have permission to set up a record. We will need to update the record after the cluster is up and running and has a dynamic endpoint defined.

There you have it! We now have a cluster running CoreOS. The script creates all the necessary AWS resources, such as **Virtual Private Clouds** (**VPCs**), security groups, and IAM roles. Now that the cluster is up and running, we can get the endpoint with the status command and update our DNS record as follows:

```
$ kube-aws status
```

Copy the entry listed next to Controller DNS Name in the output from the preceding command, and then edit your DNS records to get the domain or sub-domain you specified earlier to point to this load balancer.

If you forget which domain you specified or need to check on the configuration, you can look in the generated kubeconfig file with your favorite editor. It will look something like this:

```
apiVersion: v1
kind: Config
clusters:
- cluster:
    certificate-authority: credentials/ca.pem
    server: https://coreos.mydomain.com
  name: kube-aws-my-coreos-cluster-cluster
contexts:
- context:
    cluster: kube-aws-my-coreos-cluster-cluster
    namespace: default
    user: kube-aws-my-coreos-cluster-admin
  name: kube-aws-my-coreos-cluster-context
users:
- name: kube-aws-my-coreos-cluster-admin
  user:
    client-certificate: credentials/admin.pem
    client-key: credentials/admin-key.pem
current-context: kube-aws-my-coreos-cluster-context
```

In this case, the server line will have your domain name.

> If this is a fresh box, you will need to download kubectl separately, as it is not bundled with kube-aws:
> **$ wget**
> **https://storage.googleapis.com/kubernetes-release/release**
> **/v1.0.6/bin/linux/amd64/kubectl**

We can now use `kubectl` to see our new cluster:

```
$ ./kubectl --kubeconfig=kubeconfig get nodes
```

We should see a single node listed with the EC2 internal DNS as the name. Note `kubeconfig`, this tells Kubernetes the path to use the configuration file for the cluster that was just created instead. This is also useful if we want to manage multiple clusters from the same machine.

Tectonic

Running Kubernetes on CoreOS is a great start, but you may find that you want a higher level of support. Enter Tectonic, the CoreOS enterprise offering for running Kubernetes with CoreOS. Tectonic uses many of the components we already discussed. Both Docker and rkt runtimes are supported. In addition, Kubernetes, etcd, and flannel are packaged together to give a full stack of cluster orchestration. We discussed flannel briefly in Chapter 4, *Working with Networking, Load Balancers, and Ingress*. It is an overlay network that uses a model similar to the native Kubernetes model, and uses etcd as a backend.

Offering a support package similar to Red Hat, CoreOS also provides 24/7 support for the open source software that Tectonic is built on. Tectonic also provides regular cluster updates and a nice dashboard with views for all of the components of Kubernetes. **CoreUpdate** allows users to have more control of the automatic update process. In addition, it ships with modules for monitoring, SSO, and other security features.

As CoreOS is integrated into Red Hat, this offering will be replaced over time with a Red Hat approach.

 You can find more information and the latest instructions to install at https://coreos.com/tectonic/docs/latest/install/aws/index. html.

Dashboard highlights

Some highlights of the Tectonic dashboard are shown in the following screenshot:

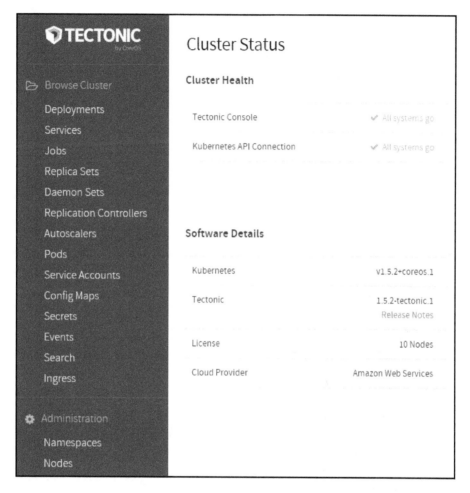

The Tectonic main dashboard

Tectonic is now generally available and the dashboard already has some nice features. As you can see in the following screenshot, we can see a lot of detail about our replication controller, and can even use the GUI to scale up and down with the click of a button:

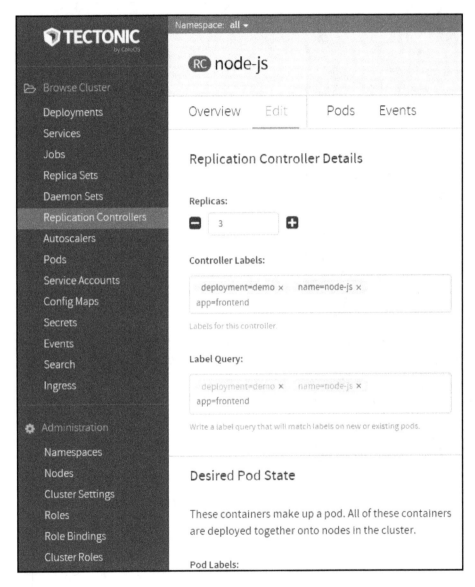

Tectonic replication controller detail

This graphic is quite large, so it's broken across two pages. The following screenshot continues from the preceding screenshot:

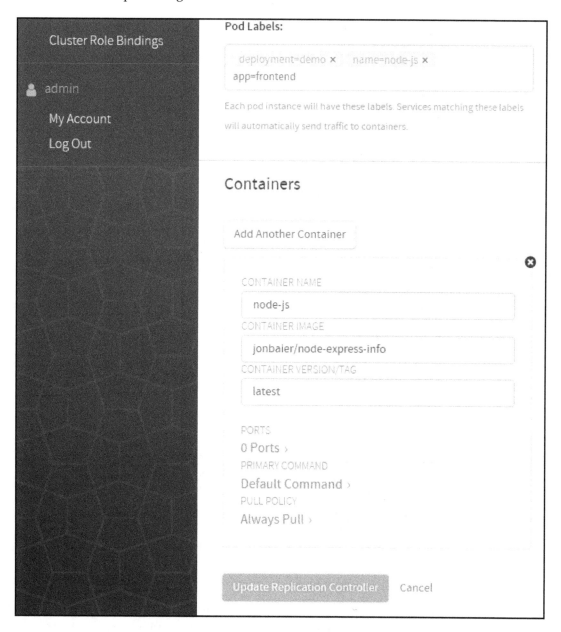

Another nice feature is the **Events** page. Here, we can watch the events live, pause them, and filter them based on event severity and resource type:

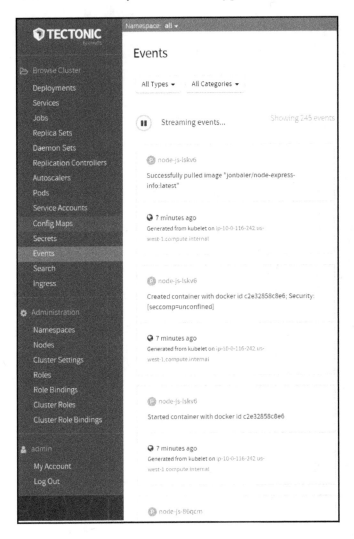

Events stream

A useful feature to browse anywhere in the dashboard system is the **Namespace:** filtering option. Simply click on the drop-down menu next to the word **Namespace:** at the top of any page that shows resources, and we can filter our views by namespace. This can be helpful if we want to filter out the Kubernetes system pods, or just look at a particular collection of resources:

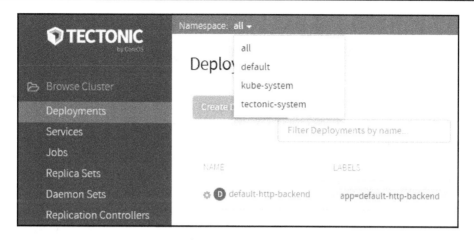

Namespace filtering

Hosted platforms

There are several options available for hosted Kubernetes in the cloud. These **Platforms as a service (PaaS)** can provide a stable operating model as you push towards production. Here's an overview of the major PaaSes provided by Amazon, Microsoft, and Google.

Amazon Web Services

Elastic Container Service (ECS) has just been launched as of the time of this chapter's writing. AWS is preparing a networking plugin to differentiate itself from other offerings, called the vpc-cni. This allows for pod networking in Kubernetes to use **Elastic Network Interfaces (ENIs)** on AWS. With ECS, you do have to pay for manager nodes, which is a different path to that taken by Microsoft and Google. ECS' startup procedure is also currently more complex and doesn't have single-command creation via the CLI.

Microsoft Azure

The Azure Container Service is the second longest running hosted Kubernetes service in the cloud after the Google Kubernetes Engine. You can use Azure templates and the Resource Manager to spin up clusters with Terraform. Microsoft offers advanced networking features, integration with Azure Active Directory, and monitoring as its standout features.

Google Kubernetes Engine

The Google Kubernetes Engine is another excellent option for running your containerized workloads. At the time of writing, it's considered to be one of the most robust offerings. GKE is able to autoscale the cluster size, while AWS and Azure offer manual scaling. GKE offers a one-command start, and is the fastest to provision a Kubernetes cluster. It also offers an *Alpha Mode* where you can try bleeding edge features in the alpha channel releases. GKE provides high availability in zones and regions, the latter of which spreads out master node zones to provide best-in-class high availability.

Summary

In this chapter, we looked at the emerging standards bodies in the container community and how they are using open specifications to shape the technology for the better. We looked at various container frameworks and runtimes. We dipped our toes into the CNCF, and tried out CRI-O.

We also took a closer look at CoreOS, a key player in both the container and Kubernetes community. We explored the technology that CoreOS is developing in order to enhance and complement container orchestration, and saw first-hand how to use some of it with Kubernetes. Finally, we looked at the supported enterprise offering of Tectonic and some of the features that are available now.

We also looked at some of the major PaaS offered by cloud service providers.

10
Creating Kubernetes Clusters

In the previous chapter, we learned what Kubernetes is all about, how it is designed, what concepts it supports, how to use its runtime engines, and how it fits within the CI/CD pipeline.

Creating a Kubernetes cluster is a non-trivial task. There are many options and tools to select from, and there are many factors to consider. In this chapter, we'll roll up our sleeves and build some Kubernetes clusters. We will also discuss and evaluate tools such as Minikube, kubeadm, kube-spray, bootkube, and stackube. We will also look into deployment environments, such as local, cloud, and bare metal. The topics we will cover are as follows:

- Creating a single-node cluster with Minikube
- Creating a multi-node cluster using kubeadm
- Creating clusters in the cloud
- Creating bare-metal clusters from scratch
- Reviewing other options for creating Kubernetes clusters

At the end of this chapter, you will have a solid understanding of the various options to create Kubernetes clusters and knowledge of the best-of-breed tools to support the creation of Kubernetes clusters; you will also build a couple of clusters, both single-node and multi-node.

A quick single-node cluster with Minikube

In this section, we will create a single-node cluster on Windows. The reason we will use Windows is that Minikube and single-node clusters are most useful for local developer machines. While Kubernetes is typically deployed on Linux in production, many developers work on Windows PCs or Macs. That said, there aren't too many differences if you do want to install Minikube on Linux:

Getting ready

There are some prerequisites to install before you can create the cluster itself. These include VirtualBox, the `kubectl` command-line interface for Kubernetes, and, of course, Minikube itself. Here is a list of the latest versions at the time of writing:

- **VirtualBox**: https://www.virtualbox.org/wiki/Downloads
- **Kubectl**: https://kubernetes.io/docs/tasks/tools/install-kubectl/
- **Minikube**: https://kubernetes.io/docs/tasks/tools/install-minikube/

On Windows

Install VirtualBox and make sure kubectl and Minikube are on your path. I personally just throw all the command-line programs I use into `c:\windows`. You may prefer another approach. I use the excellent ConEMU to manage multiple consoles, terminals, and SSH sessions. It works with `cmd.exe`, PowerShell, PuTTY, Cygwin, msys, and Git-Bash. It doesn't get much better than that on Windows.

With Windows 10 Pro, you have the option to use the Hyper-V hypervisor. This is technically a better solution than VirtualBox, but it requires the Pro version of Windows and is completely Windows-specific. When using VirtualBox, these instructions are universal and will be easy to adapt to other versions of Windows, or other operating systems altogether. If you have Hyper-V enabled, you must disable it because VirtualBox can't co-exist with Hyper-V.

I recommend using PowerShell in administrator mode. You can add the following alias and function to your PowerShell profile:

```
Set-Alias -Name k -Value kubectl
function mk
{
minikube-windows-amd64 `
--show-libmachine-logs `
--alsologtostderr            `
@args
}
```

On macOS

You can add aliases to your .bashrc file (similar to the PowerShell alias and function on Windows):

```
alias k='kubectl'
alias mk='/usr/local/bin/minikube'
```

Now I can use k and mk and type less. The flags to Minikube in the mk function provide better logging that way, and direct the output to the console, as well as to the files (similar to tee).

Type mk version to verify that Minikube is correctly installed and functioning:

```
> mk version

minikube version: v0.26.0
```

Type k version to verify that kubectl is correctly installed and functioning:

```
> k version
Client Version: version.Info{Major:"1", Minor:"9", GitVersion:"v1.9.0",
GitCommit:"925c127ec6b946659ad0fd596fa959be43f0cc05", GitTreeState:"clean",
BuildDate:"2017-12-16T03:15:38Z", GoVersion:"go1.9.2", Compiler:"gc",
Platform:"darwin/amd64"}
Unable to connect to the server: dial tcp 192.168.99.100:8443: getsockopt:
operation timed out
```

Don't worry about the error on the last line. There is no cluster running, so kubectl can't connect to anything. That's expected.

You can explore the available commands and flags for both Minikube and kubectl. I will not go over each and every one, only the commands I use.

Creating the cluster

The Minikube tool supports multiple versions of Kubernetes. At the time of writing, this is the list of supported versions:

```
> mk get-k8s-versions
The following Kubernetes versions are available when using the localkube
bootstrapper:
- v1.10.0
- v1.9.4
- v1.9.0
- v1.8.0
- v1.7.5
- v1.7.4
- v1.7.3
- v1.7.2
- v1.7.0
- v1.7.0-rc.1
- v1.7.0-alpha.2
- v1.6.4
- v1.6.3
- v1.6.0
- v1.6.0-rc.1
- v1.6.0-beta.4
- v1.6.0-beta.3
- v1.6.0-beta.2
- v1.6.0-alpha.1
- v1.6.0-alpha.0
- v1.5.3
- v1.5.2
- v1.5.1
- v1.4.5
- v1.4.3
- v1.4.2
- v1.4.1
- v1.4.0
- v1.3.7
- v1.3.6
- v1.3.5
- v1.3.4
- v1.3.3
- v1.3.0
```

I will go with 1.10.0, the latest stable release. Let's create the cluster by using the `start` command and specifying v1.10.0 as the version.

This can take a while as Minikube may need to download an image and then set up the local cluster. Just let it run. Here is the expected output (on Mac):

```
> mk start --kubernetes-version="v1.10.0"
Starting local Kubernetes v1.10.0 cluster...
Starting VM...
Getting VM IP address...
Moving files into cluster...
Finished Downloading kubeadm v1.10.0
Finished Downloading kubelet v1.10.0
Setting up certs...
Connecting to cluster...
Setting up kubeconfig...
Starting cluster components...
Kubectl is now configured to use the cluster.
Loading cached images from config file.
```

Let's review what Minikube does by following the output. You'll need to do a lot of this when creating a cluster from scratch:

1. Start a VirtualBox VM
2. Create certificates for the local machine and the VM
3. Download images
4. Set up networking between the local machine and the VM
5. Run the local Kubernetes cluster on the VM
6. Configure the cluster
7. Start all the Kubernetes control plane components
8. Configure kubectl to talk to the cluster

Troubleshooting

If something goes wrong during the process, try to follow the error messages. You can add the `--alsologtostderr` flag to get detailed error info from the console. Everything Minikube does is organized neatly under `~/.minikube`. Here is the directory structure:

```
> tree ~/.minikube -L 2
/Users/gigi.sayfan/.minikube
├── addons
├── apiserver.crt
├── apiserver.key
```

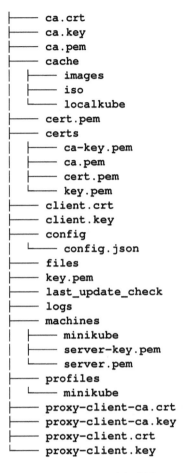

```
├─── ca.crt
├─── ca.key
├─── ca.pem
├─── cache
│    ├─── images
│    ├─── iso
│    └─── localkube
├─── cert.pem
├─── certs
│    ├─── ca-key.pem
│    ├─── ca.pem
│    ├─── cert.pem
│    └─── key.pem
├─── client.crt
├─── client.key
├─── config
│    └─── config.json
├─── files
├─── key.pem
├─── last_update_check
├─── logs
├─── machines
│    ├─── minikube
│    ├─── server-key.pem
│    └─── server.pem
├─── profiles
│    └─── minikube
├─── proxy-client-ca.crt
├─── proxy-client-ca.key
├─── proxy-client.crt
└─── proxy-client.key

13 directories, 21 files
```

Checking out the cluster

Now that we have a cluster up and running, let's peek inside.

First, let's `ssh` into the VM:

```
> mk ssh

            _ _  ( )  ( )
            _ _ ( )  ( )
   ___  ___  (_)  ___  (_)| |/')  _ _ | |_ _
  /' _ ` _ `\| |/' _ `\| || , < ( ) ( )| '_`\ /'_`\
  | ( ) ( ) || || ( ) || || |\`\ | (_) || |_) ) ( __/
  (_) (_) (_)(_)(_) (_)(_)(_) (_)`\___/'(_,__/'`\____)

$ uname -a

Linux minikube 4.9.64 #1 SMP Fri Mar 30 21:27:22 UTC 2018 x86_64 GNU/Linux$
```

Great! That works. The weird symbols are ASCII art for `minikube`. Now, let's start using `kubectl`, because it is the Swiss Army knife of Kubernetes and will be useful for all clusters (including federated clusters).

We will cover many of the `kubectl` commands on our journey. First, let's check the cluster status using `cluster-info`:

```
> k cluster-info
```

The Kubernetes master is running at `https://192.168.99.101:8443`

KubeDNS is running at `https://192.168.99.1010:8443/api/v1/namespaces/kube-system/services/kube-dns:dns/proxy`

To further debug and diagnose cluster problems, use `kubectl cluster-info dump`. You can see that the master is running properly. To see a much more detailed view of all the objects in the cluster as a JSON type, use `k cluster-info dump`. The output can be a little daunting, so let's use more specific commands to explore the cluster.

Let's check out the nodes in the cluster using `get nodes`:

```
> k get nodes
NAME        STATUS      ROLES       AGE         VERSION
NAME        STATUS      ROLES       AGE         VERSION
minikube    Ready       master      15m         v1.10.0
```

So, we have one node called `minikube`. To get a lot of information about it, type `k describe node minikube`. The output is verbose; I'll let you try it yourself.

Doing work

We have a nice empty cluster up and running (well, not completely empty, as the DNS service and dashboard run as pods in the `kube-system` namespace). It's time to run some pods. Let's use the `echo` server as an example:

```
k run echo --image=gcr.io/google_containers/echoserver:1.8 --port=8080
deployment "echo" created
```

Kubernetes created a deployment and we have a pod running. Note the `echo` prefix:

```
> k get pods
NAME                     READY     STATUS     RESTARTS     AGE
echo-69f7cfb5bb-wqgkh    1/1       Running    0            18s
```

To expose our pod as a service, type the following:

```
> k expose deployment echo --type=NodePort
  service "echo" exposed
```

Exposing the service as a `NodePort` type means that it is exposed to the host on a port, but it is not the `8080` port we ran the pod on. Ports get mapped in the cluster. To access the service, we need the cluster IP and exposed port:

```
> mk ip
192.168.99.101
> k get service echo --output='jsonpath="{.spec.ports[0].nodePort}"'
30388
```

Now we can access the `echo` service, which returns a lot of information:

```
> curl http://192.168.99.101:30388/hi
```

Congratulations! You just created a local Kubernetes cluster and deployed a service.

Examining the cluster with the dashboard

Kubernetes has a very nice web interface, which is deployed, of course, as a service in a pod. The dashboard is well designed, and provides a high-level overview of your cluster, and also drills down into individual resources, viewing logs, editing resource files, and more. It is the perfect weapon when you want to manually check out your cluster. To launch it, type `minikube dashboard`.

Minikube will open a browser window with the dashboard UI. Note that on Windows, Microsoft Edge can't display the dashboard. I had to run it myself on a different browser.

Here is the workloads view, which displays **Deployments**, **Replica Sets**, **Replication Controllers**, and **Pods**:

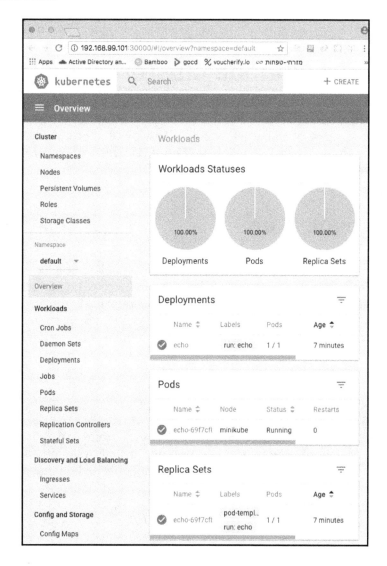

It can also display **Daemon Sets**, **Stateful Sets**, and **Jobs**, but we don't have any in this cluster.

In this section, we created a local, single-node Kubernetes cluster on Windows, explored it a little bit using `kubectl`, deployed a service, and played with the web UI. In the next section, we'll move on to a multi-node cluster.

Creating a multinode cluster using kubeadm

In this section, I'll introduce you to `kubeadm`, the recommended tool for creating Kubernetes clusters on all environments. It is still under active development, but it is the way to go because it is part of Kubernetes, and will always embody best practices. To make it accessible for the entire cluster, we will base it on VMs. This section is for readers who want a hands-on experience of deploying a multi-node cluster.

Setting expectations

Before embarking on this journey, I want to make it clear that it might *not* be a smooth ride. `kubeadm` has a difficult task: It has to follow the evolution of Kubernetes itself, which is a moving target. As a result, it is not always stable. When I wrote the first edition of *Mastering Kubernetes*, I had to dig deep and hunt for various workarounds to make it work. Guess what? I had to do the same thing for the second edition. Be prepared to make some adjustments and ask around. If you want a more streamlined solution, I will discuss some very good options later.

Getting ready

Kubeadm operates on preprovisioned hardware (physical or virtual). Before we create the Kubernetes cluster, we need to prepare a few VMs and install basic software, such as `docker`, `kubelet`, `kubeadm`, and `kubectl` (which is only needed on the master).

Preparing a cluster of vagrant VMs

The following vagrant file will create a cluster of four VMs called n1, n2, n3, and n4. Type
vagrant up to get the cluster up and running. It is based on Bento/Ubuntu versions 16.04
and not Ubuntu/Xenial, which suffers from various issues:

```ruby
# -*- mode: ruby -*-
# vi: set ft=ruby :
hosts = {
  "n1" => "192.168.77.10",
  "n2" => "192.168.77.11",
  "n3" => "192.168.77.12",
  "n4" => "192.168.77.13"
}
Vagrant.configure("2") do |config|
  # always use Vagrants insecure key
  config.ssh.insert_key = false
  # forward ssh agent to easily ssh into the different machines
  config.ssh.forward_agent = true

  check_guest_additions = false
  functional_vboxsf     = false

  config.vm.box = "bento/ubuntu-16.04"
 hosts.each do |name, ip|
    config.vm.hostname = name
    config.vm.define name do |machine|
      machine.vm.network :private_network, ip: ip
      machine.vm.provider "virtualbox" do |v|
        v.name = name
      end
    end
  end
end
```

Installing the required software

I like Ansible a lot for configuration management. I installed it on the n4 VM (running
Ubuntu 16.04). From now on I'll use n4 as my control machine, which means we're
operating in a Linux environment. I could use Ansible directly on my Mac, but since
Ansible doesn't run on Windows, I prefer a more universal approach:

```
> vagrant ssh n4
Welcome to Ubuntu 16.04.3 LTS (GNU/Linux 4.4.0-87-generic x86_64)
* Documentation:  https://help.ubuntu.com
```

```
 * Management:        https://landscape.canonical.com
 * Support:           https://ubuntu.com/advantage
0 packages can be updated.
0 updates are security updates.
vagrant@vagrant:~$ sudo apt-get -y --fix-missing install python-pip
°₀₎sshpass
vagrant@vagrant:~$ sudo pip install  ansible
```

I used version 2.5.0. You should be fine with the latest version:

```
vagrant@vagrant:~$ ansible --version
ansible 2.5.0
  config file = None
  configured module search path =
[u'/home/vagrant/.ansible/plugins/modules',
u'/usr/share/ansible/plugins/modules']
  ansible python module location = /home/vagrant/.local/lib/python2.7/site-
packages/ansible
  executable location = /home/vagrant/.local/bin/ansible
  python version = 2.7.12 (default, Dec 4 2017, 14:50:18) [GCC 5.4.0
20160609]
  python version = 2.7.12 (default, Dec 4 2017, 14:50:18) [GCC 5.4.0
20160609]
```

The `sshpass` program I installed will help `ansible` connect to all the vagrant VMs with the built-in vagrant user. This is important only for a local VM-based multi-node cluster.

I created a directory called `ansible` and put three files in it: `hosts`, `vars.yml`, and `playbook.yml`.

The host file

The `host` file is the inventory file that tells the `ansible` directory what hosts to operate on. The hosts must be SSH-accessible from the controller machine. The following are the three VMs that the cluster will be installed on:

```
[all]
192.168.77.10 ansible_user=vagrant ansible_ssh_pass=vagrant
192.168.77.11 ansible_user=vagrant ansible_ssh_pass=vagrant
192.168.77.12 ansible_user=vagrant ansible_ssh_pass=vagrant
```

The vars.yml file

The `vars.yml` file just keeps a list of the packages I want to install on each node. `vim`, `htop`, and `tmux` are my favorite packages to install on each machine I need to manage. The others are required by Kubernetes:

```
---
PACKAGES:
  - vim  - htop  - tmux  - docker.io
  - kubelet
  - kubeadm
  - kubectl
  - kubernetes-cni
```

The playbook.yml file

The `playbook.yml` file is the file you run to install the packages on all hosts:

```
---
- hosts: all
  become: true
  vars_files:
    - vars.yml
  strategy: free
  tasks:
   - name: hack to resolve Problem with MergeList Issue
     shell: 'find /var/lib/apt/lists -maxdepth 1 -type f -exec rm -v {} \;'
   - name: update apt cache directly (apt module not reliable)
     shell: 'apt-get clean && apt-get update'
   - name: Preliminary installation
     apt:  name=apt-transport-https force=yes
   - name: Add the Google signing key
     apt_key: url=https://packages.cloud.google.com/apt/doc/apt-key.gpg
state=present
   - name: Add the k8s APT repo
     apt_repository: repo='deb http://apt.kubernetes.io/ kubernetes-xenial
main' state=present
   - name: update apt cache directly (apt module not reliable)
     shell: 'apt-get update'
   - name: Install packages
     apt: name={{ item }} state=installed force=yes
     with_items: "{{ PACKAGES }}"
```

Since some of the packages are from the Kubernetes APT repository, I need to add it, along with the Google signing key:

Connect to n4:

```
> vagrant ssh n4
```

You may need to ssh once to each of the n1, n2, and n3 nodes:

```
vagrant@vagrant:~$ ssh 192.168.77.10
vagrant@vagrant:~$ ssh 192.168.77.11
vagrant@vagrant:~$ ssh 192.168.77.12
```

A more permanent solution is to add a file called ~/.ansible.cfg that contains the following:

```
[defaults]
host_key_checking = False
```

Run the playbook from n4 as follows:

```
vagrant@n4:~$ ansible-playbook -i hosts playbook.yml
```

> If you run into connection failure, try again. The Kubernetes APT repository is sometimes slow to respond. You need to do this just once per node.

Creating the cluster

It's time to create the cluster itself. We'll initialize the master on the first VM, then set up networking and add the rest of the VMs as nodes.

Initializing the master

Let's initialize the master on n1 (192.168.77.10). It is critical to use the --apiserver-advertise-address flag in case of a vagrant VM-based cloud:

```
> vagrant ssh n1
vagrant@n1:~$ sudo kubeadm init --apiserver-advertise-address 192.168.77.10
```

In Kubernetes 1.10.1, this results in the following error message:

```
[init] Using Kubernetes version: v1.10.1
[init] Using Authorization modes: [Node RBAC]
[preflight] Running pre-flight checks.
    [WARNING FileExisting-crictl]: crictl not found in system path
[preflight] Some fatal errors occurred:
    [ERROR Swap]: running with swap on is not supported. Please disable
swap
[preflight] If you know what you are doing, you can make a check non-fatal
with `--ignore-preflight-errors=...`
```

The reason is that the required cri-tools are not installed by default. We are dealing with the cutting edge of Kubernetes here. I created an additional playbook to install Go and cri-tools, turned off the swap, and fixed the hostname of the vagrant VMs:

```
---
- hosts: all
  become: true
  strategy: free
  tasks:
  - name: Add the longsleep repo for recent golang version
    apt_repository: repo='ppa:longsleep/golang-backports' state=present
  - name: update apt cache directly (apt module not reliable)
    shell: 'apt-get update'
    args:
      warn: False
  - name: Install Go
    apt: name=golang-go state=present force=yes
  - name: Install crictl
    shell: 'go get github.com/kubernetes-incubator/cri-tools/cmd/crictl'
    become_user: vagrant
  - name: Create symlink in /usr/local/bin for crictl
    file:
      src: /home/vagrant/go/bin/crictl
      dest: /usr/local/bin/crictl
      state: link
  - name: Set hostname properly
    shell: "hostname n$((1 + $(ifconfig | grep 192.168 | awk '{print $2}'
| tail -c 2)))"
   - name: Turn off swap
     shell: 'swapoff -a'

  -
```

Remember to run it on n4 again to update all the nodes in the cluster.

Here is some of the output of a successful launch of Kubernetes:

```
vagrant@n1:~$ sudo kubeadm init --apiserver-advertise-address 192.168.77.10
[init] Using Kubernetes version: v1.10.1
[init] Using Authorization modes: [Node RBAC]
[certificates] Generated ca certificate and key.
[certificates] Generated apiserver certificate and key.
[certificates] Valid certificates and keys now exist in
"/etc/kubernetes/pki"
.
.
.

[addons] Applied essential addon: kube-dns
[addons] Applied essential addon: kube-proxy
Your Kubernetes master has initialized successfully!
```

There will be a lot more information that you must write down to join other nodes to the cluster later. To start using your cluster, you need to run the following as a regular user:

```
vagrant@n1:~$ mkdir -p $HOME/.kube
vagrant@n1:~$ sudo cp -i /etc/kubernetes/admin.conf $HOME/.kube/config
vagrant@n1:~$ sudo chown $(id -u):$(id -g) $HOME/.kube/config
```

You can now join any number of machines by running a command on each node as the root. Use the command returned from kubeadm init cmmand:sudo kubeadm join --token << token>> --discovery-token-ca-cert-hash <<discvery token>> --skip-prflight-cheks.

Setting up the pod network

The networking of the cluster is the big-ticket item. The pods need to be able to talk to each other. That requires a pod network add-on. There are several options for this. Clusters generated by kubeadm, require a CNI-based add-on. I chose to use the Weave Net add-on, which supports the Network Policy resource. Your can choose whatever you like.

Run the following commands on the master VM:

```
vagrant@n1:~$ sudo sysctl net.bridge.bridge-nf-call-iptables=1
net.bridge.bridge-nf-call-iptables = 1vagrant@n1:~$ kubectl apply -f
"https://cloud.weave.works/k8s/net?k8s-version=$(kubectl version | base64 |
tr -d '\n')"
```

You should see the following:

```
serviceaccount "weave-net" created
clusterrole.rbac.authorization.k8s.io "weave-net" created
```

```
clusterrolebinding.rbac.authorization.k8s.io "weave-net" created
role.rbac.authorization.k8s.io "weave-net" created
rolebinding.rbac.authorization.k8s.io "weave-net" created
daemonset.extensions "weave-net" created
```

To verify, use the following:

```
vagrant@n1:~$ kubectl get po --all-namespaces
NAMESPACE NAME READY STATUS RESTARTS AGE
kube-system etcd-n1 1/1 Running 0 2m
kube-system kube-apiserver-n1 1/1 Running 0 2m
kube-system kube-controller-manager-n1 1/1 Running 0 2m
kube-system kube-dns-86f4d74b45-jqctg 3/3 Running 0 3m
kube-system kube-proxy-154s9 1/1 Running 0 3m
kube-system kube-scheduler-n1 1/1 Running 0 2m
kube-system weave-net-fl7wn 2/2 Running 0 31s
```

The last pod is our `weave-net-fl7wn`, which is what we're looking for, as well as the `kube-dns pod`. Both are running. All is well!

Adding the worker nodes

Now we can add worker nodes to the cluster using the token we got earlier. On each node, run the following command (don't forget `sudo`) with the tokens you got when initializing Kubernetes on the master node:

```
sudo kubeadm join --token <<token>>  --discovery-token-ca-cert-hash
<<discovery token>> --ignore-preflight-errors=all
```

At the time of writing (using Kubernetes 1.10) some preflight checks fail, but this is a false negative. Everything is actually fine, and you can skip those preflight checks by adding `--ignore-preflight-errors=all`. I hope that when you read the book, these wrinkles will be ironed out. You should see the following:

```
[discovery] Trying to connect to API Server "192.168.77.10:6443"
[discovery] Created cluster-info discovery client, requesting info from
"https://192.168.77.10:6443"
[discovery] Requesting info from "https://192.168.77.10:6443" again to
validate TLS against the pinned public key
[discovery] Cluster info signature and contents are valid and TLS
certificate validates against pinned roots, will use API Server
"192.168.77.10:6443"
[discovery] Successfully established connection with API Server
"192.168.77.10:6443"
```

This node has joined the cluster:

```
* Certificate signing request was sent to master and a response
  was received.
* The Kubelet was informed of the new secure connection details.
```

Run `kubectl get nodes` on the master to see this node join the cluster.

This might not work for some combinations because of an issue with CNI plugin initialization.

Creating clusters in the cloud (GCP, AWS, and Azure)

Creating clusters locally is fun, and important during development and when trying to troubleshoot problems locally. But in the end, Kubernetes is designed for cloud-native applications (applications that run in the cloud). Kubernetes doesn't want to be aware of individual cloud environments because that doesn't scale. Instead, Kubernetes has the concept of a cloud-provider interface. Every cloud provider can implement this interface and then host Kubernetes. Note that, as of version 1.5, Kubernetes still maintains implementations for many cloud providers in its tree, but in the future, they will be refactored out.

The cloud-provider interface

The cloud-provider interface is a collection of Go data types and interfaces. It is defined in a file called `cloud.go`, available at `http://bit.ly/2fq4NbW`. Here is the main interface:

```
type Interface interface {
    Initialize(clientBuilder controller.ControllerClientBuilder)
    LoadBalancer() (LoadBalancer, bool)
    Instances() (Instances, bool)
    Zones() (Zones, bool)
    Clusters() (Clusters, bool)
    Routes() (Routes, bool)
    ProviderName() string
    HasClusterID() bool
}
```

This is very clear. Kubernetes operates in terms of instances, `Zones`, `Clusters`, and `Routes`, and also requires access to a load balancer and provider name. The main interface is primarily a gateway. Most methods return other interfaces.

For example, the `Clusters` interface is very simple:

```
type Clusters interface {
  ListClusters() ([]string, error)
  Master(clusterName string) (string, error)
}
```

The `ListClusters()` method returns cluster names. The `Master()` method returns the IP address or DNS name of the master node.

The other interfaces are not much more complicated. The entire file is 214 lines long (at the time of writing) and includes a lot of comments. The take-home point is that it is not too complicated to implement a Kubernetes provider if your cloud utilizes those basic concepts.

Google Cloud Platform (GCP)

The **Google Cloud Platform** (**GCP**) supports Kubernetes out of the box. The so-called **Google Kubernetes Engine** (**GKE**) is a container management solution built on Kubernetes. You don't need to install Kubernetes on GCP, and you can use the Google Cloud API to create Kubernetes clusters and provision them. The fact that Kubernetes is a built-in part of the GCP means it will always be well integrated and well tested, and you don't have to worry about changes to the underlying platform breaking the cloud-provider interface.

All in all, if you plan to base your system on Kubernetes and you don't have any existing code on other cloud platforms, then GCP is a solid choice.

Amazon Web Services (AWS)

Amazon Web Services (**AWS**) has its own container-management service called ECS, but it is not based on Kubernetes. You can run Kubernetes on AWS very well. It is a supported provider, and there is a lot of documentation on how to set it up. While you could provision some VMs yourself and use `kubeadm`, I recommend using the **Kubernetes operations** (**Kops**) project. Kops is a Kubernetes project available on GitHub (`http://bit.ly/2ft5KA5`). It is not part of Kubernetes itself, but it is developed and maintained by the Kubernetes developers.

It supports the following features:

- Automated Kubernetes cluster CRUD for the cloud (AWS)
- Highly-available (HA) Kubernetes clusters
- It uses a state-sync model for dry-run and automatic idempotency
- Custom support for `kubectl` add-ons
- Kops can generate Terraform configuration
- It is based on a simple meta-model defined in a directory tree
- Easy command-line syntax
- Community support

To create a cluster, you need to do some minimal DNS configuration through `route53`, set up a S3 bucket to store the cluster configuration, and then run a single command:

```
kops create cluster --cloud=aws --zones=us-east-1c ${NAME}
```

The complete instructions can be found at `http://bit.ly/2f7r6EK`.

At the end of 2017, AWS joined the CNCF and announced two big projects regarding Kubernetes: Its own Kubernetes-based container orchestration solution (EKS) and a container-on-demand solution (Fargate).

Amazon Elastic Container Service for Kubernetes (EKS)

Amazon Elastic Container Service for Kubernetes is a fully managed and highly available Kubernetes solution. It has three masters running in three AZs. EKS also takes care of upgrades and patching. The great thing about EKS is that it runs a stock Kubernetes without any changes. This means you can use all the standard plugins and tools developed by the community. It also opens the door to convenient cluster federation with other cloud providers and/or your own on-premises Kubernetes clusters.

EKS provides deep integration with AWS infrastructure. IAM authentication is integrated with Kubernetes **role-based access control (RBAC)**.

You can also use `PrivateLink` if you want to access your Kubernetes masters directly from your own Amazon VPC. With `PrivateLink`, your Kubernetes masters and the Amazon EKS service endpoint appear as elastic network interfaces with private IP addresses in your Amazon VPC.

Another important piece of the puzzle is a special CNI plugin that lets your Kubernetes components talk to each other using AWS networking.

Fargate

Fargate lets you run containers directly without worrying about provisioning hardware. It eliminates a huge part of the operational complexity at the cost of losing some control. When using Fargate, you package your application into a container, specify CPU and memory requirements, and define networking and IAM policies, and you're off to the races. Fargate can run on top of ECS and EKS. It is a very interesting member of the serverless camp, although it's not directly related to Kubernetes.

Azure

Azure used to have its own container management service. You could use the Mesos-based DC/OS or Docker Swarm to manage them, but you could also use Kubernetes, of course. You could also provision the cluster yourself (for example, using Azure's desired-state configuration) then create the Kubernetes cluster using `kubeadm`. The recommended approach used to be to use yet another non-core Kubernetes project called `kubernetes-anywhere` (`http://bit.ly/2eCS7Ps`). The goal of `kubernetes-anywhere` is to provide a cross-platform way to create clusters in a cloud environment (at least for GCP, AWS, and Azure).

The process is pretty painless. You need to have Docker, `make`, and `kubectl` installed, and of course, your Azure subscription ID. Then, you clone the `kubernetes-anywhere` repository, run a couple of `make` commands, and your cluster is good to go.

The complete instructions to create an Azure cluster are at `http://bit.ly/2d56WdA`.

However, in the second half of 2017, Azure jumped on the Kubernetes bandwagon too and introduced AKS-Azure Container Service. It is similar to Amazon EKS, although it's a little further ahead in its implementation.

AKS provides a REST API, as well as a CLI, to manage your Kubernetes cluster, but you can use `kubectl` and any other Kubernetes tooling directly.

Here are some of the benefits of using AKS:

- Automated Kubernetes version upgrades and patching
- Easy cluster scaling
- Self-healing hosted control plane (masters)
- Cost savings—pay only for running agent pool nodes

In this section, we covered the cloud-provider interface and looked at the various recommended ways to create Kubernetes clusters on various cloud providers. The scene is still young and the tools evolving quickly. I believe convergence will happen soon. Tools and projects such as `kubeadm`, `kops`, `Kargo`, and `kubernetes-anywhere` will eventually merge and provide a uniform and easy way to bootstrap Kubernetes clusters.

Alibaba Cloud

The Chinese **Alibaba** Cloud is an up-and-comer on the cloud platform scene. It mimics AWS pretty closely, although its English documentation leaves a lot to be desired. I deployed a production application on Ali Cloud, but not one that used Kubernetes clusters. There seems to be official support for Kubernetes on Ali Cloud, but the documentation is in Chinese. I found one forum post in English that details how to deploy a Kubernetes cluster on Ali Cloud at `https://www.alibabacloud.com/forum/read-830`.

Creating a bare-metal cluster from scratch

In the previous section, we looked at running Kubernetes on cloud providers. This is the dominant deployment story for Kubernetes, but there are strong use cases for running Kubernetes on bare metal. I don't focus here on hosted versus on-premises; this is yet another dimension. If you already manage a lot of servers on-premises, you are in the best position to decide.

Use cases for bare metal

Bare-metal clusters are a beast especially if you manage them yourself. There are companies that provide commercial support for bare-metal Kubernetes clusters, such as Platform 9, but the offerings are not mature yet. A solid open-source option is Kubespray, which can deploy industrial-strength Kubernetes clusters on bare metal, AWS, GCE, Azure, and OpenStack.

Here are some use cases where it makes sense:

- **Budget concerns**: If you already manage large-scale bare clusters, it may be much cheaper to run Kubernetes clusters on your physical infrastructure
- **Low network latency**: If you must have low latency between your nodes, then the VM overhead might be too much

- **Regulatory requirements**: If you must comply with regulations, you may not be allowed to use cloud providers
- **You want total control over hardware**: Cloud providers give you many options, but you may have particular needs

When should you consider creating a bare-metal cluster?

The complexities of creating a cluster from scratch are significant. A Kubernetes cluster is not a trivial beast. There is a lot of documentation on the web about how to set up bare-metal clusters, but as the whole ecosystem moves forward, many of these guides get out of date quickly.

You should consider going down this route if you have the operational capability to take the time to debug problems at every level of the stack. Most of the problems will probably be networking-related, but filesystems and storage drivers can bite you too, as well as general incompatibilities and version mismatches between components, such as Kubernetes itself, Docker (or rkt, if you brave it), Docker images, your OS, your OS kernel, and the various add-ons and tools you use.

The process

There is a lot to do. Here is a list of some of the concerns you'll have to address:

- Implementing your own cloud provider's interface or sidestepping it
- Choosing a networking model and how to implement it (using a CNI plugin or directly compiling)
- Whether or not to use a network policy
- Select images for system components
- Security models and SSL certificates
- Admin credentials
- Templates for components such as an API server, replication controller, and scheduler
- Cluster services such as DNS, logging, monitoring, and GUI

I recommend reading the guide at the Kubernetes site (`http://bit.ly/1ToR9EC`) to get a deeper understanding of what it takes to create a cluster from scratch.

Using virtual private cloud infrastructure

If your use case falls under the bare-metal use cases, but you don't have the necessary skilled manpower or the inclination to deal with the infrastructure challenges of bare metal, you have the option of using a private cloud such as OpenStack (for example, with stackube). If you want to aim a little higher in the abstraction ladder, then Mirantis offers a cloud platform built on top of OpenStack and Kubernetes.

In this section, we considered the option of building a bare-metal cluster Kubernetes cluster. We looked into the use cases that require it and highlighted the challenges and difficulties.

Bootkube

Bootkube is very interesting too. It can launch self-hosted Kubernetes clusters. Self-hosted means that most of the cluster components run as regular pods and can be managed, monitored, and upgraded using the same tools and processes you use for your containerized applications. There are significant benefits to this approach, which simplifies the development and operation of Kubernetes clusters.

Summary

In this chapter, we got into some hands-on cluster creation. We created a single-node cluster using Minikube and a multi-node cluster using `kubeadm`. Then we looked at the many options to create Kubernetes clusters using cloud providers. Finally, we touched on the complexities of creating Kubernetes clusters on bare metal. The current state of affairs is very dynamic. The basic components are changing rapidly, the tooling is still young, and there are different options for each environment. It's not completely trivial to set up a Kubernetes cluster, but with some effort and attention to detail, you can get it done quickly.

In the next chapter, we will explore the important topics of monitoring, logging, and troubleshooting. Once your cluster is up and running and you start deploying workloads, you need to make sure that it runs properly and satisfies requirements. This requires ongoing attention and responding to various failures that happen in the real world.

11
Cluster Federation and Multi-Tenancy

This chapter will discuss the new federation capabilities and how to use them to manage multiple clusters across cloud providers. We will also cover the federated version of the core constructs. We will walk you through federated Deployments, ReplicaSets, ConfigMaps, and Events.

This chapter will discuss the following topics:

- Federating clusters
- Federating multiple clusters
- Inspecting and controlling resources across multiple clusters
- Launching resources across multiple clusters

Technical requirements

You'll need to have your Google Cloud Platform account enabled and logged in, or you can use a local Minikube instance of Kubernetes. You can also use Play with Kubernetes over the web: `https://labs.play-with-k8s.com/`. There's also the Katacoda playground at `https://www.katacoda.com/courses/kubernetes/playground`.

You'll also need GitHub credentials, the setting up of which we'll go over later in this chapter. Here's the GitHub repository for this chapter: `https://github.com/PacktPublishing/The-Complete-Kubernetes-Guide/tree/master/Chapter11`.

Introduction to federation

While federation is still very new in Kubernetes, it lays the groundwork for a highly sought after cross-cloud provider solution. Using federation, we can run multiple Kubernetes clusters on-premises and in one or more public cloud providers and manage applications utilizing the entire set of all our organizational resources.

This begins to create a path for avoiding cloud provider lock-in and highly available deployment that can place application servers in multiple clusters and allow for communication to other services located in single points among our federated clusters. We can improve isolation on outages at a particular provider or geographic location while providing greater flexibility for scaling and utilizing total infrastructure.

Currently, the federation plane supports these resources: ConfigMap, DaemonSets, Deployment, Events, Ingress, Namespaces, ReplicaSets, Secrets, and Services. Note that federation and its components are in alpha and beta phases of release, so functionality may still be a bit temperamental.

Why federation?

There are several major advantages to taking on Kubernetes cluster federation. As mentioned previously, federation allows you increase the availability and tenancy capabilities of your Kubernetes clusters. By scaling across availability zones or regions of a single **cloud service provider** (**CSP**), or by scaling across multiple CSPs, federation takes the concept of high availability to the next level. Some term this global scheduling, which will could enable you to direct traffic in order to maximize an inexpensive CSP resource that becomes available in the spot market. You could also use global scheduling to relocate workloads cluster to end use populations, improving the performance of your applications.

There is also the opportunity to treat entire clusters as if they were Kubernetes objects, and deal with failure on a per-cluster basis instead of per machine. Cluster federation could allow operators to automatically recover from entire clusters failing by routing traffic to redundant, available clusters.

It should be noted that, while federation increases the potential for high availability on your cluster, it's clear that the significant increase in complexity also lowers your potential reliability if your clusters aren't managed well. You can manage some of this complexity by using a hosted PaaS version of Kubernetes such as GKE, where leaving the cluster management to GCP will drastically lower the operational load on your teams.

Federation can also enable your team to support a hybrid environment, with on-premises clusters pairing with your resources in the cloud. Depending on your traffic routing requirements, this may require additional engineering in the form of a service mesh.

There's a number of technical features that federation supplies, which enable higher potential availability.

The building blocks of federation

Federation makes it easy to manage resources across clusters by providing two distinct types of building blocks. The first is resources and the second is service discovery:

- **Resource synchronization across clusters**: Federation is the glue that allows you to keep track of the many resources needed to run sets of applications. When you're running a lot of applications, with many resources and object types, across many clusters, federation is key to keeping your clusters organized and managed well. You may find yourself needing to keep an application deployment running in multiple clusters with a single pane of glass view.
- **Multi-cluster service discovery**: There are a number of resources that share well between clusters such as DNS, load balancers, object storage, and ingress. Federation gives you the ability to automatically configure those services with multi-cluster awareness, so you can route application traffic and manage the control plane across several clusters.

As we'll learn next, Kubernetes federation is managed by a tool named `kubefed`, which has a number of command-line flags that allow you to manage many clusters and the building blocks we discussed previously. The major building blocks of `kubefed` that we'll use are as follows:

- `kubefed init`: Initialize a federation control plane
- `kubefed join`: Join a cluster to a federation
- `kubefed options`: Print the list of flags inherited by all commands
- `kubefed unjoin`: Unjoin a cluster from a federation
- `kubefed version`: Print the client and server version information

Here's a handy list of the options that can be used:

```
        --alsologtostderr                          log to standard error
as well as files
        --as string                                Username to
impersonate for the operation
        --as-group stringArray                     Group to impersonate
for the operation, this flag can be repeated to specify multiple groups.
        --cache-dir string                         Default HTTP cache
directory (default "/Users/jrondeau/.kube/http-cache")
        --certificate-authority string             Path to a cert file
for the certificate authority
        --client-certificate string                Path to a client
certificate file for TLS
        --client-key string                        Path to a client key
file for TLS
        --cloud-provider-gce-lb-src-cidrs cidrs    CIDRs opened in GCE
firewall for LB traffic proxy & health checks (default
130.211.0.0/22,209.85.152.0/22,209.85.204.0/22,35.191.0.0/16)
        --cluster string                           The name of the
kubeconfig cluster to use
        --context string                           The name of the
kubeconfig context to use
        --default-not-ready-toleration-seconds int     Indicates the
tolerationSeconds of the toleration for notReady:NoExecute that is added by
default to every pod that does not already have such a toleration. (default
300)
        --default-unreachable-toleration-seconds int   Indicates the
tolerationSeconds of the toleration for unreachable:NoExecute that is added
by default to every pod that does not already have such a toleration.
(default 300)
    -h, --help                                     help for kubefed
        --insecure-skip-tls-verify                 If true, the server's
certificate will not be checked for validity. This will make your HTTPS
connections insecure
        --ir-data-source string                    Data source used by
InitialResources. Supported options: influxdb, gcm. (default "influxdb")
        --ir-dbname string                         InfluxDB database name
which contains metrics required by InitialResources (default "k8s")
        --ir-hawkular string                       Hawkular configuration
URL
        --ir-influxdb-host string                  Address of InfluxDB
which contains metrics required by InitialResources (default
"localhost:8080/api/v1/namespaces/kube-system/services/monitoring-
influxdb:api/proxy")
        --ir-namespace-only                        Whether the estimation
should be made only based on data from the same namespace.
        --ir-password string                       Password used for
```

```
connecting to InfluxDB (default "root")
      --ir-percentile int                          Which percentile of
samples should InitialResources use when estimating resources. For
experiment purposes. (default 90)
      --ir-user string                             User used for
connecting to InfluxDB (default "root")
      --kubeconfig string                          Path to the kubeconfig
file to use for CLI requests.
      --log-backtrace-at traceLocation             when logging hits line
file:N, emit a stack trace (default :0)
      --log-dir string                             If non-empty, write
log files in this directory
      --log-flush-frequency duration               Maximum number of
seconds between log flushes (default 5s)
      --logtostderr                                log to standard error
instead of files (default true)
      --match-server-version                       Require server version
to match client version
  -n, --namespace string                           If present, the
namespace scope for this CLI request
      --password string                            Password for basic
authentication to the API server
      --request-timeout string                     The length of time to
wait before giving up on a single server request. Non-zero values should
contain a corresponding time unit (e.g. 1s, 2m, 3h). A value of zero means
don't timeout requests. (default "0")
  -s, --server string                              The address and port
of the Kubernetes API server
      --stderrthreshold severity                   logs at or above this
threshold go to stderr (default 2)
      --token string                               Bearer token for
authentication to the API server
      --user string                                The name of the
kubeconfig user to use
      --username string                            Username for basic
authentication to the API server
  -v, --v Level                                    log level for V logs
      --vmodule moduleSpec                         comma-separated list
of pattern=N settings for file-filtered logging
```

Here's a high-level diagram that shows what all of these pieces look like when strung together:

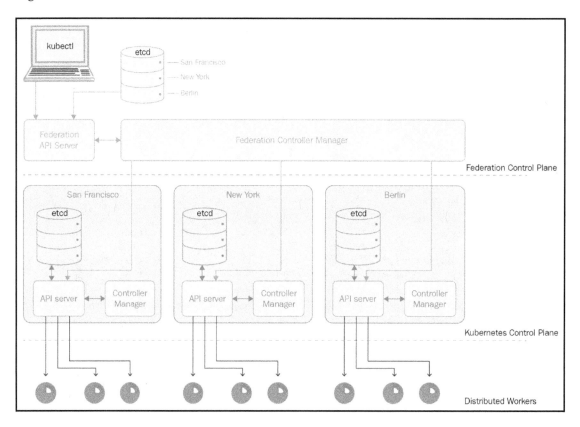

Key components

There are two key components to the federation capability within Kubernetes. These components make up the federation control plane.

The first is `federation-controller-manager`, which embeds the core control loops required to operate federation. `federation-controller-manager` watches the state of your clusters via `apiserver` and makes changes in order to reach a desired state.

The second is `federation-apiserver`, which validates and configures Kubernetes objects such as pods, services, and controllers. `federation-apiserver` is the frontend for the cluster through which all other components interact.

Federated services

Now that we have the building blocks of federation conceptualized in our mind, let's review one more facet of this before setting up federation. How exactly does a common service, deployed across multiple clusters, work?

Federated services are created in a very similar fashion to regular services: first, by sending the desired state and properties of the service to an API endpoint, which is then brought to bear by the Kubernetes architecture. There are two main differences:

- A non-federated service will make an API call directly to a cluster API endpoint
- A federated service will make the call to the Federated API endpoint at `federation/v1beta1`, which will then redirect the API call to all of the individual clusters within the federation control plane

This second type of service allows us to extend such things as DNS service discovery across cluster boundaries. The DNS `resolv` chain is able to leverage service federation and public DNS records to resolve names across multiple clusters.

 The API for a federated service is 100% compatible with regular services.

When a service is created, federation takes care of several things. First, it creates matching services in all clusters where `kubefed` specifies they reside. The health of those services is monitored so that traffic can be routed or re-routed to them. Lastly, federation ensure that there's a definitive set of public DNS records available through providers such as Route 53 or Google Cloud DNS.

Microservices residing on different pods within your Kubernetes clusters will use all of this machinery in order to locate the federated service either within their own cluster or navigate to the nearest healthy example within your federation map.

Setting up federation

While we can use the cluster we had running for the rest of the examples, I would highly recommend that you start fresh. The default naming of the clusters and contexts can be problematic for the federation system. Note that the `--cluster-context` and `--secret-name` flags are there to help you work around the default naming, but for first-time federation, it can still be confusing and less than straightforward.

Hence, starting fresh is how we will walk through the examples in this chapter. Either use new and separate cloud provider (AWS and/or GCE) accounts or tear down the current cluster and reset your Kubernetes control environment by running the following commands:

```
$ kubectl config unset contexts
$ kubectl config unset clusters
```

Double-check that nothing is listed using the following commands:

```
$ kubectl config get-contexts
$ kubectl config get-clusters
```

Next, we will want to get the `kubefed` command on our path and make it executable. Navigate back to the folder where you have the Kubernetes download extracted. The `kubefed` command is located in the `/kubernetes/client/bin` folder. Run the following commands to get in the `bin` folder and change the execution permissions:

```
$ sudo cp kubernetes/client/bin/kubefed /usr/local/bin
$ sudo chmod +x /usr/local/bin/kubefed
```

Contexts

Contexts are used by the Kubernetes control plane to keep authentication and cluster configuration stored for multiple clusters. This allows us to access and manage multiple clusters accessible from the same `kubectl`. You can always see the contexts available with the `get-contexts` command that we used earlier.

New clusters for federation

Again, make sure you navigate to wherever Kubernetes was downloaded and move into the `cluster` sub-folder:

```
$ cd kubernetes/cluster/
```

Before we proceed, make sure you have the GCE command line and the AWS command line installed, authenticated, and configured. Refer to `Chapter 1`, *Introduction to Kubernetes*, if you need assistance doing so on a new box.

First, we will create the AWS cluster. Note that we are adding an environment variable named OVERRIDE_CONTEXT, which will allow us to set the context name to something that complies with the DNS naming standards. DNS is a critical component for federation as it allows us to do cross-cluster discovery and service communication. This is important in a federated world where clusters may be in different data centers and even providers.

Run these commands to create your AWS cluster:

```
$ export KUBERNETES_PROVIDER=aws
$ export OVERRIDE_CONTEXT=awsk8s
$ ./kube-up.sh
```

Next, we will create a GCE cluster, once again using the OVERRIDE_CONTEXT environment variable:

```
$ export KUBERNETES_PROVIDER=gce
$ export OVERRIDE_CONTEXT=gcek8s
$ ./kube-up.sh
```

If we take a look at our contexts now, we will notice both awsk8s and gcek8s, which we just created. The star in front of gcek8s denotes that it's where kubectl is currently pointing and executing against:

```
$ kubectl config get-contexts
```

The preceding command should produce something like the following:

CURRENT	NAME	CLUSTER	AUTHINFO	NAMESPACE
	awsk8s	awsk8s	awsk8s	
*	gcek8s	gcek8s	gcek8s	

Initializing the federation control plane

Now that we have two clusters, let's set up the federation control plane in the GCE cluster. First, we'll need to make sure that we are in the GCE context, and then we will initialize the federation control plane:

```
$ kubectl config use-context gcek8s
$ kubefed init master-control --host-cluster-context=gcek8s --dns-zone-name="mydomain.com"
```

The preceding command creates a new context just for federation called `master-control`. It uses the `gcek8s` cluster/context to host the federation components (such as API server and controller). It assumes GCE DNS as the federation's DNS service. You'll need to update `dns-zone-name` with a domain suffix you manage.

> By default, the DNS provider is GCE. You can use `--dns-provider="aws-route53"` to set it to AWS `route53`; however, out of the box implementation still has issues for many users.

If we check our contexts once again, we will now see three contexts:

```
$ kubectl config get-contexts
```

The preceding command should produce something like the following:

```
CURRENT   NAME              CLUSTER           AUTHINFO          NAMESPACE
          awsk8s            awsk8s            awsk8s
*         gcek8s            gcek8s            gcek8s
          master-control    master-control   master-control
```

Let's make sure we have all of the federation components running before we proceed. The federation control plane uses the `federation-system` namespace. Use the `kubectl get pods` command with the namespace specified to monitor the progress. Once you see two API server pods and one controller pod, you should be set:

```
$ kubectl get pods --namespace=federation-system
```

```
NAME                                                    READY    STATUS
RESTARTS    AGE
master-control-apiserver-3595964982-s61x9               2/2      Running
0           8m
master-control-controller-manager-516854663-r8m37       1/1      Running
0           8m
```

Now that we have the federation components set up and running, let's switch to that context for the next steps:

```
$ kubectl config use-context master-control
```

Adding clusters to the federation system

Now that we have our federation control plane, we can add the clusters to the federation system. First, we will join the GCE cluster and then the AWS cluster:

```
$ kubefed join gcek8s --host-cluster-context=gcek8s --secret-name=fed-
secret-gce
$ kubefed join awsk8s --host-cluster-context=gcek8s --secret-name=fed-
secret-aws
```

Federated resources

Federated resources allow us to deploy across multiple clusters and/or regions. Currently, version 1.5 of Kubernetes support a number of core resource types in the federation API, including ConfigMap, DaemonSets, Deployment, Events, Ingress, Namespaces, ReplicaSets, Secrets, and Services.

Let's take a look at a federated deployment that will allow us to schedule pods across both AWS and GCE. Save the following file as node-js-deploy-fed.yaml:

```
apiVersion: extensions/v1beta1
kind: Deployment
metadata:
  name: node-js-deploy
  labels:
    name: node-js-deploy
spec:
  replicas: 3
  template:
    metadata:
      labels:
        name: node-js-deploy
    spec:
      containers:
      - name: node-js-deploy
        image: jonbaier/pod-scaling:latest
        ports:
        - containerPort: 80
```

Create this deployment with the following command:

```
$ kubectl create -f node-js-deploy-fed.yaml
```

Now, let's try listing the pods from this deployment:

```
$ kubectl get pods
```

```
the server doesn't have a resource type "pods"
```

We should see a message like the preceding one depicted. This is because we are still using `master-control` or federation context, which does not itself run pods. We will, however, see the deployment in the federation plane and, if we inspect the events, we will see that the deployment was in fact created on both of our federated clusters:

```
$ kubectl get deployments
$ kubectl describe deployments node-js-deploy
```

We should see something like the following. Notice that the `Events:` section shows deployments in both our GCE and AWS contexts:

```
Name:                    node-js-deploy
Namespace:               default
CreationTimestamp:       Fri, 10 Mar 2017 22:15:11 +0000
Labels:                  name=node-js-deploy
Selector:                name=node-js-deploy
Replicas:                0 updated | 3 total | 3 available | 0 unavailable
StrategyType:            RollingUpdate
MinReadySeconds:         0
RollingUpdateStrategy:   1 max unavailable, 1 max surge
Events:
    FirstSeen       LastSeen          Count    From
 SubObjectPath       Type             Reason              Message
   ---------       ---------          ------   ----
 -------------     ---------          ------   -------
     4m              4m                1               {federated-deployment-controller }
 Normal           CreateInCluster Creating deployment in cluster gcek8s
     4m              4m                1               {federated-deployment-controller }
 Normal           CreateInCluster Creating deployment in cluster awsk8s
```

We can also see the federated events using the following command:

```
$ kubectl get events
```

```
LASTSEEN    FIRSTSEEN    COUNT    NAME              KIND          SUBOBJECT    TYPE
   REASON                 SOURCE                                  MESSAGE
10m         10m          1        node-js-deploy    Deployment                 Normal
   CreateInCluster    {federated-deployment-controller }   Creating deployment in
cluster gcek8s
10m         10m          1        node-js-deploy    Deployment                 Normal
   CreateInCluster    {federated-deployment-controller }   Creating deployment in
cluster awsk8s
```

It may take a moment for all three pods to run. Once that happens, we can switch to each cluster context and see some of the pods on each. Note that we can now use get pods since we are on the individual clusters and not on the control plane:

```
$ kubectl config use-context awsk8s
$ kubectl get pods
```

```
NAME                              READY    STATUS     RESTARTS    AGE
node-js-deploy-1713031517-1661z   1/1      Running    0           7m
```

```
$ kubectl config use-context gcek8s
$ kubectl get pods
```

```
NAME                              READY    STATUS     RESTARTS    AGE
node-js-deploy-1713031517-bvdmf   1/1      Running    0           7m
node-js-deploy-1713031517-jnfnr   1/1      Running    0           7m
```

We should see the three pods spread across the clusters with two on one and a third on the other. Kubernetes has spread them across the cluster without any manual intervention. Any pods that fail will be restarted, but now we have the added redundancy of two cloud providers.

Federated configurations

In modern software development, it is common to separate configuration variables from the application code itself. In this way, it is easier to make updates to service URLs, credentials, common paths, and so on. Having these values in external configuration files means we can easily update configuration without rebuilding the entire application.

This separation solves the initial problem, but true portability comes when you can remove the dependency from the application completely. Kubernetes offers a configuration store for exactly this purpose. ConfigMaps are simple constructs that store key-value pairs.

 Kubernetes also supports Secrets for more sensitive configuration data. This will be covered in more detail in Chapter 12, *Cluster Authentication, Authorization, and Container Security*. You can use the example there in both single clusters or on the federation control plane as we are demonstrating with ConfigMaps here.

Let's take a look at an example that will allow us to store some configuration and then consume it in various pods. The following listings will work for both federated and single clusters, but we will continue using a federated setup for this example.

The ConfigMap kind can be created using literal values, flat files and directories, and finally YAML definition files. The following listing is a YAML definition of the configmap-fed.yaml file:

```
apiVersion: v1
kind: ConfigMap
metadata:
  name: my-application-config
  namespace: default
data:
  backend-service.url: my-backend-service
```

Let's first switch back to our federation plane:

```
$ kubectl config use-context master-control
```

Now, create this listing with the following command:

```
$ kubectl create -f configmap-fed.yaml
```

Let's display the configmap object that we just created. The -o yaml flag helps us to display the full information:

```
$ kubectl get configmap my-application-config -o yaml
```

```
apiVersion: v1
data:
  backend-service.url: my-backend-service
kind: ConfigMap
metadata:
  creationTimestamp: 2017-03-10T22:28:38Z
  name: my-application-config
  namespace: default
  resourceVersion: "1959"
  selfLink: /api/v1/namespaces/default/configmaps/my-application-config
  uid: e85a0028-05e0-11e7-bdf8-42010a800002
```

Now that we have a ConfigMap object, let's start up a federated ReplicaSet that can use the ConfigMap object. This will create replicas of pods across our cluster that can access the ConfigMap object. ConfigMaps can be accessed via environment variables or mount volumes. This example will use a mount volume that provides a folder hierarchy and the files for each key with the contents representing the values. Save the following file as configmap-rs-fed.yaml:

```
apiVersion: extensions/v1beta1
kind: ReplicaSet
metadata:
  name: node-js-rs
spec:
  replicas: 3
  selector:
    matchLabels:
      name: node-js-configmap-rs
  template:
    metadata:
      labels:
        name: node-js-configmap-rs
    spec:
      containers:
      - name: configmap-pod
        image: jonbaier/node-express-info:latest
        ports:
        - containerPort: 80
          name: web
        volumeMounts:
        - name: configmap-volume
          mountPath: /etc/config
```

```
volumes:
    - name: configmap-volume
      configMap:
        name: my-application-config
```

Create this pod with `kubectl create -f configmap-rs-fed.yaml`. After creation, we will need to switch contexts to one of the clusters where the pods are running. You can choose either, but we will use the GCE context here:

```
$ kubectl config use-context gcek8s
```

Now that we are on the GCE cluster specifically, let's check `configmaps` here:

```
$ kubectl get configmaps
```

As you can see, the `ConfigMap` is propagated locally to each cluster. Next, let's find a pod from our federated `ReplicaSet`:

```
$ kubectl get pods
```

```
NAME                              READY   STATUS    RESTARTS   AGE
node-js-deploy-1713031517-cmd7q   1/1     Running   0          39m
node-js-deploy-1713031517-zncxr   1/1     Running   0          39m
node-js-rs-6g7nj                  1/1     Running   0          9m
node-js-rs-f4w7b                  1/1     Running   0          9m
```

Let's take one of the `node-js-rs` pod names from the listing and run a bash shell with `kubectl exec`:

```
$ kubectl exec -it node-js-rs-6g7nj bash
```

Then, let's change directories to the `/etc/config` folder that we set up in the pod definition. Listing this directory reveals a single file with the name of the `ConfigMap` we defined earlier:

```
$ cd /etc/config
$ ls
```

If we then display the contents of the files with the following command, we should see the value we entered earlier, `my-backend-service`:

```
$ echo $(cat backend-service.url)
```

If we were to look in any of the pods across our federated cluster, we would see the same values. This is a great way to decouple configuration from an application and distribute it across our fleet of clusters.

Federated horizontal pod autoscalers

Let's look at another example of a newer resource that you can use with the federated model: **horizontal pod autoscalers (HPAs)**.

Here's what the architecture of these looks like in a single cluster:

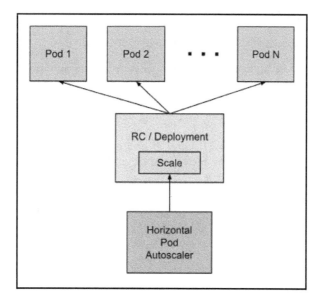

Credit: https://kubernetes.io/docs/tasks/run-application/
horizontal-pod-autoscale/#how-does-the-horizontal-pod-
autoscaler-work.

These HPAs will act in a similar fashion to normal HPAs, with the same functionality and same API-based compatibility—only, with federation, the management will traverse your clusters. This is an alpha feature, so it is not enabled by default on your cluster. In order to enable it, you'll need to run `federation-apiserver` with the `--runtime-config=api/all=true` option. Currently, the only metrics that work to manage HPAs are CPU utilization metrics.

First, let's create a file that contains the HPA configuration, called `node-hpa-fed.yaml`:

```
apiVersion: autoscaling/v1
kind: HorizontalPodAutoscaler
metadata:
  name: nodejs
  namespace: default
spec:
  scaleTargetRef:
    apiVersion: apps/v1beta1    kind: Deployment
name: nodejs
  minReplicas: 5
  maxReplicas: 20
  targetCPUUtilizationPercentage: 70
```

We can add this to our cluster with the following command:

kubectl --context=federation-cluster create -f node-hpa-fed.yaml

In this case, `--context=federation-cluster` is telling `kubectl` to send the request to `federation-apiserver` instead of `kube-apiserver`.

If, for example, you wanted to restrict this HPA to a subset of your Kubernetes clusters, you can use cluster selectors to restrict the federated object by using the `federation.alpha.kubernetes.io/cluster-selector` annotation. It's similar in function to nodeSelector, but acts upon full Kubernetes clusters. Cool! You'll need to create an annotation in JSON format. Here's a specific example of a ClusterSelector annotation:

```
metadata:
  annotations:
      federation.alpha.kubernetes.io/cluster-selector: '[{"key": "hipaa",
"operator":
        "In", "values": ["true"]}, {"key": "environment", "operator":
"NotIn", "values": ["nonprod"]}]'
```

This example is going to keep workloads with the `hipaa` label out of environments with the `nonprod` label.

For a full list of Top Level Federation API objects, see the following: `https://kubernetes.io/docs/reference/federation/`

You can check your clusters to see whether the HPA was created in an individual location by specifying the context:

```
kubectl --context=gce-cluster-01 get HPA nodejs
```

Once you're finished with the HPA, it can be deleted with the following `kubectl` command:

```
kubectl --context=federation-cluster delete HPA nodejs
```

How to use federated HPAs

HPAs used in the previous manner are an essential tool for ensuring that your clusters scale up as their workloads increase. The default behavior for HPA spreading in clusters ensure that maximum replicas are spread evenly first in all clusters. Let's say that you have 10 registered Kubernetes clusters in your federation control plane. If you have `spec.maxReplicas = 30`, each of the clusters will receive the following HPA `spec`:

```
spec.maxReplicas = 10
```

If you were to then set `spec.minReplicas = 5`, then some of the clusters will receive the following:

```
spec.minReplicas = 1
```

This is due to being unable to have a replica sum of 0. It's important to note that federation manipulates the minx/mix replicas it creates on the federated clusters, not by directly monitoring the target object metrics (in our case, CPU). The federated HPA controller is relying on HPAs within the federated cluster to monitor CPU utilization, which then makes changes to specs such as current and desired replicas.

Other federated resources

So far, we have seen federated Deployments, ReplicaSets, Events, and ConfigMaps in action. DaemonSets, Ingress, Namespaces, Secrets, and Services are also supported. Your specific setup will vary and you may have a set of clusters that differ from our example here. As mentioned earlier, these resources are still in beta, so it's worth spending some time to experiment with the various resource types and understand how well the federation constructs are supported for your particular mix of infrastructure.

Let's look at some examples that we can use to leverage other common Kubernetes API objects from a federated perspective.

Events

If you want to see what events are only stored in the federation control plane, you can use the following command:

```
kubectl --context=federation-cluster get events
```

Jobs

When you go to create a job, you'll use similar concepts as before. Here's what that looks like when you create a job within the federation context:

```
kubectl --context=federation-cluster create -f fedjob.yaml
```

You can get the list of these jobs within the federated context with the following:

```
kubectl --context=gce-cluster-01 get job fedjob
```

As with HPAs, you can spread your jobs across multiple underlying clusters with the appropriate specs. The relevant definitions are `spec.parallelism` and `spec.completions`, and they can be modified by specifying the correct `ReplicaAllocationPreferences` with the `federation.kubernetes.io/job-preferences` key.

True multi-cloud

This is an exciting space to watch. As it grows, it gives us a really good start to doing multi-cloud implementations and providing redundancy across regions, data centers, and even cloud providers.

While Kubernetes does provide an easy and exciting path to multi-cloud infrastructure, it's important to note that production multi-cloud requires much more than distributed deployments. A full set of capabilities from logging and monitoring to compliance and host-hardening, there is much to manage in a multi-provider setup.

True multi-cloud adoption will require a well-planned architecture, and Kubernetes takes a big step forward in pursuing this goal.

Getting to multi-cloud

In this exercise, we're going to unite two clusters using Istio's multi-cloud feature. Normally, we'd create two clusters from scratch, across two CSPs, but for the purposes of exploring one single isolated concept at a time, we're going to use the GKE to spin up our clusters, so we can focus on the inner workings of Istio's multi-cloud functionality.

Let's get started by logging in to your Google Cloud Project! First, you'll want to create a project in the GUI called `gsw-k8s-3`, if you haven't already, and get your Google Cloud Shell to point to it. If you're already pointed at your GCP account, you can disregard that.

Click this button for an easy way to get access to the CLI tools:

Once you've launched the shell, you can point it to your project:

```
anonymuse@cloudshell:~$ gcloud config set project gsw-k8s-3
Updated property [core/project].
anonymuse@cloudshell:~ (gsw-k8s-3)$
```

Next, we'll set up an environment variable for the project ID, which can echo back to see:

```
anonymuse@cloudshell:~ (gsw-k8s-3)$ proj=$(gcloud config list --
format='value(core.project)')
anonymuse@cloudshell:~ (gsw-k8s-3)$ echo $proj
Gsw-k8s-3
```

Now, let's create some clusters. Set some variables for the zone and cluster name:

```
zone="us-east1-b"
cluster="cluster-1"
```

First, create cluster one:

```
gcloud container clusters create $cluster --zone $zone --username "
  --cluster-version "1.10.6-gke.2" --machine-type "n1-standard-2" --image-
type "COS" --disk-size "100" \
  --scopes gke-default \
  --num-nodes "4" --network "default" --enable-cloud-logging --enable-cloud-
monitoring --enable-ip-alias --async

WARNING: Starting in 1.12, new clusters will not have a client certificate
issued. You can manually enable (or disable) the issuance of the client
```

```
certificate using the `--[no-]issue-client-certificate` flag. This will
enable the autorepair feature for nodes. Please see
https://cloud.google.com/kubernetes-engine/docs/node-auto-repair for more
information on node autorepairs.

WARNING: Starting in Kubernetes v1.10, new clusters will no longer get
compute-rw and storage-ro scopes added to what is specified in --scopes
(though the latter will remain included in the default --scopes). To use
these scopes, add them explicitly to --scopes. To use the new behavior, set
container/new_scopes_behavior property (gcloud config set
container/new_scopes_behavior true).

NAME           TYPE LOCATION    TARGET STATUS_MESSAGE   STATUS START_TIME
END_TIME
cluster-1          us-east1-b                  PROVISIONING
```

You may need to change the cluster version to a newer GKE version as updates are made. Older versions become unsupported over time. For example, you might see a message such as this:

```
ERROR: (gcloud.container.clusters.create) ResponseError:
code=400, message=EXTERNAL: Master version "1.9.6-gke.1"
is unsupported.
```

You can check this web page to find out the currently supported version of GKE: https://cloud.google.com/kubernetes-engine/release-notes.

Next, specify cluster-2:

```
cluster="cluster-2"
```

Now, create it, where you'll see messages above. We'll omit them this time around:

```
gcloud container clusters create $cluster --zone $zone --username "admin" \
--cluster-version "1.10.6-gke.2" --machine-type "n1-standard-2" --image-
type "COS" --disk-size "100" \
 --scopes gke-default \
 --num-nodes "4" --network "default" --enable-cloud-logging --enable-cloud-
monitoring --enable-ip-alias --async
```

You'll see the same messaging above. You can create another Google Cloud Shell window by clicking on the + icon in order to create some watch commands to see the clusters created. Take a minute to do this while the instances are created:

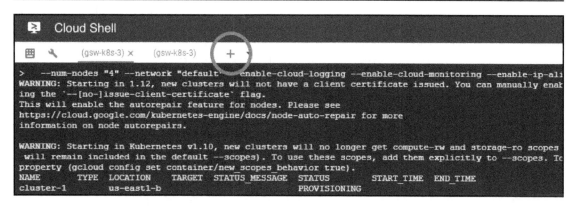

In that window, launch this command: `gcloud container clusters list`. You should see the following:

```
gcloud container clusters list
<snip>
Every 1.0s: gcloud container clusters list
cs-6000-devshell-vm-375db789-dcd6-42c6-b1a6-041afea68875: Mon Sep 3
12:26:41 2018

NAME          LOCATION MASTER_VERSION  MASTER_IP MACHINE_TYPE  NODE_VERSION
NUM_NODES STATUS
cluster-1  us-east1-b 1.10.6-gke.2    35.237.54.93 n1-standard-2  1.10.6-
gke.2 4 RUNNING
cluster-2  us-east1-b 1.10.6-gke.2    35.237.47.212 n1-standard-2  1.10.6-
gke.2 4 RUNNING
```

On the dashboard, it'll look like so:

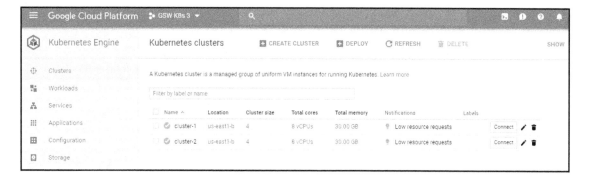

Next up, we'll grab the cluster credentials. This command will allow us to set a `kubeconfig` context for each specific cluster:

```
for clusterid in cluster-1 cluster-2; do gcloud container clusters get-
credentials $clusterid --zone $zone; done
Fetching cluster endpoint and auth data.
kubeconfig entry generated for cluster-1.
Fetching cluster endpoint and auth data.
kubeconfig entry generated for cluster-2.
```

Let's ensure that we can use `kubectl` to get the context for each cluster:

```
anonymuse@cloudshell:~ (gsw-k8s-3)$ kubectl config use-context
"gke_${proj}_${zone}_cluster-1"
Switched to context "gke_gsw-k8s-3_us-east1-b_cluster-1".
```

If you then run `kubectl get pods --all-namespaces` after executing each of the cluster context switches, you should see something similar to this for each cluster:

```
anonymuse@cloudshell:~ (gsw-k8s-3)$ kubectl get pods --all-namespaces
NAMESPACE NAME READY STATUS RESTARTS AGE
kube-system event-exporter-v0.2.1-5f5b89fcc8-2qj5c 2/2 Running 0 14m
kube-system fluentd-gcp-scaler-7c5db745fc-qxqd4 1/1 Running 0 13m
kube-system fluentd-gcp-v3.1.0-g5v24 2/2 Running 0 13m
kube-system fluentd-gcp-v3.1.0-qft92 2/2 Running 0 13m
kube-system fluentd-gcp-v3.1.0-v572p 2/2 Running 0 13m
kube-system fluentd-gcp-v3.1.0-z5wjs 2/2 Running 0 13m
kube-system heapster-v1.5.3-5c47587d4-4fsg6 3/3 Running 0 12m
kube-system kube-dns-788979dc8f-k5n8c 4/4 Running 0 13m
kube-system kube-dns-788979dc8f-ldxsw 4/4 Running 0 14m
kube-system kube-dns-autoscaler-79b4b844b9-rhxdt 1/1 Running 0 13m
kube-system kube-proxy-gke-cluster-1-default-pool-e320df41-4mnm 1/1 Running
0 13m
kube-system kube-proxy-gke-cluster-1-default-pool-e320df41-536s 1/1 Running
0 13m
kube-system kube-proxy-gke-cluster-1-default-pool-e320df41-9gqj 1/1 Running
0 13m
kube-system kube-proxy-gke-cluster-1-default-pool-e320df41-t4pg 1/1 Running
0 13m
kube-system 17-default-backend-5d5b9874d5-n44q7 1/1 Running 0 14m
kube-system metrics-server-v0.2.1-7486f5bd67-h9fq6 2/2 Running 0 13m
```

Next up, we're going to need to create a Google Cloud firewall rule so each cluster can talk to the other. We're going to need to gather all cluster networking data (tags and CIDR), and then create firewall rules with `gcloud`. The CIDR ranges will look something like this:

```
anonymuse@cloudshell:~ (gsw-k8s-3)$ gcloud container clusters list --
format='value(clusterIpv4Cidr)'
10.8.0.0/14
10.40.0.0/14
```

The tags will be per-node, resulting in eight total tags:

```
anonymuse@cloudshell:~ (gsw-k8s-3)$ gcloud compute instances list --
format='value(tags.items.[0])'
gke-cluster-1-37037bd0-node
gke-cluster-1-37037bd0-node
gke-cluster-1-37037bd0-node
gke-cluster-1-37037bd0-node
gke-cluster-2-909a776f-node
gke-cluster-2-909a776f-node
gke-cluster-2-909a776f-node
gke-cluster-2-909a776f-node
```

Let's run the full command now to create the firewall rules. Note the `join_by` function is a neat hack that allows us to join multiple elements of an array in Bash:

```
function join_by { local IFS="$1"; shift; echo "$*"; }
ALL_CLUSTER_CIDRS=$(gcloud container clusters list --
format='value(clusterIpv4Cidr)' | sort | uniq)
echo $ALL_CLUSTER_CDIRS
ALL_CLUSTER_CIDRS=$(join_by , $(echo "${ALL_CLUSTER_CIDRS}"))
echo $ALL_CLUSTER_CDIRS
ALL_CLUSTER_NETTAGS=$(gcloud compute instances list --
format='value(tags.items.[0])' | sort | uniq)
echo $ALL_CLUSTER_NETTAGS
ALL_CLUSTER_NETTAGS=$(join_by , $(echo "${ALL_CLUSTER_NETTAGS}"))
echo $ALL_CLUSTER_NETTAGS
gcloud compute firewall-rules create istio-multicluster-test-pods \
  --allow=tcp,udp,icmp,esp,ah,sctp \
  --direction=INGRESS \
  --priority=900 \
  --source-ranges="${ALL_CLUSTER_CIDRS}" \
  --target-tags="${ALL_CLUSTER_NETTAGS}"
```

That will set up our security firewall rules, which should look similar to this in the GUI when complete:

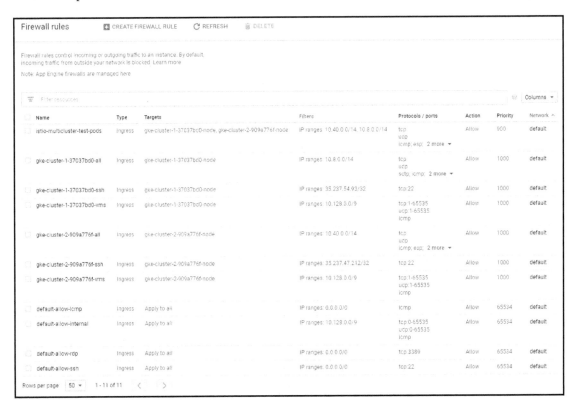

Let's create an admin role that we can use in future steps. First, set KUBE_USER to the email address associated with your GCP account with KUBE_USER="<YOUR_EMAIL>". Next, we'll create a clusterrolebinding:

```
kubectl create clusterrolebinding gke-cluster-admin-binding \
  --clusterrole=cluster-admin \
  --user="${KUBE_USER}"
clusterrolebinding "gke-cluster-admin-binding" created
```

Next up, we'll install the Istio control plane with Helm, create a namespace, and deploy Istio using a chart.

Check to make sure you're using `cluster-1` as your context with `kubectl config current-context`. Next, we'll install Helm with these commands:

```
curl https://raw.githubusercontent.com/kubernetes/helm/master/scripts/get >
get_helm.sh
 chmod 700 get_helm.sh
./get_helm.sh
Create a role for tiller to use. Youll need to clone the Istio repo first:
git clone https://github.com/istio/istio.git && cd istio
Now, create a service account for tiller.
kubectl apply -f install/kubernetes/helm/helm-service-account.yaml
And then we can intialize Tiller on the cluster.
/home/anonymuse/.helm
Creating /home/anonymuse/.helm/repository
...
To prevent this, run `helm init` with the --tiller-tls-verify flag.
For more information on securing your installation see:
https://docs.helm.sh/using_helm/#securing-your-helm-installation
Happy Helming!
anonymuse@cloudshell:~/istio (gsw-k8s-3) $
```

Now, switch to another, Istio-specific context where we'll install Istio in its own namespace:

```
kubectl config use-context "gke_${proj}_${zone}_cluster-1"
```

Copy over the installation chart for Istio into our home directory:

```
helm template install/kubernetes/helm/istio --name istio --namespace istio-
system > $HOME/istio_master.yaml
```

Create a namespace for it to be used in, install it, and enable injection:

```
kubectl create ns istio-system \
 && kubectl apply -f $HOME/istio_master.yaml \
 && kubectl label namespace default istio-injection=enabled
```

We'll now set some more environment variables to collect the IPs of our pilot, statsD, policy, and telemetry pods:

```
export PILOT_POD_IP=$(kubectl -n istio-system get pod -l istio=pilot -o
jsonpath='{.items[0].status.podIP}')
export POLICY_POD_IP=$(kubectl -n istio-system get pod -l istio=mixer -o
jsonpath='{.items[0].status.podIP}')
export STATSD_POD_IP=$(kubectl -n istio-system get pod -l istio=statsd-
prom-bridge -o jsonpath='{.items[0].status.podIP}')
export TELEMETRY_POD_IP=$(kubectl -n istio-system get pod -l istio-mixer-
type=telemetry -o jsonpath='{.items[0].status.podIP}')
```

We can now generate a manifest for our remote cluster, `cluster-2`:

```
helm template install/kubernetes/helm/istio-remote --namespace istio-system \
  --name istio-remote \
  --set global.remotePilotAddress=${PILOT_POD_IP} \
  --set global.remotePolicyAddress=${POLICY_POD_IP} \
  --set global.remoteTelemetryAddress=${TELEMETRY_POD_IP} \
  --set global.proxy.envoyStatsd.enabled=true \
  --set global.proxy.envoyStatsd.host=${STATSD_POD_IP} > $HOME/istio-remote.yaml
```

Now, we'll instill the minimal Istio components and sidecar inject in our target, `cluster-2`. Run the following commands in order:

```
kubectl config use-context "gke_${proj}_${zone}_cluster-2"
kubectl create ns istio-system
kubectl apply -f $HOME/istio-remote.yaml
kubectl label namespace default istio-injection=enabled
```

Now, we'll create more scaffolding to take advantage of the features of Istio. We'll need to create a file in which we can configure `kubeconfig` to work with Istio. First, change back into your home directory with `cd`. The `--minify` flag will ensure that you only see output associated with your current context. Now, enter the following groups of commands:

```
export WORK_DIR=$(pwd)
CLUSTER_NAME=$(kubectl config view --minify=true -o
"jsonpath={.clusters[].name}")
CLUSTER_NAME="${CLUSTER_NAME##*_}"
export KUBECFG_FILE=${WORK_DIR}/${CLUSTER_NAME}
SERVER=$(kubectl config view --minify=true -o
"jsonpath={.clusters[].cluster.server}")
NAMESPACE=istio-system
SERVICE_ACCOUNT=istio-multi
SECRET_NAME=$(kubectl get sa ${SERVICE_ACCOUNT} -n ${NAMESPACE} -o
jsonpath='{.secrets[].name}')
CA_DATA=$(kubectl get secret ${SECRET_NAME} -n ${NAMESPACE} -o
"jsonpath={.data['ca\.crt']}")
TOKEN=$(kubectl get secret ${SECRET_NAME} -n ${NAMESPACE} -o
"jsonpath={.data['token']}" | base64 --decode)
```

Create a file with the following `cat` command. This will inject the contents here into a file that's going to be located in `~/${WORK_DIR}/{CLUSTER_NAME}`:

```
cat <<EOF > ${KUBECFG_FILE}
apiVersion: v1
clusters:
```

```
      - cluster:
          certificate-authority-data: ${CA_DATA}
          server: ${SERVER}
        name: ${CLUSTER_NAME}
contexts:
      - context:
          cluster: ${CLUSTER_NAME}
          user: ${CLUSTER_NAME}
        name: ${CLUSTER_NAME}
current-context: ${CLUSTER_NAME}
kind: Config
preferences: {}
users:
      - name: ${CLUSTER_NAME}
        user:
          token: ${TOKEN}
EOF
```

Next up, we'll create a secret so that the control plane for Istio that exists on `cluster-1` can access `istio-pilot` on `cluster-2`. Switch back to the first cluster, create a Secret, and label it:

```
anonymuse@cloudshell:~ (gsw-k8s-3)$ kubectl config use-context gke_gsw-
k8s-3_us-east1-b_cluster-1
Switched to context "gke_gsw-k8s-3_us-east1-b_cluster-1".
kubectl create secret generic ${CLUSTER_NAME} --from-file ${KUBECFG_FILE} -
n ${NAMESPACE}
kubectl label secret ${CLUSTER_NAME} istio/multiCluster=true -n
${NAMESPACE}
```

Once we've completed these tasks, let's use all of this machinery to deploy one of Google's code examples, `bookinfo`, across both clusters. Run this on the first:

```
kubectl config use-context "gke_${proj}_${zone}_cluster-1"
kubectl apply -f samples/bookinfo/platform/kube/bookinfo.yaml
kubectl apply -f samples/bookinfo/networking/bookinfo-gateway.yaml
kubectl delete deployment reviews-v3
```

Now, create a file called `reviews-v3.yaml` for deploying `bookinfo` to the remote cluster. The file contents can be found in the repository directory of this chapter:

```
##############################################################################
#######################
# Ratings service
##############################################################################
#######################
apiVersion: v1
kind: Service
```

```
metadata:
 name: ratings
 labels:
 app: ratings
spec:
 ports:
 - port: 9080
 name: http
---
#########################################################################
#######################
# Reviews service
#########################################################################
#######################
apiVersion: v1
kind: Service
metadata:
 name: reviews
 labels:
 app: reviews
spec:
 ports:
 - port: 9080
 name: http
 selector:
 app: reviews
---
apiVersion: extensions/v1beta1
kind: Deployment
metadata:
 name: reviews-v3
spec:
 replicas: 1
 template:
 metadata:
 labels:
 app: reviews
 version: v3
 spec:
 containers:
 - name: reviews
 image: istio/examples-bookinfo-reviews-v3:1.5.0
 imagePullPolicy: IfNotPresent
 ports:
 - containerPort: 9080
```

Let's install this deployment on the remote cluster, `cluster-2`:

```
kubectl config use-context "gke_${proj}_${zone}_cluster-2"
kubectl apply -f $HOME/reviews-v3.yaml
```

Once this is complete, you'll need to get access to the external IP of Istio's `isto-ingressgateway` service, in order to view the data in the `bookinfo` homepage. You can run this command to open that up. You'll need to reload that page dozens of times in order to see Istio's load balancing take place. You can hold down *F5* in order to reload the page many times.

You can access `http://<GATEWAY_IP>/productpage` in order to see the reviews.

Deleting the cluster

In order to clean up the control panel once you're finished, you can run the following commands.

First, delete the firewall rules:

```
gcloud compute firewall-rules delete istio-multicluster-test-pods
The following firewalls will be deleted:
 - [istio-multicluster-test-pods]
Do you want to continue (Y/n)? y
Deleted
[https://www.googleapis.com/compute/v1/projects/gsw-k8s-3/global/firewalls/
istio-multicluster-test-pods].
anonymuse@cloudshell:~ (gsw-k8s-3)$
```

Next up, we'll delete our cluster-admin-role binding:

```
anonymuse@cloudshell:~ (gsw-k8s-3)$ kubectl delete clusterrolebinding gke-
cluster-admin-bindingclusterrolebinding "gke-cluster-admin-binding" deleted
anonymuse@cloudshell:~ (gsw-k8s-3)$
```

Lastly, let's delete our GKE clusters:

```
anonymuse@cloudshell:~ (gsw-k8s-3)$ gcloud container clusters delete
cluster-1 --zone $zone
The following clusters will be deleted. - [cluster-1] in [us-east1-b]
Do you want to continue (Y/n)? y
Deleting cluster cluster-1...done.
Deleted
[https://container.googleapis.com/v1/projects/gsw-k8s-3/zones/us-east1-b/cl
usters/cluster-1].
anonymuse@cloudshell:~ (gsw-k8s-3)
```

In the GUI, you can see the cluster being deleted:

You can also see it on the command line from your `watch` command:

Run the same command with your other cluster. You can double-check the **Compute Engine** dashboard to ensure that your instances are being deleted:

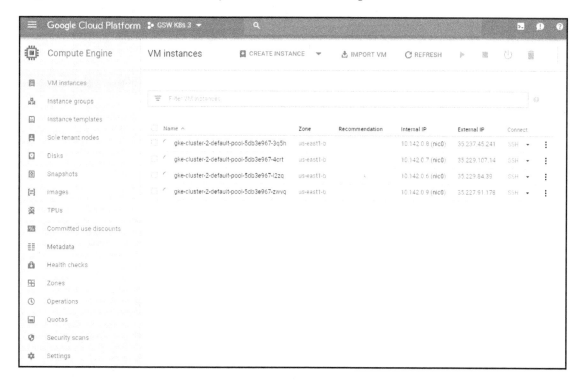

Summary

In this chapter, we looked at the new federation capabilities in Kubernetes. We saw how we can deploy clusters to multiple cloud providers and manage them from a single control plane. We also deployed an application across clusters in both AWS and GCE. While these features are new and still mainly in alpha and beta, we should now have the skills to utilize them as they evolve and become part of the standard Kubernetes operating model.

In the next chapter, we will take a look at another advanced topic: security. We will cover the basics for secure containers and also how to secure your Kubernetes cluster. We will also look at the Secrets construct, which gives us the capability to store sensitive configuration data similar to our preceding `ConfigMap` example.

12
Cluster Authentication, Authorization, and Container Security

This chapter will discuss the basics of container security from the container runtime level to the host itself. We will discuss how to apply these concepts to workloads running in a Kubernetes cluster and some of the security concerns and practices that relate specifically to running your Kubernetes cluster.

This chapter will discuss the following topics:

- Basic container security
- Container image security and continuous vulnerability scanning
- Kubernetes cluster security
- Kubernetes secrets

Basics of container security

Container security is a deep subject area and in itself can fill its own book. Having said this, we will cover some of the high-level concerns and give you a starting point so that you can start thinking about this area.

In the *A brief overview of containers* section of `Chapter 1`, *Introduction to Kubernetes*, we looked at some of the core isolation features in the Linux kernel that enable container technology. Understanding the details of how containers work is the key to grasping the various security concerns in managing them.

A good paper to dive deeper is *NCC's Whitepaper, Understanding and Hardening Linux Containers*. In *section 7*, the paper explores the various attack vectors of concern for container deployments, which I will summarize.

Keeping containers contained

One of the most obvious features that is discussed in the paper we mentioned in the preceding section is that of escaping the isolation/virtualization of the container construct. Modern container implementations guard against using namespaces to isolate processes as well as allowing the control of Linux capabilities that are available to a container. Additionally, there is an increased move toward secure default configurations of the out-of-the-box container environment. For example, by default, Docker only enables a small set of capabilities. Networking is another avenue of escape and it can be challenging since there are a variety of network options that plug into most modern container setups.

The next area discussed in the paper is that of attacks between two containers. The *User* namespace model gives us added protection here by mapping the root user within the container to a lower-level user on the host machine. Networking is, of course, still an issue, and something that requires proper diligence and attention when selecting and implementing your container networking solution.

Attacks within the container itself are another vector and, as with previous concerns, namespaces and networking are key to protection here. Another aspect that is vital in this scenario is the application security itself. The code still needs to follow secure coding practices and the software should be kept up to date and patched regularly. Finally, the efficiency of container images has an added benefit of shrinking the attack surface. The images should be built with only the packages and software that's necessary.

Resource exhaustion and orchestration security

Similar to the **denial-of-service (DoS)** attacks, we've seen in various other areas of computing that resource exhaustion is very much a pertinent concern in the container world. While cgroups provide some limitations on resource usage for things such as CPU, memory, and disk usage, there are still valid attack avenues for resource exhaustion. Tools such as Docker offer some starting defaults to the cgroups limitations, and Kubernetes also offers additional limits that can be placed on groups of containers running in the cluster. It's important to understand these defaults and to adjust for your deployments.

While the Linux kernel and the features that enable containers give us some form of isolation, they are fairly new to the Linux operating system. As such, they still contain their own bugs and vulnerabilities. The built-in mechanisms for capabilities and namespaces can and do have issues, and it is important to track these as part of your secure container operations.

The final area covered in the NCC paper is the attack of the container management layer itself. The Docker engine, image repositories, and orchestration tools are all significant vectors of attack and should be considered when developing your strategy. We'll look in more depth at how we can address the repositories and Kubernetes as an orchestration layer in the following sections.

> If you're interested in knowing more about the specific security features of Docker's implementation, take a look here: `https://docs.docker.com/engine/security/security/`.

Image repositories

Vulnerability management is a critical component of any modern day IT operation. Zero-day vulnerabilities are on the rise and even those vulnerabilities with patches can be cumbersome to remediate. First, application owners must be made aware of their vulnerabilities and potential patches. Then, these patches must be integrated into systems and code, and often this requires additional deployments or maintenance windows. Even when there is visibility to vulnerabilities, there is often a lag in remediation, often taking large organizations several months to patch.

While containers greatly improve the process of updating applications and minimizing downtime, there still remains a challenge that's inherent in vulnerability management. Especially since an attacker only needs to expose one such vulnerability, making anything less than 100% of the systems patched is a risk of compromise.

What's needed is a faster feedback loop in addressing vulnerabilities. Continuous scanning and tying into the software deployment life cycle is key to speeding up the information and remediation of vulnerabilities. Luckily, this is exactly the approach that's being built into the latest container management and security tooling.

Continuous vulnerability scanning

One such open source project that has emerged in this space is **clair**. clair is an open source project for the static analysis of vulnerabilities in appc (`https://github.com/appc/spec`) and Docker (`https://github.com/moby/moby/blob/master/image/spec/v1.md`) containers.

 You can visit clair at the following link: `https://github.com/coreos/clair`.

clair scans your code against **Common Vulnerabilities and Exploits** (**CVEs**). It can be integrated into your CI/CD pipeline and run as a response to new builds. If vulnerabilities are found, they can be taken as feedback into the pipeline, even stop deployment, and fail the build. This forces developers to be aware of and remediate vulnerabilities during their normal release process.

clair can be integrated with a number of container image repositories and CI/CD pipelines.

 clair can even be deployed on Kubernetes: `https://github.com/coreos/clair/blob/master/Documentation/running-clair.md#kubernetes-helm`.

clair is also used as the scanning mechanism in CoreOS's Quay image repository. Quay offers a number of enterprise features, including continuous vulnerability scanning (`https://quay.io/`).

Both Docker Hub and Docker Cloud support security scanning. Again, containers that are pushed to the repository are automatically scanned against CVEs, and notifications of vulnerabilities are sent as a result of any findings. Additionally, binary analysis of the code is performed to match the signature of the components with that of known versions.

There are a variety of other scanning tools that can be used as well for scanning your image repositories, including OpenSCAP, Twistlock, Aqua Sec, and many more.

Image signing and verification

Whether you are using a private image repository in-house or a public repository such as Docker Hub, it's important to know that you are only running the code that your developers have written. The potential for malicious code or man-in-the-middle attacks on downloads is an important factor in protecting your container images.

As such, both rkt and Docker support the ability to sign images and verify that the contents have not changed. Publishers can use keys to sign the images when they are pushed to the repositories, and users can verify the signature on the client side when downloading for use.

> This is from the rkt documentation:
>
> *"Before executing a remotely fetched ACI, rkt will verify it based on attached signatures generated by the ACI creator."*
>
> For more information, visit the following links:
>
> - `https://github.com/rkt/rkt/blob/master/Documentation/subcommands/trust.md`
> - `https://github.com/rkt/rkt/blob/master/Documentation/signing-and-verification-guide.md`
>
> This is from the Docker documentation:
> *"Content trust gives you the ability to verify both the integrity and the publisher of all the data received from a registry over any channel. "*
>
> For more information, visit `https://docs.docker.com/engine/security/trust/content_trust/`.
> This is from the Docker Notary GitHub page:
>
> *"The Notary project comprises a server and a client for running and interacting with trusted collections."*
>
> For more information, visit `https://github.com/docker/notary`.

Kubernetes cluster security

Kubernetes has continued to add a number of security features in their latest releases and has a well-rounded set of control points that can be used in your cluster – everything from secure node communication to pod security and even the storage of sensitive configuration data.

Secure API calls

During every API call, Kubernetes applies a number of security controls. This security life cycle is depicted here:

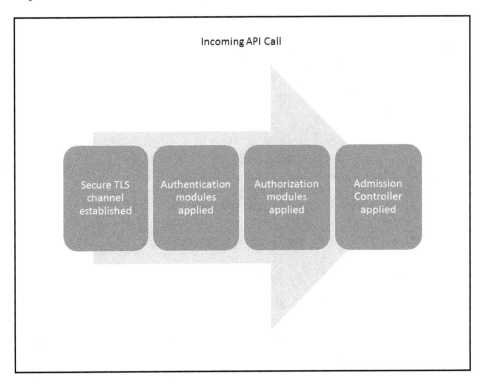

API call life cycle

After secure TLS communication is established, the API server runs through authorization and authentication. Finally, an admission controller loop is applied to the request before it reaches the API server.

Secure node communication

Kubernetes supports the use of secure communication channels between the API server and any client, including the nodes themselves. Whether it's a GUI or command-line utility such as kubectl, we can use certificates to communicate with the API server. Hence, the API server is the central interaction point for any changes to the cluster and is a critical component to secure.

In deployments such as GCE, the `kubelet` on each node is deployed for secure communication by default. This setup uses TLS bootstrapping and the new certificates' API to establish a secure connection with the API server using TLS client certificates and a **Certificate Authority (CA)** cluster.

Authorization and authentication plugins

The plugin mechanisms for authentication and authorization in Kubernetes are still being developed. They have come a long way, but still have plugins in beta stages and enhancements in the works. There are also third-party providers that integrate with the features here, so bear that in mind when building your hardening strategy.

Authentication is currently supported in the form of tokens, passwords, and certificates, with plans to add the plugin capability at a later stage. OpenID Connect tokens are supported and several third-party implementations, such as Dex from CoreOS and user account and authentication from Cloud Foundry, are available.

Authorization already supports three modes. The **role-based access control (RBAC)** mode recently went to general availability in the 1.8 release and brings the standard role-based authentication model to Kubernetes. **Attribute-based access control (ABAC)** has long been supported and lets a user define privileges via attributes in a file.

Additionally, a Webhook mechanism is supported, which allows for integration with third-party authorization via REST web service calls. Finally, we have the new node authorization method, which grants permissions to kubelets based on the pods they are scheduled to run.

You can learn more about each area at the following links:

- `http://kubernetes.io/docs/admin/authorization/`
- `http://kubernetes.io/docs/admin/authentication/`
- `https://kubernetes.io/docs/reference/access-authn-authz/node/`

Admission controllers

Kubernetes also provides a mechanism for integrating, with additional verification as a final step. This could be in the form of image scanning, signature checks, or anything that is able to respond in the specified fashion.

When an API call is made, the hook is called and that server can run its verification. Admission controllers can also be used to transform requests and add or alter the original request. Once the operations are run, a response is then sent back with a status that instructs Kubernetes to allow or deny the call.

This can be especially helpful for verifying or testing images, as we mentioned in the last section. The `ImagePolicyWebhook` plugin provides an admission controller that allows for integration with additional image inspection.

> For more information, visit the **Using Admission Controller** page in the following documentation: `https://kubernetes.io/docs/admin/admission-controllers/`.

RBAC

As mentioned earlier in this chapter, Kubernetes has now made RBAC a central component to authorization within the cluster. Kubernetes offers two levels for this kind of control. First, there is a *ClusterRole*, which provides cluster-wide authorization to resources. This is handy for enforcing access control across multiple teams, products, or to cluster-wide resources such as the underlying cluster nodes. Second, we have a *Role*, which simply provides access to resources within a specific namespace.

Once you have a role, you need a way to provide users with membership to that role. These are referred to as *Bindings*, and again we have *ClusterRoleBinding* and *RoleBinding*. As with the roles themselves, the former is meant for cluster-wide access and the latter is meant to apply within a specific namespace.

We will not dive into the details of RBAC in this book, but it is something you'll want to explore as you get ready for production grade deployments. The *PodSecurityPolicy* discussed in the next section typically utilizes Roles and RoleBindings to control which policies each user has access to.

> For more information, please refer to the documentation here: `https://kubernetes.io/docs/reference/access-authn-authz/rbac/`.

Pod security policies and context

One of the latest additions to the Kubernetes' security arsenal is that of pod security policies and contexts. These allow users to control users and groups for container processes and attached volumes, limit the use of host networks or namespaces, and even set the root filesystem to read-only. Additionally, we can limit the capabilities available and also set SELinux options for the labels that are applied to the containers in each pod.

 In addition to SELinux, Kubernetes also added beta support for using AppArmor with your pods by using annotations. For more information, refer to the following documentation page: `https://kubernetes.io/docs/admin/apparmor/`.

PodSecurityPolicies are enforced using the admission controller we spoke of earlier in this book. By default, Kubernetes doesn't enable PodSecurityPolicy, so if you have a GKE cluster running, you can try the following:

```
$ kubectl get psp
```

You should see `'No resources found.'`, assuming you haven't enabled them.

Let's try an example by using the Docker image from our previous chapters. If we use the following `run` command on a cluster with no PodSecurityPolicy applied, it will happily run:

```
$ kubectl run myroottest --image=jonbaier/node-express-info:latest
```

Follow this with `kubectl get pods` and in a minute or so we should see a pod starting with `myroottest` in the listings.

Go ahead and clean this up with the following code before proceeding:

```
$ kubectl delete deployment myroottest
```

Enabling PodSecurityPolicies

Now, let's try this with a cluster that can utilize PodSecurityPolicies. If you are using GKE, it is quite easy to create a cluster with PodSecurityPolicy enabled. Note you will need the Beta APIs enabled for this:

```
$ gcloud beta container clusters create [Cluster Name] --enable-pod-security-policy --zone=[Zone To Deploy Cluster]
```

If you have an existing GKE cluster, you can enable it with a command similar to the preceding one. Simply replace the `create` keyword with `update`.

For clusters created with `kube-up`, like we saw in Chapter 1, *Introduction to Kubernetes,* you'll need to enable the admission controller on the API server. Take a look here for more information: `https://kubernetes.io/docs/concepts/policy/pod-security-policy/#enabling-pod-security-policies`.

Once you have PodSecurityPolicy enabled, you can see the applied policies by using the following code:

```
$ kubectl get psp
```

NAME	DATA	CAPS	SELINUX	RUNASUSER	FSGROUP
gce.event-exporter	false		RunAsAny	RunAsAny	RunAsAny
gce.fluentd-gcp	false		RunAsAny	RunAsAny	RunAsAny
gce.persistent-volume-binder	false		RunAsAny	RunAsAny	RunAsAny
gce.privileged	true	*	RunAsAny	RunAsAny	RunAsAny
gce.unprivileged-addon	false		RunAsAny	RunAsAny	RunAsAny

GKE default pod security policies

You'll notice a few predefined policies that GKE has already defined. You can explore the details and the YAML used to create these policies with the following code:

```
$ kubectl get psp/[PSP Name] -o yaml
```

It's important to note that PodSecurityPolicies work with the RBAC features of Kubernetes. There are a few default roles, role bindings, and namespaces that are defined by GKE. As such, we will see different behaviors based on how we interact with Kubernetes. For example, by using `kubectl` in a GCloud Shell, you may be sending commands as a cluster admin and therefore have access to all policies, including `gce.privileged`. However, using the `kubectl run` command, as we did previously, will invoke the pods through the kube-controller-manager, which will be restricted to the policies bound to its role. Thus, if you simply create a pod with `kubectl`, it will create it without an issue, but by using the `run` command, we will be restricted.

Sticking to our previous method of using `kubectl run`, let's try the same deployment as the preceding one:

```
$ kubectl run myroottest --image=jonbaier/node-express-info:latest
```

Now, if we follow this with `kubectl get pods`, we won't see any pods prefaced with `myroottest`. We can dig a bit deeper by describing our deployment:

```
$ kubectl describe deployment myroottest
```

By using the name of the replica set listed in the output from the preceding command, we can then get the details on the failure. Run the following command:

```
$ kubectl describe rs [ReplicaSet name from deployment describe]
```

Under the events at the bottom, you will see the following pod security policy validation error:

```
Name:           myroottest-588dfdcf85
Namespace:      default
Selector:       pod-template-hash=1448987941,run=myroottest
Labels:         pod-template-hash=1448987941
                run=myroottest
Annotations:    deployment.kubernetes.io/desired-replicas=1
                deployment.kubernetes.io/max-replicas=2
                deployment.kubernetes.io/revision=1
Controlled By:  Deployment/myroottest
Replicas:       0 current / 1 desired
Pods Status:    0 Running / 0 Waiting / 0 Succeeded / 0 Failed
Pod Template:
  Labels:  pod-template-hash=1448987941
           run=myroottest
  Containers:
   myroottest:
    Image:          jonbaier/node-express-info:latest
    Port:           <none>
    Host Port:      <none>
    Environment:    <none>
    Mounts:         <none>
  Volumes:          <none>
Conditions:
  Type            Status  Reason
  ----            ------  ------
  ReplicaFailure  True    FailedCreate
Events:
  Type     Reason        Age               From                   Message
  ----     ------        ----              ----                   -------
  Warning  FailedCreate  10s (x14 over 51s)  replicaset-controller  Error creating: pods "myroottest-588dfdcf85-"
                                                                    is forbidden: unable to validate against any
                                                                    pod security policy: []
```

Replica set pod security policy validation error

Again, because the `run` command uses the controller manager and that role has no bindings that allow the use of the existing **PodSecurityPolicies**, we are unable to run any pods.

Understanding that running containers securely is not merely the task of administrators adding constraints is important. The work must be done in collaboration with developers, who will properly create the images.

You can find all of the possible parameters for PodSecurityPolicies in the source code, but I've created the following table for convenience. You can find more handy lookups like this on my new site, `http://www.kubesheets.com`:

Parameter	Type	Description	Required
`Privileged`	`bool`	Allows or disallows running a pod as privileged.	No
`DefaultAddCapabilities`	`[]v1.Capaility`	This defines a default set of capabilities that are added to the container. If the pod specifies a capability drop that will override, then add it here. Values are strings of POSIX capabilities minus the leading `CAP_`. For example, `CAP_SETUID` would be `SETUID` (`http://man7.org/linux/man-pages/man7/capabilities.7.html`).	No
`RequiredDropCapabilities`	`[]v1.Capaility`	This defines a set of capabilities that must be dropped from a container. The pod cannot specify any of these capabilities. Values are strings of POSIX capabilities minus the leading `CAP_`. For example, `CAP_SETUID` would be `SETUID` (`http://man7.org/linux/man-pages/man7/capabilities.7.html`).	No
`AllowedCapabilities`	`[]v1.Capaility`	This defines a set of capabilities that are allowed and can be added to a container. The pod can specify any of these capabilities. Values are strings of POSIX capabilities minus the leading `CAP_`. For example, `CAP_SETUID` would be `SETUID` (`http://man7.org/linux/man-pages/man7/capabilities.7.html`).	No
`Volumes`	`[]string`	This list defines which volumes can be used. Leave this empty for all types (`https://github.com/kubernetes/kubernetes/blob/release-1.5/pkg/apis/extensions/v1beta1/types.go#L1127`).	No
`HostNetwork`	`bool`	This allows or disallows the pod to use the host network.	No

HostPorts	[]HostPortRange	This lets us restrict allowable host ports that can be exposed.	No
HostPID	bool	This allows or disallows the pod to use the host PID.	No
HostIPC	bool	This allows or disallows the pod to use the host IPC.	No
SELinux	SELinuxStrategyOptions	Set it to one of the strategy options, as defined here: https://kubernetes.io/docs/concepts/policy/pod-security-policy/#selinux.	Yes
RunAsUser	RunAsUserStrategyOptions	Set it to one of the strategy options, as defined here: https://kubernetes.io/docs/concepts/policy/pod-security-policy/#users-and-groups.	Yes
SupplementalGroups	SupplementalGroupsStrategyOptions	Set it to one of the strategy options, as defined here: https://kubernetes.io/docs/concepts/policy/pod-security-policy/#users-and-groups	Yes
FSGroup	FSGroupStrategyOptions	Set it to one of the strategy options, as defined here: https://kubernetes.io/docs/user-guide/pod-security-policy/#strategies	Yes
ReadOnlyRootFilesystem	bool	Setting this to true will either deny the pod or force it to run with a read-only root filesystem.	No
allowedHostPaths	[]AllowedHostPath	This provides a whitelist of host paths that can be used at volumes.	No
allowedFlexVolumes	[]AllowedFlexVolume	This provides a whitelist of flex volumes that can be mounted.	No
allowPrivilegeEscalation	bool	This governs where setuid can be used to change the user a process is running under. Its default is true.	No
defaultAllowPrivilegeEscalation	bool	Sets the default for allowPrivilegeEscalation.	No

Additional considerations

In addition to the features we just reviewed, Kubernetes has a number of other constructs that should be considered in your overall cluster hardening process. Earlier in this book, we looked at namespaces that provide a logical separation for multi-tenancy. While the namespaces themselves do not isolate the actual network traffic, some of the network plugins, such as Calico and Canal, provide additional capability for network policies. We also looked at quotas and limits that can be set for each namespace, which should be used to prevent a single tenant or project from consuming too many resources within the cluster.

Securing sensitive application data (secrets)

Sometimes, our application needs to hold sensitive information. This can be credentials or tokens to log in to a database or service. Storing this sensitive information in the image itself is something to be avoided. Here, Kubernetes provides us with a solution in the construct of secrets.

Secrets give us a way to store sensitive information without including plaintext versions in our resource definition files. Secrets can be mounted to the pods that need them and then accessed within the pod as files with the secret values as content. Alternatively, you can also expose the secrets via environment variables.

 Given that Kubernetes still relies on plaintext etcd storage, you may want to explore integration with more mature secrets vaults, such as Vault from Hashicorp. There is even a GitHub project for integration: `https://github.com/Boostport/kubernetes-vault`.

We can easily create a secret either with YAML or on the command line. Secrets do need to be base-64 encoded, but if we use the `kubectl` command line, this encoding is done for us.

Let's start with the following secret:

```
$ kubectl create secret generic secret-phrases --from-literal=quiet-
phrase="Shh! Dont' tell"
```

We can then check for the secret with this command:

```
$ kubectl get secrets
```

Now that we have successfully created the secret, let's make a pod that can use the secret. Secrets are consumed in pods by way of attached volumes. In the following `secret-pod.yaml` file, you'll notice that we use `volumeMount` to mount the secret to a folder in our container:

```
apiVersion: v1
kind: Pod
metadata:
  name: secret-pod
spec:
  containers:
  - name: secret-pod
    image: jonbaier/node-express-info:latest
    ports:
    - containerPort: 80
      name: web
    volumeMounts:
      - name: secret-volume
        mountPath: /etc/secret-phrases
  volumes:
  - name: secret-volume
    secret:
      secretName: secret-phrases
```

Create this pod with `kubectl create -f secret-pod.yaml`. Once created, we can get a bash shell in the pod with `kubectl exec` and then change directories to the `/etc/secret-phrases` folder that we set up in the pod definition. Listing this directory reveals a single file with the name of the secret that we created earlier:

```
$ kubectl exec -it secret-pod bash
$ cd /etc/secret-phrases
$ ls
```

If we then display its contents, we should see the phrase we encoded previously, Shh! Dont' tell:

```
$ cat quiet-phrase
```

Typically, this would be used for a username and password to a database or service, or any sensitive credentials and configuration data.

Bear in mind that secrets are still in their early stages, but they are a vital component for production operations. There are several improvements being planned for future releases. At the moment, secrets are still stored in plaintext in the etcd server. However, the secrets construct does allow us to control which pods can access it, and it stores the information on the tmpfs, but does not store it at rest for each pod. You can limit users with access to etcd and perform additional wipe procedures when you decommission servers, but you'll likely want more protection in place for a production-ready system.

Summary

In this chapter, we took a look at basic container security and some essential areas of consideration. We also touched on basic image security and continuous vulnerability scanning. Later in this chapter, we looked at the overall security features of Kubernetes, including secrets for storing sensitive configuration data, secure API calls, and even setting up security policies and contexts for pods running on our cluster. You should now have a solid starting point for securing your cluster and moving toward production.

13
Running Stateful Applications with Kubernetes

In this chapter, we will look into what it takes to run stateful applications on Kubernetes. Kubernetes takes a lot of work out of our hands by automatically starting and restarting pods across the cluster nodes as needed, based on complex requirements and configurations such as namespaces, limits, and quotas. But when pods run storage-aware software, such as databases and queues, relocating a pod can cause the system to break. First, we'll understand the essence of stateful pods and why they are much more complicated to manage in Kubernetes. We will look at a few ways to manage the complexity, such as shared environment variables and DNS records. In some situations, a redundant in-memory state, a DaemonSet, or persistent storage claims can do the trick. The main solution that Kubernetes promotes for state-aware pods is the StatefulSet (previously called PetSet) resource, which allows us to manage an indexed collection of pods with stable properties. Finally, we will dive deep into a full-fledged example of running a Cassandra cluster on top of Kubernetes.

Stateful versus stateless applications in Kubernetes

A stateless Kubernetes application is an application that doesn't manage its state in the Kubernetes cluster. All of the state is stored outside the cluster and the cluster containers access it in some manner. In this section, we'll understand why state management is critical to the design of a distributed system and the benefits of managing state within the Kubernetes cluster.

Understanding the nature of distributed data-intensive apps

Let's start from the basics here. Distributed applications are a collection of processes that run on multiple machines, process inputs, manipulate data, expose APIs, and possibly have other side effects. Each process is a combination of its program, its runtime environment, and its inputs and outputs. The programs you write at school get their input as command-line arguments, maybe they read a file or access a database, and then write their results to the screen or a file or a database. Some programs keep state in-memory and can serve requests over the network. Simple programs run on a single machine, can hold all their state in memory or read from a file. Their runtime environment is their operating system. If they crash, the user has to restart them manually. They are tied to their machine. A distributed application is a different animal. A single machine is not enough to process all the data or serve all the requests fast enough. A single machine can't hold all the data. The data that needs to be processed is so large that it can't be downloaded cost-effectively into each processing machine. Machines can fail and need to be replaced. Upgrades need to be performed over all the processing machines. Users may be distributed across the globe.

Taking all these issues into account, it becomes clear that the traditional approach doesn't work. The limiting factor becomes the data. Users/client must receive only summary or processed data. All massive data processing must be done close to the data itself because transferring data is prohibitively slow and expensive. Instead, the bulk of processing code must run in the same data center and network environment of the data.

Why manage state in Kubernetes?

The main reason to manage state in Kubernetes itself as opposed to a separate cluster is that a lot of the infrastructure needed to monitor, scale, allocate, secure and operate a storage cluster is already provided by Kubernetes. Running a parallel storage cluster will lead to a lot of duplicated effort.

Why manage state outside of Kubernetes?

Let's not rule out the other option. It may be better in some situations to manage state in a separate non-Kubernetes cluster, as long as it shares the same internal network (data proximity trumps everything).

Some valid reasons are as follows:

- You already have a separate storage cluster and you don't want to rock the boat
- Your storage cluster is used by other non-Kubernetes applications
- Kubernetes support for your storage cluster is not stable or mature enough

You may want to approach stateful applications in Kubernetes incrementally, starting with a separate storage cluster and integrating more tightly with Kubernetes later.

Shared environment variables versus DNS records for discovery

Kubernetes provides several mechanisms for global discovery across the cluster. If your storage cluster is not managed by Kubernetes, you still need to tell Kubernetes pods how to find it and access it. There are two main methods:

- DNS
- Environment variables

In some cases, you may want to use both where environment variables can override DNS.

Accessing external data stores via DNS

The DNS approach is simple and straightforward. Assuming your external storage cluster is load balanced and can provide a stable endpoint, then pods can just hit that endpoint directly and connect to the external cluster.

Accessing external data stores via environment variables

Another simple approach is to use environment variables to pass connection information to an external storage cluster. Kubernetes offers the `ConfigMap` resource as a way to keep configuration separate from the container image. The configuration is a set of key-value pairs. The configuration information can be exposed as an environment variable inside the container as well as volumes. You may prefer to use secrets for sensitive connection information.

Creating a ConfigMap

The following configuration file will create a configuration file that keeps a list of addresses:

```
apiVersion: v1
kind: ConfigMap
metadata:
  name: db-config
  namespace: default
data:
  db-ip-addresses: 1.2.3.4,5.6.7.8

> kubectl create -f .\configmap.yamlconfigmap
  "db-config" created
```

The `data` section contains all the key-value pairs, in this case, just a single pair with a key name of `db-ip-addresses`. It will be important later when consuming the `configmap` in a pod. You can check out the content to make sure it's OK:

```
> kubectl get configmap db-config -o yaml
apiVersion: v1
data:
  db-ip-addresses: 1.2.3.4,5.6.7.8
kind: ConfigMap
metadata:
  creationTimestamp: 2017-01-09T03:14:07Z
  name: db-config
  namespace: default
  resourceVersion: "551258"
  selfLink: /api/v1/namespaces/default/configmaps/db-config
  uid: aebcc007-d619-11e6-91f1-3a7ae2a25c7d
```

There are other ways to create `ConfigMap`. You can directly create them using the `--from-value` or `--from-file` command-line arguments.

Consuming a ConfigMap as an environment variable

When you are creating a pod, you can specify a `ConfigMap` and consume its values in several ways. Here is how to consume our configuration map as an environment variable:

```
apiVersion: v1
kind: Pod
```

```
metadata:
  name: some-pod
spec:
  containers:
    - name: some-container
      image: busybox
      command: [ "/bin/sh", "-c", "env" ]
      env:
        - name: DB_IP_ADDRESSES
          valueFrom:
            configMapKeyRef:
              name: db-config
              key: db-ip-addresses
  restartPolicy: Never
```

This pod runs the `busybox` minimal container and executes an `env bash` command and immediately exists. The `db-ip-addresses` key from the `db-config` map is mapped to the `DB_IP_ADDRESSES` environment variable, and is reflected in the output:

```
> kubectl logs some-pod
HUE_REMINDERS_SERVICE_PORT=80
HUE_REMINDERS_PORT=tcp://10.0.0.238:80
KUBERNETES_PORT=tcp://10.0.0.1:443
KUBERNETES_SERVICE_PORT=443
HOSTNAME=some-pod
SHLVL=1
HOME=/root
HUE_REMINDERS_PORT_80_TCP_ADDR=10.0.0.238
HUE_REMINDERS_PORT_80_TCP_PORT=80
HUE_REMINDERS_PORT_80_TCP_PROTO=tcp
DB_IP_ADDRESSES=1.2.3.4,5.6.7.8
HUE_REMINDERS_PORT_80_TCP=tcp://10.0.0.238:80
KUBERNETES_PORT_443_TCP_ADDR=10.0.0.1
PATH=/usr/local/sbin:/usr/local/bin:/usr/sbin:/usr/bin:/sbin:/bin
KUBERNETES_PORT_443_TCP_PORT=443
KUBERNETES_PORT_443_TCP_PROTO=tcp
KUBERNETES_SERVICE_PORT_HTTPS=443
KUBERNETES_PORT_443_TCP=tcp://10.0.0.1:443
HUE_REMINDERS_SERVICE_HOST=10.0.0.238
PWD=/
KUBERNETES_SERVICE_HOST=10.0.0.1
```

Using a redundant in-memory state

In some cases, you may want to keep a transient state in-memory. Distributed caching is a common case. Time-sensitive information is another one. For these use cases, there is no need for persistent storage, and multiple pods accessed through a service may be just the right solution. We can use standard Kubernetes techniques, such as labeling, to identify pods that belong to the store redundant copies of the same state and expose it through a service. If a pod dies, Kubernetes will create a new one and, until it catches up, the other pods will serve the state. We can even use the pod's anti-affinity alpha feature to ensure that pods that maintain redundant copies of the same state are not scheduled to the same node.

Using DaemonSet for redundant persistent storage

Some stateful applications, such as distributed databases or queues, manage their state redundantly and sync their nodes automatically (we'll take a very deep look into Cassandra later). In these cases, it is important that pods are scheduled to separate nodes. It is also important that pods are scheduled to nodes with a particular hardware configuration or are even dedicated to the stateful application. The DaemonSet feature is perfect for this use case. We can label a set of nodes and make sure that the stateful pods are scheduled on a one-by-one basis to the selected group of nodes.

Applying persistent volume claims

If the stateful application can use effectively shared persistent storage, then using a persistent volume claim in each pod is the way to go. The stateful application will be presented with a mounted volume that looks just like a local filesystem.

Utilizing StatefulSet

The StatefulSet controller is a relatively new addition to Kubernetes (introduced as PetSets in Kubernetes 1.3 and renamed StatefulSet in Kubernetes 1.5). It is especially designed to support distributed stateful applications where the identities of the members are important, and if a pod is restarted it must retain its identity in the set. It provides ordered deployment and scaling. Unlike regular pods, the pods of a stateful set are associated with persistent storage.

When to use StatefulSet

StatefulSet is great for applications that require one or more of the following:

- Stable, unique network identifiers
- Stable, persistent storage
- Ordered, graceful deployment, and scaling
- Ordered, graceful deletion, and termination

The components of StatefulSet

There are several pieces that need to be configured correctly in order to have a working StatefulSet:

- A headless service responsible for managing the network identity of the StatefulSet pods
- The StatefulSet itself with a number of replicas
- Persistent storage provision dynamically or by an administrator

Here is an example of a service called `nginx` that will be used for a StatefulSet:

```
apiVersion: v1
kind: Service
metadata:
  name: nginx
  labels:
    app: nginx
spec:
  ports:
  - port: 80
    name: web
  clusterIP: None
  selector:
    app: nginx
```

Now, the `StatefulSet` configuration file will reference the service:

```
apiVersion: apps/v1
kind: StatefulSet
metadata:
  name: web
spec:
  serviceName: "nginx"
  replicas: 3
```

```
template:
  metadata:
    labels:
      app: nginx
```

The next part is the pod template that includes a mounted volume named www:

```
spec:
  terminationGracePeriodSeconds: 10
  containers:
  - name: nginx
    image: gcr.io/google_containers/nginx-slim:0.8
    ports:
    - containerPort: 80
      name: web
      volumeMounts:
    - name: www
      mountPath: /usr/share/nginx/html
```

Last but not least, `volumeClaimTemplates` use a claim named www matching the mounted volume. The claim requests `1Gib` of `storage` with `ReadWriteOnce` access:

```
volumeClaimTemplates:
- metadata:
    name: www
  spec:
    accessModes: [ "ReadWriteOnce" ]
    resources:
      requests:
        storage: 1Gib
```

Running a Cassandra cluster in Kubernetes

In this section, we will explore in detail a very large example of configuring a Cassandra cluster to run on a Kubernetes cluster. The full example can be accessed here:

`https://github.com/kubernetes/kubernetes/tree/master/examples/storage/cassandra`

First, we'll learn a little bit about Cassandra and its idiosyncrasies, and then follow a step-by-step procedure to get it running using several of the techniques and strategies we've covered in the previous section.

Quick introduction to Cassandra

Cassandra is a distributed columnar data store. It was designed from the get-go for big data. Cassandra is fast, robust (no single point of failure), highly available, and linearly scalable. It also has multi-data center support. It achieves all this by having a laser focus and carefully crafting the features it supports—and just as importantly—the features it doesn't support. In a previous company, I ran a Kubernetes cluster that used Cassandra as the main data store for sensor data (about 100 TB). Cassandra allocates the data to a set of nodes (node ring) based on a **distributed hash table** (**DHT**) algorithm. The cluster nodes talk to each other via a gossip protocol and learn quickly about the overall state of the cluster (what nodes joined and what nodes left or are unavailable). Cassandra constantly compacts the data and balances the cluster. The data is typically replicated multiple times for redundancy, robustness, and high-availability. From a developer's point of view, Cassandra is very good for time-series data and provides a flexible model where you can specify the consistency level in each query. It is also idempotent (a very important feature for a distributed database), which means repeated inserts or updates are allowed.

Here is a diagram that shows how a Cassandra cluster is organized and how a client can access any node and how the request will be forwarded automatically to the nodes that have the requested data:

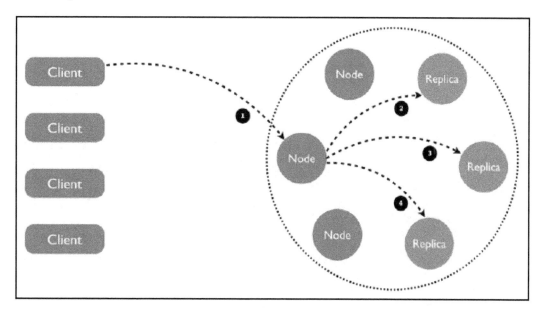

The Cassandra Docker image

Deploying Cassandra on Kubernetes as opposed to a standalone Cassandra cluster deployment requires a special Docker image. This is an important step because it means we can use Kubernetes to keep track of our Cassandra pods. The image is available here:

```
https://github.com/kubernetes/kubernetes/tree/master/examples/storage/cassandra
/image
```

Here are the essential parts of the Docker file. The image is based on Ubuntu Slim:

```
FROM gcr.io/google_containers/ubuntu-slim:0.9
```

Add and copy the necessary files (Cassandra.jar, various configuration files, run script, and read-probe script), create a data directory for Cassandra to store its SSTables, and mount it:

```
ADD files /

RUN set -e && echo 'debconf debconf/frontend select Noninteractive' |
debconf-set-selections \
  && apt-get update && apt-get -qq -y --force-yes install --no-install-
recommends \
    openjdk-8-jre-headless \
    libjemalloc1 \
    localepurge  \
    wget && \
  mirror_url=$( wget -q -O -
http://www.apache.org/dyn/closer.cgi/cassandra/ \
      | sed -n 's#.*href="\(http://.*/cassandra\/[^"]*\)".*#\1#p' \
      | head -n 1 \
  ) \
    && wget -q -O - ${mirror_url}/${CASSANDRA_VERSION}/apache-cassandra-
${CASSANDRA_VERSION}-bin.tar.gz \
      | tar -xzf - -C /usr/local \
    && wget -q -O -
https://github.com/Yelp/dumb-init/releases/download/v${DI_VERSION}/dumb-ini
t_${DI_VERSION}_amd64 > /sbin/dumb-init \
    && echo "$DI_SHA  /sbin/dumb-init" | sha256sum -c - \
    && chmod +x /sbin/dumb-init \
    && chmod +x /ready-probe.sh \
    && mkdir -p /cassandra_data/data \
    && mkdir -p /etc/cassandra \
    && mv /logback.xml /cassandra.yaml /jvm.options /etc/cassandra/ \
    && mv /usr/local/apache-cassandra-${CASSANDRA_VERSION}/conf/cassandra-
env.sh /etc/cassandra/ \
    && adduser --disabled-password --no-create-home --gecos '' --disabled-
```

```
login cassandra \
    && chown cassandra: /ready-probe.sh \
```

```
VOLUME ["/$CASSANDRA_DATA"]
```

Expose important ports for accessing Cassandra and to let Cassandra nodes gossip with each other:

```
# 7000: intra-node communication
# 7001: TLS intra-node communication
# 7199: JMX
# 9042: CQL
# 9160: thrift service

EXPOSE 7000 7001 7199 9042 9160
```

Finally, the command, which uses dumb-init, a simple container init system from yelp, eventually runs the run.sh script:

```
CMD ["/sbin/dumb-init", "/bin/bash", "/run.sh"]
```

Exploring the run.sh script

The run.sh script requires some shell skills, but it's worth the effort. Since Docker allows running only one command, it is very common with non-trivial applications to have a launcher script that sets up the environment and prepares for the actual application. In this case, the image supports several deployment options (stateful set, replication controller, DaemonSet) that we'll cover later, and the run script accommodates it all by being very configurable via environment variables.

First, some local variables are set for the Cassandra configuration file at /etc/cassandra/cassandra.yaml. The CASSANDRA_CFG variable will be used in the rest of the script:

```
set -e
CASSANDRA_CONF_DIR=/etc/cassandra
CASSANDRA_CFG=$CASSANDRA_CONF_DIR/cassandra.yaml
```

If no `CASSANDRA_SEEDS` were specified, then set the `HOSTNAME`, which is used in the StatefulSet solution:

```
# we are doing StatefulSet or just setting our seeds
if [ -z "$CASSANDRA_SEEDS" ]; then
  HOSTNAME=$(hostname -f)
Fi
```

Then comes a long list of environment variables with defaults. The syntax, `${VAR_NAME:-<default>}`, uses the `VAR_NAME` environment variable, if it's defined, or the default value.

A similar syntax, `${VAR_NAME:=<default>}`, does the same thing, but also assigns the default value to the environment variable if it's not defined.

Both variations are used here:

```
CASSANDRA_RPC_ADDRESS="${CASSANDRA_RPC_ADDRESS:-0.0.0.0}"
CASSANDRA_NUM_TOKENS="${CASSANDRA_NUM_TOKENS:-32}"
CASSANDRA_CLUSTER_NAME="${CASSANDRA_CLUSTER_NAME:='Test Cluster'}"
CASSANDRA_LISTEN_ADDRESS=${POD_IP:-$HOSTNAME}
CASSANDRA_BROADCAST_ADDRESS=${POD_IP:-$HOSTNAME}
CASSANDRA_BROADCAST_RPC_ADDRESS=${POD_IP:-$HOSTNAME}
CASSANDRA_DISK_OPTIMIZATION_STRATEGY="${CASSANDRA_DISK_OPTIMIZATION_STRATEG
Y:-ssd}"
CASSANDRA_MIGRATION_WAIT="${CASSANDRA_MIGRATION_WAIT:-1}"
CASSANDRA_ENDPOINT_SNITCH="${CASSANDRA_ENDPOINT_SNITCH:-SimpleSnitch}"
CASSANDRA_DC="${CASSANDRA_DC}"
CASSANDRA_RACK="${CASSANDRA_RACK}"
CASSANDRA_RING_DELAY="${CASSANDRA_RING_DELAY:-30000}"
CASSANDRA_AUTO_BOOTSTRAP="${CASSANDRA_AUTO_BOOTSTRAP:-true}"
CASSANDRA_SEEDS="${CASSANDRA_SEEDS:false}"
CASSANDRA_SEED_PROVIDER="${CASSANDRA_SEED_PROVIDER:-
org.apache.cassandra.locator.SimpleSeedProvider}"
CASSANDRA_AUTO_BOOTSTRAP="${CASSANDRA_AUTO_BOOTSTRAP:false}"

# Turn off JMX auth
CASSANDRA_OPEN_JMX="${CASSANDRA_OPEN_JMX:-false}"
# send GC to STDOUT
CASSANDRA_GC_STDOUT="${CASSANDRA_GC_STDOUT:-false}"
```

Then comes a section where all the variables are printed to the screen. Let's skip most of it:

```
echo Starting Cassandra on ${CASSANDRA_LISTEN_ADDRESS}
echo CASSANDRA_CONF_DIR ${CASSANDRA_CONF_DIR}
...
```

The next section is very important. By default, Cassandra uses a simple snitch, which is unaware of racks and data centers. This is not optimal when the cluster spans multiple data centers and racks.

Cassandra is rack- and data center-aware and can optimize both for redundancy and high availability while limiting communication across data centers appropriately:

```
# if DC and RACK are set, use GossipingPropertyFileSnitch
if [[ $CASSANDRA_DC && $CASSANDRA_RACK ]]; then
  echo "dc=$CASSANDRA_DC" > $CASSANDRA_CONF_DIR/cassandra-rackdc.properties
  echo "rack=$CASSANDRA_RACK" >> $CASSANDRA_CONF_DIR/cassandra-
rackdc.properties
  CASSANDRA_ENDPOINT_SNITCH="GossipingPropertyFileSnitch"
fi
```

Memory management is important, and you can control the maximum heap size to ensure Cassandra doesn't start thrashing and swapping to disk:

```
if [ -n "$CASSANDRA_MAX_HEAP" ]; then
  sed -ri "s/^(#)?-Xmx[0-9]+.*/-Xmx$CASSANDRA_MAX_HEAP/"
"$CASSANDRA_CONF_DIR/jvm.options"
  sed -ri "s/^(#)?-Xms[0-9]+.*/-Xms$CASSANDRA_MAX_HEAP/"
"$CASSANDRA_CONF_DIR/jvm.options"
fi

if [ -n "$CASSANDRA_REPLACE_NODE" ]; then
   echo "-Dcassandra.replace_address=$CASSANDRA_REPLACE_NODE/" >>
"$CASSANDRA_CONF_DIR/jvm.options"
fi
```

The rack and data center information is stored in a simple Java `properties` file:

```
for rackdc in dc rack; do
  var="CASSANDRA_${rackdc^^}"
  val="${!var}"
  if [ "$val" ]; then
  sed -ri 's/^('"$rackdc"'=).*/1 '"$val"'/' "$CASSANDRA_CONF_DIR/cassandra-
rackdc.properties"
  fi
done
```

The next section loops over all the variables defined earlier, finds the corresponding key in the `Cassandra.yaml` configuration files, and overwrites them. That ensures that each configuration file is customized on the fly just before it launches Cassandra itself:

```
for yaml in \
  broadcast_address \
```

```
      broadcast_rpc_address \
      cluster_name \
      disk_optimization_strategy \
      endpoint_snitch \
      listen_address \
      num_tokens \
      rpc_address \
      start_rpc \
      key_cache_size_in_mb \
      concurrent_reads \
      concurrent_writes \
      memtable_cleanup_threshold \
      memtable_allocation_type \
      memtable_flush_writers \
      concurrent_compactors \
      compaction_throughput_mb_per_sec \
      counter_cache_size_in_mb \
      internode_compression \
      endpoint_snitch \
      gc_warn_threshold_in_ms \
      listen_interface  \
      rpc_interface  \
      ; do
      var="CASSANDRA_${yaml^^}"
      val="${!var}"
      if [ "$val" ]; then
        sed -ri 's/^(# )?('"$yaml"':).*/\2 '"$val"'/' "$CASSANDRA_CFG"
      fi
done

echo "auto_bootstrap: ${CASSANDRA_AUTO_BOOTSTRAP}" >> $CASSANDRA_CFG
```

The next section is all about setting the seeds or seed provider depending on the deployment solution (StatefulSet or not). There is a little trick for the first pod to bootstrap as its own seed:

```
# set the seed to itself.  This is only for the first pod, otherwise
# it will be able to get seeds from the seed provider
if [[ $CASSANDRA_SEEDS == 'false' ]]; then
  sed -ri 's/- seeds:.*/- seeds: "'"$POD_IP"'"/' $CASSANDRA_CFG
else # if we have seeds set them.  Probably StatefulSet
  sed -ri 's/- seeds:.*/- seeds: "'"$CASSANDRA_SEEDS"'"/' $CASSANDRA_CFG
fi

sed -ri 's/- class_name: SEED_PROVIDER/- class_name:
'"$CASSANDRA_SEED_PROVIDER"'/' $CASSANDRA_CFG
```

The following section sets up various options for remote management and JMX monitoring. It's critical in complicated distributed systems to have proper administration tools. Cassandra has deep support for the ubiquitous **Java Management Extensions (JMX)** standard:

```
# send gc to stdout
if [[ $CASSANDRA_GC_STDOUT == 'true' ]]; then
  sed -ri 's/ -Xloggc:\/var\/log\/cassandra\/gc\.log//'
$CASSANDRA_CONF_DIR/cassandra-env.sh
fi

# enable RMI and JMX to work on one port
echo "JVM_OPTS=\"\$JVM_OPTS -Djava.rmi.server.hostname=$POD_IP\"" >>
$CASSANDRA_CONF_DIR/cassandra-env.sh

# getting WARNING messages with Migration Service
echo "-
Dcassandra.migration_task_wait_in_seconds=${CASSANDRA_MIGRATION_WAIT}" >>
$CASSANDRA_CONF_DIR/jvm.options
echo "-Dcassandra.ring_delay_ms=${CASSANDRA_RING_DELAY}" >>
$CASSANDRA_CONF_DIR/jvm.options

if [[ $CASSANDRA_OPEN_JMX == 'true' ]]; then
  export LOCAL_JMX=no
  sed -ri 's/ -Dcom\.sun\.management\.jmxremote\.authenticate=true/ -
Dcom\.sun\.management\.jmxremote\.authenticate=false/'
$CASSANDRA_CONF_DIR/cassandra-env.sh
  sed -ri 's/ -
Dcom\.sun\.management\.jmxremote\.password\.file=\/etc\/cassandra\/jmxremot
e\.password//' $CASSANDRA_CONF_DIR/cassandra-env.sh
fi
```

Finally, the CLASSPATH is set to the Cassandra JAR file, and it launches Cassandra in the foreground (not daemonized) as the Cassandra user:

```
export CLASSPATH=/kubernetes-cassandra.jar
su cassandra -c "$CASSANDRA_HOME/bin/cassandra -f"
```

Hooking up Kubernetes and Cassandra

Connecting Kubernetes and Cassandra takes some work because Cassandra was designed to be very self-sufficient, but we want to let it hook Kubernetes at the right time to provide capabilities, such as automatically restarting failed nodes, monitoring, allocating Cassandra pods, and providing a unified view of the Cassandra pods side by side with other pods. Cassandra is a complicated beast and has many knobs to control it. It comes with a `Cassandra.yaml` configuration file, and you can override all the options with environment variables.

Digging into the Cassandra configuration

There are two settings that are particularly relevant: the seed provider and the snitch. The seed provider is responsible for publishing a list of IP addresses (seeds) of nodes in the cluster. Every node that starts running connects to the seeds (there are usually at least three) and if it successfully reaches one of them they immediately exchange information about all the nodes in the cluster. This information is updated constantly for each node as the nodes gossip with each other.

The default seed provider configured in `Cassandra.yaml` is just a static list of IP addresses, in this case just the loopback interface:

```
seed_provider:
    - class_name: SEED_PROVIDER
      parameters:
          # seeds is actually a comma-delimited list of addresses.
          # Ex: "<ip1>,<ip2>,<ip3>"
          - seeds: "127.0.0.1"
```

The other important setting is the snitch. It has two roles:

- It teaches Cassandra enough about your network topology to route requests efficiently.
- It allows Cassandra to spread replicas around your cluster to avoid correlated failures. It does this by grouping machines into data centers and racks. Cassandra will do its best not to have more than one replica on the same rack (which may not actually be a physical location).

Cassandra comes pre-loaded with several snitch classes, but none of them are Kubernetes-aware. The default is `SimpleSnitch`, but it can be overridden:

```
# You can use a custom Snitch by setting this to the full class
# name of the snitch, which will be assumed to be on your classpath.
endpoint_snitch: SimpleSnitch
```

The custom seed provider

When running Cassandra nodes as pods in Kubernetes, Kubernetes may move pods around, including seeds. To accommodate that, a Cassandra seed provider needs to interact with the Kubernetes API server.

Here is a short snippet from the custom `KubernetesSeedProvider` Java class that implements the Cassandra `SeedProvider` API:

```
public class KubernetesSeedProvider implements SeedProvider {
    ...
    /**
     * Call kubernetes API to collect a list of seed providers
     * @return list of seed providers
     */
    public List<InetAddress> getSeeds() {
        String host = getEnvOrDefault("KUBERNETES_PORT_443_TCP_ADDR",
"kubernetes.default.svc.cluster.local");
        String port = getEnvOrDefault("KUBERNETES_PORT_443_TCP_PORT",
"443");
        String serviceName = getEnvOrDefault("CASSANDRA_SERVICE",
"cassandra");
        String podNamespace = getEnvOrDefault("POD_NAMESPACE", "default");
        String path = String.format("/api/v1/namespaces/%s/endpoints/",
podNamespace);
        String seedSizeVar = getEnvOrDefault("CASSANDRA_SERVICE_NUM_SEEDS",
"8");
        Integer seedSize = Integer.valueOf(seedSizeVar);
        String accountToken = getEnvOrDefault("K8S_ACCOUNT_TOKEN",
"/var/run/secrets/kubernetes.io/serviceaccount/token");
        List<InetAddress> seeds = new ArrayList<InetAddress>();
        try {
            String token = getServiceAccountToken(accountToken);

            SSLContext ctx = SSLContext.getInstance("SSL");
            ctx.init(null, trustAll, new SecureRandom());

            String PROTO = "https://";
            URL url = new URL(PROTO + host + ":" + port + path +
```

```
serviceName);
            logger.info("Getting endpoints from " + url);
            HttpsURLConnection conn =
(HttpsURLConnection)url.openConnection();

            conn.setSSLSocketFactory(ctx.getSocketFactory());
            conn.addRequestProperty("Authorization", "Bearer " + token);
            ObjectMapper mapper = new ObjectMapper();
            Endpoints endpoints = mapper.readValue(conn.getInputStream(),
Endpoints.class);     }
            . . .
        }
        . . .
    return Collections.unmodifiableList(seeds);
}
```

Creating a Cassandra headless service

The role of the headless service is to allow clients in the Kubernetes cluster to connect to the Cassandra cluster through a standard Kubernetes service instead of keeping track of the network identities of the nodes or putting a dedicated load balancer in front of all the nodes. Kubernetes provides all that out of the box through its services.

Here is the configuration file:

```
apiVersion: v1
kind: Service
metadata:
  labels:
    app: cassandra
  name: cassandra
spec:
  clusterIP: None
  ports:
    - port: 9042
  selector:
    app: Cassandra
```

The app: Cassandra label will group all the pods to participate in the service. Kubernetes will create endpoint records and the DNS will return a record for discovery. The clusterIP is None, which means the service is headless and Kubernetes will not do any load balancing or proxying. This is important because Cassandra nodes do their own communication directly.

The `9042` port is used by Cassandra to serve CQL requests. Those can be queries, inserts/updates (it's always an upsert with Cassandra), or deletes.

Using StatefulSet to create the Cassandra cluster

Declaring a StatefulSet is not trivial. It is arguably the most complex Kubernetes resource. It has a lot of moving parts: standard metadata, the stateful set spec, the pod template (which is often pretty complex itself), and volume claim templates.

Dissecting the stateful set configuration file

Let's go methodically over this example stateful set configuration file that declares a three-node Cassandra cluster.

Here is the basic metadata. Note the `apiVersion` string is `apps/v1` (StatefulSet became generally available from Kubernetes 1.9):

```
apiVersion: "apps/v1"
kind: StatefulSet
metadata:
  name: cassandra
```

The stateful set `spec` defines the headless service name, how many pods there are in the stateful set, and the pod template (explained later). The `replicas` field specifies how many pods are in the stateful set:

```
spec:
  serviceName: cassandra
  replicas: 3
  template: ...
```

The term `replicas` for the pods is an unfortunate choice because the pods are not replicas of each other. They share the same pod template, but they have a unique identity and they are responsible for different subsets of the state in general. This is even more confusing in the case of Cassandra, which uses the same term, `replicas`, to refer to groups of nodes that redundantly duplicate some subset of the state (but are not identical, because each can manage additional state too). I opened a GitHub issue with the Kubernetes project to change the term from `replicas` to `members`:

https://github.com/kubernetes/kubernetes.github.io/issues/2103

The pod template contains a single container based on the custom Cassandra image. Here is the pod template with the `app: cassandra` label:

```
template:
  metadata:
    labels:
        app: cassandra
  spec:
    containers: ...
```

The container spec has multiple important parts. It starts with a `name` and the `image` we looked at earlier:

```
containers:
    - name: cassandra
        image: gcr.io/google-samples/cassandra:v12
        imagePullPolicy: Always
```

Then, it defines multiple container ports needed for external and internal communication by Cassandra nodes:

```
ports:
- containerPort: 7000
  name: intra-node
- containerPort: 7001
  name: tls-intra-node
- containerPort: 7199
  name: jmx
- containerPort: 9042
  name: cql
```

The resources section specifies the CPU and memory needed by the container. This is critical because the storage management layer should never be a performance bottleneck due to `cpu` or `memory`.

```
resources:
  limits:
    cpu: "500m"
    memory: 1Gi
  requests:
    cpu: "500m"
    memory: 1Gi
```

Cassandra needs access to IPC, which the container requests through the security content's capabilities:

```
securityContext:
capabilities:
  add:
       - IPC_LOCK
```

The env section specifies environment variables that will be available inside the container. The following is a partial list of the necessary variables. The CASSANDRA_SEEDS variable is set to the headless service, so a Cassandra node can talk to seeds on startup and discover the whole cluster. Note that in this configuration we don't use the special Kubernetes seed provider. POD_IP is interesting because it utilizes the Downward API to populate its value via the field reference to status.podIP:

```
env:
  - name: MAX_HEAP_SIZE
    value: 512M
  - name: CASSANDRA_SEEDS
    value: "cassandra-0.cassandra.default.svc.cluster.local"
 - name: POD_IP
   valueFrom:
     fieldRef:
       fieldPath: status.podIP
```

The container has a readiness probe, too, to ensure the Cassandra node doesn't receive requests before it's fully online:

```
readinessProbe:
  exec:
    command:
    - /bin/bash
    - -c
    - /ready-probe.sh
  initialDelaySeconds: 15
  timeoutSeconds: 5
```

Cassandra needs to read and write the data, of course. The cassandra-data volume mount is where it's at:

```
volumeMounts:
- name: cassandra-data
  mountPath: /cassandra_data
```

That's it for the container spec. The last part is the volume claim template. In this case, dynamic provisioning is used. It's highly recommended to use SSD drives for Cassandra storage, and especially its journal. The requested storage in this example is 1 Gi. I discovered through experimentation that 1-2 TB is ideal for a single Cassandra node. The reason is that Cassandra does a lot of data shuffling under the covers, compacting and rebalancing the data. If a node leaves the cluster or a new one joins the cluster, you have to wait until the data is properly rebalanced before the data from the node that left is properly re-distributed or a new node is populated. Note that Cassandra needs a lot of disk space to do all this shuffling. It is recommended to have 50% free disk space. When you consider that you also need replication (typically 3x), then the required storage space can be 6x your data size. You can get by with 30% free space if you're adventurous and maybe use just 2x replication depending on your use case. But don't get below 10% free disk space, even on a single node. I learned the hard way that Cassandra will simply get stuck and will be unable to compact and rebalance such nodes without extreme measures.

The access mode is, of course, ReadWriteOnce:

```
volumeClaimTemplates:
- metadata:
  name: cassandra-data
  annotations:
    volume.beta.kubernetes.io/storage-class: fast
spec:
  accessModes: [ "ReadWriteOnce" ]
  resources:
    requests:
      storage: 1Gi
```

When deploying a stateful set, Kubernetes creates the pod in order per its index number. When scaling up or down, it also does it in order. For Cassandra, this is not important because it can handle nodes joining or leaving the cluster in any order. When a Cassandra pod is destroyed, the persistent volume remains. If a pod with the same index is created later, the original persistent volume will be mounted into it. This stable connection between a particular pod and its storage enables Cassandra to manage the state properly.

Using a replication controller to distribute Cassandra

A StatefulSet is great, but, as mentioned earlier, Cassandra is already a sophisticated distributed database. It has a lot of mechanisms for automatically distributing, balancing, and replicating the data around the cluster. These mechanisms are not optimized for working with network persistent storage. Cassandra was designed to work with the data stored directly on the nodes. When a node dies, Cassandra can recover having redundant data stored on other nodes. Let's look at a different way to deploy Cassandra on a Kubernetes cluster, which is more aligned with Cassandra's semantics. Another benefit of this approach is that if you have an existing Kubernetes cluster; you don't have to upgrade it to the latest and greatest just to use a stateful set.

We will still use the headless service, but instead of a stateful set we'll use a regular replication controller. There are some important differences:

- Replication controller instead of a stateful set
- Storage on the node the pod is scheduled to run on
- The custom Kubernetes seed provider class is used

Dissecting the replication controller configuration file

The metadata is pretty minimal, with just a name (labels are not required):

```
apiVersion: v1
kind: ReplicationController
metadata:
  name: cassandra
  # The labels will be applied automatically
  # from the labels in the pod template, if not set
  # labels:
    # app: Cassandra
```

The `spec` specifies the number of `replicas`:

```
spec:
  replicas: 3
  # The selector will be applied automatically
  # from the labels in the pod template, if not set.
  # selector:
      # app: Cassandra
```

The pod template's metadata is where the `app: Cassandra` label is specified. The replication controller will keep track and make sure that there are exactly three pods with that label:

```
template:
    metadata:
        labels:
            app: Cassandra
```

The pod template's `spec` describes the list of containers. In this case, there is just one container. It uses the same Cassandra Docker image named `cassandra` and runs the `run.sh` script:

```
spec:
  containers:
    - command:
        - /run.sh
      image: gcr.io/google-samples/cassandra:v11
      name: cassandra
```

The resources section just requires `0.5` units of CPU in this example:

```
resources:
            limits:
                cpu: 0.5
```

The environment section is a little different. The `CASSANDRA_SEED_PROVDIER` specifies the custom Kubernetes seed provider class we examined earlier. Another new addition here is `POD_NAMESPACE`, which uses the Downward API again to fetch the value from the metadata:

```
env:
    - name: MAX_HEAP_SIZE
      value: 512M
    - name: HEAP_NEWSIZE
      value: 100M
    - name: CASSANDRA_SEED_PROVIDER
      value: "io.k8s.cassandra.KubernetesSeedProvider"
```

```
- name: POD_NAMESPACE
  valueFrom:
    fieldRef:
      fieldPath: metadata.namespace
- name: POD_IP
  valueFrom:
    fieldRef:
      fieldPath: status.podIP
```

The `ports` section is identical, exposing the intra-node communication ports (`7000` and `7001`), the `7199` JMX port used by external tools, such as Cassandra OpsCenter, to communicate with the Cassandra cluster, and of course the `9042` CQL port, through which clients communicate with the cluster:

```
ports:
  - containerPort: 7000
    name: intra-node
  - containerPort: 7001
    name: tls-intra-node
  - containerPort: 7199
    name: jmx
  - containerPort: 9042
    name: cql
```

Once again, the volume is mounted into `/cassandra_data`. This is important because the same Cassandra image configured properly just expects its `data` directory to be at a certain path. Cassandra doesn't care about the backing storage (although you should care, as the cluster administrator). Cassandra will just read and write using filesystem calls:

```
volumeMounts:
  - mountPath: /cassandra_data
    name: data
```

The volumes section is the biggest difference from the stateful set solution. A stateful set uses persistent storage claims to connect a particular pod with a stable identity to a particular persistent volume. The replication controller solution just uses an `emptyDir` on the hosting node:

```
volumes:
  - name: data
    emptyDir: {}
```

This has many ramifications. You have to provision enough storage on each node. If a Cassandra pod dies, its storage goes away. Even if the pod is restarted on the same physical (or virtual) machine, the data on disk will be lost because emptyDir is deleted once its pod is removed. Note that container restarts are OK because emptyDir survives container crashes. So, what happens when the pod dies? The replication controller will start a new pod with empty data. Cassandra will detect that a new node was added to the cluster, assign it some portion of the data, and start rebalancing automatically by moving data from other nodes. This is where Cassandra shines. It constantly compacts, rebalances, and distributes the data evenly across the cluster. It will just figure out what to do on your behalf.

Assigning pods to nodes

The main problem with the replication controller approach is that multiple pods can get scheduled on the same Kubernetes node. What if you have a replication factor of three and all three pods that are responsible for some range of the keyspace are all scheduled to the same Kubernetes node? First, all requests for read or writes of that range of keys will go to the same node, creating more pressure. But, even worse, we just lost our redundancy. We have a **single point of failure** (SPOF). If that node dies, the replication controller will happily start three new pods on some other Kubernetes node, but none of them will have data, and no other Cassandra node in the cluster (the other pods) will have data to copy from.

This can be solved using a Kubernetes scheduling concept called anti-affinity. When assigning pods to nodes, a pod can be annotated so that the scheduler will not schedule it to a node that already has a pod with a particular set of labels. Add this to the pod spec to ensure that at most a single Cassandra pod will be assigned to a node:

```
spec:
  affinity:
    podAntiAffinity:
      requiredDuringSchedulingIgnoredDuringExecution:
      - labelSelector:
          matchExpressions:
          - key: app
            operator: In
            values:
            - cassandra
        topologyKey: kubernetes.io/hostname
```

Using DaemonSet to distribute Cassandra

A better solution to the problem of assigning Cassandra pods to different nodes is to use a DaemonSet. A DaemonSet has a pod template like a replication controller. But a DaemonSet has a node selector that determines on which nodes to schedule its pods. It doesn't have a certain number of replicas, it just schedules a pod on each node that matches its selector. The simplest case is to schedule a pod on each node in the Kubernetes cluster. But the node selector can also use match expressions against labels to deploy to a particular subset of nodes. Let's create a DaemonSet for deploying our Cassandra cluster onto the Kubernetes cluster:

```
apiVersion: apps/v1
kind: DaemonSet
metadata:
  name: cassandra-daemonset
```

The `spec` of the DaemonSet contains a regular pod template. The `nodeSelector` section is where the magic happens, and it ensures that one and exactly one pod will always be scheduled to each node with a label of `app: Cassandra`:

```
spec:
  template:
    metadata:
      labels:
        app: cassandra
    spec:
      # Filter only nodes with the label "app: cassandra":
      nodeSelector:
        app: cassandra
      containers:
```

The rest is identical to the replication controller. Note that `nodeSelector` is expected to be deprecated in favor of affinity. When that will happen, it's not clear.

Summary

In this chapter, we covered the topic of stateful applications and how to integrate them with Kubernetes. We discovered that stateful applications are complicated and considered several mechanisms for discovery, such as DNS and environment variables. We also discussed several state management solutions, such as in-memory redundant storage and persistent storage. The bulk of the chapter revolved around deploying a Cassandra cluster inside a Kubernetes cluster using several options, such as a stateful set, a replication controller, and a DaemonSet. Each approach has its own pros and cons. At this point, you should have a thorough understanding of stateful applications and how to apply them in your Kubernetes-based system. You are armed with multiple methods for various use cases, and maybe you've even learned a little bit about Cassandra.

In the next chapter, we will continue our journey and explore the important topic of scalability, in particular auto-scalability, and how to deploy and do live upgrades and updates as the cluster dynamically grows. These issues are very intricate, especially when the cluster has stateful apps running on it.

14
Rolling Updates, Scalability, and Quotas

In this chapter, we will explore the automated pod scalability that Kubernetes provides, how it affects rolling updates, and how it interacts with quotas. We will touch on the important topic of provisioning and how to choose and manage the size of the cluster. Finally, we will go over how the Kubernetes team tests the limits of Kubernetes with a 5,000-node cluster. Here are the main points we will cover:

- Horizontal pod autoscaling
- Performing rolling updates with autoscaling
- Handling scarce resources with quotas and limits
- Pushing the envelope with Kubernetes performance

By the end of this chapter, you will have the ability to plan a large-scale cluster, provision it economically, and make informed decisions about the various trade-offs between performance, cost, and availability. You will also understand how to set up horizontal pod auto-scaling and use resource quotas intelligently to let Kubernetes automatically handle intermittent fluctuations in volume.

Horizontal pod autoscaling

Kubernetes can watch over your pods and scale them when the CPU utilization or some other metric crosses a threshold. The autoscaling resource specifies the details (percentage of CPU, how often to check) and the corresponding autoscale controller adjusts the number of replicas, if needed.

The following diagram illustrates the different players and their relationships:

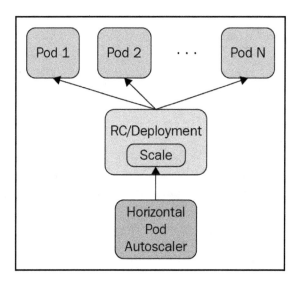

As you can see, the horizontal pod autoscaler doesn't create or destroy pods directly. It relies instead on the replication controller or deployment resources. This is very smart because you don't need to deal with situations where autoscaling conflicts with the replication controller or deployments trying to scale the number of pods, unaware of the autoscaler's efforts.

The autoscaler automatically does what we had to do ourselves before. Without the autoscaler, if we had a replication controller with replicas set to 3, but we determined that based on average CPU utilization we actually needed 4, then we would update the replication controller from 3 to 4 and keep monitoring the CPU utilization manually in all pods. The autoscaler will do it for us.

Declaring horizontal pod autoscaler

To declare a horizontal pod autoscaler, we need a replication controller, or a deployment, and an autoscaling resource. Here is a simple replication controller configured to maintain three `nginx` pods:

```
apiVersion: v1
kind: ReplicationController
metadata:
  name: nginx
```

```
spec:
  replicas: 3
  template:
    metadata:
      labels:
        run: nginx
    spec:
      containers:
      - name: nginx
        image: nginx
        ports:
        - containerPort: 80
```

The `autoscaling` resource references the NGINX replication controller in `scaleTargetRef`:

```
apiVersion: autoscaling/v1
kind: HorizontalPodAutoscaler
metadata:
  name: nginx
  namespace: default
spec:
  maxReplicas: 4
  minReplicas: 2
  targetCPUUtilizationPercentage: 90
  scaleTargetRef:
    apiVersion: v1
    kind: ReplicationController
    name: nginx
```

`minReplicas` and `maxReplicas` specify the range of scaling. This is needed to avoid runaway situations that could occur because of some problem. Imagine that, due to some bug, every pod immediately uses 100% CPU regardless of the actual load. Without the `maxReplicas` limit, Kubernetes will keep creating more and more pods until all cluster resources are exhausted. If we are running in a cloud environment with autoscaling of VMs then we will incur a significant cost. The other side of this problem is that, if there are no `minReplicas` and there is a lull in activity, then all pods could be terminated, and, when new requests come in, all the pods will have to be created and scheduled again. If there are patterns of on and off activity, then this cycle can repeat multiple times. Keeping the minimum of replicas running can smooth this phenomenon. In the preceding example, `minReplicas` is set to 2 and `maxReplicas` is set to 4. Kubernetes will ensure that there are always between 2 to 4 NGINX instances running.

The **target CPU** utilization percentage is a mouthful. Let's abbreviate it to **TCUP**. You specify a single number like 80%. This could lead to constant thrashing if the average load hovers around the TCUP. Kuberentes will alternate frequently between adding more replicas and removing replicas. This is often not a desired behavior. To address this concern, you can specify a delay for either scaling up or scaling down. There are two flags to the `kube-controller-manager` to support this:

- `--horizontal-pod-autoscaler-downscale-delay`: The value for this option is a duration that specifies how long the autoscaler has to wait before another downscale operation can be performed after the current one has completed. The default value is 5 minutes (5m0s).
- `--horizontal-pod-autoscaler-upscale-delay`: The value for this option is a duration that specifies how long the autoscaler has to wait before another upscale operation can be performed after the current one has completed. The default value is 3 minutes (3m0s).

Custom metrics

CPU utilization is an important metric to gauge whether pods that are bombarded with too many requests should be scaled up, or whether they are mostly idle and can be scaled down. But the CPU is not the only and sometimes not even the best metric to keep track of. Memory may be the limiting factor, and there are more specialized metrics, such as the depth of a pod's internal on-disk queue, the average latency on a request, or the average number of service timeouts.

The horizontal pod custom metrics were added as an alpha extension in version 1.2. In version 1.6 they were upgraded to beta status. You can now autoscale your pods based on multiple custom metrics. The autoscaler will evaluate all the metrics and will autoscale based on the largest number of replicas required, so the requirements of all the metrics are respected.

Using custom metrics

Using the horizontal pod autoscaler with custom metrics requires some configuration when launching your cluster. First, you need to enable the API aggregation layer. Then you need to register your resource metrics API and your custom metrics API. Heapster provides an implementation of the resource metrics API you can use. Just start Heapster with the `--api-server` flag set to `true`. You need to run a separate server that exposes the custom metrics API. A good starting point is this:
`https://github.com/kubernetes-incubator/custom-metrics-apiserver`.

The next step is to start the `kube-controller-manager` with the following flags:

```
--horizontal-pod-autoscaler-use-rest-clients=true
--kubeconfig <path-to-kubeconfig> OR --master <ip-address-of-apiserver>
```

The `--master` flag will override `--kubeconfig` if both are specified. These flags specify the location of the API aggregation layer, allowing the controller manager to communicate to the API server.

In Kubernetes 1.7, the standard aggregation layer that Kubernetes provides runs in-process with the `kube-apiserver`, so the target IP address can be found with this:

```
> kubectl get pods --selector k8s-app=kube-apiserver --namespace kube-
system -o jsonpath='{.items[0].status.podIP}'
```

Autoscaling with kubectl

`kubectl` can create an autoscale resource using the standard `create` command and accepting a configuration file. But `kubectl` also has a special command, `autoscale`, that lets you easily set an autoscaler in one command without a special configuration file:

1. First, let's start a replication controller that makes sure there are three replicas of a simple pod that just runs an infinite `bash-loop`:

```
apiVersion: v1
kind: ReplicationController
metadata:
   name: bash-loop-rc
spec:
   replicas: 3
   template:
     metadata:
       labels:
         name: bash-loop-rc
```

```
    spec:
      containers:
        - name: bash-loop
          image: ubuntu
          command: ["/bin/bash", "-c", "while true; do sleep 10;
                    done"]
```

2. Let's create a replication controller:

```
> kubectl create -f bash-loop-rc.yaml
replicationcontroller "bash-loop-rc" created
```

3. Here is the resulting replication controller:

```
> kubectl get rc
NAME            DESIRED     CURRENT     READY       AGE
bash-loop-rc       3           3          3         1m
```

4. You can see that the desired and current count are both three, meaning three pods are running. Let's make sure:

```
> kubectl get pods
NAME                    READY     STATUS      RESTARTS      AGE
bash-loop-rc-8h59t      1/1       Running     0             50s
bash-loop-rc-1svtd      1/1       Running     0             50s
bash-loop-rc-z7wt5      1/1       Running     0             50s
```

5. Now, let's create an autoscaler. To make it interesting, we'll set the minimum number of replicas to 4 and the maximum number to 6:

```
> kubectl autoscale rc bash-loop-rc --min=4 --max=6 --cpu-
percent=50
replicationcontroller "bash-loop-rc" autoscaled
```

6. Here is the resulting horizontal pod autoscaler (you can use hpa). It shows the referenced replication controller, the target and current CPU percentage, and the min/max pods. The name matches the referenced replication controller:

```
> kubectl get hpa
NAME            REFERENCE       TARGETS   MINPODS   MAXPODS   REPLICAS
AGE
bash-loop-rc  bash-loop-rc     50%         4         6           4
16m
```

7. Originally, the replication controller was set to have three replicas, but the autoscaler has a minimum of four pods. What's the effect on the replication controller? That's right. Now the desired number of replicas is four. If the average CPU utilization goes above 50%, then it may climb to five, or even six:

```
> kubectl get rc
NAME               DESIRED   CURRENT   READY     AGE
bash-loop-rc       4         4         4         21m
```

8. Just to make sure everything works, here is another look at the pods. Note the new pod (17 minutes old) that was created because of the autoscaling:

```
> kubectl get pods
NAME                  READY   STATUS    RESTARTS   AGE
bash-loop-rc-8h59t    1/1     Running   0          21m
bash-loop-rc-gjv4k    1/1     Running   0          17m
bash-loop-rc-lsvtd    1/1     Running   0          21m
bash-loop-rc-z7wt5    1/1     Running   0          21m
```

9. When we delete the horizontal pod autoscaler, the replication controller retains the last desired number of replicas (four in this case). Nobody remembers that the replication controller was created with three replicas:

```
> kubectl  delete hpa bash-loop-rc
horizontalpodautoscaler "bash-loop-rc" deleted
```

10. As you can see, the replication controller wasn't reset and still maintains four pods even when the autoscaler is gone:

```
> kubectl get rc
NAME               DESIRED   CURRENT   READY     AGE
bash-loop-rc       4         4         4         28m
```

Let's try something else. What happens if we create a new horizontal pod autoscaler with a range of 2 to 6 and the same CPU target of 50%?

```
> kubectl autoscale rc bash-loop-rc --min=2 --max=6 --cpu-percent=50
    replicationcontroller "bash-loop-rc" autoscaled
```

Well, the replication controller still maintains its four replicas, which is within the range:

```
> kubectl get rc
NAME               DESIRED   CURRENT   READY     AGE
bash-loop-rc       4         4         4         29m
```

However, the actual CPU utilization is zero, or close to zero. The replica count should have been scaled down to two replicas, but because the horizontal pod autoscaler didn't receive CPU metrics from Heapster it doesn't know it needs to scale down the number of replicas in the replication controller.

Performing rolling updates with autoscaling

Rolling updates are the cornerstone of managing large clusters. Kubernetes support rolling updates at the replication controller level and by using deployments. Rolling updates using replication controllers are incompatible with the horizontal pod autoscaler. The reason is that, during the rolling deployment, a new replication controller is created and the horizontal pod autoscaler remains bound to the old replication controller. Unfortunately, the intuitive `kubectl rolling-update` command triggers a replication controller rolling update.

Since rolling updates are such an important capability, I recommend that you always bind horizontal pod autoscalers to a deployment object instead of a replication controller or a replica set. When the horizontal pod autoscaler is bound to a deployment, it can set the replicas in the deployment spec and let the deployment take care of the necessary underlying rolling update and replication.

Here is a deployment configuration file we've used for deploying the `hue-reminders` service:

```
apiVersion: extensions/v1beta1
kind: Deployment
metadata:
  name: hue-reminders
spec:
  replicas: 2
  template:
    metadata:
      name: hue-reminders
      labels:
        app: hue-reminders
    spec:
      containers:
      - name: hue-reminders
        image: g1g1/hue-reminders:v2.2
        ports:
        - containerPort: 80
```

To support it with autoscaling and ensure we always have between 10 to 15 instances running, we can create an `autoscaler` configuration file:

```
apiVersion: autoscaling/v1
 kind: HorizontalPodAutoscaler
 metadata:
   name: hue-reminders
   namespace: default
 spec:
   maxReplicas: 15
   minReplicas: 10
   targetCPUUtilizationPercentage: 90
   scaleTargetRef:
     apiVersion: v1
     kind: Deployment
     name: hue-reminders
```

The `kind` of the `scaleTargetRef` field is now `Deployment` instead of `ReplicationController`. This is important because we may have a replication controller with the same name. To disambiguate and ensure that the horizontal pod autoscaler is bound to the correct object, the `kind` and the `name` must match.

Alternatively, we can use the `kubectl autoscale` command:

```
> kubectl autoscale deployment hue-reminders --min=10--max=15
--cpu-percent=90
```

Handling scarce resources with limits and quotas

With the horizontal pod autoscaler creating pods on the fly, we need to think about managing our resources. Scheduling can easily get out of control, and inefficient use of resources is a real concern. There are several factors that can interact with each other in subtle ways:

- Overall cluster capacity
- Resource granularity per node
- Division of workloads per namespace
- DaemonSets
- StatefulSets
- Affinity, anti-affinity, taints, and tolerations

First, let's understand the core issue. The Kubernetes scheduler has to take into account all these factors when it schedules pods. If there are conflicts or a lot of overlapping requirements, then Kubernetes may have a problem finding room to schedule new pods. For example, a very extreme yet simple scenario is that a daemon set runs on every node a pod that requires 50% of the available memory. Now, Kubernetes can't schedule any pod that needs more than 50% memory because the daemon set pod gets priority. Even if you provision new nodes, the daemon set will immediately commandeer half of the memory.

Stateful sets are similar to daemon sets in that they require new nodes to expand. The trigger to adding new members to the stateful set is growth in data, but the impact is taking resources from the pool available for Kubernetes to schedule other members. In a multi-tenant situation, the noisy neighbor problem can rear its head in a provisioning or resource allocation context. You may plan exact rations meticulously in your namespace between different pods and their resource requirements, but you share the actual nodes with your neighbors from other namespaces that you may not even have visibility into.

Most of these problems can be mitigated by judiciously using namespace resource quotas and careful management of the cluster capacity across multiple resource types, such as CPU, memory, and storage.

Enabling resource quotas

Most Kubernetes distributions support resource quota out of the box. The API servers' `--admission-control` flag must have `ResourceQuota` as one of its arguments. You will also have to create a `ResourceQuota` object to enforce it. Note that there may be at most one `ResourceQuota` object per namespace to prevent potential conflicts. This is enforced by Kubernetes.

Resource quota types

There are different types of quota we can manage and control. The categories are compute, storage, and objects.

Compute resource quota

Compute resources are CPU and memory. For each one, you can specify a limit or request a certain amount. Here is the list of compute related fields. Note that `requests.cpu` can be specified as just `cpu`, and `requests.memory` can be specified as just memory:

- `limits.cpu`: Across all pods in a non-terminal state, the sum of CPU limits cannot exceed this value
- `limits.memory`: Across all pods in a non-terminal state, the sum of memory limits cannot exceed this value
- `requests.cpu`: Across all pods in a non-terminal state, the sum of CPU requests cannot exceed this value
- `requests.memory`: Across all pods in a non-terminal state, the sum of memory requests cannot exceed this value

Storage resource quota

The storage resource quota type is a little more complicated. There are two entities you can restrict per namespace: the amount of storage and the number of persistent volume claims. However, in addition to just globally setting the quota on total storage or total number of persistent volume claims, you can also do that per `storage` class. The notation for `storage` class resource quota is a little verbose, but it gets the job done:

- `requests.storage`: Across all persistent volume claims, the sum of storage requests cannot exceed this value
- `persistentvolumeclaims`: The total number of persistent volume claims that can exist in the namespace
- `<storage-class>.storageclass.storage.k8s.io/requests.storage`: Across all persistent volume claims associated with the `storage-class-name`, the sum of storage requests cannot exceed this value
- `<storage-class>.storageclass.storage.k8s.io/persistentvolumeclaims`: Across all persistent volume claims associated with the `storage-class-name`, this is the total number of persistent volume claims that can exist in the namespace

Kubernetes 1.8 added alpha support for ephemeral storage quotas too:

- `requests.ephemeral-storage`: Across all pods in the namespace, the sum of local ephemeral storage requests cannot exceed this value
- `limits.ephemeral-storage`: Across all pods in the namespace, the sum of local ephemeral storage limits cannot exceed this value

Object count quota

Kubernetes has another category of resource quotas, which is API objects. My guess is that the goal is to protect the Kubernetes API server from having to manage too many objects. Remember that Kubernetes does a lot of work under the hood. It often has to query multiple objects to authenticate, authorize, and ensure that an operation doesn't violate any of the many policies that may be in place. A simple example is pod scheduling based on replication controllers. Imagine that you have 1 billion replication controller objects. Maybe you just have three pods and most of the replication controllers have zero replicas. Still, Kubernetes will spend all its time just verifying that indeed all those billion replication controllers have no replicas of their pod template and that they don't need to kill any pods. This is an extreme example, but the concept applies. Too many API objects means a lot of work for Kubernetes.

The overage of objects that can be restricted is a little spotty. For example, you can limit the number of replication controllers, but not replica sets, which are almost an improved version of replication controller that can do exactly the same damage if too many of them are around.

The most glaring omission is namespaces. There is no limit to the number of namespaces. Since all limits are per namespace, you can easily overwhelm Kubernetes by creating too many namespaces, as each namespace has only a small number of API objects.

Here are all the supported objects:

- `ConfigMaps`: The total number of configuration maps that can exist in the namespace.
- `PersistentVolumeClaims`: The total number of persistent volume claims that can exist in the namespace.
- `Pods`: The total number of pods in a non-terminal state that can exist in the namespace. A pod is in a terminal state if `status.phase` in (`Failed`, `Succeeded`) is `true`.

- ReplicationControllers: The total number of replication controllers that can exist in the namespace.
- ResourceQuotas: The total number of resource quotas that can exist in the namespace.
- Services: The total number of services that can exist in the namespace.
- Services.LoadBalancers: The total number of load balancer services that can exist in the namespace.
- Services.NodePorts: The total number of node port services that can exist in the namespace.
- Secrets: The total number of secrets that can exist in the namespace.

Quota scopes

Some resources, such as pods, may be in different states, and it is useful to have different quotas for these different states. For example, if there are many pods that are terminating (this happens a lot during rolling updates) then it is OK to create more pods even if the total number exceeds the quota. This can be achieved by only applying a pod object count quota to non-terminating pods. Here are the existing scopes:

- Terminating: Match pods where spec.activeDeadlineSeconds >= 0
- NotTerminating: Match pods where spec.activeDeadlineSeconds is nil
- BestEffort: Match pods that have best effort quality of service
- NotBestEffort: Match pods that do not have best effort quality of service

While the BestEffort scope applies only to pods, the Terminating, NotTerminating, and NotBestEffort scopes apply to CPU and memory, too. This is interesting because a resource quota limit can prevent a pod from terminating. Here are the supported objects:

- cpu
- limits.cpu
- limits.memory
- memory
- pods
- requests.cpu
- requests.memory

Requests and limits

The meaning of requests and limits in the context of resource quotas is that it requires the containers to explicitly specify the target attribute. This way, Kubernetes can manage the total quota because it knows exactly what range of resources is allocated to each container.

Working with quotas

Let's create a `namespace` first:

```
> kubectl create namespace ns
namespace "ns" created
```

Using namespace-specific context

When working with namespaces other than default, I prefer to use a `context`, so I don't have to keep typing `--namespace=ns` for every command:

```
> kubectl config set-context ns --cluster=minikube --user=minikube --
namespace=ns
Context "ns" set.
> kubectl config use-context ns
Switched to context "ns".
```

Creating quotas

1. Create a `compute quota` object:

```
apiVersion: v1
kind: ResourceQuota
metadata:
  name: compute-quota
spec:
  hard:
    pods: "2"
    requests.cpu: "1"
    requests.memory: 20Mi
    limits.cpu: "2"
    limits.memory: 2Gi
> kubectl create -f compute-quota.yaml
resourcequota "compute-quota" created
```

2. Next, let's add a `count quota` object:

```
apiVersion: v1
kind: ResourceQuota
metadata:
  name: object-counts-quota
spec:
  hard:
    configmaps: "10"
    persistentvolumeclaims: "4"
    replicationcontrollers: "20"
    secrets: "10"
    services: "10"
    services.loadbalancers: "2"
> kubectl create -f object-count-quota.yaml
resourcequota "object-counts-quota" created
```

3. We can observe all the quotas:

```
> kubectl get quota
NAME                        AGE
compute-resources           17m
object-counts               15m
```

4. And we can even get all the information using `describe`:

```
> kubectl describe quota compute-quota
Name:             compute-quota
Namespace:        ns
Resource          Used  Hard
--------          ----  ----
limits.cpu        0     2
limits.memory     0     2Gi
pods              0     2
requests.cpu      0     1
requests.memory   0     20Mi
> kubectl describe quota object-counts-quota
Name:                   object-counts-quota
Namespace:              ns
Resource                Used  Hard
--------                ----  ----
configmaps              0     10
persistentvolumeclaims  0     4
replicationcontrollers  0     20
secrets                 1     10
services                0     10
services.loadbalancers  0     2
```

This view gives us an instant understanding of the global resource usage of important resources across the cluster without diving into too many separate objects.

1. Let's add an NGINX server to our namespace:

```
> kubectl run nginx --image=nginx --replicas=1
deployment "nginx" created
> kubectl get pods
No resources found.
```

2. Uh-oh. No resources found. But there was no error when the deployment was created. Let's check out the deployment resource:

```
> kubectl describe deployment nginx
Name:                   nginx
Namespace:              ns
CreationTimestamp:      Sun, 11 Feb 2018 16:04:42 -0800
Labels:                 run=nginx
Annotations:            deployment.kubernetes.io/revision=1
Selector:               run=nginx
Replicas:               1 desired | 0 updated | 0 total | 0 available |
1 unavailable
StrategyType:           RollingUpdate
MinReadySeconds:        0
RollingUpdateStrategy:  1 max unavailable, 1 max surge
Pod Template:
  Labels:  run=nginx
  Containers:
   nginx:
    Image:         nginx
    Port:          <none>
    Environment:   <none>
    Mounts:        <none>
  Volumes:         <none>
Conditions:
  Type                Status  Reason
  ----                ------  ------
  Available           True    MinimumReplicasAvailable
  ReplicaFailure      True    FailedCreate
OldReplicaSets:       <none>
NewReplicaSet:        nginx-8586cf59 (0/1 replicas created)
Events:
  Type    Reason            Age  From                   Message
  ----    ------            ---- ----                   -------
Normal  ScalingReplicaSet  16m  deployment-controller  Scaled up replica
set nginx-8586cf59 to 1
```

There it is, in the `conditions` section. The `ReplicaFailure` status is `True` and the reason is `FailedCreate`. You can see that the deployment created a new replica set called `nginx-8586cf59`, but it couldn't create the pod it was supposed to create. We still don't know why. Let's check out the replica set:

```
> kubectl describe replicaset nginx-8586cf59
Name:           nginx-8586cf59
Namespace:      ns
Selector:       pod-template-hash=41427915,run=nginx
Labels:         pod-template-hash=41427915
                run=nginx
Annotations:    deployment.kubernetes.io/desired-replicas=1
                deployment.kubernetes.io/max-replicas=2
                deployment.kubernetes.io/revision=1
Controlled By:  Deployment/nginx
Replicas:       0 current / 1 desired
Pods Status:    0 Running / 0 Waiting / 0 Succeeded / 0 Failed
Conditions:
  Type             Status  Reason
  ----             ------  ------
  ReplicaFailure   True    FailedCreate
Events:
  Type      Reason        Age                   From
Message
  ----      ------        ----                  ----                      ----
---
  Warning   FailedCreate  17m (x8 over 22m)     replicaset-controller
(combined from similar events): Error creating: pods "nginx-8586cf59-sdwxj"
is forbidden: failed quota: compute-quota: must specify
limits.cpu,limits.memory,requests.cpu,requests.memory
```

The output is very wide, so it overlaps several lines, but the message is crystal clear. Since there is a compute quota in the namespace, every container must specify its CPU, memory requests, and limit. The quota controller must account for every container compute resources usage to ensure the total namespace quota is respected.

OK. We understand the problem, but how to resolve it? One way is to create a dedicated `deployment` object for each pod type we want to use and carefully set the CPU and memory requests and limit. But what if we're not sure? What if there are many pod types and we don't want to manage a bunch of `deployment` configuration files?

Another solution is to specify the limit on the command line when we run the `deployment`:

```
> kubectl run nginx \
  --image=nginx \
  --replicas=1 \
```

```
  --requests=cpu=100m,memory=4Mi \
  --limits=cpu=200m,memory=8Mi \
  --namespace=ns
```

That works, but creating deployments on the fly with lots of arguments is a very fragile way to manage your cluster:

```
> kubectl get pods
NAME                      READY     STATUS     RESTARTS    AGE
nginx-2199160687-zkc2h    1/1       Running    0           2m
```

Using limit ranges for default compute quotas

1. A better way is to specify default compute limits. Enter limit ranges. Here is a configuration file that sets some defaults for containers:

```
apiVersion: v1
kind: LimitRange
metadata:
  name: limits
spec:
  limits:
  - default:
      cpu: 200m
      memory: 6Mi
    defaultRequest:
      cpu: 100m
      memory: 5Mi
    type: Container
> kubectl create -f limits.yaml
limitrange "limits" created
```

2. Here are the current default `limits`:

```
> kubectl describe limits limitsName:   limits
Namespace:   ns
Type Resource Min Max Default Request Default Limit Max
Limit/Request Ratio
----         --------        ---      ---      ----------------
-------------    ----------------------
Container cpu      -    -    100m              200m          -
Container memory   -    -              5Mi     6Mi                     -
```

3. Now, let's run NGINX again without specifying any CPU or memory requests and limits. But first, let's delete the current NGINX deployment:

```
> kubectl delete deployment nginx
deployment "nginx" deleted
> kubectl run nginx --image=nginx --replicas=1
deployment "nginx" created
```

4. Let's see if the pod was created. Yes, it was:

```
> kubectl get pods
NAME                    READY    STATUS     RESTARTS   AGE
nginx-8586cf59-p4dp4    1/1      Running    0          16m
```

Choosing and managing the cluster capacity

With Kubernetes' horizontal pod autoscaling, daemon sets, stateful sets, and quotas, we can scale and control our pods, storage, and other objects. However, in the end, we're limited by the physical (virtual) resources available to our Kubernetes cluster. If all your nodes are running at 100% capacity, you need to add more nodes to your cluster. There is no way around it. Kubernetes will just fail to scale. On the other hand, if you have very dynamic workloads then Kubernetes can scale down your pods, but if you don't scale down your nodes correspondingly, you will still pay for the excess capacity. In the cloud, you can stop and start instances.

Choosing your node types

The simplest solution is to choose a single node type with a known quantity of CPU, memory, and local storage. But that is typically not the most efficient and cost-effective solution. It makes capacity planning simple because the only question is how many nodes are needed. Whenever you add a node, you add a known quantity of CPU and memory to your cluster, but most Kubernetes clusters and components within the cluster handle different workloads. We may have a stream processing pipeline where many pods receive some data and process it in one place. This workload is CPU-heavy and may or may not need a lot of memory. Other components, such as a distributed memory cache, need a lot of memory, but very little CPU. Other components, such as a Cassandra cluster, need multiple SSD disks attached to each node.

For each type of node, you should consider proper labeling and making sure that Kubernetes schedules the pods that are designed to run on that node type.

Choosing your storage solutions

Storage is a huge factor in scaling a cluster. There are three categories of scalable storage solution:

- Roll your own
- Use your cloud platform storage solution
- Use an out-of-cluster solution

When you use roll your own, you install some type of storage solution in your Kubernetes cluster. The benefits are flexibility and full control, but you have to manage and scale it yourself.

When you use your cloud platform storage solution, you get a lot out of the box, but you lose control, you typically pay more, and, depending on the service, you may be locked in to that provider.

When you use an out-of-cluster solution, the performance and cost of data transfer may be much greater. You typically use this option if you need to integrate with an existing system.

Of course, large clusters may have multiple data stores from all categories. This is one of the most critical decisions you have to make, and your storage needs may change and evolve over time.

Trading off cost and response time

If money is not an issue you can just over-provision your cluster. Every node will have the best hardware configuration available, you'll have way more nodes than are needed to process your workloads, and you'll have copious amounts of available storage. Guess what? Money is always an issue!

You may get by with over-provisioning when you're just starting and your cluster doesn't handle a lot of traffic. You may just run five nodes, even if two nodes are enough most of the time. Multiply everything by 1,000 and someone will come asking questions if you have thousands of idle machines and petabytes of empty storage.

OK. So, you measure and optimize carefully and you get 99.99999% utilization of every resource. Congratulations, you just created a system that can't handle an iota of extra load or the failure of a single node without dropping requests on the floor or delaying responses.

You need to find the middle ground. Understand the typical fluctuations of your workloads and consider the cost/benefit ratio of having excess capacity versus having reduced response time or processing ability.

Sometimes, if you have strict availability and reliability requirements, you can build redundancy into the system and then you over-provision by design. For example, you want to be able to hot swap a failed component with no downtime and no noticeable effects. Maybe you can't lose even a single transaction. In this case, you'll have a live backup for all critical components, and that extra capacity can be used to mitigate temporary fluctuations without any special actions.

Using effectively multiple node configurations

Effective capacity planning requires you to understand the usage patterns of your system and the load each component can handle. That may include a lot of data streams generated inside the system. When you have a solid understanding of the typical workloads, you can look at workflows and which components handle which parts of the load. Then you can compute the number of pods and their resource requirements. In my experience, there are some relatively fixed workloads, some workloads that vary predictably (such as office hours versus non-office hours), and then you have your completely crazy workloads that behave erratically. You have to plan according to each workload, and you can design several families of node configurations that can be used to schedule pods that match a particular workload.

Benefiting from elastic cloud resources

Most cloud providers let you scale instances automatically, which is a perfect complement to Kubernetes' horizontal pod autoscaling. If you use cloud storage, it also grows magically without you having to do anything. However, there are some gotchas that you need to be aware of.

Autoscaling instances

All the big cloud providers have instance autoscaling in place. There are some differences, but scaling up and down based on CPU utilization is always available, and sometimes custom metrics are available too. Sometimes, load balancing is offered as well. As you can see, there is some overlap with Kubernetes here. If your cloud provider doesn't have adequate autoscaling with proper control, it is relatively easy to roll your own, so that you monitor your cluster resource usage and invoke cloud APIs to add or remove instances. You can extract the metrics from Kubernetes.

Here is a diagram that shows how two new instances are added based on a CPU load monitor:

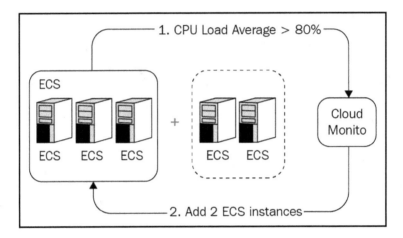

Mind your cloud quotas

When working with cloud providers, some of the most annoying things are quotas. I've worked with four different cloud providers (AWS, GCP, Azure, and Alibaba Cloud) and I was always bitten by quotas at some point. The quotas exist to let the cloud providers do their own capacity planning (and also to protect you from inadvertently starting 1 million instances that you won't be able to pay for), but from your point of view it is yet one more thing that can trip you up. Imagine that you set up a beautiful autoscaling system that works like magic, and suddenly the system doesn't scale when you hit 100 nodes. You quickly discover that you are limited to 100 nodes and you open a support request to increase the quota. However, a human must approve quota requests, and that can take a day or two. In the meantime, your system is unable to handle the load.

Manage regions carefully

Cloud platforms are organized in regions and availability zones. Some services and machine configurations are available only in some regions. Cloud quotas are also managed at the regional level. The performance and cost of data transfers within regions is much lower (often free) than across regions. When planning your cluster, you should consider your geo-distribution strategy carefully. If you need to run your cluster across multiple regions, you may have some tough decisions to make regarding redundancy, availability, performance, and cost.

Considering Hyper.sh (and AWS Fargate)

`Hyper.sh` is a container-aware hosting service. You just start containers. The service takes care of allocating the hardware. Containers start within seconds. You never need to wait minutes for a new VM. Hypernetes is Kubernetes on Hyper.sh, and it completely eliminates the need to scale the nodes because there are no nodes as far as you're concerned. There are only containers (or pods).

In the following diagram, you can see on the right how **Hyper Containers** run directly on a multi-tenant bare-metal container cloud:

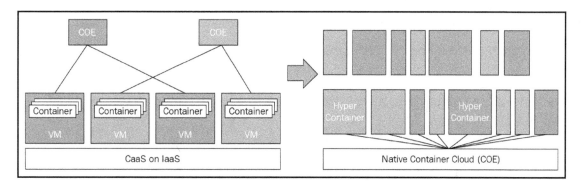

AWS recently released Fargate, which similarly abstracts away the underlying instances and just let you schedule containers in the cloud. In combination with EKS, it may become the most popular way to deploy Kubernetes.

Pushing the envelope with Kubernetes

In this section, we will see how the Kubernetes team pushes Kubernetes to its limit. The numbers are quite telling, but some of the tools and techniques, such as Kubemark, are ingenious, and you may even use them to test your clusters. In the wild, there are some Kubernetes clusters with 3,000 nodes. At CERN, the OpenStack team achieved 2 million requests per second:

`http://superuser.openstack.org/articles/scaling-magnum-and-kubernetes-2-million-requests-per-second/`.

Mirantis conducted a performance and scaling test in their scaling lab where they deployed 5,000 Kubernetes nodes (in VMs) on 500 physical servers.

 For more detail on Mirantis, please refer to: `http://bit.ly/2oijqQY`.

OpenAI scaled their machine learning Kubernetes cluster to 2,500 nodes and learned some valuable lessons, such as minding the query load of logging agents and storing events in a separate `etcd` cluster:

`https://blog.openai.com/scaling-kubernetes-to-2500-nodes/`

At the end of this section, you'll appreciate the effort and creativity that goes into improving Kubernetes on a large scale, you will know how far you can push a single Kubernetes cluster and what performance to expect, and you'll get an inside look at some of the tools and techniques that can help you evaluate the performance of your own Kubernetes clusters.

Improving the performance and scalability of Kubernetes

The Kubernetes team focused heavily on performance and scalability in Kubernetes 1.6. When Kubernetes 1.2 was released, it supported clusters of up to 1,000 nodes within the Kubernetes service-level objectives. Kubernetes 1.3 doubled the number to 2,000 nodes, and Kubernetes 1.6 brought it to a staggering 5,000 nodes per cluster. We will get into the numbers later, but first let's look under the hood and see how Kubernetes achieved these impressive improvements.

Caching reads in the API server

Kubernetes keeps the state of the system in etcd, which is very reliable, though not superfast (although etcd3 delivered a massive improvement specifically in order to enable larger Kubernetes clusters). The various Kubernetes components operate on snapshots of that state and don't rely on real-time updates. That fact allows the trading of some latency for throughput. All the snapshots used to be updated by etcd watches. Now, the API server has an in-memory read cache that is used for updating state snapshots. The in-memory read cache is updated by etcd watches. These schemes significantly reduce the load on etcd and increase the overall throughput of the API server.

The pod life cycle event generator

Increasing the number of nodes in a cluster is key for horizontal scalability, but pod density is crucial too. Pod density is the number of pods that the Kubelet can manage efficiently on one node. If pod density is low, then you can't run too many pods on one node. That means that you might not benefit from more powerful nodes (more CPU and memory per node) because the Kubelet will not be able to manage more pods. The other alternative is to force the developers to compromise their design and create coarse-grained pods that do more work per pod. Ideally, Kubernetes should not force your hand when it comes to pod granularity. The Kubernetes team understands this very well and has invested a lot of work in improving pod density.

In Kubernetes 1.1, the official (tested and advertised) number was 30 pods per node. I actually ran 40 pods per node on Kubernetes 1.1, but I paid for it with an excessive kubelet overhead that stole CPU from the worker pods. In Kubernetes 1.2, the number jumped to 100 pods per node.

The kubelet used to poll the container runtime constantly for each pod in its own go routine. That put a lot of pressure on the container runtime so that, during performance peaks, there were reliability issues, particularly with CPU utilization. The solution was the **Pod Lifecycle Event Generator** (**PLEG**). The way the PLEG works is that it lists the state of all the pods and containers and compares it to the previous state. This is done once for all the pods and containers. Then, by comparing the state to the previous state, the PLEG knows which pods need to sync again and invokes only those pods. That change resulted in a significant four times lower CPU usage by the Kubelet and the container runtime. It also reduced the polling period, which improves responsiveness.

The following diagram shows the **CPU utilization for 120 pods** on Kubernetes 1.1 versus Kubernetes 1.2. You can see the 4x factor very clearly:

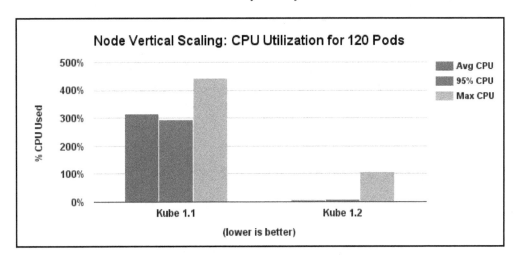

Serializing API objects with protocol buffers

The API server has a REST API. REST APIs typically use JSON as their serialization format, and the Kubernetes API server was no different. However, JSON serialization implies marshaling and unmarshaling JSON to native data structures. This is an expensive operation. In a large-scale Kubernetes cluster, a lot of components need to query or update the API server frequently. The cost of all that JSON parsing and composition adds up quickly. In Kubernetes 1.3, the Kubernetes team added an efficient protocol buffers serialization format. The JSON format is still there, but all internal communication between Kubernetes components uses the protocol buffers serialization format.

etcd3

Kubernetes switched from etcd2 to etcd3 in Kubernetes 1.6. This was a big deal. Scaling Kubernetes to 5,000 nodes wasn't possible due to limitations of etcd2, especially related to the watch implementation. The scalability needs of Kubernetes drove many of the improvements of etcd3, as CoreOS used Kubernetes as a measuring stick. Some of the big ticket items are as follows:

- GRPC instead of REST-etcd2 has a REST API, etcd3 has a gRPC API (and a REST API via gRPC gateway). The http/2 protocol at the base of gRPC can use a single TCP connection for multiple streams of requests and responses.

- Leases instead of TTLs-etcd2 uses **time to live** (**TTL**) per key as the mechanism to expire keys, and etcd3 uses leases with TTLs, where multiple keys can share the same key. This reduces significantly keep alive traffic.
- The watch implementation of etcd3 takes advantage of GRPC bi-directional streams and maintains a single TCP connection to send multiple events, which reduced the memory footprint by at least an order of magnitude.
- With etcd3, Kubernetes started storing all the state as protobug, which eliminated a lot of wasteful JSON serialization overhead.

Other optimizations

The Kubernetes team made many other optimizations:

- Optimizing the scheduler (which resulted in 5-10x higher scheduling throughput)
- Switching all controllers to a new recommended design using shared informers, which reduced resource consumption of controller-manager-for reference see this document at `https://github.com/kubernetes/community/blob/master/contributors/devel/controllers.md`
- Optimizing individual operations in the API server (conversions, deep-copies, patch)
- Reducing memory allocation in the API server (which significantly impacts the latency of API calls)

Measuring the performance and scalability of Kubernetes

In order to improve performance and scalability, you need a sound idea of what you want to improve and how you're going to measure the improvements. You must also make sure that you don't violate basic properties and guarantees in the quest for improved performance and scalability. What I love about performance improvements is that they often buy you scalability improvements for free. For example, if a pod needs 50% of the CPU of a node to do its job and you improve performance so that the pod can do the same work using 33% of the CPU, then you can suddenly run three pods instead of two on that node, and you've improved the scalability of your cluster by 50% overall (or reduced your cost by 33%).

The Kubernetes SLOs

Kubernetes has **Service Level Objectives** (**SLOs**). These guarantees must be respected when trying to improve performance and scalability. Kubernetes has a one-second response time for API calls. That's 1,000 milliseconds. It actually achieves an order of magnitude faster response time most of the time.

Measuring API responsiveness

The API has many different endpoints. There is no simple API responsiveness number. Each call has to be measured separately. In addition, due to the complexity and the distributed nature of the system, not to mention networking issues, there can be a lot of volatility to the results. A solid methodology is to break the API measurements into separate endpoints, then run a lot of tests over time and look at percentiles (which is standard practice).

It's also important to use enough hardware to manage a large number of objects. The Kubernetes team used a 32-core VM with 120 GB for the master in this test.

The following diagram describes the 50th, 90th, and 99th percentile of various important API call latencies for Kubernetes 1.3. You can see that the 90th percentile is very low, below 20 milliseconds. Even the 99th percentile is less than 125 milliseconds for the DELETE pods operation, and less than 100 milliseconds for all other operations:

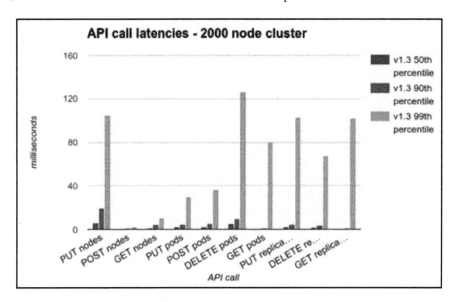

Another category of API calls is LIST operations. Those calls are more expansive because they need to collect a lot of information in a large cluster, compose the response, and send a potential large response. This is where performance improvements such as the in-memory read-cache and the protocol buffers serialization really shine. The response time is understandably greater than the single API calls, but it is still way below the SLO of one second (1,000 milliseconds):

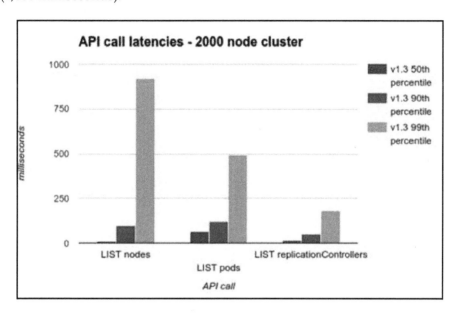

This is excellent, but check out the API call latencies with Kubernetes 1.6 on a 5,000 nodes cluster:

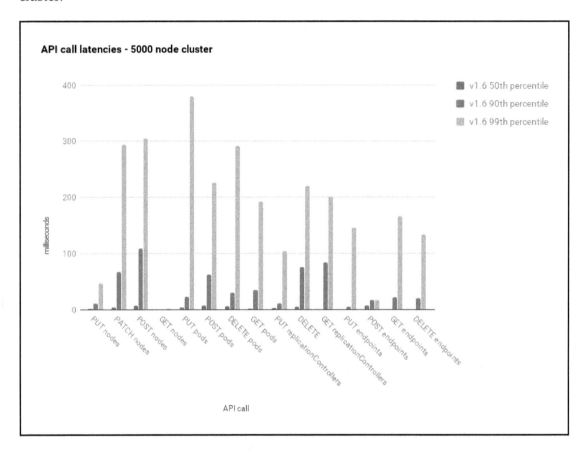

Measuring end-to-end pod startup time

One of the most important performance characteristics of a large dynamic cluster is end-to-end pod startup time. Kubernetes creates, destroys, and shuffles pods around all the time. You could say that the primary function of Kubernetes is to schedule pods.

In the following diagram, you can see that pod startup time is less volatile than API calls. This makes sense since there is a lot of work that needs to be done, such as launching a new instance of a runtime that doesn't depend on cluster size. With Kubernetes 1.2 on a 1,000-node cluster, the 99th percentile end-to-end time to launch a pod was less than 3 seconds. With Kubernetes 1.3, the 99th percentile end-to-end time to launch a pod was a little over 2.5 seconds. It's remarkable that the time is very close, but a little better with Kubernetes 1.3 on a 2,000-node cluster versus a 1,000-node cluster:

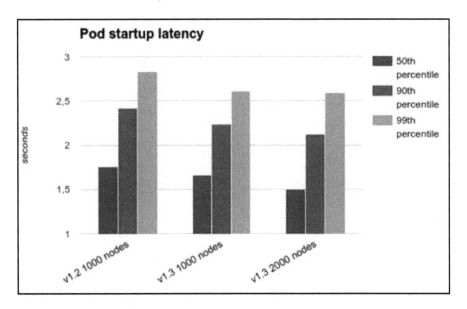

Kubernetes 1.6 takes it to the next level and does even better on a larger cluster:

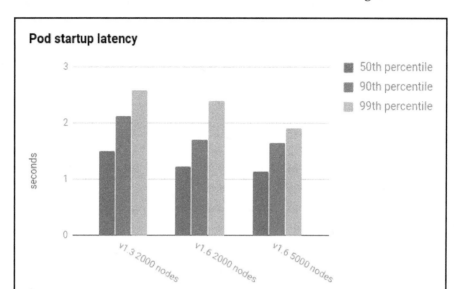

Testing Kubernetes at scale

Clusters with thousands of nodes are expensive. Even a project such as Kubernetes that enjoys the support of Google and other industry giants still needs to come up with reasonable ways to test without breaking the bank.

The Kubernetes team runs a full-fledged test on a real cluster at least once per release to collect real-world performance and scalability data. However, there is also a need for a lightweight and cheaper way to experiment with potential improvements and to detect regressions. Enter the Kubemark.

Introducing the Kubemark tool

The Kubemark is a Kubernetes cluster that runs mock nodes called hollow nodes used for running lightweight benchmarks against large-scale (hollow) clusters. Some of the Kubernetes components that are available on a real node such as the kubelet is replaced with a hollow kubelet. The hollow kubelet fakes a lot of the functionality of a real kubelet. A hollow kubelet doesn't actually start any containers, and it doesn't mount any volumes. But from the Kubernetes cluster point of view -the state stored in etcd- all those objects exist and you can query the API server. The hollow kubelet is actually the real kubelet with an injected mock Docker client that doesn't do anything.

Another important hollow component is the `hollow-proxy`, which mocks the Kubeproxy component. It again uses the real Kubeproxy code with a mock proxier interface that does nothing and avoids touching iptables.

Setting up a Kubemark cluster

A Kubemark cluster uses the power of Kubernetes. To set up a Kubemark cluster, perform the following steps:

1. Create a regular Kubernetes cluster where we can run `N hollow-nodes`.
2. Create a dedicated VM to start all master components for the Kubemark cluster.
3. Schedule `N hollow-node` pods on the base Kubernetes cluster. Those hollow-nodes are configured to talk to the Kubemark API server running on the dedicated VM.
4. Create add-on pods by scheduling them on the base cluster and configuring them to talk to the Kubemark API server.

A full-fledged guide on GCP is available at `http://bit.ly/2nPMkwc`.

Comparing a Kubemark cluster to a real-world cluster

The performance of Kubemark clusters is pretty similar to the performance of real clusters. For the pod startup end-to-end latency, the difference is negligible. For the API-responsiveness, the differences are higher, though generally less than a factor of two. However, trends are exactly the same: an improvement/regression in a real cluster is visible as a similar percentage drop/increase in metrics in Kubemark.

Summary

In this chapter, we've covered many topics relating to scaling Kubernetes clusters. We discussed how the horizontal pod autoscaler can automatically manage the number of running pods-based CPU utilization or other metrics, how to perform rolling updates correctly and safely in the context of auto-scaling, and how to handle scarce resources via resource quotas. Then we moved on to overall capacity planning and management of the cluster's physical or virtual resources. Finally, we delved into a real-world example of scaling a single Kubernetes cluster to handle 5,000 nodes.

At this point, you have a good understanding of all the factors that come into play when a Kubernetes cluster is facing dynamic and growing workloads. You have multiple tools to choose from for planning and designing your own scaling strategy.

In the next chapter, we will dive into advanced Kubernetes networking. Kubernetes has a networking model based on the **Common Networking Interface** (**CNI**) and supports multiple providers.

15
Advanced Kubernetes Networking

In this chapter, we will examine the important topic of networking. Kubernetes, as an orchestration platform, manages containers/pods running on different machines (physical or virtual) and requires an explicit networking model. We will look at the following topics:

- The Kubernetes networking model
- Standard interfaces that Kubernetes supports, such as EXEC, Kubenet, and, in particular, CNI
- Various networking solutions that satisfy the requirements of Kubernetes networking
- Network policies and load balancing options
- Writing a custom CNI plugin

At the end of this chapter, you will understand the Kubernetes approach to networking and be familiar with the solution space for aspects such as standard interfaces, networking implementations, and load balancing. You will even be able to write your very own CNI plugin if you wish.

Understanding the Kubernetes networking model

The Kubernetes networking model is based on a flat address space. All pods in a cluster can directly see each other. Each pod has its own IP address. There is no need to configure any NAT. In addition, containers in the same pod share their pod's IP address and can communicate with each other through localhost. This model is pretty opinionated, but, once set up, it simplifies life considerably both for developers and administrators. It makes it particularly easy to migrate traditional network applications to Kubernetes. A pod represents a traditional node and each container represents a traditional process.

Intra-pod communication (container to container)

A running pod is always scheduled on one (physical or virtual) node. That means that all the containers run on the same node and can talk to each other in various ways, such as the local filesystem, any IPC mechanism, or using localhost and well-known ports. There is no danger of port collision between different pods because each pod has its own IP address, and when a container in the pod uses localhost, it applies to the pod's IP address only. So, if container 1 in pod 1 connects to port 1234, which container 2 listens to on pod 1, it will not conflict with another container in pod 2 running on the same node that also listens on port 1234. The only caveat is that if you're exposing ports to the host then you should be careful about pod-to-node affinity. This can be handled using several mechanisms, such as DaemonSet and pod anti-affinity.

Inter-pod communication (pod to pod)

Pods in Kubernetes are allocated a network-visible IP address (not private to the node). Pods can communicate directly without the aid of network address translation, tunnels, proxies, or any other obfuscating layer. Well-known port numbers can be used for a configuration-free communication scheme. The pod's internal IP address is the same as its external IP address that other pods see (within the cluster network; not exposed to the outside world). This means that standard naming and discovery mechanisms such as DNS work out of the box.

Pod-to-service communication

Pods can talk to each other directly using their IP addresses and well-known ports, but that requires the pods to know each other's IP addresses. In a Kubernetes cluster, pods can be destroyed and created constantly. The service provides a layer of indirection that is very useful because the service is stable even if the set of actual pods that respond to requests is ever-changing. In addition, you get automatic, highly-available load balancing because the Kube-proxy on each node takes care of redirecting traffic to the correct pod:

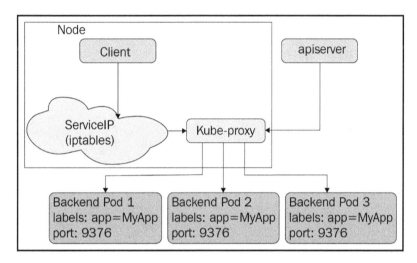

External access

Eventually, some containers need to be accessible from the outside world. The pod IP addresses are not visible externally. The service is the right vehicle, but external access typically requires two redirects. For example, cloud provider load balancers are Kubernetes-aware, so they can't direct traffic to a particular service directly to a node that runs a pod that can process the request. Instead, the public load balancer just directs traffic to any node in the cluster and the Kube-proxy on that node will redirect again to an appropriate pod if the current node doesn't run the necessary pod.

The following diagram shows how all that the external load balancer on the right side does is send traffic to all nodes that reach the proxy, which takes care of further routing, if it's needed:

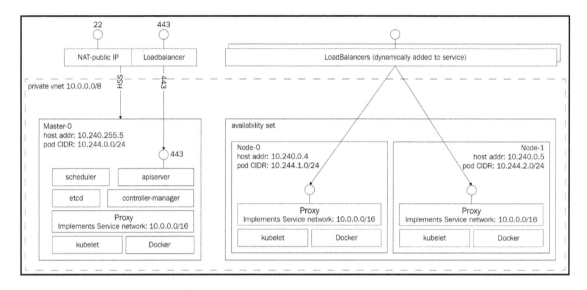

Kubernetes networking versus Docker networking

Docker networking follows a different model, although over time it has gravitated towards the Kubernetes model. In Docker networking, each container has its own private IP address from the 172.xxx.xxx.xxx address space confined to its own node. It can talk to other containers on the same node via their own 172.xxx.xxx.xxx IP addresses. This makes sense for Docker because it doesn't have the notion of a pod with multiple interacting containers, so it models every container as a lightweight VM that has its own network identity. Note that with Kubernetes, containers from different pods that run on the same node can't connect over localhost (except by exposing host ports, which is discouraged). The whole idea is that, in general, Kubernetes can kill and create pods anywhere, so different pods shouldn't rely, in general, on other pods available on the node. Daemon sets are a notable exception, but the Kubernetes networking model is designed to work for all use cases and doesn't add special cases for direct communication between different pods on the same node.

How do Docker containers communicate across nodes? The container must publish ports to the host. This obviously requires port coordination because if two containers try to publish the same host port, they'll conflict with each other. Then containers (or other processes) connect to the host's port that get channeled into the container. A big downside is that containers can't self-register with external services because they don't know what their host's IP address is. You could work around it by passing the host's IP address as an environment variable when you run the container, but that requires external coordination and complicates the process.

The following diagram shows the networking setup with Docker. Each container has its own IP address; Docker creates the docker0 bridge on every node:

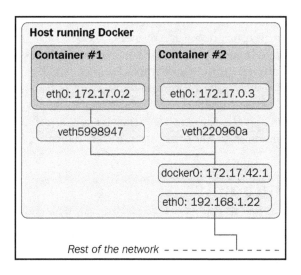

Lookup and discovery

In order for pods and containers to communicate with each other, they need to find each other. There are several ways for containers to locate other containers or announce themselves. There are also some architectural patterns that allow containers to interact indirectly. Each approach has its own pros and cons.

Self-registration

We've mentioned self-registration several times. Let's understand exactly what it means. When a container runs, it knows its pod's IP address. Each container that wants to be accessible to other containers in the cluster can connect to some registration service and register its IP address and port. Other containers can query the registration service for the IP addresses and port of all registered containers and connect to them. When a container is destroyed (gracefully), it will unregister itself. If a container dies ungracefully then some mechanism needs to be established to detect that. For example, the registration service can periodically ping all registered containers, or the containers are required periodically to send a keepalive message to the registration service.

The benefit of self-registration is that once the generic registration service is in place (no need to customize it for different purposes), there is no need to worry about keeping track of containers. Another huge benefit is that containers can employ sophisticated policies and decide to unregister temporarily if they are unavailable because of local conditions, such as if a container is busy and doesn't want to receive any more requests at the moment. This sort of smart and decentralized dynamic load balancing can be very difficult to achieve globally. The downside is that the registration service is yet another non-standard component that containers need to know about in order to locate other containers.

Services and endpoints

Kubernetes services can be considered as a registration service. Pods that belong to a service are registered automatically based on their labels. Other pods can look up the endpoints to find all the service pods or take advantage of the service itself and directly send a message to the service that will get routed to one of the backend pods. Although most of the time, pods will just send their message to the service itself, which will forward it to one of the backing pods.

Loosely coupled connectivity with queues

What if containers can talk to each other without knowing their IP addresses and ports or even service IP addresses or network names? What if most of the communication can be asynchronous and decoupled? In many cases, systems can be composed of loosely coupled components that are not only unaware of the identities of other components, but they are unaware that other components even exist. Queues facilitate such loosely coupled systems. Components (containers) listen to messages from the queue, respond to messages, perform their jobs, and post messages to the queue about progress, completion status, and errors. Queues have many benefits:

- Easy to add processing capacity without coordination; just add more containers that listen to the queue
- Easy to keep track of overall load by queue depth
- Easy to have multiple versions of components running side by side by versioning messages and/or topics
- Easy to implement load balancing as well as redundancy by having multiple consumers process requests in different modes

The downsides of queues are the following:

- Need to make sure that the queue provides appropriate durability and high availability so it doesn't become a critical SPOF
- Containers need to work with the async queue API (could be abstracted away)
- Implementing request-response requires the somewhat cumbersome listening on response queues

Overall, queues are an excellent mechanism for large-scale systems and they can be utilized in large Kubernetes clusters to ease coordination.

Loosely coupled connectivity with data stores

Another loosely coupled method is to use a data store (for example, Redis) to store messages and then other containers can read them. While possible, this is not the design objective of data stores and the result is often cumbersome, fragile, and doesn't have the best performance. Data stores are optimized for data storage and not for communication. That being said, data stores can be used in conjunction with queues, where a component stores some data in a data store and then sends a message to the queue that data is ready for processing. Multiple components listen to the message and all start processing the data in parallel.

Kubernetes ingress

Kubernetes offers an ingress resource and controller that is designed to expose Kubernetes services to the outside world. You can do it yourself, of course, but many tasks involved in defining ingress are common across most applications for a particular type of ingress, such as a web application, CDN, or DDoS protector. You can also write your own ingress objects.

The `ingress` object is often used for smart load balancing and TLS termination. Instead of configuring and deploying your own NGINX server, you can benefit from the built-in ingress. If you need a refresher, hop on to `Chapter 5`, *Using Critical Kubernetes Resources*, where we discussed the ingress resource with examples.

Kubernetes network plugins

Kubernetes has a network plugin system, because networking is so diverse and different people would like to implement it in different ways. Kubernetes is flexible enough to support any scenario. The primary network plugin is CNI, which we will discuss in depth. But Kubernetes also comes with a simpler network plugin called Kubenet. Before we go over the details, let's get on the same page with the basics of Linux networking (just the tip of the iceberg).

Basic Linux networking

Linux, by default, has a single shared network space. The physical network interfaces are all accessible in this namespace, but the physical namespace can be divided into multiple logical namespaces, which is very relevant to container networking.

IP addresses and ports

Network entities are identified by their IP address. Servers can listen to incoming connections on multiple ports. Clients can connect (TCP) or send data (UDP) to servers within their network.

Network namespaces

Namespaces group a bunch of network devices such that they can reach other servers in the same namespace, but not other servers even if they are physically on the same network. Linking networks or network segments can be done through bridges, switches, gateways, and routing.

Subnets, netmasks, and CIDRs

Granular division of network segments is very useful when designing and maintaining networks. Dividing networks in to smaller subnets with a common prefix is a common practice. These subnets can be defined by bitmasks that represent the size of the subnet (how many hosts it can contain). For example, a netmask of 255.255.255.0 means that the first three octets are used for routing and only 256 (actually 254) individual hosts are available. The Classless Inter-Domain Routing (CIDR) notation is often used for this purpose because it is more concise, encodes more information, and also allows combining hosts from multiple legacy classes (A, B, C, D, E). For example, 172.27.15.0/24 means that the first 24 bits (three octets) are used for routing.

Virtual Ethernet devices

Virtual Ethernet (veth) devices represent physical network devices. When you create a veth that's linked to a physical device, you can assign that veth (and by extension the physical device) into a namespace in which devices from other namespaces can't reach it directly, even if physically they are on the same local network.

Bridges

Bridges connect multiple network segments to an aggregate network, so all the nodes can communicate with each other. Bridging is done at the L1 (physical) and L2 (data link) layers of the OSI network model.

Routing

Routing connects separate networks, typically based on routing tables that instruct network devices how to forward packets to their destination. Routing is done through various network devices, such as routers, bridges, gateways, switches, and firewalls, including regular Linux boxes.

Maximum transmission unit

The **maximum transmission unit (MTU)** determines how big packets can be. On Ethernet networks, for example, the MTU is 1,500 bytes. The bigger the MTU, the better the ratio between payload and headers, which is a good thing. The downside is that minimum latency is reduced because you have to wait for the entire packet to arrive and, furthermore, if there's a failure, you have to retransmit the entire packet.

Pod networking

Here is a diagram that describes the relationship between pod, host, and the global internet at the networking level through veth0:

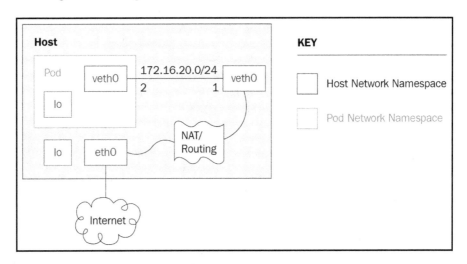

Kubenet

Back to Kubernetes. Kubenet is a network plugin; it's very rudimentary and just creates a Linux bridge called cbr0 and a veth for each pod. Cloud providers typically use it to set up routing rules for communication between nodes, or in single-node environments. The veth pair connects each pod to its host node using an IP address from the host's IP address range.

Requirements

The Kubenet plugin has the following requirements:

- The node must be assigned a subnet to allocate IP addresses for its pods
- The standard CNI bridge, lo, and host-local plugins are required for version 0.2.0 or greater
- The Kubelet must be run with the --network-plugin=kubenet argument
- The Kubelet must be run with the --non-masquerade-cidr=<clusterCidr> argument

Setting the MTU

The MTU is critical for network performance. Kubernetes network plugins such as Kubenet make their best efforts to deduce optimal MTU, but sometimes they need help. If an existing network interface (for example, the Docker `docker0` bridge) sets a small MTU, then Kubenet will reuse it. Another example is IPSEC, which requires lowering the MTU due to the extra overhead from IPSEC encapsulation overhead, but the Kubenet network plugin doesn't take it into consideration. The solution is to avoid relying on the automatic calculation of the MTU and just tell the Kubelet what MTU should be used for network plugins through the `--network-plugin-mtu` command-line switch, which is provided to all network plugins. However, at the moment, only the Kubenet network plugin accounts for this command-line switch.

Container Networking Interface (CNI)

CNI is a specification as well as a set of libraries for writing network plugins to configure network interfaces in Linux containers (not just Docker). The specification actually evolved from the rkt network proposal. There is a lot of momentum behind CNI and it's on a fast track to become the established industry standard. Some of the organizations that use CNI are:

- Kubernetes
- Kurma
- Cloud foundry
- Nuage
- RedHat
- Mesos

The CNI team maintains some core plugins, but there are a lot of third-party plugins too that contribute to the success of CNI:

- **Project Calico**: A layer 3 virtual network
- **Weave**: A multi-host Docker network
- **Contiv networking**: Policy-based networking
- **Cilium**: BPF and XDP for containers
- **Multus**: A Multi plugin
- **CNI-Genie**: A generic CNI network plugin
- **Flannel**: A network fabric for containers, designed for Kubernetes
- **Infoblox**: Enterprise IP address management for containers

Container runtime

CNI defines a plugin spec for networking application containers, but the plugin must be plugged into a container runtime that provides some services. In the context of CNI, an application container is a network-addressable entity (has its own IP address). For Docker, each container has its own IP address. For Kubernetes, each pod has its own IP address and the pod is the CNI container and not the containers within the pod.

Likewise, rkt's app containers are similar to Kubernetes pods in that they may contain multiple Linux containers. If in doubt, just remember that a CNI container must have its own IP address. The runtime's job is to configure a network and then execute one or more CNI plugins, passing them the network configuration in JSON format.

The following diagram shows a container runtime using the CNI plugin interface to communicate with multiple CNI plugins:

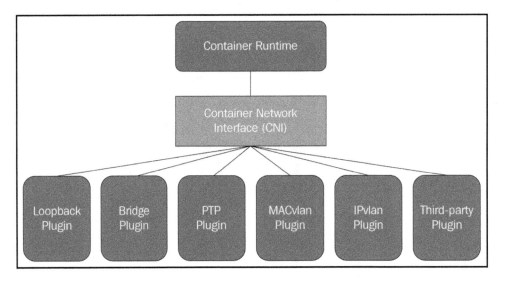

CNI plugin

The CNI plugin's job is to add a network interface into the container network namespace and bridge the container to the host via a `veth` pair. It should then assign an IP address through an IPAM (IP address management) plugin and set up routes.

The container runtime (Docker, rkt, or any other CRI-compliant runtime) invokes the CNI plugin as an executable. The plugin needs to support the following operations:

- Add a container to the network
- Remove a container from the network
- Report version

The plugin uses a simple command-line interface, standard input/output, and environment variables. The network configuration in JSON format is passed to the plugin through standard input. The other arguments are defined as environment variables:

- CNI_COMMAND: Indicates the desired operation; ADD, DEL, or VERSION.
- CNI_CONTAINERID: Container ID.
- CNI_NETNS: Path to network namespace file.
- * CNI_IFNAME: Interface name to set up; the plugin must honor this interface name or return an error.
- * CNI_ARGS: Extra arguments passed in by the user at invocation time. Alphanumeric key-value pairs are separated by semicolons, for example, FOO=BAR;ABC=123.
- CNI_PATH: List of paths to search for CNI plugin executables. Paths are separated by an OS-specific list separator, for example, : on Linux and ; on Windows.

If the command succeeds, the plugin returns a zero exit code and the generated interfaces (in the case of the ADD command) are streamed to standard output as JSON. This low-tech interface is smart in the sense that it doesn't require any specific programming language, or component technology, or binary API. CNI plugin writers can use their favorite programming language too.

The result of invoking the CNI plugin with the ADD command is as follows:

```
{
  "cniVersion": "0.3.0",
  "interfaces": [ (this key omitted by IPAM plugins)
      {
          "name": "<name>",
          "mac": "<MAC address>", (required if L2 addresses are meaningful)
          "sandbox": "<netns path or hypervisor identifier>" (required for
  container/hypervisor interfaces, empty/omitted for host interfaces)
      }
  ],
  "ip": [
      {
          "version": "<4-or-6>",
```

```
                "address": "<ip-and-prefix-in-CIDR>",
                "gateway": "<ip-address-of-the-gateway>", (optional)
                "interface": <numeric index into 'interfaces' list>
        },
        ...
    ],
    "routes": [ (optional)
        {
                "dst": "<ip-and-prefix-in-cidr>",
                "gw": "<ip-of-next-hop>" (optional)
        },
        ...
    ]
    "dns": {
      "nameservers": <list-of-nameservers> (optional)
      "domain": <name-of-local-domain> (optional)
      "search": <list-of-additional-search-domains> (optional)
      "options": <list-of-options> (optional)
    }
}
```

The input network configuration contains a lot of information: `cniVersion`, name, type, `args` (optional), `ipMasq` (optional), `ipam`, and `dns`. The `ipam` and `dns` parameters are dictionaries with their own specified keys. Here is an example of a network configuration:

```
{
  "cniVersion": "0.3.0",
  "name": "dbnet",
  "type": "bridge",
  // type (plugin) specific
  "bridge": "cni0",
  "ipam": {
    "type": "host-local",
    // ipam specific
    "subnet": "10.1.0.0/16",
    "gateway": "10.1.0.1"
  },
  "dns": {
    "nameservers": [ "10.1.0.1" ]
  }
}
```

Note that additional plugin-specific elements can be added. In this case, the `bridge: cni0` element is a custom one that the specific `bridge` plugin understands.

The `CNI spec` also supports network configuration lists where multiple CNI plugins can be invoked in order. Later, we will dig into a fully-fledged implementation of a CNI plugin.

Kubernetes networking solutions

Networking is a vast topic. There are many ways to set up networks and connect devices, pods, and containers. Kubernetes can't be opinionated about it. The high-level networking model of a flat address space for pods is all that Kubernetes prescribes. Within that space, many valid solutions are possible, with various capabilities and policies for different environments. In this section, we'll examine some of the available solutions and understand how they map to the Kubernetes networking model.

Bridging on bare metal clusters

The most basic environment is a raw bare-metal cluster with just an L2 physical network. You can connect your containers to the physical network with a Linux bridge device. The procedure is quite involved and requires familiarity with low-level Linux network commands such as `brctl`, `ip addr`, `ip route`, `ip link`, `nsenter`, and so on. If you plan to implement it, this guide can serve as a good start (search for the *With Linux Bridge devices* section): `http://blog.oddbit.com/2014/08/11/four-ways-to-connect-a-docker/`.

Contiv

Contiv is a general-purpose network plugin for container networking and it can be used with Docker directly, Mesos, Docker Swarm, and of course Kubernetes, through a CNI plugin. Contiv is focused on network policies that overlap somewhat with Kubernetes' own network policy object. Here are some of the capabilities of the Contiv net plugin:

- Supports both libnetwork's CNM and the CNI specification
- A feature-rich policy model to provide secure, predictable application deployment
- Best-in-class throughput for container workloads
- Multi-tenancy, isolation, and overlapping subnets

- Integrated IPAM and service discovery
- A variety of physical topologies:
    - Layer2 (VLAN)
    - Layer3 (BGP)
    - Overlay (VXLAN)
    - Cisco SDN solution (ACI)
- IPv6 support
- Scalable policy and route distribution
- Integration with application blueprints, including the following:
    - Docker-compose
    - Kubernetes deployment manager
    - Service load balancing is built in east-west microservice load balancing
    - Traffic isolation for storage, control (for example, `etcd/consul`), network, and management traffic
- Contiv has many features and capabilities. I'm not sure if it's the best choice for Kubernetes due to its broad surface area and the fact that it caters to multiple platforms.

Open vSwitch

Open vSwitch is a mature software-based virtual switch solution endorsed by many big players. The **Open Virtualization Network (OVN)** solution lets you build various virtual networking topologies. It has a dedicated Kubernetes plugin, but it is not trivial to set up, as demonstrated by this guide: `https://github.com/openvswitch/ovn-kubernetes`. The Linen CNI plugin may be easier to set up, although it doesn't support all the features of OVN: `https://github.com/John-Lin/linen-cni`. Here is a diagram of the Linen CNI plugin:

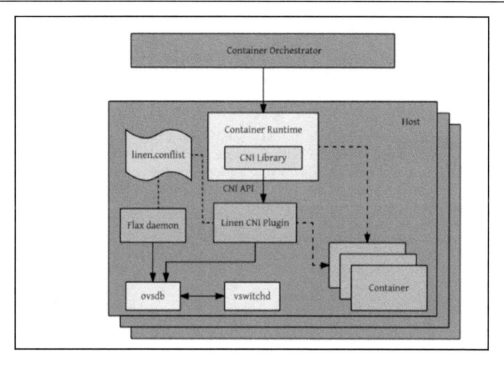

Open vSwitch can connect bare-metal servers, VMs, and pods/containers using the same logical network. It actually supports both overlay and underlay modes.

Here are some of its key features:

- Standard 802.1Q VLAN model with trunk and access ports
- NIC bonding with or without LACP on upstream switch
- NetFlow, sFlow(R), and mirroring for increased visibility
- QoS (Quality of Service) configuration, plus policing
- Geneve, GRE, VXLAN, STT, and LISP tunneling
- 802.1ag connectivity fault management
- OpenFlow 1.0 plus numerous extensions
- Transactional configuration database with C and Python bindings
- High-performance forwarding using a Linux kernel module

Nuage networks VCS

The **Virtualized Cloud Services** (VCS) product from Nuage networks provides a highly scalable policy-based **Software-Defined Networking** (SDN) platform. It is an enterprise-grade offering that builds on top of the open source Open vSwitch for the data plane along with a feature-rich SDN controller built on open standards.

The Nuage platform uses overlays to provide seamless policy-based networking between Kubernetes Pods and non-Kubernetes environments (VMs and bare metal servers). Nuage's policy abstraction model is designed with applications in mind and makes it easy to declare fine-grained policies for applications. The platform's real-time analytics engine enables visibility and security monitoring for Kubernetes applications.

In addition, all VCS components can be installed in containers. There are no special hardware requirements.

Canal

Canal is a mix of two open source projects: Calico and Flannel. The name **Canal** is a portmanteau of the project names. Flannel, by CoreOS, is focused on container networking, and **Calico** is focused on network policy. Originally, they were developed independently, but users wanted to use them together. The open source Canal project is currently a deployment pattern to install both projects as separate CNI plugins. **Tigera**—a company formed by Calico's founders—is shepherding both projects now and had plans for tighter integration, but since they released their secure application connectivity solution for Kubernetes the focus seemed to shift to contribute back to Flannel and Calico to ease configuration and integration rather than providing a unified solution. The following diagram demonstrates the present status of Canal and how it relates to container orchestrators such as Kubernetes and Mesos:

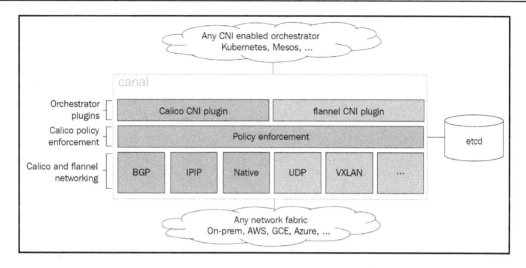

Note that when integrating with Kubernetes, Canal doesn't use etcd directly anymore, instead it relies on the Kubernetes API server.

Flannel

Flannel is a virtual network that gives a subnet to each host for use with container runtimes. It runs a `flaneld` agent on each host, which allocates a subnet to the node from a reserved address space stored in etcd. Forwarding packets between containers and, ultimately, hosts is done by one of multiple backends. The most common backend uses UDP over a TUN device that tunnels through port `8285` by default (make sure it's open in your firewall).

The following diagram describes in detail the various components of Flannel, the virtual network devices it creates, and how they interact with the host and the pod through the `docker0` bridge. It also shows the UDP encapsulation of packets and how they are transmitted between hosts:

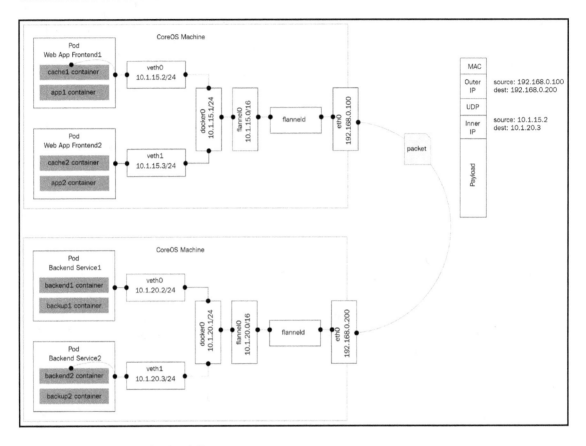

Other backends include the following:

- `vxlan`: Uses in-kernel VXLAN to encapsulate the packets.
- `host-gw`: Creates IP routes to subnets via remote machine IPs. Note that this requires direct layer2 connectivity between hosts running Flannel.
- `aws-vpc`: Creates IP routes in an Amazon VPC route table.

- `gce`: Creates IP routes in a Google compute engine network.
- `alloc`: Only performs subnet allocation (no forwarding of data packets).
- `ali-vpc`: Creates IP routes in an alicloud VPC route table.

Calico project

Calico is a versatile virtual networking and network security solution for containers. Calico can integrate with all the primary container orchestration frameworks and runtimes:

- Kubernetes (CNI plugin)
- Mesos (CNI plugin)
- Docker (libnework plugin)
- OpenStack (Neutron plugin)

Calico can also be deployed on-premises or on public clouds with its full feature set. Calico's network policy enforcement can be specialized for each workload and make sures that traffic is controlled precisely and packets always go from their source to vetted destinations. Calico can automatically map network policy concepts from orchestration platforms to its own network policy. The reference implementation of Kubernetes' network policy is Calico.

Romana

Romana is a modern cloud-native container networking solution. It operates at layer 3, taking advantage of standard IP address management techniques. Whole networks can become the unit of isolation as Romana uses Linux hosts to create gateways and routes to the networks. Operating at layer 3 level means that no encapsulation is needed. Network policy is enforced as a distributed firewall across all endpoints and services. Hybrid deployments across cloud platforms and on-premises deployments are easier as there is no need to configure virtual overlay networks.

New Romana virtual IPs allow on-premise users to expose services on layer 2 LANs through external IPs and service specs.

Romana claims that their approach brings significant performance improvements. The following diagram shows how Romana eliminates a lot of the overhead associated with VXLAN encapsulation:

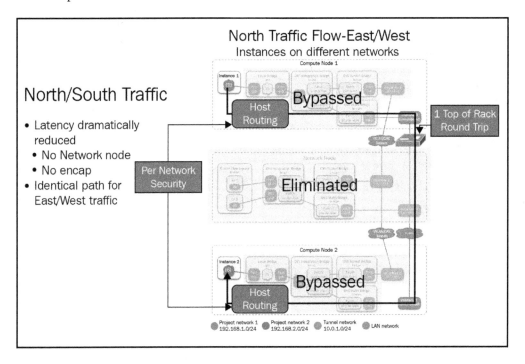

Weave net

Weave net is all about ease of use and zero configuration. It uses VXLAN encapsulation under the covers and micro DNS on each node. As a developer, you operate at a high abstraction level. You name your containers, and Weave net lets you connect to and use standard ports for services. This helps you to migrate existing applications into containerized applications and microservices. Weave net has a CNI plugin for interfacing with Kubernetes (and Mesos). On Kubernetes 1.4 and higher, you can integrate Weave net with Kubernetes by running a single command that deploys a DaemonSet:

```
kubectl apply -f https://git.io/weave-kube
```

The Weave net pods on every node will take care of attaching any new pod you create to the Weave network. Weave net supports the network policy API as well providing a complete yet easy-to-set-up solution.

Using network policies effectively

The Kubernetes network policy is about managing network traffic to selected pods and namespaces. In a world of hundreds of deployed and orchestrated microservices, as is often the case with Kubernetes, managing networking and connectivity between pods is essential. It's important to understand that it is not primarily a security mechanism. If an attacker can reach the internal network, they will probably be able to create their own pods that comply with the network policy in place and communicate freely with other pods. In the previous section, we looked at different Kubernetes networking solutions and focused on the container networking interface. In this section, the focus is on network policy, although there are strong connections between the networking solution and how network policy is implemented on top of it.

Understanding the Kubernetes network policy design

A network policy is a specification of how selections of pods can communicate with each other and other network endpoints. `NetworkPolicy` resources use labels to select pods and define whitelist rules that allow traffic to the selected pods in addition to what is allowed by the isolation policy for a given namespace.

Network policies and CNI plugins

There is an intricate relationship between network policies and CNI plugins. Some CNI plugins implement both network connectivity and network policy, while others implement just one aspect, but they can collaborate with another CNI plugin that implements the other aspect (for example, Calico and Flannel).

Configuring network policies

Network policies are configured through the `NetworkPolicy` resource. Here is a sample network policy:

```
apiVersion: networking.k8s.io/v1kind: NetworkPolicy
metadata:
 name: test-network-policy
 namespace: default
spec:
 podSelector:
```

```
        matchLabels:
          role: db
    ingress:
    - from:
        - namespaceSelector:
            matchLabels:
              project: awesome-project
        - podSelector:
            matchLabels:
              role: frontend
      ports:
      - protocol: tcp
        port: 6379
```

Implementing network policies

While the network policy API itself is generic and is part of the Kubernetes API, the implementation is tightly coupled to the networking solution. That means that on each node, there is a special agent or gatekeeper that does the following:

- Intercepts all traffic coming into the node
- Verifies that it adheres to the network policy
- Forwards or rejects each request

Kubernetes provides the facility to define and store network policies through the API. Enforcing the network policy is left to the networking solution or a dedicated network policy solution that is tightly integrated with the specific networking solution. Calico and Canal are good examples of this approach. Calico has its own networking solution and a network policy solution that work together, but it can also provide network policy enforcement on top of Flannel as part of Canal. In both cases, there is tight integration between the two pieces. The following diagram shows how the Kubernetes policy controller manages the network policies and how agents on the nodes execute it:

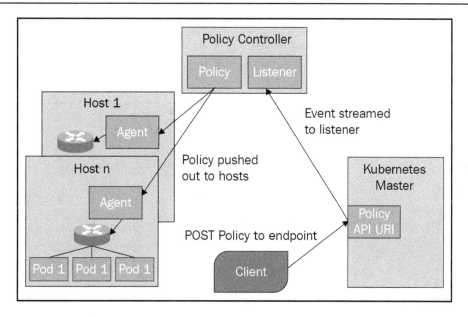

Load balancing options

Load balancing is a critical capability in dynamic systems such as a Kubernetes cluster. Nodes, VMs, and pods come and go, but the clients can't keep track of which individual entities can service their requests. Even if they could, it would require a complicated dance of managing a dynamic map of the cluster, refreshing it frequently, and handling disconnected, unresponsive, or just slow nodes. Load balancing is a battle-tested and well-understood mechanism that adds a layer of indirection that hides the internal turmoil from the clients or consumers outside the cluster. There are options for external as well as internal load balancers. You can also mix and match and use both. The hybrid approach has its own particular pros and cons, such as performance versus flexibility.

External load balancer

An external load balancer is a load balancer that runs outside the Kubernetes cluster. There must be an external load balancer provider that Kubernetes can interact with to configure the external load balancer with health checks, firewall rules, and to get the external IP address of the load balancer.

The following diagram shows the connection between the load balancer (in the cloud), the Kubernetes API server, and the cluster nodes. The external load balancer has an up-to-date picture of which pods run on which nodes, and it can direct external service traffic to the right pods:

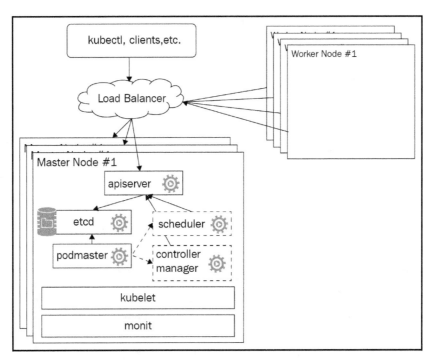

Configuring an external load balancer

An external load balancer is configured via the service configuration file or directly through Kubectl. We use a service type of LoadBalancer instead of using a service type of ClusterIP, which directly exposes a Kubernetes node as a load balancer. This depends on an external load balancer provider being properly installed and configured in the cluster. Google's GKE is the most well-tested provider, but other cloud platforms provide their integrated solution on top of their cloud load balancer.

Via configuration file

Here is an example service configuration file that accomplishes this goal:

```
{
    "kind": "Service",
    "apiVersion": "v1",
    "metadata": {
      "name": "example-service"
    },
    "spec": {
      "ports": [{
        "port": 8765,
        "targetPort": 9376
      }],
      "selector": {
        "app": "example"
      },
      "type": "LoadBalancer"
    }
}
```

Via Kubectl

You can also accomplish the same result using a direct `kubectl` command:

```
> kubectl expose rc example --port=8765 --target-port=9376 \
--name=example-service --type=LoadBalancer
```

The decision whether to use a `service` configuration file or `kubectl` command is usually determined by the way you set up the rest of your infrastructure and deploy your system. Configuration files are more declarative and arguably more appropriate for production usage, where you want a versioned, auditable, and repeatable way to manage your infrastructure.

Finding the load balancer IP addresses

The load balancer will have two IP addresses of interest. The internal IP address can be used inside the cluster to access the service. Clients outside the cluster will use the external IP address. It's a good practice to create a DNS entry for the external IP address. To get both addresses, use the `kubectl describe` command. The `IP` will denote the internal IP address. `LoadBalancer ingress` will denote the external IP address:

```
> kubectl describe services example-service
    Name:   example-service
```

```
Selector:    app=example
Type:        LoadBalancer
IP:        10.67.252.103
LoadBalancer Ingress: 123.45.678.9
Port:        <unnamed> 80/TCP
NodePort:    <unnamed> 32445/TCP
Endpoints:      10.64.0.4:80,10.64.1.5:80,10.64.2.4:80
Session Affinity: None
No events.
```

Preserving client IP addresses

Sometimes, the service may be interested in the source IP address of the clients. Up until Kubernetes 1.5, this information wasn't available. In Kubernetes 1.5, there is a beta feature available only on GKE through an annotation to get the source IP address. In Kubernetes 1.7, the capability to preserve the original client IP was added to the API.

Specifying original client IP address preservation

You need to configure the following two fields of the service spec:

- `service.spec.externalTrafficPolicy`: This field determines whether the service should route external traffic to a node-local endpoint or a cluster-wide endpoint, which is the default. The cluster option doesn't reveal the client source IP and might add a hop to a different node, but spreads the load well. The Local option keeps the client source IP and doesn't add an extra hop as long as the service type is `LoadBalancer` or `NodePort`. Its downside is it might not balance the load very well.
- `service.spec.healthCheckNodePort`: This field is optional. If used, then the service health check will use this port number. The default is the allocate node port. It has an effect for services of type `LoadBalancer` whose `externalTrafficPolicy` is set to `Local`.

Here is an example:

```
{
  "kind": "Service",
  "apiVersion": "v1",
  "metadata": {
    "name": "example-service"
  },
  "spec": {
    "ports": [{
      "port": 8765,
```

```
      "targetPort": 9376
    }],
    "selector": {
      "app": "example"
    },
    "type": "LoadBalancer"
    "externalTrafficPolicy: "Local"
  }
}
```

Understanding potential in even external load balancing

External load balancers operate at the node level; while they direct traffic to a particular pod, the load distribution is done at the node level. That means that if your service has four pods, and three of them are on node A and the last one is on node B, then an external load balancer is likely to divide the load evenly between node A and node B. This will have the three pods on node A handle half of the load (1/6 each) and the single pod on node B handle the other half of the load on its own. Weights may be added in the future to address this issue.

Service load balancer

Service load balancing is designed for funneling internal traffic within the Kubernetes cluster and not for external load balancing. This is done by using a service type of clusterIP. It is possible to expose a service load balancer directly via a pre-allocated port by using service type of NodePort and use it as an external load balancer, but it wasn't designed for that use case. For example, desirable features such as SSL termination and HTTP caching will not be readily available.

The following diagram shows how the service load balancer (the yellow cloud) can route traffic to one of the backend pods it manages (through labels, of course):

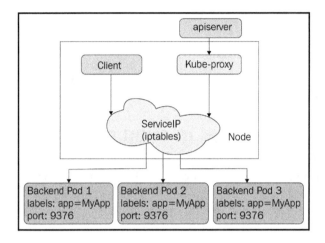

Ingress

Ingress in Kubernetes is, at its core, a set of rules that allow inbound connections to reach cluster services. In addition, some ingress controllers support the following:

- Connection algorithms
- Request limits
- URL rewrites and redirects
- TCP/UDP load balancing
- SSL termination
- Access control and authorization

Ingress is specified using an ingress resource and is serviced by an ingress controller. It's important to note that ingress is still in beta and it doesn't yet cover all of the necessary capabilities. Here is an example of an ingress resource that manages traffic into two services. The rules map the externally visible `http:// foo.bar.com/foo` to the `s1` service and `http://foo.bar.com/bar` to the `s2` service:

```
apiVersion: extensions/v1beta1
kind: Ingress
metadata:
  name: test
spec:
  rules:
```

```
- host: foo.bar.com
  http:
    paths:
    - path: /foo
      backend:
         serviceName: s1
         servicePort: 80
    - path: /bar
      backend:
         serviceName: s2
         servicePort: 80
```

There are two official ingress controllers right now. One of them is an L7 ingress controller for GCE only, the other is a more general-purpose NGINX ingress controller that lets you configure NGINX through a ConfigMap. The NGNIX ingress controller is very sophisticated and brings to bear a lot of features that are not available yet through the ingress resource directly. It uses the endpoints API to directly forward traffic to pods. It supports Minikube, GCE, AWS, Azure, and bare-metal clusters. For a detailed review, check out `https://github.com/kubernetes/ingress-nginx`.

HAProxy

We discussed using a cloud provider external load balancer using service type of `LoadBalancer` and using the internal service load balancer inside the cluster using `ClusterIP`. If we want a custom external load balancer, we can create a custom external load balancer provider and use `LoadBalancer` or use the third service type, `NodePort`. **High Availability (HA)** Proxy is a mature and battle-tested load balancing solution. It is considered the best choice for implementing external load balancing with on-premises clusters. This can be done in several ways:

- Utilize `NodePort` and carefully manage port allocations
- Implement custom load balancer provider interface
- Run HAProxy inside your cluster as the only target of your frontend servers at the edge of the cluster (load balanced or not)

You can use all approaches with HAProxy. Regardless, it is still recommended to use ingress objects. The `service-loadbalancer` project is a community project that implemented a load balancing solution on top of HAProxy. You can find it at: `https://github.com/kubernetes/contrib/tree/master/service-loadbalancer`.

Utilizing the NodePort

Each service will be allocated a dedicated port from a predefined range. This usually is a high range, such as 30,000 and above, to avoid clashing with other applications using low known ports. HAProxy will run outside the cluster in this case, and it will be configured with the correct port for each service. Then it can just forward any traffic to any nodes and Kubernetes through the internal service, and the load balancer will route it to a proper pod (double load balancing). This is, of course, sub-optimal because it introduces another hop. The way to circumvent it is to query the Endpoints API and dynamically manage for each service the list of its backend pods and directly forward traffic to the pods.

Custom load balancer provider using HAProxy

This approach is a little more complicated, but the benefit is that it is better integrated with Kubernetes and can make the transition to/from on-premises from/to the cloud easier.

Running HAProxy Inside the Kubernetes cluster

In this approach, we use the internal HAProxy load balancer inside the cluster. There may be multiple nodes running HAProxy, and they will share the same configuration to map incoming requests and load balance them across the backend servers (the Apache servers in the following diagram):

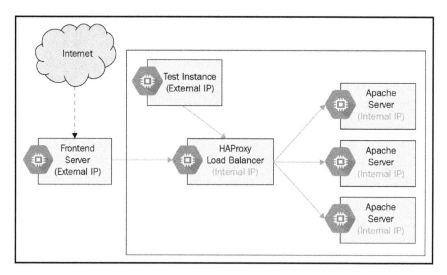

Keepalived VIP

Keepalived **VirtualIP** (**VIP**) is not necessarily a load balancing solution of its own. It can be a complement to the NGINX ingress controller or the HAProxy-based service `LoadBalancer`. The main motivation is that pods move around in Kubernetes, including your load balancer(s). That creates a problem for clients outside the network that require a stable endpoint. DNS is often not good enough due to performance issues. Keepalived provides a high-performance virtual IP address that can serve as the address to the NGINX ingress controller or the HAProxy load balancer. Keepalived utilizes core Linux networking facilities such as IPVS (IP virtual server) and implements high availability through **Virtual Redundancy Router Protocol** (**VRRP**). Everything runs at layer 4 (TCP/UDP). It takes some effort and attention to detail to configure it. Luckily, there is a Kubernetes `contrib` project that can get you started,
at `https://github.com/kubernetes/contrib/tree/master/keepalived-vip`.

Træfic

Træfic is a modern HTTP reverse proxy and load balancer. It was designed to support microservices. It works with many backends, including Kubernetes, to manage its configuration automatically and dynamically. This is a game changer compared to traditional load balancers. It has an impressive list of features:

- It's fast
- Single Go executable
- Tiny official Docker image
- Rest API
- Hot-reloading of configuration; no need to restart the process
- Circuit breakers, retry
- Round Robin, rebalancer load-balancers
- Metrics (Rest, Prometheus, Datadog, Statsd, InfluxDB)
- Clean AngularJS Web UI
- Websocket, HTTP/2, GRPC ready
- Access Logs (JSON, CLF)
- Let's Encrypt support (Automatic HTTPS with renewal)
- High availability with cluster mode

Writing your own CNI plugin

In this section, we will look at what it takes to actually write your own CNI plugin. First, we will look at the simplest plugin possible – the loopback plugin. Then, we will examine the plugin skeleton that implements most of the boilerplate associated with writing a CNI plugin. Finally, we will review the implementation of the bridge plugin. Before we dive in, here is a quick reminder of what a CNI plugin is:

- A CNI plugin is an executable
- It is responsible for connecting new containers to the network, assigning unique IP addresses to CNI containers, and taking care of routing
- A container is a network namespace (in Kubernetes, a pod is a CNI container)
- Network definitions are managed as JSON files, but stream to the plugin through standard input (no files are being read by the plugin)
- Auxiliary information can be provided via environment variables

First look at the loopback plugin

The loopback plugin simply adds the loopback interface. It is so simple that it doesn't require any network configuration information. Most CNI plugins are implemented in Golang, and the loopback CNI plugin is no exception. The full source code is available at:

```
https://github.com/containernetworking/plugins/blob/master/plugins/main/loopback
```

Let's look at the imports first. There are multiple packages from the container networking project on GitHub that provide many of the building blocks necessary to implement CNI plugins and the `netlink` package for adding and removing interfaces, as well as setting IP addresses and routes. We will look at the `skel` package soon:

```
package main
import (
  "github.com/containernetworking/cni/pkg/ns"
  "github.com/containernetworking/cni/pkg/skel"
  "github.com/containernetworking/cni/pkg/types/current"
  "github.com/containernetworking/cni/pkg/version"
  "github.com/vishvananda/netlink"
)
```

Then, the plugin implements two commands, cmdAdd and cmdDel, which are called when a `container` is added to or removed from the network. Here is the cmdAdd command:

```go
func cmdAdd(args *skel.CmdArgs) error {
  args.IfName = "lo"
  err := ns.WithNetNSPath(args.Netns, func(_ ns.NetNS) error {
    link, err := netlink.LinkByName(args.IfName)
    if err != nil {
      return err // not tested
    }

    err = netlink.LinkSetUp(link)
    if err != nil {
      return err // not tested
    }

    return nil
  })
  if err != nil {
    return err // not tested
  }

  result := current.Result{}
  return result.Print()
}
```

The core of this function is setting the interface name to lo (for loopback) and adding the link to the container's network namespace. The del command does the opposite:

```go
func cmdDel(args *skel.CmdArgs) error {
  args.IfName = "lo"
  err := ns.WithNetNSPath(args.Netns, func(ns.NetNS) error {
    link, err := netlink.LinkByName(args.IfName)
    if err != nil {
      return err // not tested
    }

    err = netlink.LinkSetDown(link)
    if err != nil {
      return err // not tested
    }

    return nil
  })
  if err != nil {
    return err // not tested
  }
}
```

```
    result := current.Result{}
    return result.Print()

}
```

The `main` function simply calls the `skel` package, passing the command functions. The `skel` package will take care of running the CNI plugin executable and will invoke the `addCmd` and `delCmd` functions at the right time:

```
func main() {
    skel.PluginMain(cmdAdd, cmdDel, version.All)
}
```

Building on the CNI plugin skeleton

Let's explore the `skel` package and see what it does under the covers. Starting with the `PluginMain()` entry point, it is responsible for invoking `PluginMainWithError()`, catching errors, printing them to standard output, and exiting:

```
func PluginMain(cmdAdd, cmdDel func(_ *CmdArgs) error, versionInfo
version.PluginInfo) {
    if e := PluginMainWithError(cmdAdd, cmdDel, versionInfo); e != nil {
        if err := e.Print(); err != nil {
            log.Print("Error writing error JSON to stdout: ", err)
        }
        os.Exit(1)
    }
}
```

The `PluginErrorWithMain()` instantiates a dispatcher, sets it up with all the I/O streams and the environment, and invokes its `PluginMain()` method:

```
func PluginMainWithError(cmdAdd, cmdDel func(_ *CmdArgs) error, versionInfo
version.PluginInfo) *types.Error {
    return ( dispatcher{
        Getenv: os.Getenv,
        Stdin:  os.Stdin,
        Stdout: os.Stdout,
        Stderr: os.Stderr,
    }).pluginMain(cmdAdd, cmdDel, versionInfo)
}
```

Here is, finally, the main logic of the skeleton. It gets the `cmd` arguments from the environment (which includes the configuration from standard input), detects which `cmd` is invoked, and calls the appropriate `plugin` function (`cmdAdd` or `cmdDel`). It can also return version information:

```
func (t *dispatcher) pluginMain(cmdAdd, cmdDel func(_ *CmdArgs) error,
versionInfo version.PluginInfo) *types.Error {
  cmd, cmdArgs, err := t.getCmdArgsFromEnv()
  if err != nil {
    return createTypedError(err.Error())
  }

  switch cmd {
  case "ADD":
    err = t.checkVersionAndCall(cmdArgs, versionInfo, cmdAdd)
  case "DEL":
    err = t.checkVersionAndCall(cmdArgs, versionInfo, cmdDel)
  case "VERSION":
    err = versionInfo.Encode(t.Stdout)
  default:
    return createTypedError("unknown CNI_COMMAND: %v", cmd)
  }

  if err != nil {
    if e, ok := err.(*types.Error); ok {
      // don't wrap Error in Error
      return e
    }
    return createTypedError(err.Error())
  }
  return nil
}
```

Reviewing the bridge plugin

The bridge plugin is more substantial. Let's look at some of the key parts of its implementation. The full source code is available at:

`https://github.com/containernetworking/plugins/blob/master/plugins/main/bridge.`

It defines a network configuration `struct` with the following fields:

```
type NetConf struct {
  types.NetConf
  BrName               string `json:"bridge"`
  IsGW                 bool   `json:"isGateway"`
```

```
    IsDefaultGW          bool    `json:"isDefaultGateway"`
    ForceAddress         bool    `json:"forceAddress"`
    IPMasq                    bool    `json:"ipMasq"`
    MTU                       int     `json:"mtu"`
    HairpinMode          bool    `json:"hairpinMode"`
    PromiscMode          bool    `json:"promiscMode"`
}
```

We will not cover what each parameter does and how it interacts with the other parameters due to space limitations. The goal is to understand the flow and have a starting point if you want to implement your own CNI plugin. The configuration is loaded from JSON through the `loadNetConf()` function. It is called at the beginning of the `cmdAdd()` and `cmdDel()` functions:

```
    n, cniVersion, err := loadNetConf(args.StdinData)
```

Here is the core of the `cmdAdd()` function. It uses information from network configuration, sets up a `veth`, interacts with the IPAM plugin to add a proper IP address, and returns the results:

```
hostInterface, containerInterface, err := setupVeth(netns, br, args.IfName,
n.MTU,
n.HairpinMode)
  if err != nil {
    return err
  }

  // run the IPAM plugin and get back the config to apply
  r, err := ipam.ExecAdd(n.IPAM.Type, args.StdinData)
  if err != nil {
    return err
  }

  // Convert the IPAM result was into the current Result type
  result, err := current.NewResultFromResult(r)
  if err != nil {
    return err
  }

  if len(result.IPs) == 0 {
    return errors.New("IPAM returned missing IP config")
  }

  result.Interfaces = []*current.Interface{brInterface, hostInterface,
containerInterface}
```

This is just part of the full implementation. There is also route setting and hardware IP allocation. I encourage you to pursue the full source code, which is quite extensive, to get the full picture.

Summary

In this chapter, we covered a lot of ground. Networking is such a vast topic and there are so many combinations of hardware, software, operating environments, and user skills that coming up with a comprehensive networking solution that is robust, secure, performs well, and is easy to maintain, is a very complicated endeavor. For Kubernetes clusters, the cloud providers mostly solve these issues. But if you run on-premise clusters or need a tailor-made solution, you get a lot of options to choose from. Kubernetes is a very flexible platform, designed for extension. Networking, in particular, is totally pluggable. The main topics we discussed were the Kubernetes networking model (flat address space where pods can reach others and shared localhost between all containers inside a pod), how lookup and discovery work, the Kubernetes network plugins, various networking solutions at different levels of abstraction (a lot of interesting variations), using network policies effectively to control the traffic inside the cluster, the spectrum of load balancing solutions, and finally we looked at how to write a CNI plugin by dissecting a real-world implementation.

At this point, you are probably overwhelmed, especially if you're not a subject-matter expert. You should have a good grasp of the internals of Kubernetes networking, be aware of all the interlocking pieces required to implement a fully-fledged solution, and be able to craft your own solution based on trade-offs that make sense for your system.

16
Kubernetes Infrastructure Management

In this chapter, we'll discuss how to make changes to the infrastructure that powers your Kubernetes infrastructure, whether or not it is a purely public cloud platform or a hybrid installation. We'll discuss methods for handling underlying instance and resource instability, and strategies for running highly available workloads on partially available underlying hardware. We'll cover a few key topics in this chapter in order to build your understanding of how to manage infrastructure in this way:

- How do we plan to deploy Kubernetes components?
- How do we secure Kubernetes infrastructure?
- How do we upgrade the cluster and `kubeadm`?
- How do we scale up the cluster?
- What external resources are available to us?

In this chapter, you'll learn about the following:

- Cluster upgrades
- How to manage `kubeadm`
- Cluster scaling
- Cluster maintenance
- The SIG Cluster Lifecycle group

Technical requirements

You'll need to have your Google Cloud Platform account enabled and logged in, or you can use a local Minikube instance of Kubernetes. You can also use Play with Kubernetes over the web: `https://labs.play-with-k8s.com/`.

Here's the GitHub repository for this chapter: `https://github.com/PacktPublishing/The-Complete-Kubernetes-Guide/tree/master/Chapter16`.

Planning a cluster

Looking back over the work we've done up till now in this book, there are a lot of options when it comes to building a cluster with Kubernetes. Let's briefly highlight the options you have available to you when you're planning on building your cluster. We have a few key areas to investigate when planning ahead.

Picking what's right

The first and arguably most important step when choosing a cluster is to pick the right hosted platform for your Kubernetes cluster. At a high level, here are the choices you have:

- Local solutions include the following:
    - **Minikube**: A single-node Kubernetes cluster
    - **Ubuntu on LXD**: This uses LXD to deploy a nine-instance cluster of Kubernetes
    - **IBM's Cloud Private-CE**: This uses VirtualBox to deploy Kubernetes on *n+1* instances
    - `kubeadm-dind` (Docker-in-Docker): This allows for multi-node Kubernetes clusters
- Hosted solutions include the following:
    - Google Kubernetes Engine
    - Amazon Elastic Container Services
    - Azure Kubernetes Service
    - Stackpoint
    - Openshift online
    - IBM Cloud Kubernetes Services
    - Giant Swarm
- On all of the aforementioned clouds and more, there are many turnkey solutions that allow you to spin up full clusters with community-maintained scripts

As of this book's publishing, here's a list of projects and solutions:

IaaS Provider	Config. Mgmt.	OS	Networking
any	any	multi-support	any CNI
Google Kubernetes Engine			GCE
Stackpoint.io		multi-support	multi-support
AppsCode.com	Saltstack	Debian	multi-support
Madcore.Ai	Jenkins DSL	Ubuntu	flannel
Platform9		multi-support	multi-support
Kublr	custom	multi-support	multi-support
Kubermatic		multi-support	multi-support
IBM Cloud Kubernetes Service		Ubuntu	IBM Cloud Networking + Calico
Giant Swarm		CoreOS	flannel and/or Calico
GCE	Saltstack	Debian	GCE
Azure Kubernetes Service		Ubuntu	Azure
Azure (IaaS)		Ubuntu	Azure
Bare-metal	custom	Fedora	*none*
Bare-metal	custom	Fedora	flannel

Check out this link for more turnkey solutions: `https://kubernetes.io/docs/setup/pick-right-solution/#turnkey-cloud-solutions`.

Securing the cluster

As we've discussed, there are several areas of focus when securing a cluster. Ensure that you have read through and made configuration changes (in code) to your cluster configuration in the following areas:

- **Logging**: Ensure that your Kubernetes logs are enabled. You can read more about audit logging here: `https://kubernetes.io/docs/tasks/debug-application-cluster/audit/`.

- Make sure you have authentication enabled so that your users, operators, and services identify themselves as unique identifiers. Read more about authentication here: `https://kubernetes.io/docs/reference/access-authn-authz/authentication/`.

- Ensure that you have proper separation of duties, role-based access control, and fine grained privileges using authorization. You can read more about HTTP-based controls here: `https://kubernetes.io/docs/reference/access-authn-authz/authorization/`.

- Make sure that you have locked down the API to specific permissions and groups. You can read more about access to the API here: `https://kubernetes.io/docs/reference/access-authn-authz/controlling-access/`.

- When appropriate, enable an admission controller to further re-validate requests after they pass through the authentication and authorization controls. These controllers can take additional, business-logic based validation steps in order to secure your cluster further. Read more about admission controllers here: `https://kubernetes.io/docs/reference/access-authn-authz/controlling-access`.

- Tune Linux system parameters via the `sysctl` interface. This allows you to modify kernel parameters for node-level and namespaced `sysctl` features. There are safe and unsafe system parameters. There are several subsystems that can be tweaked with `sysctls`. Possible parameters are as follows:
  - `abi`: Execution domains and personalities
  - `fs`: Specific filesystems, filehandle, inode, dentry, and quota tuning
  - `kernel`: Global kernel information/tuning
  - `net`: Networking
  - `sunrpc`: SUN **Remote Procedure Call (RPC)**
  - `vm`: Memory management tuning, buffer, and cache management
  - `user`: Per user per user namespace limits

You can read more about `sysctl` calls here: `https://kubernetes.io/docs/tasks/administer-cluster/sysctl-cluster/`.

You can enable unsafe `sysctl` values by running the following command:

```
kubelet --allowed-unsafe-sysctls 'net.ipv4.route.min_pmtu'
```

Here's a diagram of the authorization, authentication, and admission control working together:

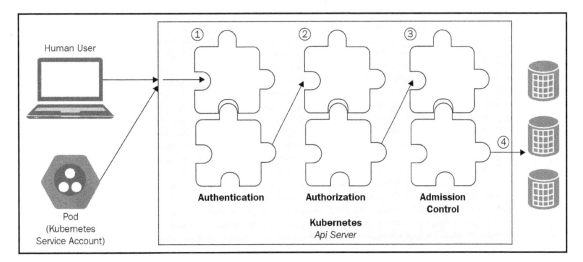

Tuning examples

If you'd like to experiment with modifying `sysctls`, you can set a security context as follows, per pod:

```
apiVersion: v1
kind: Pod
metadata:
 name: sysctl-example
spec:
 securityContext:
   sysctls:
   - name: kernel.shm_rmid_forced
     value: "0"
   - name: net.core.somaxconn
     value: "10000"
```

```
- name: kernel.msgmax
  value: "65536"
- name: ipv4.ip_local_port_range
   value: '1024 65535'
```

You can also tune variables such as the ARP cache, as Kubernetes consumes a lot of IPs at scale, which can exhaust space in the ARP cache. Changing these settings is common in large scale HPC clusters and can help with address exhaustion with Kubernetes as well. You can set these values, as follows:

```
net.ipv4.neigh.default.gc_thresh1 = 90000
net.ipv4.neigh.default.gc_thresh2 = 100000
net.ipv4.neigh.default.gc_thresh3 = 120000
```

Upgrading the cluster

In order to run your cluster over long periods of time, you'll need to update your cluster as needed. There are several ways to manage cluster upgrades, and the difficulty level of the upgrades is determined by the platform you've chosen previously. As a general rule, hosted **Platform as a service (PaaS)** options are simpler, while roll your own options rely on you to manage your cluster upgrades.

Upgrading PaaS clusters

Upgrading PaaS clusters is a lot simpler than updating your hand-rolled clusters. Let's check out how the major cloud service providers update their hosted Kubernetes platforms.

With Azure, it's relatively straightforward to manage an upgrade of both the control plane and nodes of your cluster. You can check which upgrades are available for your cluster with the following command:

```
az aks get-upgrades --name "myAKSCluster" --resource-group myResourceGroup -
-output table
Name ResourceGroup MasterVersion NodePoolVersion Upgrades

------- --------------- --------------- ------------------ ------------------
--

default gsw-k8s-aks 1.8.10 1.8.10 1.9.1, 1.9.2, 1.9.6
```

When upgrading AKS clusters, you have to upgrade through minor versions. AKS handles adding a new node to your cluster and manages to cordon and drain process in order to prevent any disruption to your running applications. You can see how the drain process works in a following section.

You can run the `upgrade` command as follows. You should experiment with this feature before running on production workloads so you can understand the impact on running applications:

```
az aks upgrade --name myAKSCluster --resource-group myResourceGroup --
kubernetes-version 1.9.6
```

You should see a lot of output that identifies the update, which will look something like this:

```
{
  "id": "/subscriptions/<Subscription
ID>/resourcegroups/myResourceGroup/providers/Microsoft.ContainerService/man
agedClusters/myAKSCluster",
  "location": "eastus",
  "name": "myAKSCluster",
  "properties": {
    "accessProfiles": {
      "clusterAdmin": {
        "kubeConfig": "..."
      },
      "clusterUser": {
        "kubeConfig": "..."
      }
    },
    "agentPoolProfiles": [
      {
        "count": 1,
        "dnsPrefix": null,
        "fqdn": null,
        "name": "myAKSCluster",
        "osDiskSizeGb": null,
        "osType": "Linux",
        "ports": null,
        "storageProfile": "ManagedDisks",
        "vmSize": "Standard_D2_v2",
        "vnetSubnetId": null
      }
    ],
    "dnsPrefix": "myK8sClust-myResourceGroup-4f48ee",
    "fqdn": "myk8sclust-
myresourcegroup-4f48ee-406cc140.hcp.eastus.azmk8s.io",
```

```
      "kubernetesVersion": "1.9.6",
      "linuxProfile": {
        "adminUsername": "azureuser",
        "ssh": {
          "publicKeys": [
            {
              "keyData": "..."
            }
          ]
        }
      },
      "provisioningState": "Succeeded",
      "servicePrincipalProfile": {
        "clientId": "e70c1c1c-0ca4-4e0a-be5e-aea5225af017",
        "keyVaultSecretRef": null,
        "secret": null
      }
    },
    "resourceGroup": "myResourceGroup",
    "tags": null,
    "type": "Microsoft.ContainerService/ManagedClusters"
  }
```

You can additionally show the current version:

```
az aks show --name myAKSCluster --resource-group myResourceGroup --output
table
```

To upgrade a GCE cluster, you'll follow a similar procedure. In GCE's case, there are two mechanisms that allow you update your cluster:

- For manager node upgrades, GCP deletes and recreates the master nodes using the same **Persistent Disk** (**PD**) to preserve your state across upgrades
- With your worker nodes, you'll use GCP's manage instance groups and perform a rolling upgrade of your cluster, wherein each node is destroyed and replaced to avoid interruption to your workloads

You can upgrade your cluster master to a specific version:

```
cluster/gce/upgrade.sh -M v1.0.2
```

Or, you can update your full cluster with this command:

```
cluster/gce/upgrade.sh -M v1.0.2
```

To upgrade a Google Kubernetes Engine cluster, you have a simple, user-initiated option. You'll need to set your project ID:

```
gcloud config set project [PROJECT_ID]
```

And, make sure that you have the latest set of gcloud components:

```
gcloud components update
```

When updating Kubernetes clusters on GCP, you get the following benefits. You can downgrade your nodes, but you cannot downgrade your master:

- GKE will handle node and pod drainage without application interruption
- Replacement nodes will be recreated with the same node and configuration as their predecessors
- GKE will update software for the following pieces of the cluster:
  - kubelet
  - kube-proxy
  - Docker daemon
  - OS

You can see what options your server has for upgrades with this command:

```
gcloud container get-server-config
```

Keep in mind that data stored in the hostPath and emptyDir directories will be deleted during the upgrade, and only PDs will be preserved during it. You can turn on automatic node updates for your cluster with GKE, or you can perform them manually.

 To turn on automatic node automatic upgrades read this: https://cloud. google.com/kubernetes-engine/docs/concepts/node-auto-upgrades.

You can also create clusters with this set to default with the --enable-autoupgrade command:

```
gcloud container clusters create [CLUSTER_NAME] --zone [COMPUTE_ZONE] \
  --enable-autoupgrade
```

If you'd like to update your clusters manually, you can issue specific commands. It is recommended for production systems to turn off automatic upgrades and to perform them during periods of low traffic or during maintenance windows to ensure minimal disruption for your applications. Once you build confidence in updates, you may be able to experiment with auto-upgrades.

To manually kick off a node upgrade, you can run the following command:

```
gcloud container clusters upgrade [CLUSTER_NAME]
```

If you'd like to upgrade to a specific version of Kubernetes, you can add the --cluster-version tag.

You can see a running list of operations on your cluster to keep track of the update operation:

```
gcloud beta container operations list
NAME TYPE ZONE TARGET STATUS_MESSAGE STATUS START_TIME END_TIME
operation-1505407677851-8039e369 CREATE_CLUSTER us-west1-a my-cluster DONE
20xx-xx-xxT16:47:57.851933021Z 20xx-xx-xxT16:50:52.898305883Z
operation-1505500805136-e7c64af4 UPGRADE_CLUSTER us-west1-a my-cluster DONE
20xx-xx-xxT18:40:05.136739989Z 20xx-xx-xxT18:41:09.321483832Z
operation-1505500913918-5802c989 DELETE_CLUSTER us-west1-a my-cluster DONE
20xx-xx-xxT18:41:53.9188825764Z 20xx-xx-xxT18:43:48.639506814Z
```

You can then describe your particular upgrade operation with the following:

```
gcloud beta container operations describe [OPERATION_ID]
```

The previous command will tell you details about the cluster upgrade action:

```
gcloud beta container operations describe operation-1507325726639-981f0ed6
endTime: '20xx-xx-xxT21:40:05.324124385Z'
name: operation-1507325726639-981f0ed6
operationType: UPGRADE_CLUSTER
selfLink:
https://container.googleapis.com/v1/projects/.../kubernetes-engine/docs/zon
es/us-central1-a/operations/operation-1507325726639-981f0ed6
startTime: '20xx-xx-xxT21:35:26.639453776Z'
status: DONE
targetLink:
https://container.googleapis.com/v1/projects/.../kubernetes-engine/docs/zon
es/us-central1-a/clusters/...
zone: us-central1-a
```

Scaling the cluster

As with PaaS versus hosted clusters, you have several options for scaling up your production Kubernetes cluster.

On GKE and AKS

When upgrading a GKE cluster, all you need to do is issue a scaling command that modifies the number of instances in your minion group. You can resize the node pools that control your cluster with the following:

```
gcloud container clusters resize [CLUSTER_NAME] \
  --node-pool [POOL_NAME]
  --size [SIZE]
```

Keep in mind that new nodes are created with the same configuration as the current machines in your node pool. When additional pods are scheduled, they'll be scheduled on the new nodes. Existing pods will not be relocated or rebalanced to the new nodes.

Scaling up the AKS cluster engine is a similar exercise, where you'll need to specify the `--resource-group` node count to your required number of nodes:

```
az aks scale --name myAKSCluster --resource-group gsw-k8s-group --node-
count 1
```

DIY clusters

When you add resources to your hand-rolled Kubernetes cluster, you'll need to do more work. In order to have nodes join in as you add them automatically via a scaling group, or manually via Infrastructure as code, you'll need to ensure that automatic registration of nodes is enabled via the `--register-node` flag. If this flag is turned on, new nodes will attempt to auto-register themselves. This is the default behavior.

You can also join nodes manually, using a pre-vetted token, to your clusters. If you initialize `kubeadm` with the following token:

```
kubeadm init --token=101tester101 --kubernetes-version $(kubeadm version -o
short)
```

You can then add additional nodes to your clusters with this command:

```
kubeadm join --discovery-token-unsafe-skip-ca-verification --
token=101tester101:6443
```

Normally in a production install of `kubeadm`, you would not specify the token and need to extract it and store it from the `kubeadm init` command.

Node maintenance

If you're scaling your cluster up or down, it's essential to know how the manual process of node deregistration and draining works. We'll use the `kubectl` drain command here to remove all pods from your node before removing the node from your cluster. Removing all pods from your nodes ensures that there are not running workloads on your instance or VM when you remove it.

Let's get a list of available nodes using the following command:

```
kubectl get nodes
```

Once we have the node list, the command to drain nodes is fairly simple:

```
kubectl drain <node>
```

This command will take some time to execute, as it has to reschedule the workloads on the node onto other machines that have available resources. Once the draining is complete, you can remove the node via your preferred programmatic API. If you're merely removing the node for maintenance, you can add it back to the available nodes with the `uncordon` command:

```
kubectl uncordon <node>
```

Additional configuration options

Once you've built up an understanding of how Kubernetes cluster configuration is managed, it's a good idea to explore the additional tools that offer enhanced mechanisms or abstractions to configure the state of your clusters.

ksonnet is one such tool, which allows you to build a structure around your various configurations in order to keep many environments configured. ksonnet uses another powerful tool called Jsonnet in order to maintain the state of the cluster. ksonnet is a different approach to cluster management that's different from the Helm approach we discussed in earlier chapters, in that it doesn't define packages by dependency, but instead takes a composable prototype approach, where you build JSON templates that are rendered by the ksonnet CLI to apply state on the cluster. You start with parts that create prototypes, which becomes a component once it's configured, and those components can then get combined into applications. This helps avoid repeated code in your code base. Check it out here: `https://ksonnet.io/`.

Summary

In this chapter, we discussed how to make changes to the infrastructure that provides compute, storage, and networking capacity to your Kubernetes infrastructure, whether it be a purely public cloud platform or a hybrid installation. In observing the public cloud platforms, we discussed methods for handling underlying instance and resource instability, and strategies for running highly available workloads on partially available underlying hardware.

Additionally, we covered a key topic on how to build infrastructure using tools such as `kubeadm`, `kubectl`, and public cloud provider tools that can scale up and down your clusters.

Customizing Kubernetes - API and Plugins

17

In this chapter, we will dig deep into the guts of Kubernetes. We will start with the Kubernetes API and learn how to work with Kubernetes programmatically via direct access to the API, the Python client, and then we will automate Kubectl. Then, we'll look into extending the Kubernetes API with custom resources. The last part is all about the various plugins Kubernetes supports. Many aspects of the Kubernetes operation are modular and designed for extension. We will examine several types of plugins, such as custom schedulers, authorization, admission control, custom metrics, and volumes. Finally, we'll look into extending Kubectl and adding your own commands.

The topics we cover are as follows:

- Working with the Kubernetes API
- Extending the Kubernetes API
- Writing Kubernetes and Kubectl plugins
- Writing webhooks

Working with the Kubernetes API

The Kubernetes API is comprehensive and encompasses the entire functionality of Kubernetes. As you may expect, it is huge. But it is designed very well using best practices, and it is consistent. If you understand the basic principles, you can discover everything you need to know.

Understanding OpenAPI

OpenAPI allows API providers to define their operations and models, and enables developers to automate their tools and generate their favorite language's client to talk to that API server. Kubernetes has supported Swagger 1.2 (an older version of the OpenAPI spec) for a while, but the spec was incomplete and invalid, making it hard to generate tools/clients based on it.

In Kubernetes 1.4, alpha support was added for the OpenAPI spec (formerly known as **Swagger 2.0** before it was donated to the OpenAPI Initiative) and current models and operations were updated. In Kubernetes 1.5, support for the OpenAPI spec has been completed by auto-generating the spec directly from the Kubernetes source, which keeps the spec and documentation completely in sync with future changes in operations/models.

The new spec enables better API documentation and an auto-generated Python client that we will explore later.

The spec is modular and divided by group version. This is future-proof. You can run multiple API servers that support different versions. Applications can transition gradually to newer versions.

The structure of the spec is explained in detail in the OpenAPI spec definition. The Kubernetes team used the operation's tags to separate each group version and fill in as much information as possible about paths/operations and models. For a specific operation, all parameters, calling methods, and responses are documented. The result is impressive.

Setting up a proxy

To simplify access, you can use Kubectl to set up a proxy:

```
> kubectl proxy --port 8080
```

Now, you can access the API server at `http://localhost:8080` and it will reach the same Kubernetes API server that Kubectl is configured for.

Exploring the Kubernetes API directly

The Kubernetes API is easy to find out about. You can just browse to the URL of the API server at `http://localhost:8080` and get a nice JSON document that describes all the available operations under the paths key.

Here is a partial list due to space constraints:

```
{
  "paths": [
    "/api",
    "/api/v1",
    "/apis",
    "/apis/apps",
    "/apis/storage.k8s.io/v1",
        .
        .
        .
    "/healthz",
    "/healthz/ping",
    "/logs",
    "/metrics",
    "/swaggerapi/",
    "/ui/",
    "/version"
  ]
}
```

You can drill down any one of the paths. For example, here is the response from the `/api/v1/namespaces/default` endpoint:

```
{
    "apiVersion": "v1",
    "kind": "Namespace",
    "metadata": {
        "creationTimestamp": "2017-12-25T10:04:26Z",
        "name": "default",
        "resourceVersion": "4",
        "selfLink": "/api/v1/namespaces/default",
        "uid": "fd497868-e95a-11e7-adce-080027c94384"
    },
    "spec": {
        "finalizers": [
            "kubernetes"
        ]
    },
    "status": {
        "phase": "Active"
    }
}
```

I discovered this endpoint by going first to `/api`, then discovered `/api/v1`, which told me there is `/api/v1/namespaces`, which pointed me to `/api/v1/namespaces/default`.

Using Postman to explore the Kubernetes API

Postman (`https://www.getpostman.com`) is a very polished application for working with RESTful APIs. If you lean more to the GUI side, you may find it extremely useful.

The following screenshot shows the available endpoints under the batch `V1` API group:

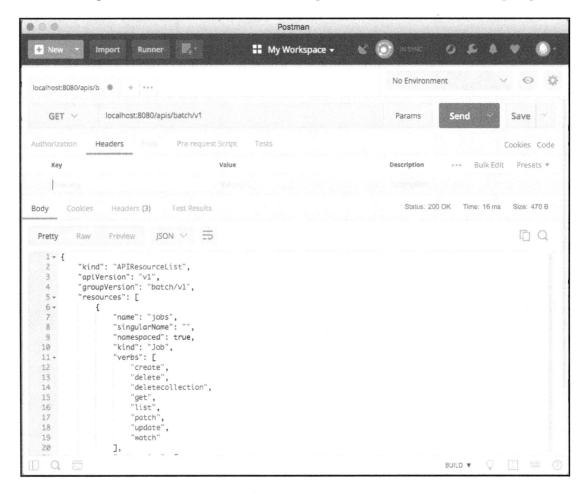

Postman has a lot of options, and it organizes the information in a very pleasing way. Give it a try.

Filtering the output with httpie and jq

The output from the API can be too verbose sometimes. Often, you're interested just in one value out of a huge chunk of JSON responses. For example, if you want to get the names of all running services, you can hit the `/api/v1/services` endpoint. The response, however, includes a lot of additional information that is irrelevant. Here is a very partial subset of the output:

```
$ http http://localhost:8080/api/v1/services
{
    "apiVersion": "v1",
    "items": [
        {
            "metadata": {
                "creationTimestamp": "2018-03-03T05:18:30Z",
                "labels": {
                    "component": "apiserver",
                    "provider": "kubernetes"
                },
                "name": "kubernetes",
                ...
            },
            "spec": {
                ...
            },
            "status": {
                "loadBalancer": {}
            }
        },
        ...
    ],
    "kind": "ServiceList",
    "metadata": {
        "resourceVersion": "1076",
        "selfLink": "/api/v1/services"
    }
}
```

The complete output is 121 lines long! Let's see how to use `httpie` and `jq` to gain full control over the output and show only the names of the services. I prefer (https://httpie.org/) over CURL for interacting with REST APIs on the command line. The `jq` (https://stedolan.github.io/jq/) command-line JSON processor is great for slicing and dicing JSON.

Examining the full output, you can see that the service names are in the metadata sections of each item in the items array. The `jq` expression that will select just the `name` is as follows:

```
.items[].metadata.name
```

Here is the full command and output:

```
$ http http://localhost:8080/api/v1/services | jq .items[].metadata.name
"kubernetes"
"kube-dns"
"kubernetes-dashboard"
```

Creating a pod via the Kubernetes API

The API can be used for creating, updating, and deleting resources too, given the following pod manifest in `nginx-pod.json`:

```json
{
    "kind": "Pod",
    "apiVersion": "v1",
    "metadata":{
        "name": "nginx",
        "namespace": "default",
        "labels": {
            "name": "nginx"
        }
    },
    "spec": {
        "containers": [{
            "name": "nginx",
            "image": "nginx",
            "ports": [{"containerPort": 80}]
        }]
    }
}
```

The following command will create the pod through the API:

```
> http POST http://localhost:8080/api/v1/namespaces/default/pods @nginx-pod.json
```

To verify that it worked, let's extract the name and status of the current pods. The endpoint is as follows:

```
/api/v1/namespaces/default/pods
```

The `jq` expression is as follows:

```
items[].metadata.name,.items[].status.phase
```

Here is the full command and output:

```
> FILTER='.items[].metadata.name,.items[].status.phase'
> http http://localhost:8080/api/v1/namespaces/default/pods | jq $FILTER
"nginx"
"Running"
```

Accessing the Kubernetes API via the Python client

Exploring the API interactively using `httpie` and `jq` is great, but the real power of API comes when you consume and integrate it with other software. The Kubernetes incubator project provides a full-fledged and very well-documented Python `client` library. It is available at `https://github.com/kubernetes-incubator/client-python`.

First, make sure you have Python installed (either 2.7 or 3.5+). Then install the Kubernetes package:

```
> pip install kubernetes
```

To start talking to a Kubernetes cluster, you need to connect to it. Start an interactive Python session:

```
> python
Python 3.6.4 (default, Mar  1 2018, 18:36:42)
[GCC 4.2.1 Compatible Apple LLVM 9.0.0 (clang-900.0.39.2)] on darwin
Type "help", "copyright", "credits" or "license" for more information.
>>>
```

The Python client can read your Kubectl config:

```
>>> from kubernetes import client, config
>>> config.load_kube_config()
>>> v1 = client.CoreV1Api()
```

Or it can connect directly to an already running proxy:

```
>>> from kubernetes import client, config
>>> client.Configuration().host = 'http://localhost:8080'
>>> v1 = client.CoreV1Api()
```

Note that the client module provides methods to get access to different group versions, such as `CoreV1API`.

Dissecting the CoreV1API group

Let's dive in and understand the `CoreV1API` group. The Python object has `481 public attributes`:

```
>>> attributes = [x for x in dir(v1) if not x.startswith('__')]
>>> len(attributes)
481
```

Ignore the `attributes` that starts with double underscores because those are special `class/instance` methods unrelated to Kubernetes.

Let's pick ten random methods and see what they look like:

```
>>> import random
>>> from pprint import pprint as pp
>>> pp(random.sample(attributes, 10))
['patch_namespaced_pod',
 'connect_options_node_proxy_with_path_with_http_info',
 'proxy_delete_namespaced_pod_with_path',
 'delete_namespace',
 'proxy_post_namespaced_pod_with_path_with_http_info',
 'proxy_post_namespaced_service',
 'list_namespaced_pod_with_http_info',
 'list_persistent_volume_claim_for_all_namespaces',
 'read_namespaced_pod_log_with_http_info',
 'create_node']
```

Very interesting. The `attributes` begin with a verb such as list, patch, or read. Many of them have this notion of a `namespace`, and many have a `with_http_info` suffix. To understand the better, let's count how many verbs exist and how many `attributes` use each verb (where the verb is the first token before the underscore):

```
>>> from collections import Counter
>>> verbs = [x.split('_')[0] for x in attributes]
>>> pp(dict(Counter(verbs)))
{'api': 1,
```

```
'connect': 96,
'create': 36,
'delete': 56,
'get': 2,
'list': 56,
'patch': 48,
'proxy': 84,
'read': 52,
'replace': 50}
```

We can drill further and look at the interactive help for a specific `attribute`:

```
>>> help(v1.create_node)
Help on method create_node in module kuber-netes.client.apis.core_v1_api:

create_node(body, **kwargs) method of kuber-
netes.client.apis.core_v1_api.CoreV1Api instance
 create a Node
 This method makes a synchronous HTTP request by default. To make an
 asynchronous HTTP request, please pass async=True
 >>> thread = api.create_node(body, async=True)
 >>> result = thread.get()

 :param async bool
 :param V1Node body: (required)
 :param str pretty: If 'true', then the output is pretty printed.
 :return: V1Node
 If the method is called asynchronously,
 returns the request thread.
```

You can poke around yourself and learn more about the API. Let's look at some common operations, such as listing, creating, watching, and deleting objects.

Listing objects

You can list different kinds of object. The method names start with `list_`. Here is an example listing all namespaces:

```
>>> for ns in v1.list_namespace().items:
...     print(ns.metadata.name)
...
default
kube-public
kube-system
```

Creating objects

To create an object, you need to pass a body parameter to the create method. The body must be a Python dictionary that is equivalent to a YAML configuration file you would use with Kubectl. The easiest way to do it is to actually use a YAML and then use the Python YAML module (this is not part of the standard library and must be installed separately) to read the YAML file and load it into a dictionary. For example, to create an nginx-deployment with 3 replicas, we can use this YAML configuration file:

```yaml
apiVersion: apps/v1
kind: Deployment
metadata:
  name: nginx-deployment
spec:
  replicas: 3
  template:
    metadata:
      labels:
        app: nginx
    spec:
      containers:
      - name: nginx
        image: nginx:1.7.9
        ports:
        - containerPort: 80
```

To install the yaml Python module, type this command:

```
> pip install yaml
```

Then the following Python program will create the deployment:

```python
from os import path
import yaml
from kubernetes import client, config

def main():
    # Configs can be set in Configuration class directly or using
    # helper utility. If no argument provided, the config will be
    # loaded from default location.
    config.load_kube_config()

    with open(path.join(path.dirname(__file__),
                        'nginx-deployment.yaml')) as f:
        dep = yaml.load(f)
        k8s = client.AppsV1Api()
        status = k8s_beta.create_namespaced_deployment(
```

```
            body=dep, namespace="default").status
        print("Deployment created. status='{}'".format(status))


if __name__ == '__main__':
    main()
```

Watching objects

Watching objects is an advanced capability. It is implemented using a separate watch module. Here is an example to watch for 10 namespace events and print them to the screen:

```
from kubernetes import client, config, watch

# Configs can be set in Configuration class directly or using helper
utility
config.load_kube_config()
v1 = client.CoreV1Api()
count = 10
w = watch.Watch()
for event in w.stream(v1.list_namespace, _request_timeout=60):
    print(f"Event: {event['type']} {event['object'].metadata.name}")
    count -= 1
    if count == 0:
        w.stop()

print('Done.')
```

Invoking Kubectl programmatically

If you're not a Python developer and don't want to deal with the REST API directly, you have another option. Kubectl is used mostly as an interactive command-line tool, but nothing is stopping you from automating it and invoking it through scripts and programs. Here are some of the benefits of using Kubectl as your Kubernetes API client:

- Easy to find examples for any usage
- Easy to experiment on the command line to find the right combination of commands and arguments
- Kubectl supports output in JSON or YAML for quick parsing
- Authentication is built-in via Kubectl configuration

Using Python subprocess to run Kubectl

I'll use Python again, so you can compare using the official Python client with rolling your own. Python has a module called `subprocess` that can run external processes such as Kubectl and capture the output. Here is a Python 3 example running Kubectl on its own and displaying the beginning of the usage output:

```
>>> import subprocess
>>> out = subprocess.check_output('kubectl').decode('utf-8')
>>> print(out[:276])
```

Kubectl controls the Kubernetes cluster manager. Find more information at `https://github.com/kubernetes/kubernetes`.

Here are some basic commands for beginners:

- `create`: Create a resource using the filename or `stdin`
- `expose`: Take a replication controller, service, deployment, or pod

The `check_checkout()` function captures the output as a bytes array that needs to be decoded to `utf-8` to display it properly. We can generalize it a little bit and create a convenience function called `k` that accepts parameters it feeds to Kubectl, and then decodes the output and returns it:

```
from subprocess import check_output
def k(*args):
    out = check_output(['kubectl'] + list(args))
    return out.decode('utf-8')
Let's use it to list all the running pods in the default namespace:
>>> print(k('get', 'po'))
NAME                                    Ready   Status    Restarts      Age
nginx-deployment-6c54bd5869-9mp2g       1/1     Running   0             18m
nginx-deployment-6c54bd5869-lgs84       1/1     Running   0             18m
nginx-deployment-6c54bd5869-n7468       1/1     Running   0           . 18m
```

This is nice for display, but Kubectl already does that. The real power comes when you use the structured output options with the `-o` flag. Then the result can be converted automatically to a Python object. Here is a modified version of the `k()` function that accepts a Boolean `use_json` keyword argument (default is `False`); if `True` adds `-o json` and then parses the JSON output to a Python object (dictionary):

```
from subprocess import check_output
import json

def k(use_json=False, *args):
```

```
cmd = ['kubectl']
cmd += list(args)
if use_json:
    cmd += ['-o', 'json']
out = check_output(cmd)
if use_json:
    out = json.loads(out)
else:
    out = out.decode('utf-8')
return out
```

That returns a full-fledged API object, which can be navigated and drilled down just like when accessing the REST API directly or using the official Python client:

```
result = k('get', 'po', use_json=True)
for r in result['items']:
    print(r['metadata']['name'])
nginx-deployment-6c54bd5869-9mp2g
nginx-deployment-6c54bd5869-lgs84
nginx-deployment-6c54bd5869-n7468
```

Let's see how to delete the deployment and wait until all the pods are gone. The Kubectl delete command doesn't accept the -o json option (although it has -o name), so let's leave out use_json:

```
k('delete', 'deployment', 'nginx-deployment')
while len(k('get', 'po', use_json=True)['items']) > 0:
    print('.')
print('Done.')
Done.
```

Extending the Kubernetes API

Kubernetes is an extremely flexible platform. It allows you to extend its own API with new types of resources called custom resources. If that is not enough you can even provide your API server that integrates with the Kubernetes API server in a mechanism called API aggregation. What can you do with custom resources? Plenty. You can use them to manage the Kubernetes API resources that live outside the Kubernetes cluster, which your pods communicate with.

By adding those external resources as custom resources, you get a full picture of your system and you benefit from many Kubernetes API features such as the following:

- Custom CRUD REST endpoints
- Versioning
- Watches
- Automatic integration with generic Kubernetes tooling

Other use cases for custom resources are metadata for custom controllers and automation programs.

Custom resources that were introduced in Kubernetes 1.7 are a significant improvement over the now deprecated third-party resources. Let's dive in and see what custom resources are all about.

Understanding the structure of a custom resource

In order to play nice with the Kubernetes API server, third-party resources must conform to some basic requirements. Similar to built-in API objects, they must have the following fields:

- apiVersion: apiextensions.k8s.io/v1beta1
- metadata: Standard Kubernetes object metadata
- kind: CustomResourceDefinition
- spec: Describes how the resource appears in the API and tools
- status: Indicates the current status of the CRD

The spec has an internal structure that includes fields like group, names, scope, validation, and version. The status includes the fields acceptedNames and Conditions. In the next section, I'll show you an example that clarifies the meaning of these fields.

Developing custom resource definitions

You develop your custom resources using custom resource definitions, aslo known as CRD. The intention is for CRDs to integrate smoothly with Kubernetes, its API, and its tooling, so you need to provide a lot of information. Here is an example for a custom resource called Candy:

```
apiVersion: apiextensions.k8s.io/v1beta1
kind: CustomResourceDefinition
metadata:
  # name must match the spec fields below, and be in the form:
<plural>.<group>
  name: candies.awesome.corp.com
spec:
  # group name to use for REST API: /apis/<group>/<version>
  group: awesome.corp.com
  # version name to use for REST API: /apis/<group>/<version>
  version: v1
  # either Namespaced or Cluster
  scope: Namespaced
  names:
    # plural name to be used in the URL: /apis/<group>/<version>/<plural>
    plural: candies
    # singular name to be used as an alias on the CLI and for display
    singular: candy
    # kind is normally the CamelCased singular type. Your resource
manifests use this.
    kind: Candy
    # shortNames allow shorter string to match your resource on the CLI
    shortNames:
    - cn
```

Let's create it:

```
> kubectl create -f crd.yaml
customresourcedefinition "candies.awesome.corp.com" created
```

Note that the metadata name with the plural notation is returned. Now, let's verify that we can access it:

```
> kubectl get crd
NAME                              AGE
candies.awesome.corp.com          17m
```

There is also a new API endpoint for managing this new resource:

```
/apis/awesome.corp.com/v1/namespaces/<namespace>/candies/
```

Let's use our Python code to access it:

```
>>> config.load_kube_config()
>>> print(k('get', 'thirdpartyresources'))
NAME                                    AGE
candies.awesome.corp.com                24m
```

Integrating custom resources

Once the `CustomResourceDefinition` object has been created, you can create custom resources of that resource kind in particular, `Candy` in this case (`candy` becomes `CamelCase Candy`). `Candy` objects can contain arbitrary fields with arbitrary JSON. In the following example, a `flavor` custom field is set on the `Candy` object. The `apiVersion` field is derived from the CRD spec's group and version fields:

```
apiVersion: "awesome.corp.com/v1"
kind: Candy
metadata:
  name: chocolatem
spec:
  flavor: "sweeeeeeet"
```

You can add arbitrary fields to your custom resources. The values can be any JSON values. Note that these fields are not defined in the CRD. Different objects can have different fields. Let's create it:

```
> kubectl create -f candy.yaml
candy "chocolate" created
```

At this point, `kubectl` can operate on `Candy` objects just like it works on built-in objects. Note that resource names are case-insensitive when using `kubectl`:

```
$ kubectl get candies
NAME            AGE
chocolate       2m
```

We can also view the raw JSON data using the standard `-o json` flag. I'll use the short name `cn` this time:

```
> kubectl get cn -o json
{
    "apiVersion": "v1",
    "items": [
        {
            "apiVersion": "awesome.corp.com/v1",
            "kind": "Candy",
            "metadata": {
                "clusterName": "",
                "creationTimestamp": "2018-03-07T18:18:42Z",
                "name": "chocolate",
                "namespace": "default",
                "resourceVersion": "4791773",
                "selfLink":
"/apis/awesome.corp.com/v1/namespaces/default/candies/chocolate",
                "uid": "f7a6fd80-2233-11e8-b432-080027c94384"
            },
            "spec": {
                "flavor": "sweeeeeeet"
            }
        }
    ],
    "kind": "List",
    "metadata": {
        "resourceVersion": "",
        "selfLink": ""
    }
}
```

Finalizing custom resources

Custom resources support finalizers just like standard API objects. A finalizer is a mechanism where objects are not deleted immediately but have to wait for special controllers that run in the background and watch for deletion requests. The controller may perform any necessary cleanup options and then remove its finalizer from the target object. There may be multiple finalizers on an object. Kubenetes will wait until all finalizers have been removed and only then delete the object. The finalizers in the metadata are just arbitrary strings that their corresponding controller can identify. Here is an example with a `Candy` object that has two finalizers, `eat-me` and `drink-me`:

```
apiVersion: "awesome.corp.com/v1"
kind: Candy
```

```
metadata:
  name: chocolate
  finalizers:
  - eat-me
  - drink-me
spec:
  flavor: "sweeeeeet"
```

Validating custom resources

You can add any field to a CRD. This may cause invalid definitions. Kubernetes 1.9 introduced a validation mechanism for CRDs based on the OpenAPI V3 schema. It's still in beta and can be disabled using a feature gate when starting the API server:

```
--feature-gates=CustomResourceValidation=false
```

In your CRD, you add a validation section to the spec:

```
validation:
    openAPIV3Schema:
      properties:
        spec:
          properties:
            cronSpec:
              type: string
              pattern: '^(\d+|\*)(/\d+)?(\s+(\d+|\*)(/\d+)?){4}$'
            replicas:
              type: integer
              minimum: 1
              maximum: 10
```

If you try to create objects that violate the validation in the spec, you'll get an error message. You can read more about the OpenAPI schema here: http://bit.ly/2FsBfWA.

Understanding API server aggregation

CRDs are great when all you need is some CRUD operations on your own types. You can just piggyback on the Kubernetes API server, which will store your objects and provide API support and integration with tooling such as Kubectl. You can run controllers that watch for your objects and perform some operations when they are created, updated, or deleted. But CRDs have limitations. If you need more advanced features and customization, you can use API server aggregation and write your own API server that the Kubernetes API server will delegate to.

Your API server will use the same API machinery as the Kubernetes API server itself. Some of the advanced capabilities are as follows:

- Controlling the storage of your objects
- Multi-versioning
- Custom operations beyond CRUD (such as exec or scale)
- Using protocol buffer payloads

Writing an extension API server is a non-trivial effort. If you decide you need all that power, I recommend using the API builder project:

```
https://github.com/kubernetes-incubator/apiserver-builder
```

It is a young project, but it takes care of a lot of the necessary boilerplate code. The API builder provides the following capabilities:

- Bootstrap complete type definitions, controllers, and tests, as well as documentation
- You can run the extension control plane locally, inside Minikube, or on an actual remote cluster
- Your generated controllers will be able to watch and update API objects
- Adding resources (including sub-resources)
- Default values you can override if needed

Utilizing the service catalog

The Kubernetes service catalog project allows you to integrate smoothly and painlessly any external service that support the Open Service Broker API specification:

```
https://github.com/openservicebrokerapi/servicebroker
```

The intention of the open service broker API is to expose external services to any cloud environment through a standard specification with supporting documentation and a comprehensive test suite. That lets providers implement a single specification and supports multiple cloud environments. The current environments include Kubernetes and CloudFoundry. The project works towards broad industry adoption.

The service catalog is particularly useful for integrating the services of cloud platform providers. Here are some examples of such services:

- Microsoft Azure Cloud Queue
- Amazon Simple Queue Service
- Google Cloud Pub/Sub

This capability is a boon for organizations that are committed to the cloud. You get to build your system on Kubernetes, but you don't have to deploy, manage, and maintain every service in your cluster yourself. You can offload that to your cloud provider, enjoy deep integration, and focus on your application.

The service catalog can potentially make your Kubernetes cluster fully autonomous by allowing you to provision cloud resources through service brokers. We're not there yet, but the direction is very promising.

This concludes our discussion of accessing and extending Kubernetes from the outside. In the next section, we will direct our gaze inward and look into customizing the inner workings of Kubernetes itself via plugins.

Writing Kubernetes plugins

In this section, we will dive into the guts of Kubernetes and learn how to take advantage of its famous flexibility and extensibility. We will learn about the different aspects that can be customized via plugins, and how to implement such plugins and integrate them with Kubernetes.

Writing a custom scheduler plugin

Kubernetes defines itself as a container scheduling and management system. As such, the scheduler is the most important component of Kubernetes. Kubernetes comes with a default scheduler, but allows for writing additional schedulers. To write your own custom scheduler, you need to understand what the scheduler does, how it is packaged, how to deploy your custom scheduler, and how to integrate your scheduler. The scheduler source code is available here:

```
https://github.com/kubernetes/kubernetes/tree/master/pkg/scheduler
```

In the rest of this section, we will dive deep into the source and examine data types, algorithms, and code.

Understanding the design of the Kubernetes scheduler

The job of the scheduler is to find a node for newly created or restarted pods, and create a binding in the API server and run it there. If the scheduler can't find a suitable node for the pod, it will remain in pending state.

The scheduler

Most of the work of the scheduler is pretty generic—it figures out which pods need to be scheduled, updates their state, and runs them on the selected node. The custom part is how to map pods to nodes. The Kubernetes team recognized the need for custom scheduling, and the generic scheduler can be configured with different scheduling algorithms.

The main data type is the Scheduler `struct` that contains a `Config` `struct` with lots of properties (this will soon be replaced by a `configurator` interface):

```
type Scheduler struct {
    config *Config
}
```

Here is the `Config` struct:

```
type Config struct {
    SchedulerCache schedulercache.Cache
    Ecache        *core.EquivalenceCache
    NodeLister algorithm.NodeLister
    Algorithm   algorithm.ScheduleAlgorithm
    GetBinder  func(pod *v1.Pod) Binder
    PodConditionUpdater PodConditionUpdater
    PodPreemptor PodPreemptor
    NextPod func() *v1.Pod
    WaitForCacheSync func() bool
    Error func(*v1.Pod, error)
    Recorder record.EventRecorder
    StopEverything chan struct{}
    VolumeBinder *volumebinder.VolumeBinder
}
```

Most of these are interfaces, so you can configure the scheduler with custom functionality. In particular, the scheduler algorithm is relevant if you want to customize pod scheduling.

Registering an algorithm provider

The scheduler has the concept of an algorithm provider and an algorithm. Together, they let you use the substantial functionality of the built-in scheduler in order to replace the core scheduling algorithm.

The algorithm provider lets you register new algorithm providers with the factory. There is already one custom provider registered, called ClusterAutoScalerProvider. We will see later how the scheduler knows which algorithm provider to use. The key file is as follows:

https://github.com/kubernetes/kubernetes/blob/master/pkg/scheduler/algorithmprovider/defaults/defaults.go

The init() function calls the registerAlgorithmProvider(), which you should extend to include your algorithm provider in addition to the default and autoscaler providers:

```
func registerAlgorithmProvider(predSet, priSet sets.String) {
    // Registers algorithm providers. By default we use 'DefaultProvider'
    // but user can specify one to be used by specifying flag.
    factory.RegisterAlgorithmProvider(factory.DefaultProvider, predSet,
priSet)
    // Cluster autoscaler friendly scheduling algorithm.
    factory.RegisterAlgorithmProvider(ClusterAutoscalerProvider, predSet,
        copyAndReplace(priSet, "LeastRequestedPriority",
"MostRequestedPriority"))
}
```

In addition to registering the provider, you also need to register a fit predicate and a priority function, which are used to actually perform the scheduling.

You can use the factory's RegisterFitPredicate() and RegisterPriorityFunction2() functions.

Configuring the scheduler

The scheduler algorithm is provided as part of the configuration. Custom schedulers can implement the ScheduleAlgorithm interface:

```
type ScheduleAlgorithm interface {
    Schedule(*v1.Pod, NodeLister) (selectedMachine string, err error)
    Preempt(*v1.Pod, NodeLister, error) (selectedNode *v1.Node,
                                          preemptedPods []*v1.Pod,
                                          cleanupNominatedPods []*v1.Pod,
                                          err error)
    Predicates() map[string]FitPredicate
```

```
        Prioritizers() []PriorityConfig
    }
```

When you run the scheduler, you can provide the name of the custom scheduler or a custom algorithm provider as a command-line argument. If none are provided, the default algorithm provider will be used. The command-line arguments to the scheduler are `--algorithm-provider` and `--scheduler-name`.

Packaging the scheduler

The custom scheduler runs as a pod inside the same Kubernetes cluster it oversees. It needs to be packaged as a container image. Let's use a copy of the standard Kubernetes scheduler for demonstration purposes. We can build Kubernetes from the source to get a scheduler image:

```
git clone https://github.com/kubernetes/kubernetes.git
cd kubernetes
make
```

Create the following Dockerfile:

```
FROM busybox
ADD ./_output/bin/kube-scheduler /usr/local/bin/kube-scheduler
```

Use it to `build` a Docker image type:

```
docker build -t custom-kube-scheduler:1.0 .
```

Finally, push the image to a container registry. I'll use DockerHub here. You'll need to create an account on DockerHub and log in before pushing your image:

```
> docker login
> docker push g1g1/custom-kube-scheduler
```

Note that I built the scheduler locally, and in the Dockerfile I just copy it from the host into the image. That works when you deploy on the same OS that you build with. If this is not the case, then it may be better to insert the build commands into the Dockerfile. The price you pay is that you need to pull all of Kubernetes into the image.

Deploying the custom scheduler

Now that the scheduler image is built and available in the registry, we need to create a Kubernetes deployment for it. The scheduler is, of course, critical, so we can use Kubernetes itself to ensure that it is always running. The following YAML file defines a deployment with a single replica and a few other bells and whistles, such as liveness and readiness probes:

```
apiVersion: apps/v1
kind: Deployment
metadata:
  labels:
    component: scheduler
    tier: control-plane
  name: custom-scheduler
  namespace: kube-system
spec:
  replicas: 1
  template:
    metadata:
      labels:
        component: scheduler
        tier: control-plane
        version: second
    spec:
      containers:
      - command:
        - /usr/local/bin/kube-scheduler
        - --address=0.0.0.0
        - --leader-elect=false
        - --scheduler-name=custom-scheduler
        image: g1g1/custom-kube-scheduler:1.0
        livenessProbe:
          httpGet:
            path: /healthz
            port: 10251
          initialDelaySeconds: 15
        name: kube-second-scheduler
        readinessProbe:
          httpGet:
            path: /healthz
            port: 10251
        resources:
          requests:
            cpu: '0.1'
```

The name of the scheduler (`custom-scheduler` here) is important and must be unique. It will be used later to associate pods with the scheduler to schedule them. Note that the custom scheduler belongs in the `kube-system` namespace.

Running another custom scheduler in the cluster

Running another custom scheduler is as simple as creating the deployment. This is the beauty of this encapsulated approach. Kubernetes is going to run a second scheduler, which is a big deal, but Kubernetes is unaware of what's going on. It just deploys a pod like any other pod, except this pod happens to be a custom scheduler:

```
$ kubectl create -f custom-scheduler.yaml
```

Let's verify that the scheduler pod is running:

```
$ kubectl get pods --namespace=kube-system
NAME                                 READY   STATUS    RESTARTS   AGE
. . . .
custom-scheduler-7cfc49d749-lwzxj    1/1     Running   0          2m
. . .
```

Our custom scheduler is running.

Assigning pods to the custom scheduler

OK. The custom scheduler is running alongside the default scheduler. But how does Kubernetes choose which scheduler to use when a pod needs scheduling? The answer is that the pod decides and not Kubernetes. The pod spec has an optional scheduler name field. If it's missing, the default scheduler is used; otherwise, the specified scheduler is used. This is the reason the custom scheduler names must be unique. The name of the default scheduler is `default-scheduler`, in case you want to be explicit in your pod spec. Here is a pod definition that will be scheduled using the default scheduler:

```
apiVersion: v1
kind: Pod
metadata:
  name: some-pod
  labels:
    name: some-pod
spec:
  containers:
  - name: some-container
    image: gcr.io/google_containers/pause:2.0
```

To have the `custom-scheduler` schedule this pod, change the pod spec to the following:

```
apiVersion: v1
kind: Pod
metadata:
  name: some-pod
  labels:
    name: some-pod
spec:
  schedulerName: custom-scheduler
  containers:
  - name: some-container
    image: gcr.io/google_containers/pause:2.0
```

Verifying that the pods were scheduled using the custom scheduler

There are two primary ways to verify pods get scheduled by the correct scheduler. First, you can create pods that need to be scheduled by the custom scheduler before deploying the custom scheduler. The pods will remain in the pending state. Then, deploy the custom scheduler and the pending pods will be scheduled and start running.

The other method is to check the event logs and look for scheduled events using this command:

```
$ kubectl get events
```

Employing access control webhooks

Kubernetes always provided ways for you to customize access control. In Kubernetes access control can be denoted as triple-A: Authentication, Authorization, and Admission control. In early versions, it was done through plugins that required Go programming, installing into your cluster, registration, and other invasive procedures. Now, Kubernetes lets you customize authentication, authorization, and admission control webhooks.

Using an authentication webhook

Kubernetes lets you extend the authentication process by injecting a webhook for bearer tokens. It requires two pieces of information: how to access the remote authentication service and the duration of the authentication decision (it defaults to two minutes).

To provide this information and enable authentication webhooks, start the API server with the following command-line arguments:

- `--runtime-config=authentication.k8s.io/v1beta1=true`
- `--authentication-token-webhook-config-file`
- `--authentication-token-webhook-cache-ttl`

The configuration file uses the `kubeconfig` file format. Here is an example:

```
clusters:
  - name: remote-authentication-service
    cluster:
      certificate-authority: /path/to/ca.pem
      server: https://example.com/authenticate

users:
  - name: k8s-api-server
    user:
      client-certificate: /path/to/cert.pem
      client-key: /path/to/key.pem

current-context: webhook
contexts:
- context:
    cluster: remote-authentication-service
    user: k8s-api-sever
  name: webhook
```

Note that a client certificate and key must be provided to Kubernetes for mutual authentication against the remote authentication service.

The cache TTL is useful because often users will make multiple consecutive requests to Kubernetes. Having the authentication decision cached can save a lot of round trips to the remote authentication service.

When an API HTTP request comes in, Kubernetes extracts the bearer token from its headers and posts a `TokenReview` JSON request to the remote authentication service through the webhook:

```
{
    "apiVersion": "authentication.k8s.io/v1beta1",
    "kind": "TokenReview",
    "spec": {
        "token": "<bearer token from original request headers>"
    }
}
```

The remote authentication service will respond with a decision. The status authentication will either be true or false. Here is an example of a successful authentication:

```
{
    "apiVersion": "authentication.k8s.io/v1beta1",
    "kind": "TokenReview",
    "status": {
        "authenticated": true,
        "user": {
            "username": "gigi@gg.com",
            "uid": "42",
            "groups": [
                "developers",
            ],
            "extra": {
                "extrafield1": [
                    "extravalue1",
                    "extravalue2"
                ]
            }
        }
    }
}
```

A rejected response is much more concise:

```
{
    "apiVersion": "authentication.k8s.io/v1beta1",
    "kind": "TokenReview",
    "status": {
        "authenticated": false
    }
}
```

Using an authorization webhook

The authorization webhook is very similar to the authentication webhook. It just requires a configuration file that is in the same format as the authentication webhook configuration file. There is no authorization caching because unlike authentication, the same user may make lots of requests to different API endpoints with different parameters and authorization decisions may be different, so caching is not a viable option.

You configure the webhook by passing the following command-line arguments to the API server:

- `--runtime-config=authorization.k8s.io/v1beta1=true`
- `--authorization-webhook-config-file=<configuration filename>`

When a request passes authentication, Kubernetes will send a `SubjectAccessReview` JSON object to the remote authorization service. It will contain the request user as well as requested resource and other request attributes:

```
{
  "apiVersion": "authorization.k8s.io/v1beta1",
  "kind": "SubjectAccessReview",
  "spec": {
    "resourceAttributes": {
      "namespace": "awesome-namespace",
      "verb": "get",
      "group": "awesome.example.org",
      "resource": "pods"
    },
    "user": "gigi@gg.com",
    "group": [
      "group1",
      "group2"
    ]
  }
}
```

The request will be allowed:

```
{
  "apiVersion": "authorization.k8s.io/v1beta1",
  "kind": "SubjectAccessReview",
  "status": {
    "allowed": true
  }
}
```

Or it will be disallowed (with a reason):

```
{
  "apiVersion": "authorization.k8s.io/v1beta1",
  "kind": "SubjectAccessReview",
  "status": {
    "allowed": false,
    "reason": "user does not have read access to the namespace"
  }
}
```

A user may be authorized to access a resource, but not non-resource attributes such as /api, /apis, /metrics, /resetMetrics, /logs, /debug, /healthz, /swagger-ui/, /swaggerapi/, /ui, and /version.

Here is how to request access to the logs:

```
{
  "apiVersion": "authorization.k8s.io/v1beta1",
  "kind": "SubjectAccessReview",
  "spec": {
    "nonResourceAttributes": {
      "path": "/logs",
      "verb": "get"
    },
    "user": "gigi@gg.com",
    "group": [
      "group1",
      "group2"
    ]
  }
}
```

Using an admission control webhook

Dynamic admission control supports webhooks too. It is still in alpha. You need to enable the generic admission webhook by passing the following command-line arguments to the API server:

- --admission-control=GenericAdmissionWebhook
- --runtime-config=admissionregistration.k8s.io/v1alpha1

Configuring webhook admission controller on the fly

The authentication and authorization webhooks must be configured when you start the API server. The admission control webhooks can be configured dynamically by creating `externaladmissionhookconfiguration` objects:

```
apiVersion: admissionregistration.k8s.io/v1alpha1
kind: ExternalAdmissionHookConfiguration
metadata:
  name: example-config
externalAdmissionHooks:
- name: pod-image.k8s.io
  rules:
  - apiGroups:
    - ""
    apiVersions:
    - v1
    operations:
    - CREATE
    resources:
    - pods
  failurePolicy: Ignore
  clientConfig:
    caBundle: <pem encoded ca cert that signs the server cert used by the
webhook>
    service:
      name: <name of the front-end service>
      namespace: <namespace of the front-end service>
```

Providing custom metrics for horizontal pod autoscaling

Prior to Kubernetes 1.6, custom metrics were implemented as a Heapster model. In Kubernetes 1.6, a new custom metrics API landed and matured gradually. As of Kubernetes 1.9, they are enabled by default. Custom metrics rely on API aggregation. The recommended path is to start with the custom metrics API server boilerplate available here:

```
https://github.com/kubernetes-incubator/custom-metrics-apiserver
```

Then, you implement the `CustomMetricsProvider` interface:

```
type CustomMetricsProvider interface {
    GetRootScopedMetricByName(groupResource schema.GroupResource,
                              name string,
                              metricName string)
(*custom_metrics.MetricValue, error)
    GetRootScopedMetricBySelector(groupResource schema.GroupResource,
                                  selector labels.Selector,
                                  metricName string)
(*custom_metrics.MetricValueList,
                                                            error)
    GetNamespacedMetricByName(groupResource schema.GroupResource,
                              namespace string,
                              name string,
                              metricName string)
(*custom_metrics.MetricValue, error)
    GetNamespacedMetricBySelector(groupResource schema.GroupResource,
                                                    namespace
string,
                                                    selector
labels.Selector,
                                                    metricName
string)   (*MetricValueList, error)
    ListAllMetrics() []MetricInfo
}
```

Extending Kubernetes with custom storage

Volume plugins are yet another type of plugin. Prior to Kubernetes 1.8, you had to write a Kublet plugin that required implementing, registration with Kubernetes, and linking with the Kubelet. Kubernetes 1.8 introduced the FlexVolume, which is much more versatile. Kubernetes 1.9 took it to the next level with the **Container Storage Interface** (**CSI**).

Taking advantage of FlexVolume

Kubernetes volume plugins are designed to support a particular type of storage or storage provider. There are numerous volume plugins, which we covered in `Chapter 7`, *Handling Kubernetes Storage*. The existing volume plugins are more than enough for most users, but if you need to integrate with a storage solution that is not supported you must implement your own volume plugin, which is not trivial. If you want it to get accepted as an official Kubernetes plugin then you have to get through a rigorous approval process. But `FlexVolume` provides another path. It is a generic plugin that allows you to hook up your unsupported storage backend without deep integration with Kubernetes itself.

`FlexVolume` lets you add arbitrary attributes to the spec, and it communicates with your backend via a callout interface that includes the following operations:

- **Attach**: Attaches a volume to the Kubernetes Kubelet node
- **Detach**: Detaches the volume from the Kubernetes Kubelet node
- **Mount**: Mounts the attached volume
- **Unmount**: Unmounts the attached volume

Each operation is implemented by the backend driver as a binary that the FlexVolume invokes at the right time. The driver must be installed in `/usr/libexec/kubernetes/kubelet-plugins/volume/exec/<vendor>~<driver>/<driver>`.

Benefitting from CSI

FlexVolume provides out-of-tree plugin capability, but it still requires the FlexVolume plugin itself and a somewhat cumbersome installation and invocation model. The CSI will improve on it significantly by having the vendor implement it directly. The best thing about it is that you, as a developer, don't have to create and maintain those plugins. It is the responsibility of the storage solution provider to implement and maintain the CSI, and it's in their interest to make it as robust as possible so that people don't choose a different storage solution that works out of the box on Kubernetes (and other platforms that integrate with CSI).

Summary

In this chapter, we covered three major topics: working with the Kubernetes API, extending the Kubernetes API, and writing Kubernetes plugins. The Kubernetes API supports the OpenAPI spec and is a great example of REST API design that follows all current best practices. It is very consistent, well organized, and well documented, yet it is a big API and is not easy to understand. You can access the API directly via REST over HTTP, using client libraries including the official Python client, and even by invoking Kubectl.

Extending the Kubernetes API involves defining your own custom resources and optionally extending the API server itself via API aggregation. Custom resources are most effective when you combine them with additional custom plugins or controllers when you query and update them externally.

Plugins and webhooks are the foundation of Kubernetes design. Kubernetes was always meant to be extended by users to accommodate any need. We looked at various plugins and webhooks you can write and how to register and integrate them seamlessly with Kubernetes.

We also looked at custom metrics and even how to extend Kubernetes with custom storage options.

At this point, you should be well aware of all the major mechanisms to extend, customize, and control Kubernetes through API access, custom resources, and custom plugins. You are in a great position to take advantage of these capabilities to augment the existing functionality of Kubernetes and adapt it to your needs and your systems.

In the next chapter, we'll look at Helm, the Kubernetes package manager, and its charts. As you may have realized, deploying and configuring complex systems on Kubernetes is far from simple. Helm allows the grouping together of a bunch of manifests into a chart, which can be installed as a single unit.

18
Handling the Kubernetes Package Manager

In this chapter, we are going to look into Helm, the Kubernetes package manager. Every successful and important platform must have a good packaging system. Helm was developed by Deis (acquired by Microsoft in April 2017) and later contributed to the Kubernetes project directly. We will start by understanding the motivation for Helm, its architecture, and its components. Then, we'll get hands-on experience and see how to use Helm and its charts within Kubernetes. This includes finding, installing, customizing, deleting, and managing charts. Last but not least, we'll cover how to create your own charts and handle versioning, dependencies, and templating.

The following topics will be covered:

- Understanding Helm
- Using Helm
- Creating your own charts

Understanding Helm

Kubernetes provides many ways to organize and orchestrate your containers at runtime, but it lacks a higher-level organization of grouping sets of images together. This is where Helm comes in. In this section, we'll go over the motivation for Helm, its architecture and components, and discuss what has changed in the transition from Helm Classic to Helm.

The motivation for Helm

Helm provides support for several important use cases:

- Managing complexity
- Easy upgrades
- Simple sharing
- Safe rollbacks

Charts can describe even the most complex apps, provide repeatable application installation, and serve as a single point of authority. In-place upgrades and custom hooks allow easy updates. It's simple to share charts that can be versioned and hosted on public or private servers. When you need to roll back recent upgrades, Helm provides a single command to roll back a cohesive set of changes to your infrastructure.

The Helm architecture

Helm is designed to perform the following:

- Create new charts from scratch
- Package charts into chart archive (`tgz`) files
- Interact with chart repositories where charts are stored
- Install and uninstall charts into an existing Kubernetes cluster
- Manage the release cycle of charts that have been installed with Helm

Helm uses a client-server architecture to achieve these goals.

Helm components

Helm has a server component that runs on your Kubernetes cluster and a client component that you run on a local machine.

The Tiller server

The server is responsible for managing releases. It interacts with the Helm clients as well as the Kubernetes API server. Its main functions are as follows:

- Listening for incoming requests from the Helm client
- Combining a chart and configuration to build a release
- Installing charts into Kubernetes
- Tracking the subsequent release
- Upgrading and uninstalling charts by interacting with Kubernetes

The Helm client

You install the Helm client on your machine. It is responsible for the following:

- Local chart development
- Managing repositories
- Interacting with the Tiller server
- Sending charts to be installed
- Asking for information about releases
- Requesting upgrades or uninstallation of existing releases

Using Helm

Helm is a rich package management system that lets you perform all the necessary steps to manage the applications installed on your cluster. Let's roll up our sleeves and get going.

Installing Helm

Installing Helm involves installing the client and the server. Helm is implemented in Go, and the same binary executable can serve as either client or server.

Installing the Helm client

You must have Kubectl configured properly to talk to your Kubernetes cluster, because the Helm client uses the Kubectl configuration to talk to the Helm server (Tiller).

Helm provides binary releases for all platforms, at
`https://github.com/kubernetes/helm/releases/latest`.

For Windows, you can also use the `chocolatey` package manager, but it may be a little behind the official version,
`https://chocolatey.org/packages/kubernetes-helm/<version>`.

For macOS and Linux, you can install the client from a script:

```
$ curl https://raw.githubusercontent.com/kubernetes/helm/master/scripts/get
> get_helm.sh
$ chmod 700 get_helm.sh
$ ./get_helm.sh
```

On macOS X, you can also use Homebrew:

```
brew install kubernetes-helm
```

Installing the Tiller server

Tiller typically runs inside your cluster. For development, it is sometimes easier to run Tiller locally.

Installing Tiller in-cluster

The easiest way to install Tiller is from a machine where the Helm client is installed. Run the following command:

```
helm init
```

This will initialize both the client and the Tiller server on the remote Kubernetes cluster. When the installation is done, you will have a running Tiller pod in the `kube-system` namespace of your cluster:

```
> kubectl get po --namespace=kube-system -l name=tiller
NAME                              READY   STATUS    RESTARTS   AGE
tiller-deploy-3210613906-2j5sh    1/1     Running   0          1m
```

You can also run `helm version` to check out both the client's and the server's version:

```
> helm version
Client: &version.Version{SemVer:"v2.2.3",
GitCommit:"1402a4d6ec9fb349e17b912e32fe259ca21181e3", GitTreeState:"clean"}
Server: &version.Version{SemVer:"v2.2.3",
GitCommit:"1402a4d6ec9fb349e17b912e32fe259ca21181e3", GitTreeState:"clean"}
```

Installing Tiller locally

If you want to run Tiller locally, you need to build it first. This is supported on Linux and macOS:

```
> cd $GOPATH
> mkdir -p src/k8s.io
> cd src/k8s.io
> git clone https://github.com/kubernetes/helm.git
> cd helm
> make bootstrap build
```

The bootstrap target will attempt to install dependencies, rebuild the `vendor/` tree, and validate configuration.

The build target will compile Helm and place it in `bin/helm`. Tiller is also compiled and is placed in `bin/tiller`.

Now you can just run `bin/tiller`. Tiller will connect to the Kubernetes cluster via your Kubectl configuration.

You need to tell the Helm client to connect to the local Tiller server. You can do it by setting an environment variable:

```
> export HELM_HOST=localhost:44134
```

Otherwise, you can pass it as a command-line argument: `--host localhost:44134`.

Using Alternative Storage Backend

Helm 2.7.0 added the option to store release information as **secrets**. Earlier versions always stored release information in ConfigMaps. The secrets backend increases the security of charts. It's a complement to general Kubernetes encryption at rest. To use the Secrets backend, you need to run Helm with the following command line:

```
> helm init --override
'spec.template.spec.containers[0].command'='{/tiller,--storage=secret}'
```

Finding charts

In order to install useful applications and software with Helm, you need to find their charts first. This is where the `helm search` command comes in. Helm, by default, searches the official Kubernetes `chart repository`, which is named `stable`:

```
>  helm search
NAME                             VERSION      DESCRIPTION
stable/acs-engine-autoscaler     2.1.1        Scales worker nodes within
agent pools
stable/aerospike                 0.1.5        A Helm chart for Aerospike in
Kubernetes
stable/artifactory               6.2.4        Universal Repository Manager
supporting all maj...
stable/aws-cluster-autoscaler    0.3.2        Scales worker nodes within
autoscaling groups.
stable/buildkite                 0.2.0        Agent for Buildkite
stable/centrifugo                2.0.0        Centrifugo is a real-time
messaging server.
stable/chaoskube                 0.6.1        Chaoskube periodically kills
random pods in you...
stable/chronograf                0.4.0        Open-source web application
written in Go and R..
stable/cluster-autoscaler        0.3.1        Scales worker nodes within
autoscaling groups.
```

The official repository has a rich library of charts that represent all modern open source databases, monitoring systems, Kubernetes-specific helpers, and a slew of other offerings, such as a Minecraft server. You can search for specific charts, for example, let's search for charts that contain `kube` in their name or description:

```
> helm search kube
NAME                             VERSION      DESCRIPTION
stable/chaoskube                 0.6.1        Chaoskube periodically kills
random pods in you...
stable/kube-lego                 0.3.0        Automatically requests
certificates from Let's ...
stable/kube-ops-view             0.4.1        Kubernetes Operational View -
read-only system ...
stable/kube-state-metrics        0.5.1        Install kube-state-metrics to
generate and expo...
stable/kube2iam                  0.6.1        Provide IAM credentials to pods
based on annota...
stable/kubed                     0.1.0        Kubed by AppsCode - Kubernetes
daemon
stable/kubernetes-dashboard      0.4.3        General-purpose web UI for
Kubernetes clusters
```

```
stable/sumokube              0.1.1      Sumologic Log Collector
stable/aerospike             0.1.5      A Helm chart for Aerospike in
Kubernetes
stable/coredns               0.8.0      CoreDNS is a DNS server that
chains plugins and...
stable/etcd-operator         0.6.2      CoreOS etcd-operator Helm chart
for Kubernetes
stable/external-dns          0.4.4      Configure external DNS servers
(AWS Route53...
stable/keel                  0.2.0      Open source, tool for automating
Kubernetes dep...
stable/msoms                 0.1.1      A chart for deploying omsagent as
a daemonset...
stable/nginx-lego            0.3.0      Chart for nginx-ingress-
controller and kube-lego
stable/openvpn               2.0.2      A Helm chart to install an
openvpn server insid...
stable/risk-advisor          2.0.0      Risk Advisor add-on module for
Kubernetes
stable/searchlight           0.1.0      Searchlight by AppsCode - Alerts
for Kubernetes
stable/spartakus             1.1.3      Collect information about
Kubernetes clusters t...
stable/stash                 0.2.0      Stash by AppsCode - Backup your
Kubernetes Volumes
stable/traefik               1.15.2     A Traefik based Kubernetes
ingress controller w...
stable/voyager               2.0.0       Voyager by AppsCode - Secure
Ingress Controller...
stable/weave-cloud           0.1.2      Weave Cloud is a add-on to
Kubernetes which pro...
stable/zetcd                 0.1.4      CoreOS zetcd Helm chart for
Kubernetes
stable/buildkite             0.2.0      Agent for Buildkite
```

Let's try another search:

```
> helm search mysql
NAME                         VERSION    DESCRIPTION
stable/mysql                 0.3.4      Fast, reliable, scalable, and easy to
use open-...
stable/percona               0.3.0      free, fully compatible, enhanced, open
source d...
stable/gcloud-sqlproxy       0.2.2      Google Cloud SQL Proxy
stable/mariadb               2.1.3       Fast, reliable, scalable, and easy to
use open-...
```

What happened? Why does `mariadb` show up in the results? The reason is that `mariadb` (which is a fork of MySQL) mentions MySQL in its description, even though you can't see it in the truncated output. To get the full description, use the `helm inspect` command:

```
> helm inspect stable/mariadb
appVersion: 10.1.30
description: Fast, reliable, scalable, and easy to use open-source
relational database
   system. MariaDB Server is intended for mission-critical, heavy-load
production systems
   as well as for embedding into mass-deployed software.
engine: gotpl
home: https://mariadb.org
icon:
https://bitnami.com/assets/stacks/mariadb/img/mariadb-stack-220x234.png
keywords:
- mariadb
- mysql
- database
- sql
- prometheus
maintainers:
- email: containers@bitnami.com
   name: bitnami-bot
name: mariadb
sources:
- https://github.com/bitnami/bitnami-docker-mariadb
- https://github.com/prometheus/mysqld_exporter
version: 2.1.3
```

Installing packages

OK. You've found the package of your dreams. Now, you probably want to install it on your Kubernetes cluster. When you install a package, Helm creates a release that you can use to keep track of the installation progress. Let's install `MariaDB` using the `helm install` command. Let's go over the output in detail. The first part of the output lists the name of the release - `cranky-whippet` in this case (you can choose your own with the `--name` flag), the namespace, and the deployment status:

```
> helm install stable/mariadb
NAME:    cranky-whippet
LAST DEPLOYED: Sat Mar 17 10:21:21 2018
NAMESPACE: default
STATUS: DEPLOYED
```

The second part of the output lists all the resources created by this chart. Note that the resource names are all derived from the release name:

```
RESOURCES:
==> v1/Service
NAME                       TYPE        CLUSTER-IP       EXTERNAL-IP   PORT(S)
AGE
cranky-whippet-mariadb     ClusterIP   10.106.206.108   <none>        3306/TCP
1s
==> v1beta1/Deployment
NAME                       DESIRED   CURRENT   UP-TO-DATE   AVAILABLE   AGE
cranky-whippet-mariadb     1         1         1            0           1s
==> v1/Pod(related)
NAME                                         READY   STATUS     RESTARTS   AGE
cranky-whippet-mariadb-6c85fb4796-mttf7      0/1     Init:0/1   0          1s
==> v1/Secret
NAME                       TYPE      DATA   AGE
cranky-whippet-mariadb     Opaque    2      1s
==> v1/ConfigMap
NAME                             DATA   AGE
cranky-whippet-mariadb           1      1s
cranky-whippet-mariadb-tests     1      1s
==> v1/PersistentVolumeClaim
NAME                       STATUS   VOLUME
CAPACITY   ACCESS MODES    STORAGECLASS   AGE
cranky-whippet-mariadb     Bound    pvc-9cb7e176-2a07-11e8-9bd6-080027c94384
8Gi        RWO             standard       1s
```

The last part is notes that provide easy-to-understand instructions on how to use MariaDB in the context of your Kubernetes cluster:

```
NOTES:
MariaDB can be accessed via port 3306 on the following DNS name from within
your cluster:
cranky-whippet-mariadb.default.svc.cluster.local
To get the root password run:
MARIADB_ROOT_PASSWORD=$(kubectl get secret --namespace default cranky-
whippet-mariadb -o jsonpath="{.data.mariadb-root-password}" | base64 --
decode)
To connect to your database:
1. Run a pod that you can use as a client:
kubectl run cranky-whippet-mariadb-client --rm --tty -i --env
MARIADB_ROOT_PASSWORD=$MARIADB_ROOT_PASSWORD --image bitnami/mariadb --
command -- bash
2. Connect using the mysql cli, then provide your password:
mysql -h cranky-whippet-mariadb -p$MARIADB_ROOT_PASSWORD
```

Checking installation status

Helm doesn't wait for the installation to complete because it may take a while. The `helm status` command displays the latest information on a release in the same format as the output of the initial `helm install` command. In the output of the `install` command, you can see that the `PersistentVolumeClaim` had a `PENDING` status. Let's check it out now:

```
> helm status cranky-whippet | grep Persist -A 3
==> v1/PersistentVolumeClaim
NAME STATUS VOLUME CAPACITY ACCESS MODES STORAGECLASS  AGE
cranky-whippet-mariadbBoundpvc-9cb7e176-2a07-11e8-9bd6-080027c943848Gi
RWO                        standard                    5m
```

Hooray! It is bound now, and there is a volume attached with 8 GB capacity.

Let's try to connect and verify that `mariadb` is indeed accessible. Let's modify the suggested commands a little bit from the notes to connect. Instead of running `bash` and then running `mysql`, we can directly run the `mysql` command on the container:

```
> kubectl run cranky-whippet-mariadb-client --rm --tty -i --image
bitnami/mariadb --command -- mysql -h cranky-whippet-mariadb
```

If you don't see a command prompt, try pressing *Enter*.

```
MariaDB [(none)]> show databases;
+--------------------+
| Database           |
+--------------------+
| information_schema |
| mysql              |
| performance_schema |
+--------------------+
3 rows in set (0.00 sec)
```

Customizing a chart

Very often, as a user, you want to customize or configure the charts you install. Helm fully supports customization through `config` files. To learn about possible customizations, you can use the `helm inspect` command again, but this time, focus on the values. Here is a partial output:

```
> helm inspect values stable/mariadb
## Bitnami MariaDB image version
## ref: https://hub.docker.com/r/bitnami/mariadb/tags/
```

```
##
## Default: none
image: bitnami/mariadb:10.1.30-r1
## Specify an imagePullPolicy (Required)
## It's recommended to change this to 'Always' if the image tag is 'latest'
## ref: http://kubernetes.io/docs/user-guide/images/#updating-images
imagePullPolicy: IfNotPresent
## Use password authentication
usePassword: true
## Specify password for root user
## Defaults to a random 10-character alphanumeric string if not set and
usePassword is true
## ref:
https://github.com/bitnami/bitnami-docker-mariadb/blob/master/README.md#set
ting-the-root-password-on-first-run
##
# mariadbRootPassword:
## Create a database user
## Password defaults to a random 10-character alphanumeric string if not
set and usePassword is true
## ref:
https://github.com/bitnami/bitnami-docker-mariadb/blob/master/README.md#cre
ating-a-database-user-on-first-run
##
# mariadbUser:
# mariadbPassword:
## Create a database
## ref:
https://github.com/bitnami/bitnami-docker-mariadb/blob/master/README.md#cre
ating-a-database-on-first-run
##
# mariadbDatabase:
```

For example, if you want to set a root password and create a database when installing `mariadb`, you can create the following YAML file and save it as `mariadb-config.yaml`:

```
mariadbRootPassword: supersecret
mariadbDatabase: awesome_stuff
```

Then, run `helm` and pass it the `yaml` file:

```
> helm install -f config.yaml stable/mariadb
```

You can also set individual values on the command line with `--set`. If both `--f` and `--set` try to set the same values, then `--set` takes precedence. For example, in this case, the root password will be `evenbettersecret`:

```
helm install -f config.yaml --set mariadbRootPassword=evenbettersecret
stable/mariadb
```

You can specify multiple values using comma-separated lists: `--set a=1,b=2`.

Additional installation options

The `helm install` command can install from several sources:

- A `chart repository` (as we've seen)
- A local chart archive (`helm install foo-0.1.1.tgz`)
- An unpacked `chart` directory (`helm install path/to/foo`)
- A full URL (`helm install https://example.com/charts/foo-1.2.3.tgz`)

Upgrading and rolling back a release

You may want to upgrade a package you installed to the latest and greatest version. Helm provides the `upgrade` command, which operates intelligently and only updates things that have changed. For example, let's check the current values of our `mariadb` installation:

```
> helm get values cranky-whippet
mariadbDatabase: awesome_stuff
mariadbRootPassword: evenbettersecret
```

Now, let's run, upgrade, and change the name of the database:

```
> helm upgrade cranky-whippet --set mariadbDatabase=awesome_sauce
stable/mariadb
$ helm get values cranky-whippet
mariadbDatabase: awesome_sauce
```

Note that we've lost our `root` password. All the existing values are replaced when you upgrade. OK, let's roll back. The `helm history` command shows us all the available revisions we can roll back to:

```
> helm history cranky-whippet
REVISION         STATUS            CHART             DESCRIPTION
1                SUPERSEDED        mariadb-2.1.3     Install complete
2                SUPERSEDED        mariadb-2.1.3     Upgrade complete
```

```
3            SUPERSEDED       mariadb-2.1.3        Upgrade complete
4            DEPLOYED         mariadb-2.1.3        Upgrade complete
```

Let's roll back to revision 3:

```
> helm rollback cranky-whippet 3
Rollback was a success! Happy Helming!
> helm history cranky-whippet
REVISION        STATUS           CHART             DESCRIPTION
1               SUPERSEDED       mariadb-2.1.3     Install complete
2               SUPERSEDED       mariadb-2.1.3     Upgrade complete
3               SUPERSEDED       mariadb-2.1.3     Upgrade complete
4               SUPERSEDED       mariadb-2.1.3     Upgrade complete
5               DEPLOYED         mariadb-2.1.3     Rollback to 3
```

Let's verify that our changes were rolled back:

```
> helm get values cranky-whippet
mariadbDatabase: awesome_stuff
mariadbRootPassword: evenbettersecret
```

Deleting a release

You can, of course, delete a release too using the `helm delete` command.

First, let's examine the list of releases. We have only `cranky-whippet`:

```
> helm list
NAME                REVISION       STATUS       CHART           NAMESPACE
cranky-whippet      5              DEPLOYED     mariadb-2.1.3   default
```

Now, let's delete it:

```
> helm delete cranky-whippet
release "cranky-whippet" deleted
```

So, no more releases:

```
> helm list
```

However, Helm keeps track of deleted releases too. You can see them using the `--all` flag:

```
> helm list --all
NAME                REVISION    STATUS       CHART           NAMESPACE
cranky-whippet      5           DELETED      mariadb-2.1.3   default
```

To delete a release completely, add the `--purge` flag:

```
> helm delete --purge cranky-whippet
```

Working with repositories

Helm stores charts in repositories that are simple HTTP servers. Any standard HTTP server can host a Helm repository. In the cloud, the Helm team verified that AWS S3 and Google Cloud storage can both serve as Helm repositories in web-enabled mode. Helm also comes bundled with a local package server for developer testing. It runs on the client machine, so it's inappropriate for sharing. In a small team, you may run the Helm package server on a shared machine on the local network accessible to all team members.

To use the local package server, type `helm serve`. Do it in a separate terminal window because it is blocking. Helm will start serving charts from `~/.helm/repository/local` by default. You can put your charts there and generate an index file with `helm index`.

The generated `index.yaml` file lists all the charts.

Note that Helm doesn't provide tools to upload charts to remote repositories because that would require the remote server to understand Helm, to know where to put the chart, and how to update the `index.yaml` file.

On the client's side, the `helm repo` command lets you `list`, `add`, `remove`, `index`, and `update`:

```
> helm repo
```

This command consists of multiple subcommands to interact with `chart` repositories.

It can be used to `add`, `remove`, `list`, and `index` chart repositories:

- **Example usage:**

  ```
  $ helm repo add [NAME] [REPO_URL]
  ```

- **Usage:**

  ```
  helm repo [command]
  ```

- Available commands:

```
add          add a chart repository
index        generate an index file for a given a directory
list         list chart repositories
remove       remove a chart repository
update       update information on available charts
```

Managing charts with Helm

Helm provides several commands to manage charts. It can create a new chart for you:

```
> helm create cool-chart
Creating cool-chart
```

Helm will create the following files and directories under `cool-chart`:

```
-rw-r--r--  1 gigi.sayfan  gigi.sayfan    333B Mar 17 13:36 .helmignore
-rw-r--r--  1 gigi.sayfan  gigi.sayfan     88B Mar 17 13:36 Chart.yaml
drwxr-xr-x  2 gigi.sayfan  gigi.sayfan     68B Mar 17 13:36 charts
drwxr-xr-x  7 gigi.sayfan  gigi.sayfan    238B Mar 17 13:36 templates
-rw-r--r--  1 gigi.sayfan  gigi.sayfan    1.1K Mar 17 13:36 values.yaml
```

Once you have edited your chart, you can package it into a tar `gzipped` archive:

```
> helm package cool-chart
```

Helm will create an archive named `cool-chart-0.1.0.tgz` and store both in the `local` directory and in the `local repository`.

You can also use helm to help you find issues with your chart's formatting or information:

```
> helm lint cool-chart
==> Linting cool-chart
[INFO] Chart.yaml: icon is recommended
1 chart(s) linted, no failures
```

Taking advantage of starter packs

The `helm create` command takes an optional `--starter` flag that lets you specify a starter chart.

Starters are regular charts located in $HELM_HOME/starters. As a chart developer, you may author charts that are specifically designed to be used as starters. Such charts should be designed with the following considerations in mind:

- The Chart.yaml will be overwritten by the generator
- Users will expect to modify such a chart's contents, so documentation should indicate how users can do so

At the moment, there is no way to install charts to $HELM_HOME/starters, the user must copy it manually. Make sure to mention that in your chart's documentation if you develop starter pack charts.

Creating your own charts

A chart is a collection of files that describe a related set of Kubernetes resources. A single chart might be used to deploy something simple, such as a memcached pod, or something complex, such as a full web app stack with HTTP servers, databases, and caches.

Charts are created as files laid out in a particular directory tree. Then, they can be packaged into versioned archives to be deployed. The key file is Chart.yaml.

The Chart.yaml file

The Chart.yaml file is the main file of a Helm chart. It requires a name and version fields:

- name: The name of the chart (same as the directory name)
- version: A SemVer 2 version

It may also contain various optional fields:

- kubeVersion: A SemVer range of compatible Kubernetes versions
- description: A single-sentence description of this project
- keywords: A list of keywords about this project
- home: The URL of this project's home page
- sources: A list of URLs to source code for this project

- maintainers:
  - name: The maintainer's name (required for each maintainer)
  - email: The maintainer's email (optional)
  - url: A URL for the maintainer (optional)
- engine: The name of the template engine (defaults to gotpl)
- icon: A URL to an SVG or PNG image to be used as an icon
- appVersion: The version of the app that this contains
- deprecated: Is this chart deprecated? (Boolean)
- tillerVersion: The version of Tiller that this chart requires

Versioning charts

The version field inside the Chart.yaml is used by the CLI and the Tiller server. The helm package command will use the version that it finds in the Chart.yaml when constructing the package name. The version number in the chart package name must match the version number in the Chart.yaml.

The appVersion field

The appVersion field is not related to the version field. It is not used by Helm and serves as metadata or documentation for users that want to understand what they are deploying. Correctness is not enforced by Helm.

Deprecating charts

From time to time, you may want to deprecate a chart. You can mark a chart as deprecated by setting the deprecated field in Chart.yaml to true. It's enough to deprecate the latest version of a chart. You can later reuse the chart name and publish a newer version that is not deprecated. The workflow used by the kubernetes/charts project is:

- Update the chart's Chart.yaml to mark the chart as deprecated and bump the version
- Release a new version of the chart
- Remove the chart from the source repository

Chart metadata files

Charts may contain various metadata files, such as `README.md`, `LICENSE`, and `NOTES.txt`, that describe the installation, configuration, usage, and license of a chart. The `README.md` file should be formatted as markdown. It should provide the following information:

- A description of the application or service the chart provides
- Any prerequisites or requirements to run the chart
- Descriptions of options in `values.yaml` and default values
- Any other information that may be relevant to the installation or configuration of the chart

The `templates/NOTES.txt` file will be displayed after installation or when viewing the release status. You should keep the `NOTES` concise and point to the `README.md` for detailed explanations. It's common to put usage notes and next steps such as information about connecting to a database or accessing a web UI.

Managing chart dependencies

In Helm, a chart may depend on any number of other charts. These dependencies are expressed explicitly by listing them in a `requirements.yaml` file or by copying the dependency charts into the charts/ sub-directory during installation.

A dependency can be either a chart archive (`foo-1.2.3.tgz`) or an unpacked chart directory. However, its name cannot start with _ or .. Such files are ignored by the chart loader.

Managing dependencies with requirements.yaml

Instead of manually placing charts in the `charts/` subdirectory, it is better to declare dependencies using a `requirements.yaml` file inside your chart.

A `requirements.yaml` file is a simple file for listing the chart dependencies:

```
dependencies:
  - name: foo
    version: 1.2.3
    repository: http://example.com/charts
  - name: bar
    version: 4.5.6
    repository: http://another.example.com/charts
```

The `name` field is the name of the chart you want.

The `version` field is the version of the chart you want.

The `repository` field is the full URL to the `chart repository`. Note that you must also use `helm repo` to add that `repository` locally.

Once you have a dependencies file, you can run the `helm dep up` and it will use your dependency file to download all of the specified charts into the charts subdirectory for you:

```
$ helm dep up foo-chart
Hang tight while we grab the latest from your chart repositories...
...Successfully got an update from the "local" chart repository
...Successfully got an update from the "stable" chart repository
...Successfully got an update from the "example" chart repository
...Successfully got an update from the "another" chart repository
Update Complete. Happy Helming!
Saving 2 charts
Downloading Foo from repo http://example.com/charts
Downloading Bar from repo http://another.example.com/charts
```

Helm stores dependency charts retrieves during helm dependency update as chart archives in the `charts/` directory. For the preceding example, these files will be present in the `charts` directory:

```
charts/
  foo-1.2.3.tgz
  bar-4.5.6.tgz
```

Managing charts and their dependencies with `requirements.yaml` is a best practice, both for explicitly documenting dependencies, sharing across the team, and support automated pipelines.

Using special fields in requirements.yaml

Each entry in the `requirements.yaml` file may also contain the optional `fields` tags and condition.

These fields can be used to dynamically control the loading of charts (by default, all charts are loaded). When tags or condition are present, Helm will evaluate them and determine if the target chart should be loaded:

- condition: The condition field holds one or more YAML paths (delimited by commas). If this path exists in the top parent's values and resolves to a Boolean value, the chart will be enabled or disabled based on that Boolean value. Only the first valid path found in the list is evaluated, and if no paths exist, then the condition has no effect.
- tags: The tags field is a YAML list of labels to associate with this chart. In the top parent's values, all charts with tags can be enabled or disabled by specifying the tag and a Boolean value.
- Here is an example of requirements.yaml and values.yaml that make good use of conditions and tags to enable and disable the installation of dependencies. The requirements.yaml file defines two conditions for installing its dependencies based on the value of the global enabled field and the specific sub-charts enabled field:

```
# parentchart/requirements.yaml
dependencies:
     - name: subchart1
       repository: http://localhost:10191
       version: 0.1.0
       condition: subchart1.enabled, global.subchart1.enabled
       tags:
         - front-end
         - subchart1
     - name: subchart2
       repository: http://localhost:10191
       version: 0.1.0
       condition: subchart2.enabled,global.subchart2.enabled
       tags:
         - back-end
         - subchart2
```

The values.yaml file assigns values to some of the condition variables. The subchart2 tag doesn't get a value, so it is considered enabled:

```
# parentchart/values.yaml
  subchart1:
   enabled: true
  tags:
   front-end: false
   back-end: true
```

You can set tag and conditions values from the command line too when installing a chart, and they'll take precedence over the `values.yaml` file:

```
helm install --set subchart2.enabled=false
```

The resolution of tags and conditions is as follows:

- Conditions (when set in values) always override tags. The first condition path that exists wins, and subsequent ones for that chart are ignored.
- If any of the chart's tags are true then enable the chart.
- Tags and condition values must be set in the top parent's values.
- The tags: key-in values must be a top-level key. Globals and nested tags are not supported.

Using templates and values

Any important application will require configuration and adaptation to the specific use case. Helm charts are templates that use the Go template language to populate placeholders. Helm supports additional functions from the `Sprig` library and a few other specialized functions. The template files are stored in the `templates/` subdirectory of the chart. Helm will use the template engine to render all files in this directory and apply the provided value files.

Writing template files

Template files are just text files that follow the Go template language rules. They can generate Kubernetes configuration files. Here is the service template file from the artifactory chart:

```
kind: Service
apiVersion: v1
kind: Service
metadata:
  name: {{ template "artifactory.fullname" . }}
  labels:
    app: {{ template "artifactory.name" . }}
    chart: {{ .Chart.Name }}-{{ .Chart.Version }}
    component: "{{ .Values.artifactory.name }}"
    heritage: {{ .Release.Service }}
    release: {{ .Release.Name }}
{{- if .Values.artifactory.service.annotations }}
  annotations:
```

```
{{ toYaml .Values.artifactory.service.annotations | indent 4 }}
{{- end }}
spec:
  type: {{ .Values.artifactory.service.type }}
  ports:
  - port: {{ .Values.artifactory.externalPort }}
    targetPort: {{ .Values.artifactory.internalPort }}
    protocol: TCP
    name: {{ .Release.Name }}
  selector:
    app: {{ template "artifactory.name" . }}
    component: "{{ .Values.artifactory.name }}"
    release: {{ .Release.Name }}
```

Using pipelines and functions

Helm allows rich and sophisticated syntax in the template files through the built-in Go template functions, sprig functions, and pipelines. Here is an example template that takes advantage of these capabilities. It uses the repeat, quote, and upper functions for the food and drink keys, and it uses pipelines to chain multiple functions together:

```
apiVersion: v1
kind: ConfigMap
metadata:
  name: {{ .Release.Name }}-configmap
data:
  greeting: "Hello World"
  drink: {{ .Values.favorite.drink | repeat 3 | quote }}
  food: {{ .Values.favorite.food | upper | quote }}
```

See if the values file has the following section:

```
favorite:
  drink: coffee
  food: pizza
```

If it does, then the resulting chart would be as follows:

```
apiVersion: v1
kind: ConfigMap
metadata:
  name: cool-app-configmap
data:
  greeting: "Hello World"
  drink: "coffeecoffeecoffee"
  food: "PIZZA"
```

Embedding predefined values

Helm provides some predefined values which you can use in your templates. In the previous artifactory chart template, `Release.Name`, `Release.Service`, `Chart.Name`, and `Chart.Version` are examples of Helm predefined values. Other predefined values are as follows:

- `Release.Time`
- `Release.Namespace`
- `Release.IsUpgrade`
- `Release.IsInstall`
- `Release.Revision`
- `Chart`
- `Files`
- `Capabilities`

The chart is the content of `Chart.yaml`. The files and capabilities predefined values are `map-like` objects that allow access through various functions. Note that unknown fields in `Chart.yaml` are ignored by the template engine and cannot be used to `pass` arbitrary structured data to templates.

Feeding values from a file

Here is part of the `artifactory` default values file. The values from this file are used to populate multiple templates. For example, the `artifactory name` and `internalPort` values are used in the preceding service template:

```
artifactory:
  name: artifactory
   replicaCount: 1
   image:
   # repository: "docker.bintray.io/jfrog/artifactory-oss"
   repository: "docker.bintray.io/jfrog/artifactory-pro"
   version: 5.9.1
   pullPolicy: IfNotPresent
    service:
     name: artifactory
      type: ClusterIP
      annotations: {}
      externalPort: 8081
      internalPort: 8081
      persistence:
```

```
        mountPath: "/var/opt/jfrog/artifactory"
        enabled: true
        accessMode: ReadWriteOnce
        size: 20Gi
```

You can provide your own YAML values files to override the defaults during the install command:

```
> helm install --values=custom-values.yaml gitlab-ce
```

Scope, dependencies, and values

Value files can declare values for the top-level chart, as well as for any of the charts that are included in that chart's `charts/` directory. For example, the `artifactory-ce` `values.yaml` file contains some default values for its dependency chart `postgresql`:

```
## Configuration values for the postgresql dependency
## ref:
https://github.com/kubernetes/charts/blob/master/stable/postgressql/README.
md
##
postgresql:
postgresUser: "artifactory"
postgresPassword: "artifactory"
postgresDatabase: "artifactory"
persistence:
 enabled: true
```

The top-level chart has access to values of its dependent charts, but not vice versa. There is also a global value that is accessible to all charts. For example, you could add something like this:

```
global:
 app: cool-app
```

When a global is present, it will be replicated to each dependent chart's values as follows:

```
global:
  app: cool-app
 postgresql:
   global:
     app: cool-app
     . . .
```

Summary

In this chapter, we took a look at Helm, the Kubernetes package manager. Helm gives Kubernetes the ability to manage complicated software composed of many Kubernetes resources with interdependencies. It serves the same purpose as an OS package manager. It organizes packages and lets you search charts, install and upgrade charts, and share charts with collaborators. You can develop your charts and store them in repositories.

At this point, you should understand the important role that Helm serves in the Kubernetes ecosystem and community. You should be able to use it productively and even develop and share your own charts.

In the next chapter, we will look ahead to the future of Kubernetes and examine its roadmap and a few personal items from my wish list.

19
The Future of Kubernetes

In this chapter, we look at the future of Kubernetes from multiple angles. We'll start with the roadmap and forthcoming product features, including diving into the design process of Kubernetes. Then, we'll cover the momentum of Kubernetes since its inception, including dimensions such as community, ecosystem, and mindshare. A big part of Kubernetes' future will be determined by how it fares against its competition. Education will play a major role too, as container orchestration is new, fast-moving, and not a well-understood domain. Then, we'll discuss a capability at the top of my wish list—dynamic plugins.

The covered topics are as follows:

- The road ahead
- Competition
- The Kubernetes momentum
- Education and training
- Modularization and out-of-tree plugins
- Service meshes and serverless frameworks

The road ahead

Kubernetes is a large open source project. Let's look at some of the planned features and upcoming releases, as well the various special interest groups that focus on specific areas.

Kubernetes releases and milestones

Kubernetes has fairly regular releases. The current release, as of April 2018, is 1.10. The next release, 1.11, is currently 33% complete. Here are a couple of issues from the 1.11 releases to give you a taste of the work being done:

- Update to Go 1.10.1 and default `etcd` server to 3.2
- Support out-of-tree authentication providers
- Migrate kublet flags to `kublet.config.k8s.io`
- Add support of Azure Standard Load Balancer and public IP
- Add kubectl `api-resources` command
- Minor releases are released every 3 months, and patch releases plug holes and issues until the next minor release. Here are the release dates of the three most recent releases:
  - 10.0 released on March 26, 2018, and 1.9.6 released on March, 21 2018
  - 9.0 released on Dec 15, 2017, and 1.8.5 released on December, 7 2017
  - 8.0 and 1.7.7 released on Sep 28, 2017 (my birthday!)

Another good way to look at what is coming is to look at the work being done on the alpha and beta releases. You can check the change log here: `https://github.com/kubernetes/kubernetes/blob/master/CHANGELOG.md`.

Here are some of the major themes of the 1.10 release:

- Node
- Network
- Storage
- Windows
- OpenStack
- API machinery
- Auth
- Azure
- CLI

Kubernetes special interest and working groups

As a large open source community project, most of the development work on Kubernetes takes place in multiple working groups. The complete list is here:

`https://github.com/kubernetes/community/blob/master/sig-list.md`

The planning for future releases is done mostly within these SIGs and working groups because Kubernetes is too big to handle it all centrally. SIGs meet regularly and discuss.

Competition

The first edition of *Mastering Kubernetes* was published in May 2017. The competitive landscape of Kubernetes was very different then. Here is what I wrote back then:

> *"Kubernetes operates in one of the hottest technology areas of container orchestration. The future of Kubernetes must be considered as part of the whole market. As you will see, some of the possible competitors may also be partners that promote both their own offering as well as Kubernetes (or at least, Kubernetes can run on their platform)."*

In less than a year, the situation has changed drastically. In short, Kubernetes won. All the cloud providers offer managed Kubernetes services. IBM provides support for Kubernetes on bare metal clusters. Companies that develop software and add-ons for container orchestration focus on Kubernetes as opposed to creating products that support multiple orchestration solutions.

The value of bundling

Container orchestration platforms such as Kubernetes compete directly and indirectly with larger and smaller scopes. For example, Kubernetes may be available on a particular Cloud platform, such as AWS, but may not be the default/go-to solution. On the other hand, Kubernetes is at the core of GKE on the Google Cloud Platform. Developers who choose a higher level of abstraction, such as a cloud platform or even PaaS, will more often than not go with the default solution. But some developers or organizations worry about vendor lock-in or need to run on multiple cloud platforms or a hybrid public/private. Kubernetes has a strong advantage here. Bundling was a potential serious threat to Kubernetes adoption, but the momentum was too great, and now every major player offers Kubernetes directly on their platform or solution.

Docker Swarm

Docker is currently the de facto standard for containers (although CoreOS rkt is gathering steam), and often people say Docker when they mean containers. Docker wants to get a piece of the orchestration cake and released the Docker Swarm product. The main benefit of Docker Swarm is that it comes as part of the Docker installation and uses standard Docker APIs. So, the learning curve is not as steep, and it's easier to get started. However, Docker Swarm is way behind Kubernetes in terms of capabilities and maturity. In addition, Docker's reputation is not great when it comes to high-quality engineering and security. Organizations and developers that are concerned with the stability of their systems may shy away from Docker Swarm. Docker is aware of the problem and is taking steps to address it. It released an Enterprise offering and also reworked Docker's internals as a set of independent components through the Moby project. But, recently Docker acknowledged the prominent place of Kubernetes as the container orchestration platform. Docker now supports Kubernetes directly side-by-side with Docker swarm. My guess is that Docker swarm will fizzle out, and it will be used just for very small prototyping.

Mesos/Mesosphere

Mesosphere is the company behind the open source Apache Mesos, and the DC/OS product is the incumbent that runs containers and big data in the cloud. The technology is mature and Mesosphere evolves it, but they don't have the resources and momentum that Kubernetes has. I believe that Mesosphere will do very well because it is a big market, but it will not threaten Kubernetes as the number one container orchestration solution. In addition, Mesosphere also recognized that they can't beat Kubernetes and opted to join it. In DC/OS 1.11, you get Kubernetes-as-a-Service. The DC/OS offering is a highly available, easy to set up, and secure by default deployment of Kubernetes that was tested on Google, AWS, and Azure.

Cloud platforms

A large contingent of organizations and developers flock to public cloud platforms to avoid the headaches of low-level management of their infrastructure. Those companies' primary motivation is often to move fast and focus on their core competency. As such, they'll often go with the default deployment solution offered by their Cloud provider because the integration is the most seamless and streamlined.

AWS

Kubernetes runs very well on AWS through the official Kubernetes Kops project: `https://github.com/kubernetes/kops`.

Some of Kops, features are as follows:

- Automate the provisioning of Kubernetes clusters in AWS
- Deploy highly-available Kubernetes masters
- The ability to generate Terraform configurations

However, Kops is not an official AWS solution. If you manage your infrastructure through the AWS console and APIs, the path of least resistance used to be AWS **Elastic Container Service** (**ECS**)—a built-in container orchestration solution that is not based on Kubernetes.

Now, AWS is fully committed to Kubernetes and is in the process of releasing **Elastic Kubernetes Service** (**EKS**), which is a fully managed and highly available upstream Kubernetes cluster, with no modifications, but with tight integration through add-ons and plugins to AWS services.

I speculated in the first edition that AWS would stick to its guns and stand behind ECS, but I was wrong. Even the mighty AWS deferred to Kubernetes; ECS will stick around because a lot of organizations invested in it and might not want to migrate to Kubernetes. However, over time, I predict that ECS will be relegated to legacy service status, maintained to support organizations that don't have enough incentive to move to Kubernetes.

Azure

Azure provides the Azure container service, and they don't pick favorites. You can choose if you want to use Kubernetes, Docker Swarm, or DC/OS. This is interesting because, initially, Azure was based on Mesosphere DC/OS and they added Kubernetes and Docker Swarm as orchestration options later. As Kubernetes pulls forward in capabilities, maturity, and mindshare, I believe it will become the number one orchestration option on Azure too.

In the second half of 2017, Azure officially released **Azure Kubernetes Service** (**AKS**) and Microsoft got fully behind Kubernetes as the container orchestration solution. It is very active in the Kubernetes community, acquired Deis (the Helm developers), and contributes a lot of tools, code fixes, and integrations. The Windows support for Kubernetes keeps improving as well as integration with Azure.

Alibaba Cloud

Alibaba Cloud is the Chinese AWS in more ways than one. Their APIs are intentionally very much like AWS APIs. Alibaba Cloud used to provide a container management service based on Docker Swarm. I've deployed some applications at a small scale on Alibaba Cloud, and they seem to be able to keep up with the changes in the field and quickly follow the big players. Over the past year, Alibaba Cloud (Aliyun) joined the ranks of Kubernetes supporters. There are several resources for deploying and managing Kubernetes clusters on the Alibaba cloud including an implementation on GitHub of the cloud provider interface.

The Kubernetes momentum

Kubernetes has tremendous momentum behind it; the community is super strong. Users flock to Kubernetes as its mindshare increases, the technical press acknowledges its number one leadership position, the ecosystem is sizzling, and a lot of big corporations and companies (in addition to Google) actively support it and many more evaluate it and run it in production.

Community

The Kubernetes community is one of its greatest assets. Kubernetes recently became the first project to graduate from the **Cloud Native Computing Foundation (CNCF)**.

GitHub

Kubernetes is developed on GitHub and is one of the top projects on GitHub. It is in the top 0.01 percent in stars and number one in terms of activity. Note that over the past year, Kubernetes became more modular, and many pieces of the puzzle are now developed separately.

More professionals list Kubernetes in their LinkedIn profile than any other comparable offering by a wide margin.

A year ago, Kubernetes had ~1,100 contributors and ~34,000 commits. Now, the number exploded to more than 1,600 contributors and more than 63,000 commits.

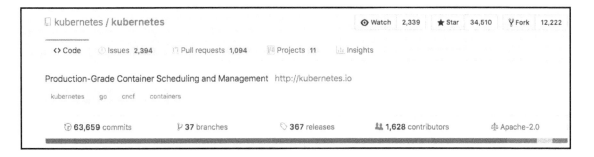

Conferences and meetups

Another indication of Kubernetes momentum is the number of conferences, meetups, and attendees. KubeCon is growing quickly and new Kubernetes meetups open up every day.

Mindshare

Kubernetes is getting a lot of attention and deployments. Large and small companies that get into the containers/DevOps/microservices arena adopt Kubernetes and the trend is clear. One interesting metric is the number of stack overflow questions over time. The community steps in to answer questions and foster collaboration. The growth dwarfs its rivals, and the trend is very clear:

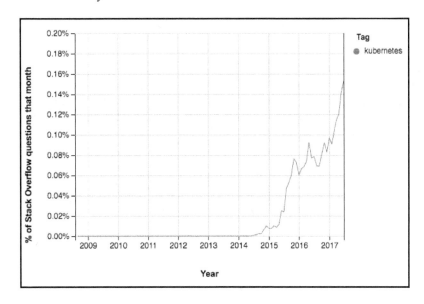

Ecosystem

The Kubernetes ecosystem is very impressive, from cloud providers to PaaS platforms and startups that offer a streamlined environment.

Public cloud providers

All the major cloud providers support Kubernetes directly. Obviously, Google is leading the pack with GKE, which is the native container engine on the Google Cloud Platform. The Kops project, mentioned earlier, is a well-supported, maintained, and documented solution on AWS, and EKS is just around the corner. Azure offers AKS. The IBM container cloud service is powered by Kubernetes. Oracle tracks Kubernetes closely and offers Oracle container services for Kubernetes based on upstream Kubernetes and Kubeadm.

OpenShift

OpenShift is RedHat's container application product that's built on top of the open source OpenShift origin, which is based on Kubernetes. OpenShift adds application life cycle management and DevOps tooling on top of Kubernetes and contributes a lot to Kubernetes (such as autoscaling). This type of interaction is very healthy and encouraging. RedHat recently acquired CoreOS and the merging of CoreOS Tectonic with OpenShift may provide great synergy.

OpenStack

OpenStack is the open source private cloud platform, and it has recently decided to standardize on Kubernetes as the underlying orchestration platform. This is a big deal because large enterprises that want to deploy across a mix of public and private Clouds will have a much better integration with Kubernetes cloud federation on one end and OpenStack as a private cloud platform using Kubernetes under the hood.

The latest OpenStack survey from November 2017 shows that Kubernetes is by far the most popular solution for container orchestration:

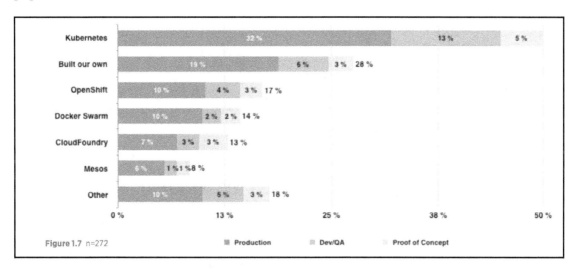

Figure 1.7 n=272

Other players

There are a number of other companies that use Kubernetes as a foundation, such as Rancher and Apprenda. A large number of startups develop add-ons and services that run inside the Kubernetes cluster. The future is bright.

Education and training

Education will be critical. As the early adopters of Kubernetes make way to the majority, it is very important to have the right resources for organizations and developers to pick up Kubernetes and be productive quickly. There are already some pretty good resources, and, in the future, I predict that the number and quality will just increase. Of course, the book you're reading right now is part of this drive.

The official Kubernetes documentation is getting better and better. The online tutorials are great for getting started:

- The CNCF has a free introductory Kubernetes course (as well as more advanced paid courses), at `https://www.cncf.io/certification/training/`.

- Google has created a few Udacity courses on Kubernetes. Check them out at `https://www.udacity.com/course/scalable-microservices-with-kubernetes--ud615`.

- Another excellent resource is KataCoda, which provides a completely free Kubernetes playground, where you can get a private cluster within seconds, in addition to multiple hands-on tutorials on advanced topics, at `https://www.katacoda.com/courses/kubernetes`.

There are also a lot of paid training options for Kubernetes. As the popularity of Kubernetes grows even further, more and more options will be available.

Modularization and out-of-tree plugins

Kubernetes has made great strides toward modularization since the first edition. Kubernetes was always a paragon of flexibility and extensibility. However, originally you had to build and link your code into the Kubernetes API server or the Kublet (with the exception of CNI plugins). You also had to get your code vetted and integrated with the main Kubernetes codebase to make it available to other developers. At the time, I was very excited about Go 1.8 dynamic plugins and how they could be used to extend Kubernetes in a much more agile way. The Kubernetes developers and community took a different path and decided to make Kubernetes proper a general-purpose and versatile engine where almost every aspect can be customized or extended from the outside through standard interfaces. You've seen many examples in `Chapter 17`, *Customizing Kubernetes - APIs and Plugins*. The out-of-tree approach means that you integrate a plugin or extension with Kubernetes that lives outside of the Kubernetes code tree on GitHub. There are several mechanisms in use:

- CNI plugins use standard input and out through a separate executables
- CSI plugins use pods gRPC
- Kubectl plugins use YAML descriptors and binary commands
- API aggregators use custom API servers
- Webhooks use remote HTTP interfaces
- Various other plugins can be deployed as pods
- External credential providers

Service meshes and serverless frameworks

Kubernetes helps with a lot of the heavy lifting involved in container orchestration and cost reduction due to efficient scheduling. But, there are two trends that gain momentum in cloud native world. Service meshes fit Kubernetes like a glove, and running a serverless framework plays to Kubernetes strengths as well.

Service meshes

A service mesh operates at a higher level than container orchestration. A service mesh manages services. The service mesh provides various capabilities that are very necessary when running systems with hundreds and thousands different services such as:

- Dynamic routing
- Latency-aware east-west load balancing (inside the cluster)
- Auto retries of idempotent requests
- Operational metrics

In the past, applications had to address those responsibilities on top of their core functionality. Now, service meshes take the load off and provide an infrastructure layer so that applications can focus on their primary goals.

The most well-known service mesh is Linkered by Buoyant. Linkered supports Kubernetes as well as other orchestrators. But, given the momentum of Kubernetes.

Buoyant decided to develop a new Kubernetes-only service mesh named Conduit (in Rust). This is another testament to the traction of Kubernetes where all the innovation takes place. Another Kubernetes service mesh is Istio. Istio was founded by teams from Google, IBM, and Lyft. It's built on top of Lyft's Envoy and it's moving fast.

Serverless frameworks

Serverless computing is an exciting new trend in the cloud native landscape. AWS Lambda functions are the most popular, but all cloud platforms provide them now. The idea is that you don't have to provision hardware, instances, and storage. Instead you just write your code, package it (often in a container), and invoke it whenever you want. The cloud platform takes care of allocating resources to run your code at invocation time and deallocate the resources when the code finished running. This can save a lot of costs (you only pay for the resources you use) and eliminate the need to provision and manage infrastructure. However, the serverless capabilities provided by cloud providers often come with strings attached (runtime and memory limits), or they are not flexible enough (can't control the hardware your code will run on). Kubernetes can also provide serverless capabilities once your cluster is provisioned. There are multiple frameworks at different levels of maturity available, as follows:

- Fast-netes
- Nuclio.io
- Apache OpenWhisk
- Platform9 Fission
- Kubless.io

This is great news for people running Kubernetes on bare metal or who need more flexibility than cloud platforms provide.

Summary

In this chapter, we looked at the future of Kubernetes, and it looks great! The technical foundation, the community, the broad support, and the momentum are all very impressive. Kubernetes is still young, but the pace of innovation and stabilization is very encouraging. The modularization and extensibility principles of Kubernetes let it become the universal foundation for modern cloud native applications.

At this point, you should have a clear idea of where Kubernetes is right now and where it's going from here. You should have confidence that Kubernetes is not just here to stay but that it will be the leading container orchestration platform for many years to come and will integrate with larger offerings and environments.

Now, it's up to you to use what you have learned and build amazing things with Kubernetes!

Other Books You May Enjoy

If you enjoyed this book, you may be interested in these other books by Packt:

Kubernetes for Developers
Joseph Heck

ISBN: 978-1-78883-475-9

- Build your software into containers.
- Deploy and debug software running in containers within Kubernetes.
- Declare and add configuration through Kubernetes.
- Define how your application fits together, using internal and external services.
- Add feedback to your code to help Kubernetes manage your services
- Monitor and measure your services through integration testing and in production deployments.

DevOps with Kubernetes
Hideto Saito, Hui-Chuan Chloe Lee, Cheng-Yang Wu

ISBN: 978-1-78839-664-6

- Learn fundamental and advanced DevOps skills and tools
- Get a comprehensive understanding for container
- Learn how to move your application to container world
- Learn how to manipulate your application by Kubernetes
- Learn how to work with Kubernetes in popular public cloud
- Improve time to market with Kubernetes and Continuous Delivery
- Learn how to monitor, log, and troubleshoot your application with Kubernetes

Kubernetes Cookbook - Second Edition

Hideto Saito, Hui-Chuan Chloe Lee, Ke-Jou Carol Hsu

ISBN: 978-1-78883-760-6

- Build your own container cluster
- Deploy and manage highly scalable, containerized applications with Kubernetes
- Build high-availability Kubernetes clusters
- Build a continuous delivery pipeline for your application
- Track metrics and logs for every container running in your cluster
- Streamline the way you deploy and manage your applications with large-scale container orchestration

Leave a review - let other readers know what you think

Please share your thoughts on this book with others by leaving a review on the site that you bought it from. If you purchased the book from Amazon, please leave us an honest review on this book's Amazon page. This is vital so that other potential readers can see and use your unbiased opinion to make purchasing decisions, we can understand what our customers think about our products, and our authors can see your feedback on the title that they have worked with Packt to create. It will only take a few minutes of your time, but is valuable to other potential customers, our authors, and Packt. Thank you!

Index

U

Ubuntu LXD
  about 312
  reference 312
Ubuntu Snappy
  about 311
  reference 311
union filesystems 13
unique ID (UID) 72

V

values, charts
  declaring 570
  dependency 570
  feeding, from file 569
  predefined values, embedding 569
  scope 570
  using 567
virtual Ethernet (veth) devices 467
Virtual Extensible LAN (VXLAN) 146
virtual IP (VIP) 114, 149
virtual machines 67
Virtual Private Cloud (VPC) 50, 315
virtual private cloud infrastructure
  Bootkube 346

  using 346
Virtual Redundancy Router Protocol (VRRP) 491
VirtualBox
  reference 20
  URL 324
Virtualized Cloud Services (VCS) 476
VMware Photon
  about 312
  reference 312
volumes
  about 74
  reference 210

W

Weave net 480
Weave
  about 146
  reference 146
Windows
  single-node cluster, creating 324
workflows, Hue
  automatic workflows 182
  budget-aware workflows 183
  human workflows 183
  planning 182